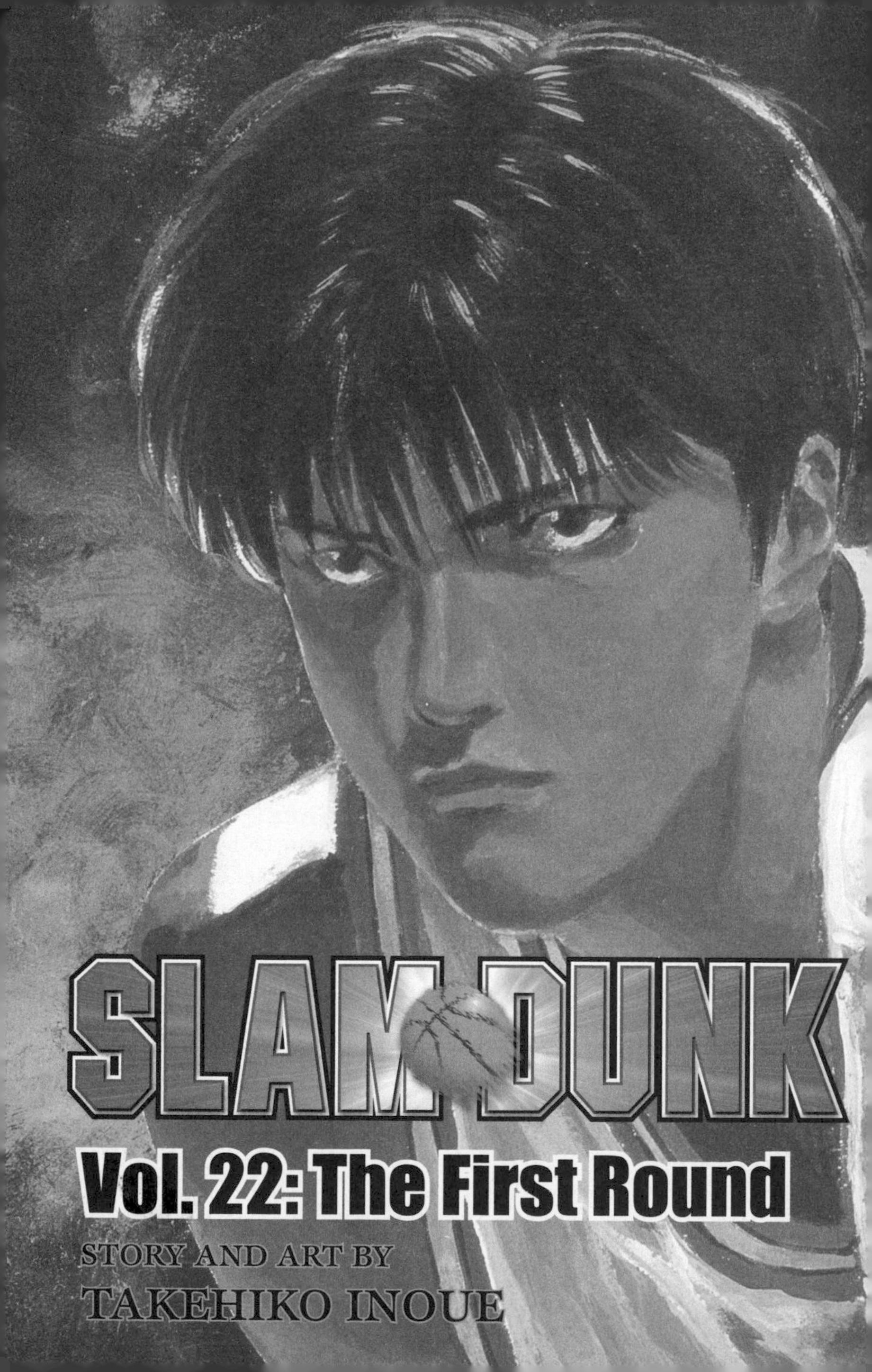
SLAM DUNK
Vol. 22: The First Round
STORY AND ART BY
TAKEHIKO INOUE

Character Introduction

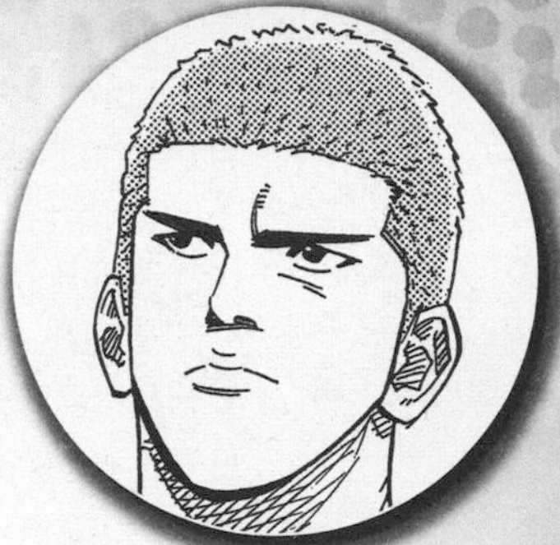

Hanamichi Sakuragi
A first-year at Shohoku High School, Sakuragi is in love with Haruko Akagi.

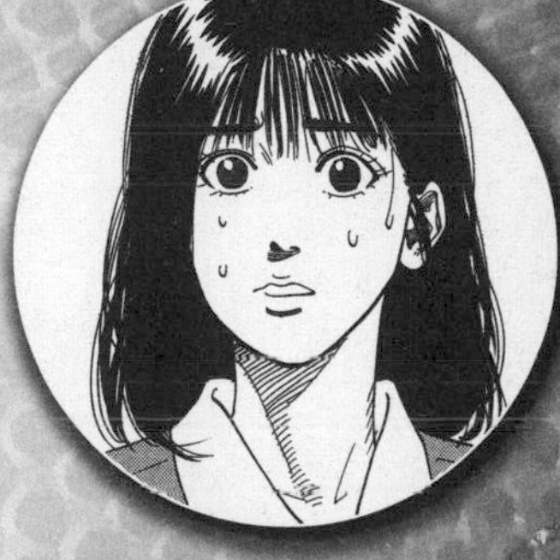

Haruko Akagi
Also a first-year at Shohoku, Takenori Akagi's little sister has a crush on Kaede Rukawa.

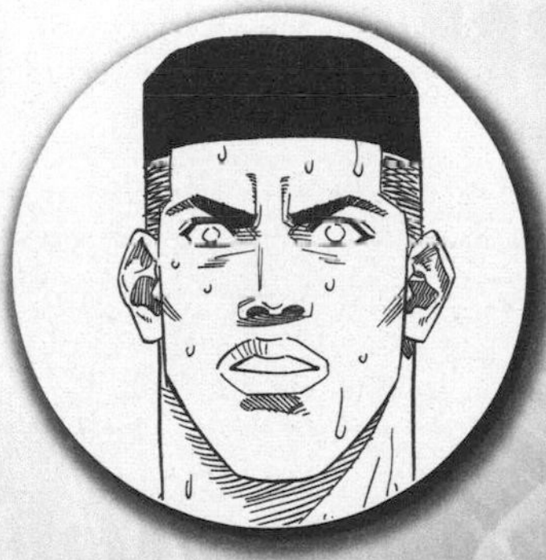

Takenori Akagi
A third-year and the basketball team's captain, Akagi has an intense passion for his sport.

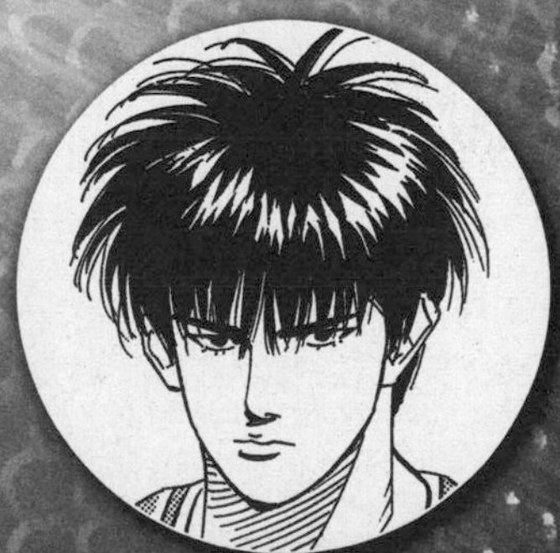

Kaede Rukawa
The object of Haruko's affection (and that of many of Shohoku's female students!), this first-year has been a star player since junior high.

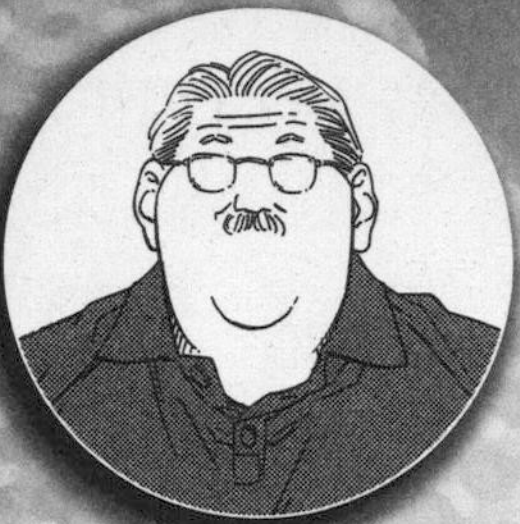

Coach Anzai
Shohoku High School
Basketball Coach

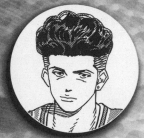

Ryota Miyagi
A problem child with
a thing for Ayako.

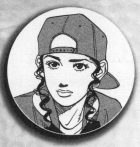

Ayako
Basketball Team
Manager

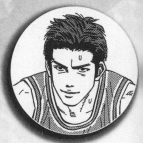

Hisashi Mitsui
An MVP during
junior high.

Our Story Thus Far

Hanamichi Sakuragi is rejected by close to 50 girls during his three years in junior high. He joins the basketball team to be closer to Haruko Akagi, but his frustration mounts when all he does is practice day after day.

Shohoku advances through the Prefectural Tournament to face Kainan University, but loses by two points.

Kainan, last year's champions, face Ryonan in the second round and defeat them in overtime to advance to the National Tournament. In the game for the final spot in the nationals, Shohoku is in the lead, but thanks to Sendoh's brilliant play, Ryonan chips away at the point spread. In the end, Sakuragi's dunk with just eight seconds remaining gives Shohoku the victory.

Vol. 22
The First Round

Table of Contents

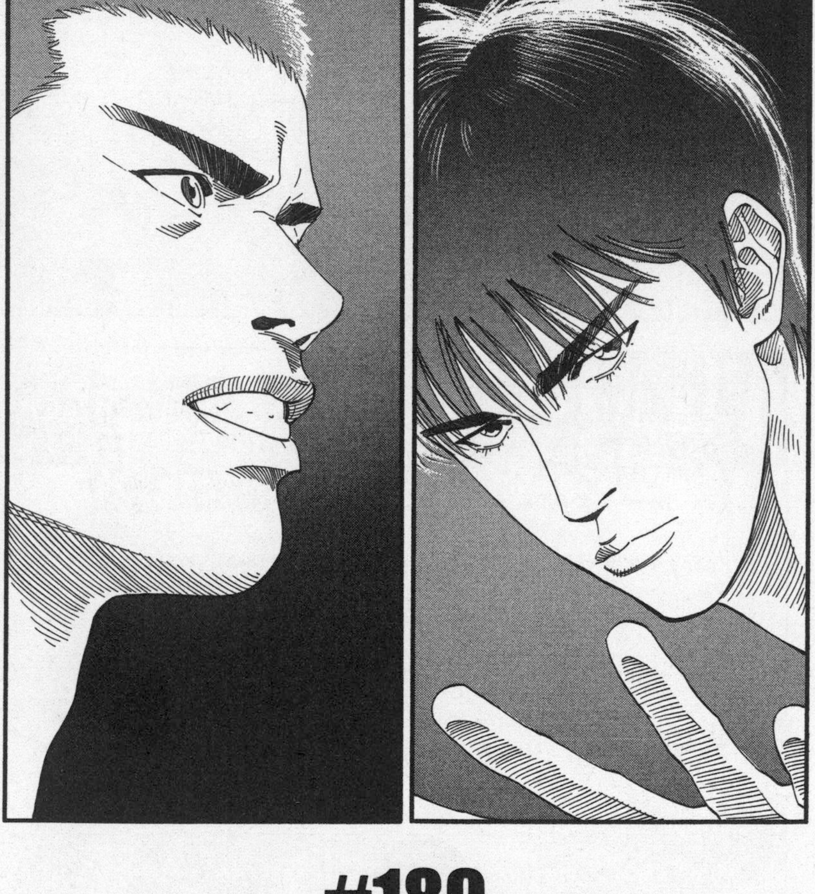

#189
THE LAND OF BASKETBALL

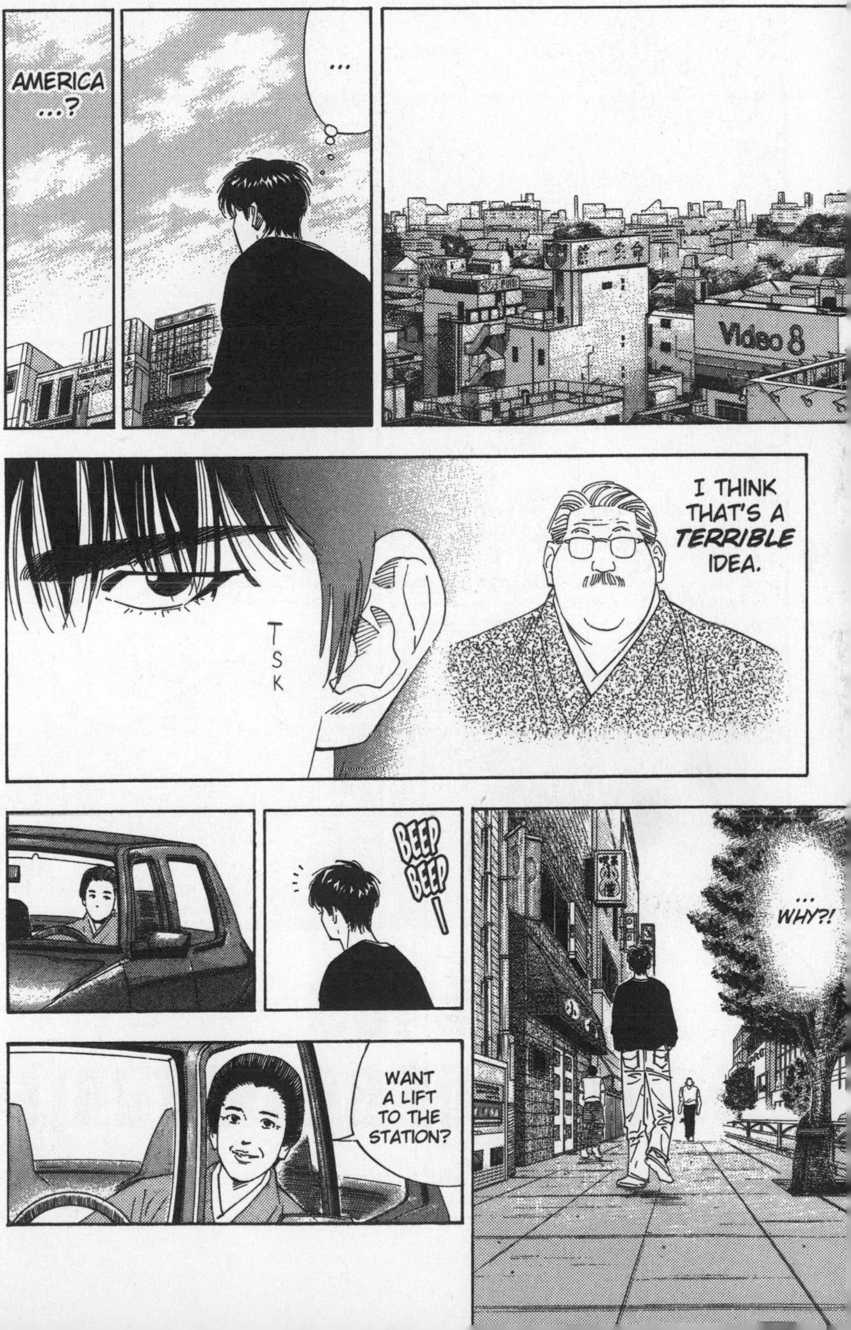
Video 8
...
AMERICA ...?
I THINK THAT'S A TERRIBLE IDEA.
TSK
... WHY?!
BEEP BEEP
WANT A LIFT TO THE STATION?

READ THIS WAY

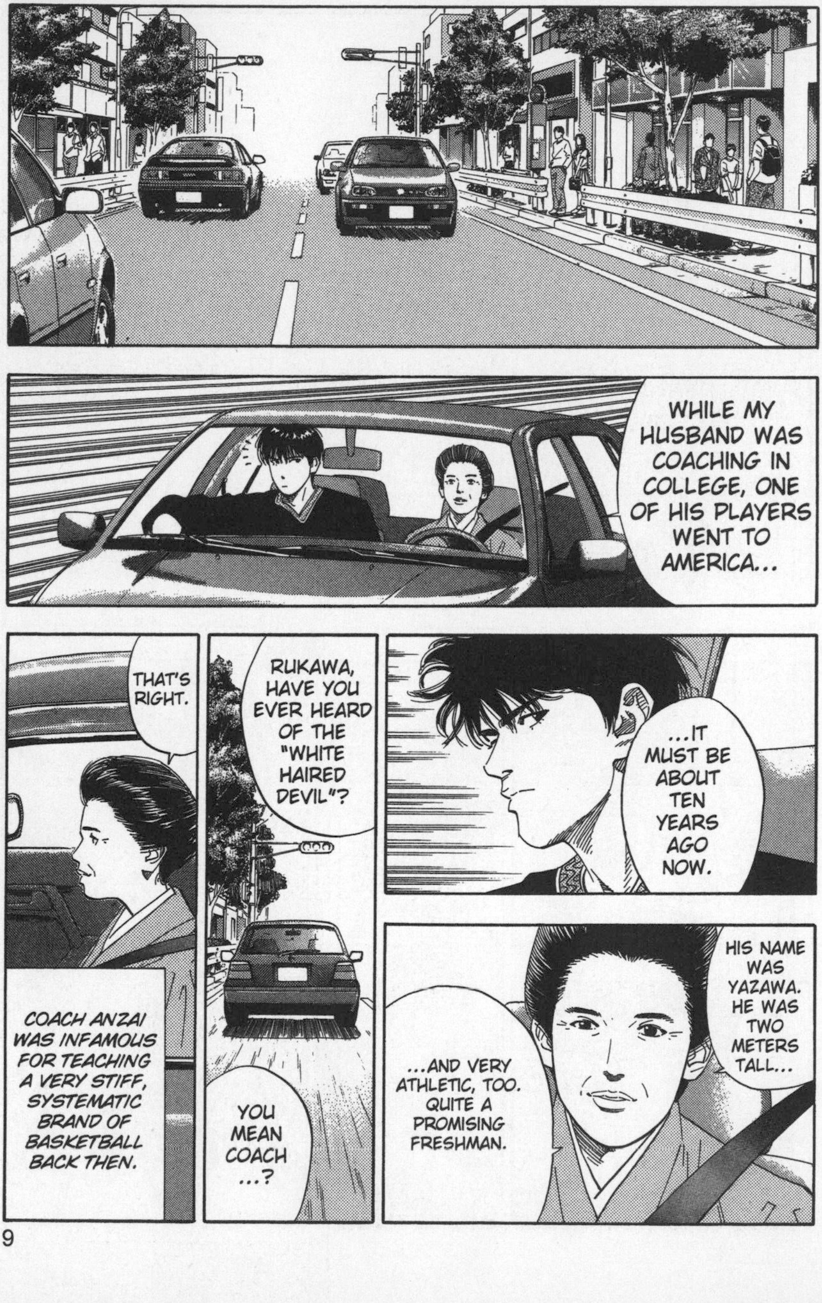

WHILE MY HUSBAND WAS COACHING IN COLLEGE, ONE OF HIS PLAYERS WENT TO AMERICA...
...IT MUST BE ABOUT TEN YEARS AGO NOW.
HIS NAME WAS YAZAWA. HE WAS TWO METERS TALL...
...AND VERY ATHLETIC, TOO. QUITE A PROMISING FRESHMAN.
RUKAWA, HAVE YOU EVER HEARD OF THE "WHITE HAIRED DEVIL"?
YOU MEAN COACH ...?
THAT'S RIGHT.
COACH ANZAI WAS INFAMOUS FOR TEACHING A VERY STIFF, SYSTEMATIC BRAND OF BASKETBALL BACK THEN.

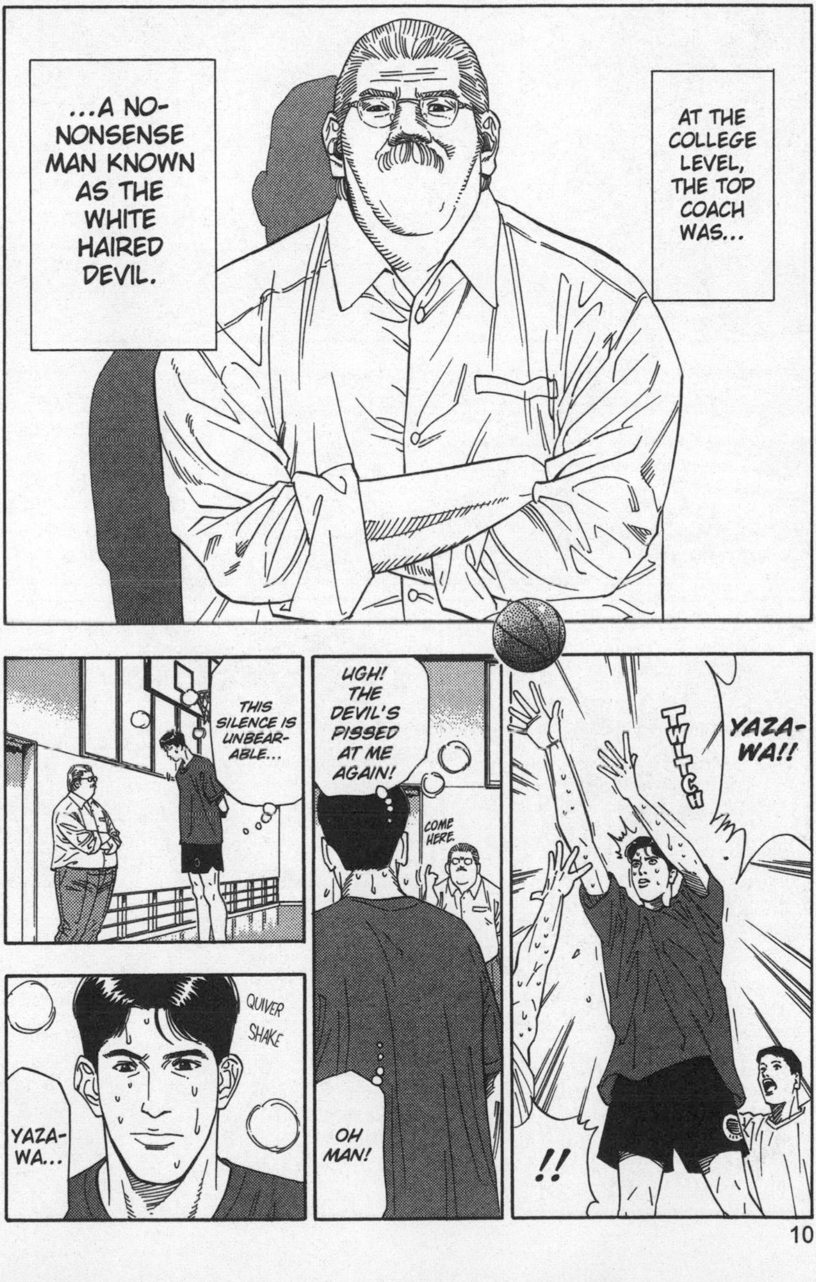
AT THE COLLEGE LEVEL, THE TOP COACH WAS...
...A NO-NONSENSE MAN KNOWN AS THE WHITE HAIRED DEVIL.
YAZA-WA!!
TWITCH
!!
UGH! THE DEVIL'S PISSED AT ME AGAIN!
COME HERE.
OH MAN!
THIS SILENCE IS UNBEARABLE...
QUIVER
SHAKE
YAZA-WA...

READ THIS WAY

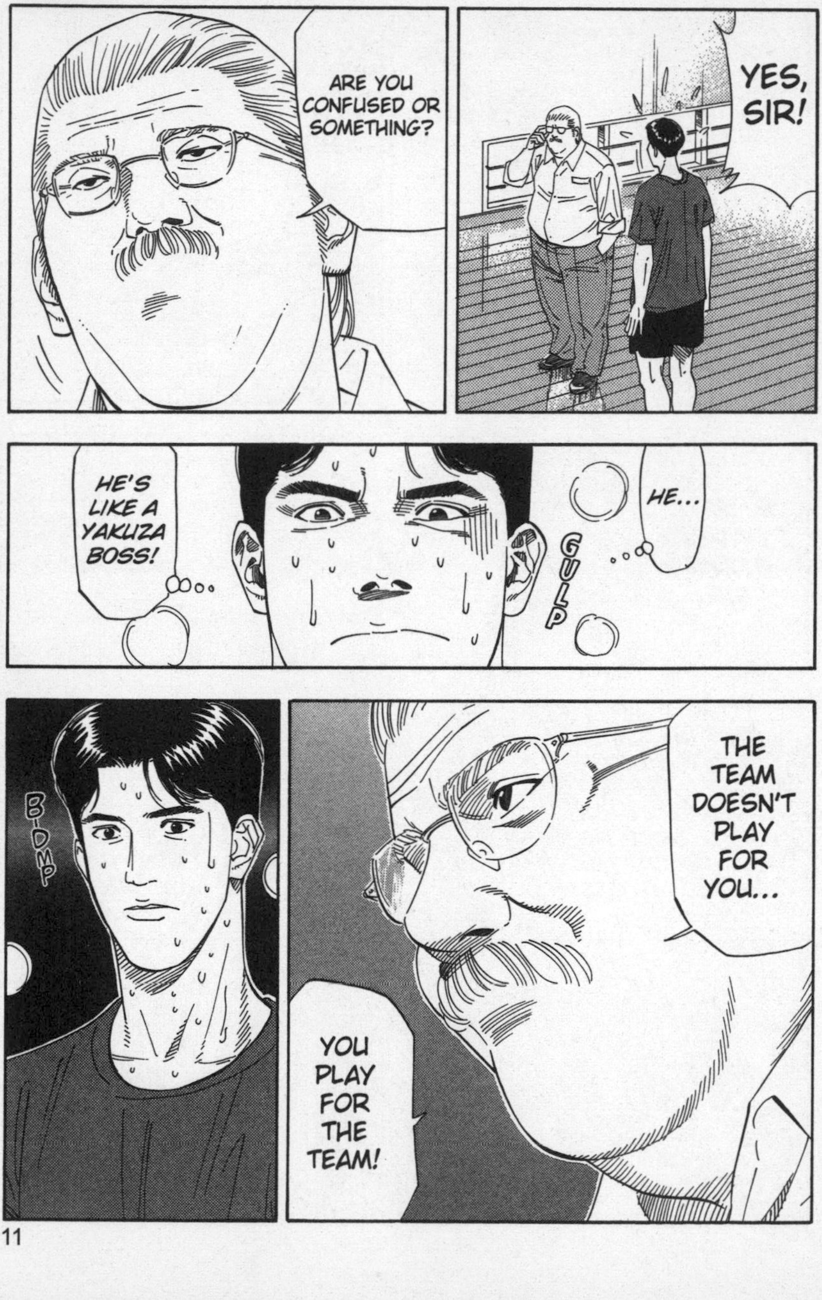
YES, SIR!
ARE YOU CONFUSED OR SOMETHING?
HE...
GULP
HE'S LIKE A YAKUZA BOSS!
THE TEAM DOESN'T PLAY FOR YOU...
YOU PLAY FOR THE TEAM!
B-DMP

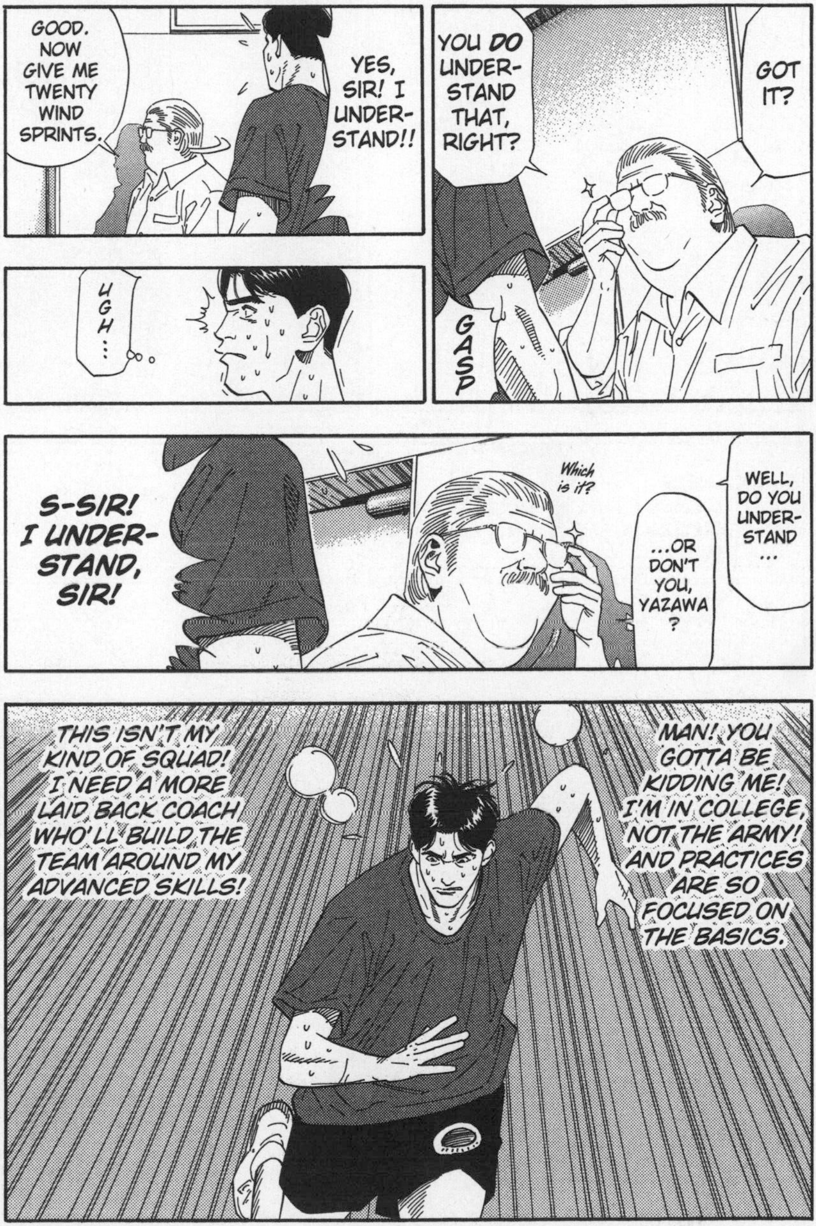
GOT IT?
YOU DO UNDERSTAND THAT, RIGHT?
GASP
YES, SIR! I UNDERSTAND!!
GOOD. NOW GIVE ME TWENTY WIND SPRINTS.
UGH...
WELL, DO YOU UNDERSTAND...
...OR DON'T YOU, YAZAWA?
Which is it?
S-SIR! I UNDERSTAND, SIR!
MAN! YOU GOTTA BE KIDDING ME! I'M IN COLLEGE, NOT THE ARMY! AND PRACTICES ARE SO FOCUSED ON THE BASICS.
THIS ISN'T MY KIND OF SQUAD! I NEED A MORE LAID BACK COACH WHO'LL BUILD THE TEAM AROUND MY ADVANCED SKILLS!

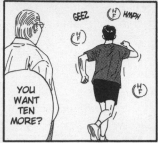

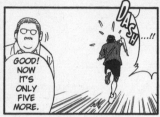

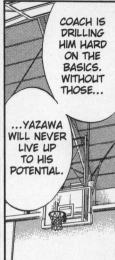

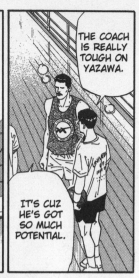

READ THIS WAY

THE COACH IS REALLY TOUGH ON YAZAWA.
IT'S CUZ HE'S GOT SO MUCH POTENTIAL.
COACH IS DRILLING HIM HARD ON THE BASICS. WITHOUT THOSE...
...YAZAWA WILL NEVER LIVE UP TO HIS POTENTIAL.
HMPH
HF
GEEZ
HF
YOU WANT TEN MORE?
HF
...!!
DASH
GOOD! NOW IT'S ONLY FIVE MORE.
...
HNF
HF
THAT'S IT! I'M OUTTA HERE! HE DOESN'T KNOW ANYTHING ABOUT THE GAME I WANT TO PLAY!
AMERICA! THIS IS MY CHANCE TO GO AND PLAY IN AMERICA! BUT CAN I CUT IT IN AMERICA? MAYBE NOT RIGHT AWAY. BUT GIVE ME A YEAR OR TWO ON THE COURTS IN THE MECCA OF BASKETBALL AND I'LL BE A PLAYER THE DEVIL CAN'T EVEN IMAGINE! I'M SURE OF IT! I'M GONNA TEST MYSELF IN AMERICA!

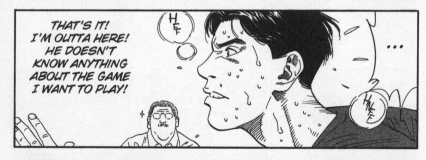

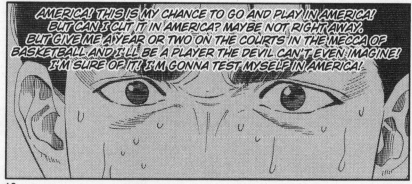

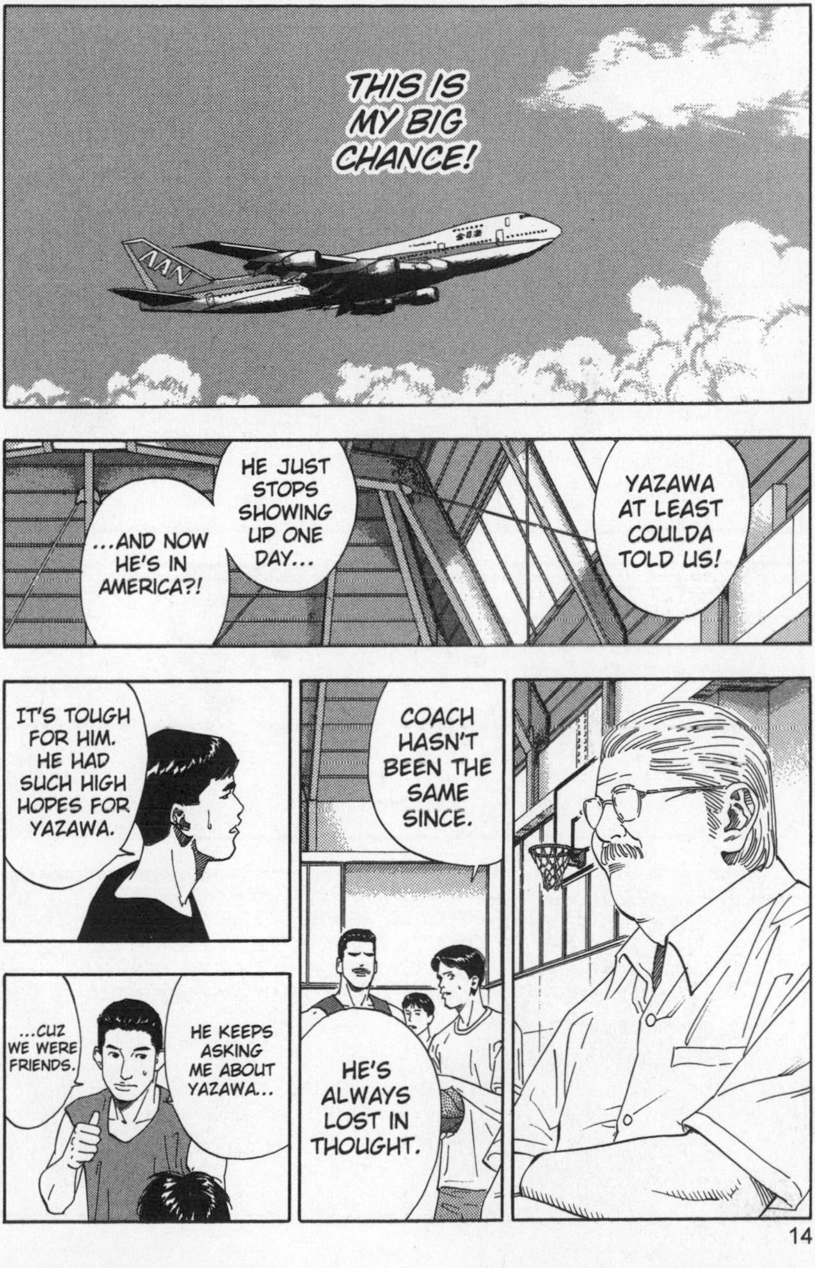
THIS IS MY BIG CHANCE!
YAZAWA AT LEAST COULDA TOLD US!
HE JUST STOPS SHOWING UP ONE DAY...
...AND NOW HE'S IN AMERICA?!
COACH HASN'T BEEN THE SAME SINCE.
HE'S ALWAYS LOST IN THOUGHT.
IT'S TOUGH FOR HIM. HE HAD SUCH HIGH HOPES FOR YAZAWA.
HE KEEPS ASKING ME ABOUT YAZAWA...
...CUZ WE WERE FRIENDS.

READ THIS WAY

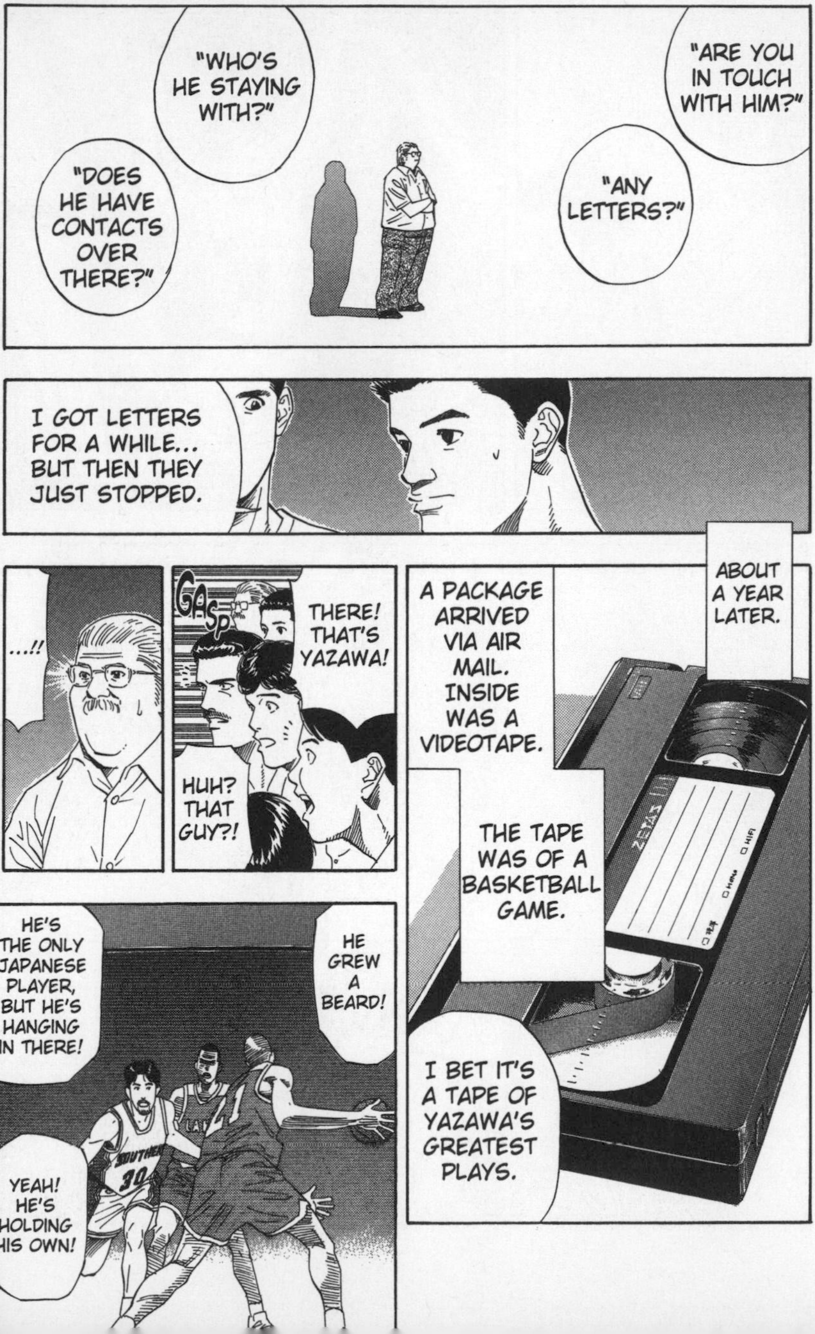
"ARE YOU IN TOUCH WITH HIM?"
"WHO'S HE STAYING WITH?"
"ANY LETTERS?"
"DOES HE HAVE CONTACTS OVER THERE?"
I GOT LETTERS FOR A WHILE... BUT THEN THEY JUST STOPPED.
ABOUT A YEAR LATER.
A PACKAGE ARRIVED VIA AIR MAIL. INSIDE WAS A VIDEOTAPE.
THE TAPE WAS OF A BASKETBALL GAME.
I BET IT'S A TAPE OF YAZAWA'S GREATEST PLAYS.
THERE! THAT'S YAZAWA!
GASP
HUH? THAT GUY?!
...!!
HE GREW A BEARD!
HE'S THE ONLY JAPANESE PLAYER, BUT HE'S HANGING IN THERE!
YEAH! HE'S HOLDING HIS OWN!

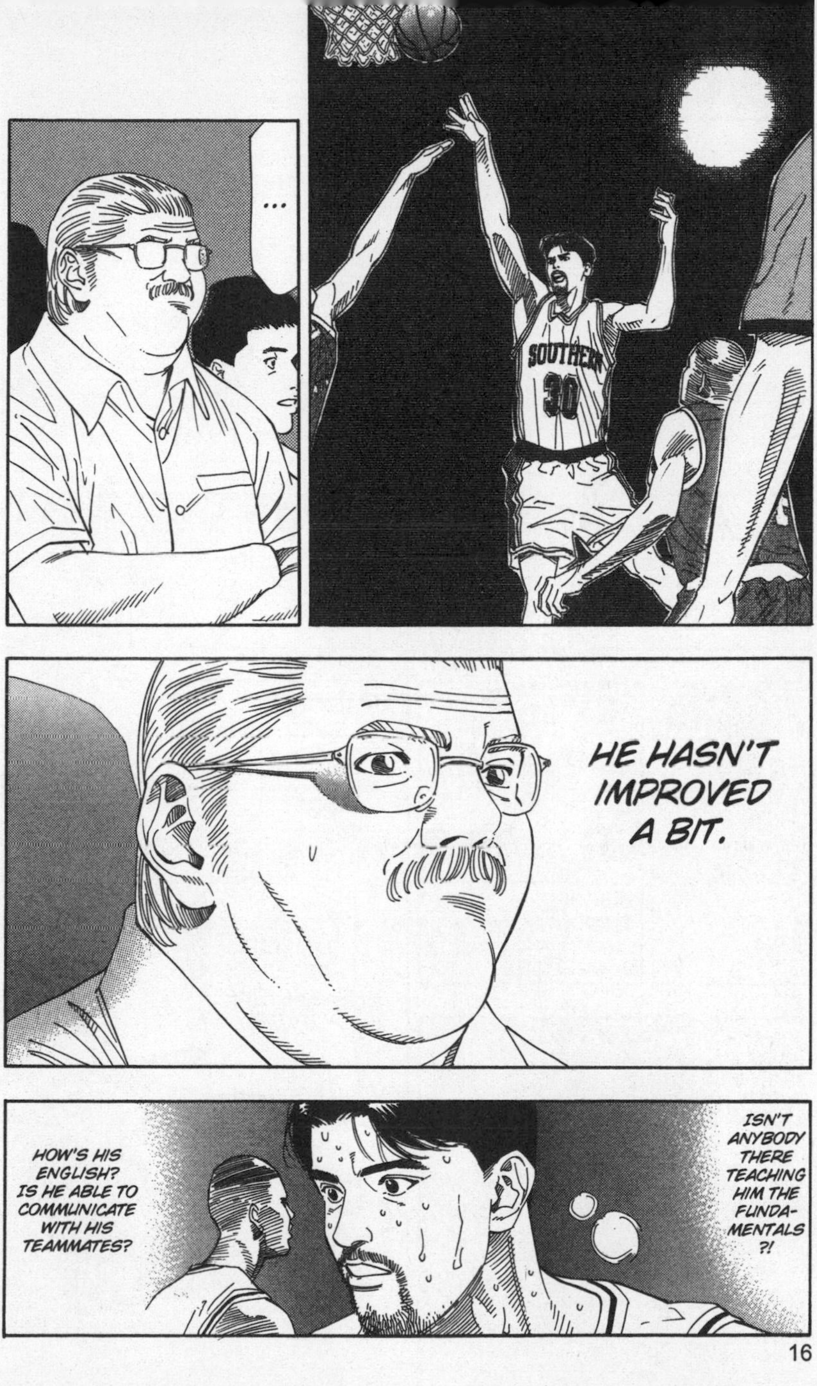
...
HE HASN'T IMPROVED A BIT.
ISN'T ANYBODY THERE TEACHING HIM THE FUNDA-MENTALS?!
HOW'S HIS ENGLISH? IS HE ABLE TO COMMUNICATE WITH HIS TEAMMATES?

READ THIS WAY

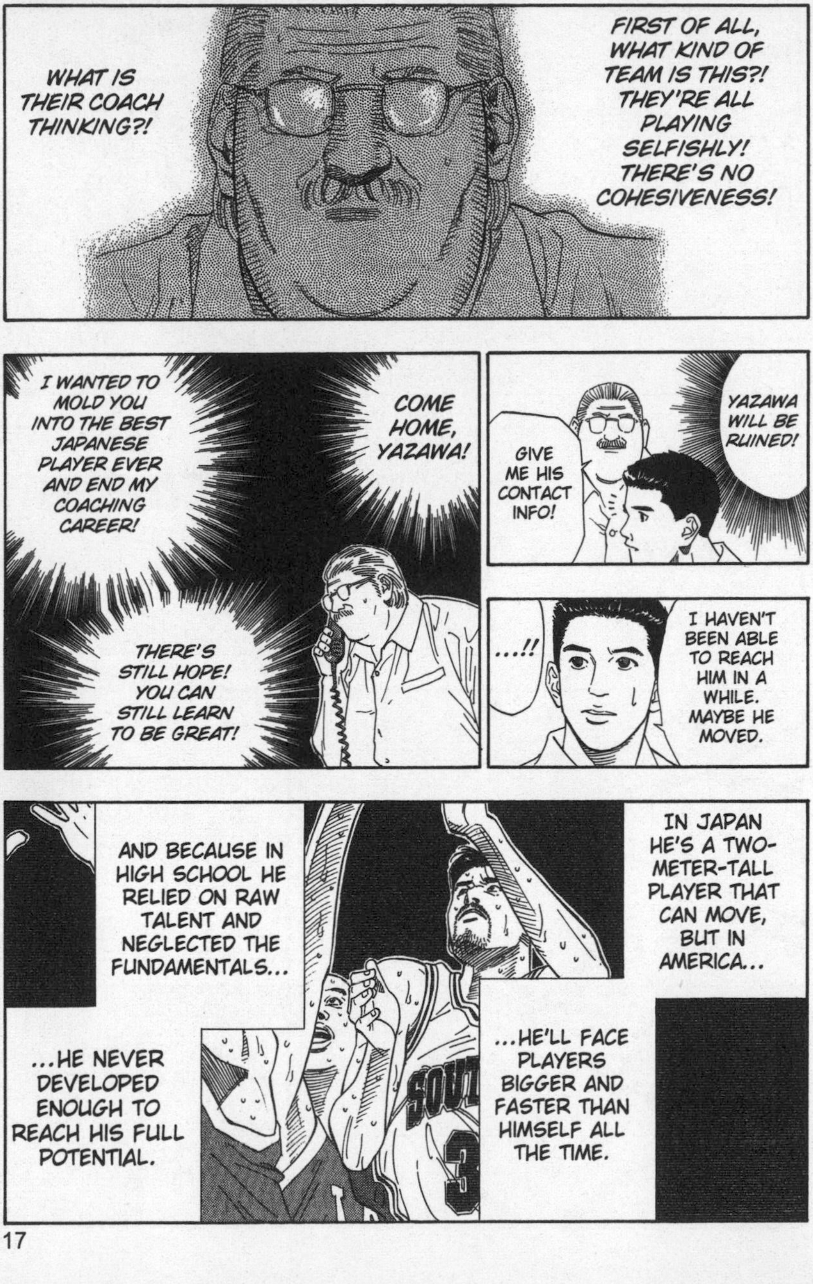
FIRST OF ALL, WHAT KIND OF TEAM IS THIS?! THEY'RE ALL PLAYING SELFISHLY! THERE'S NO COHESIVENESS!
WHAT IS THEIR COACH THINKING?!
YAZAWA WILL BE RUINED!
GIVE ME HIS CONTACT INFO!
I HAVEN'T BEEN ABLE TO REACH HIM IN A WHILE. MAYBE HE MOVED.
...!!
COME HOME, YAZAWA!
I WANTED TO MOLD YOU INTO THE BEST JAPANESE PLAYER EVER AND END MY COACHING CAREER!
THERE'S STILL HOPE! YOU CAN STILL LEARN TO BE GREAT!
IN JAPAN HE'S A TWO-METER-TALL PLAYER THAT CAN MOVE, BUT IN AMERICA...
...HE'LL FACE PLAYERS BIGGER AND FASTER THAN HIMSELF ALL THE TIME.
AND BECAUSE IN HIGH SCHOOL HE RELIED ON RAW TALENT AND NEGLECTED THE FUNDAMENTALS...
...HE NEVER DEVELOPED ENOUGH TO REACH HIS FULL POTENTIAL.
SOUT
3

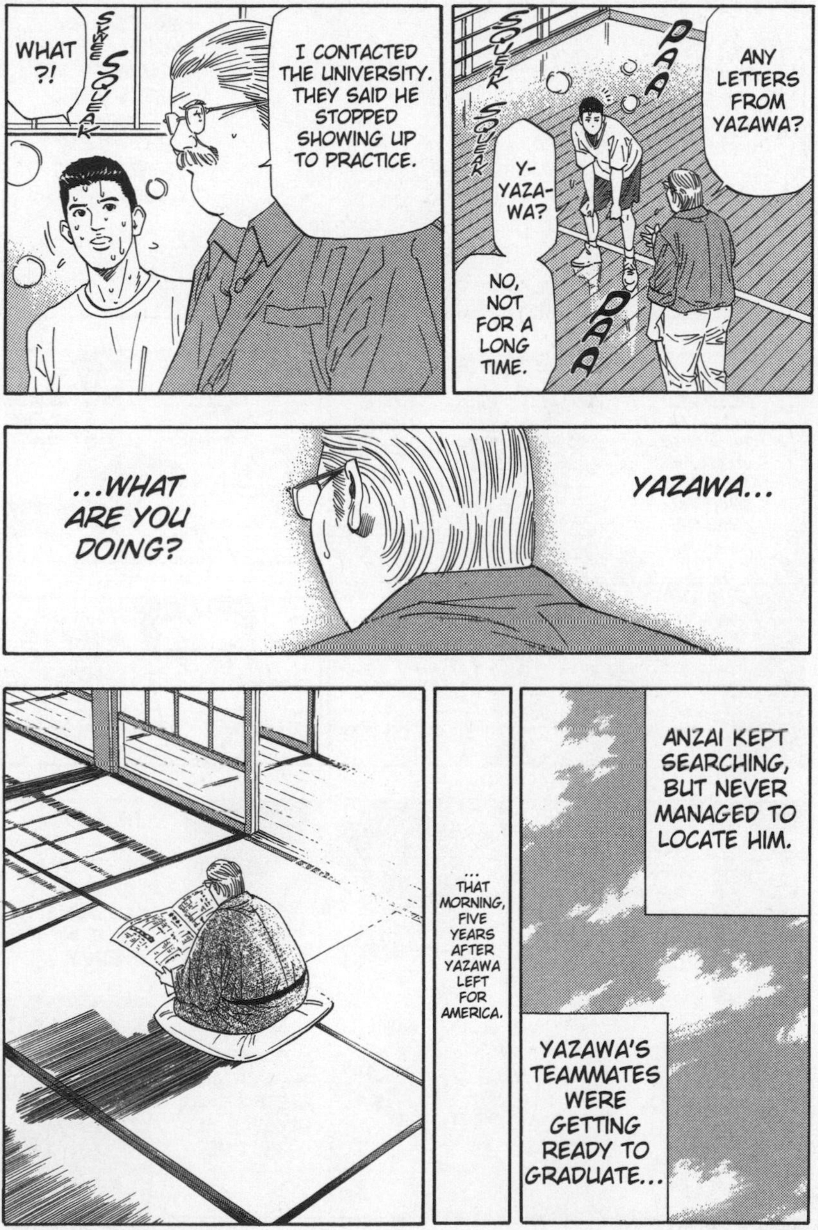
ANY LETTERS FROM YAZAWA?
SQUEAK SQUEAK
PAA
Y-YAZAWA?
NO, NOT FOR A LONG TIME.
PAA
I CONTACTED THE UNIVERSITY. THEY SAID HE STOPPED SHOWING UP TO PRACTICE.
WHAT?!
SQUEAK
YAZAWA...
...WHAT ARE YOU DOING?
ANZAI KEPT SEARCHING, BUT NEVER MANAGED TO LOCATE HIM.
YAZAWA'S TEAMMATES WERE GETTING READY TO GRADUATE...
...THAT MORNING, FIVE YEARS AFTER YAZAWA LEFT FOR AMERICA.

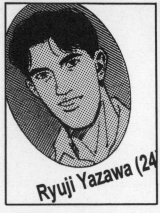

Ryuji Yazawa (24)

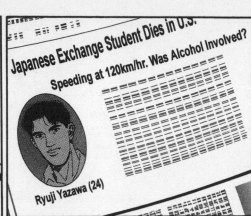

Japanese Exchange Student Dies in U.S.

Speeding at 120km/hr. Was Alcohol Involved?

Ryuji Yazawa (24)

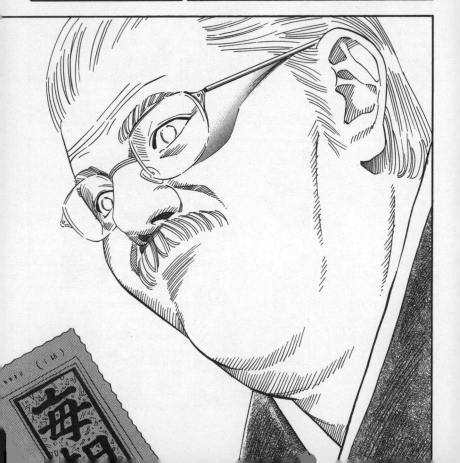

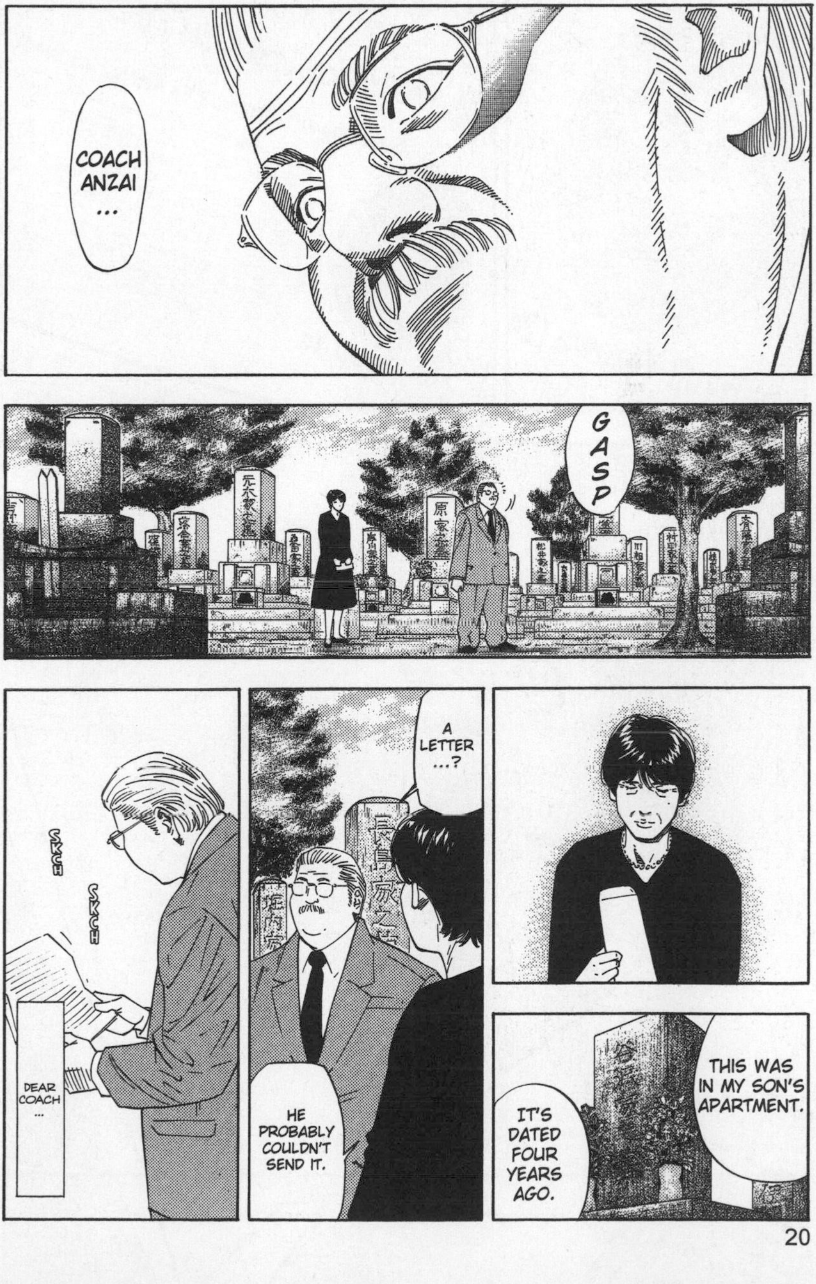

COACH ANZAI ...
GASP
THIS WAS IN MY SON'S APARTMENT.
IT'S DATED FOUR YEARS AGO.
A LETTER ...?
HE PROBABLY COULDN'T SEND IT.
SKCH
SKCH
DEAR COACH ...

READ THIS WAY

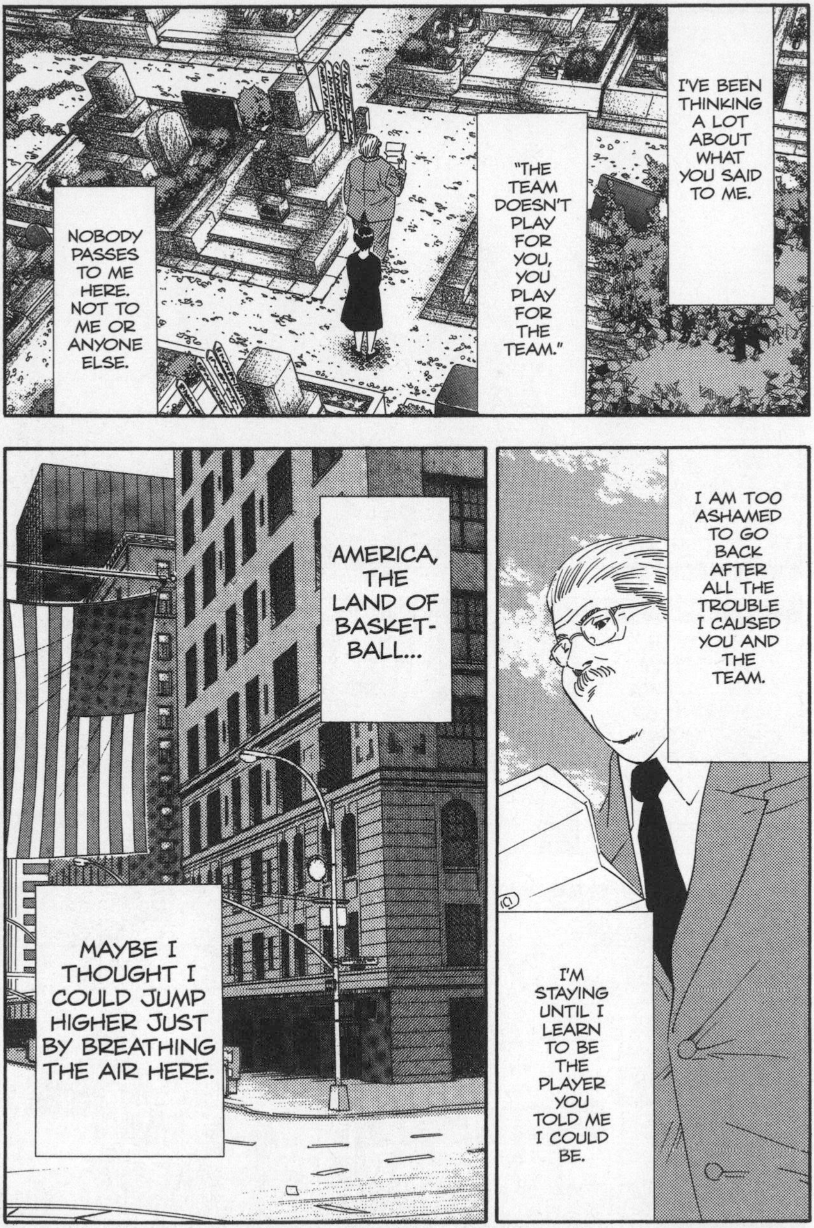
I'VE BEEN THINKING A LOT ABOUT WHAT YOU SAID TO ME.
"THE TEAM DOESN'T PLAY FOR YOU, YOU PLAY FOR THE TEAM."
NOBODY PASSES TO ME HERE. NOT TO ME OR ANYONE ELSE.
I AM TOO ASHAMED TO GO BACK AFTER ALL THE TROUBLE I CAUSED YOU AND THE TEAM.
I'M STAYING UNTIL I LEARN TO BE THE PLAYER YOU TOLD ME I COULD BE.
AMERICA, THE LAND OF BASKET-BALL...
MAYBE I THOUGHT I COULD JUMP HIGHER JUST BY BREATHING THE AIR HERE.

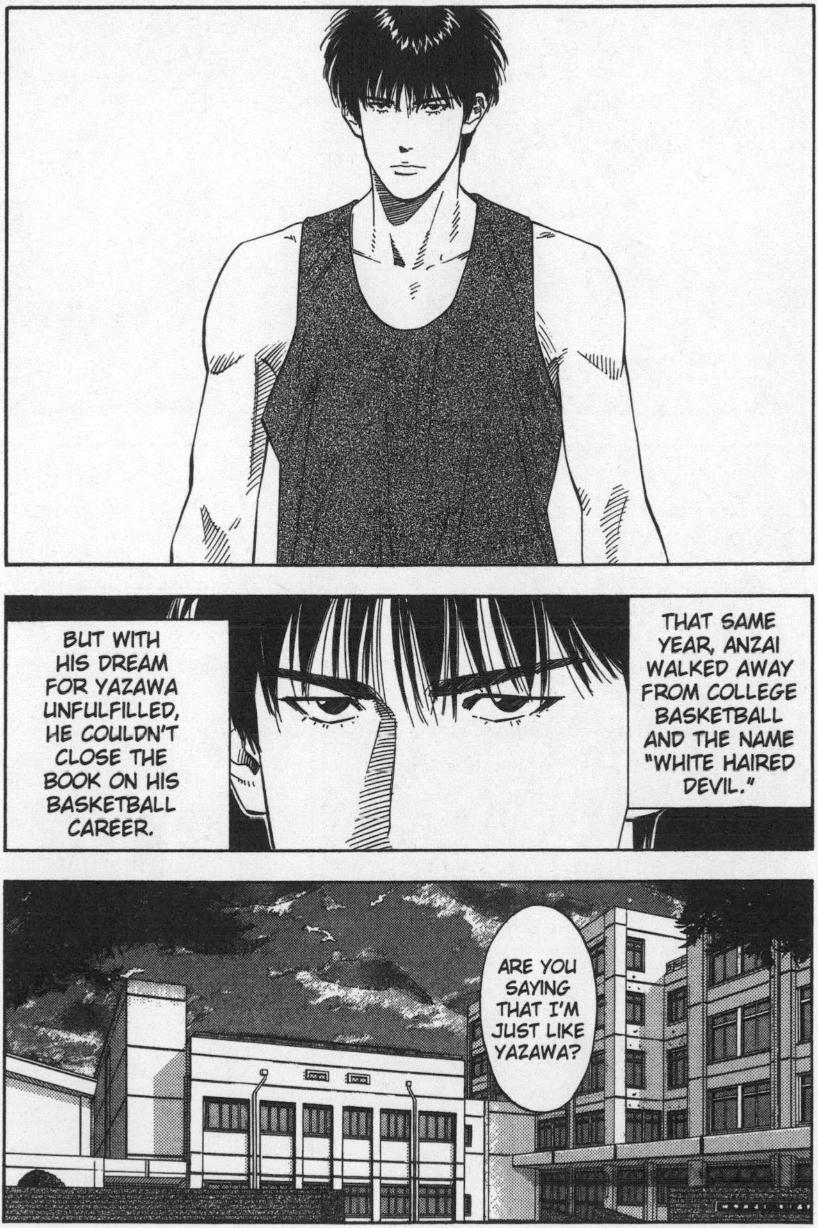
THAT SAME YEAR, ANZAI WALKED AWAY FROM COLLEGE BASKETBALL AND THE NAME "WHITE HAIRED DEVIL."
BUT WITH HIS DREAM FOR YAZAWA UNFULFILLED, HE COULDN'T CLOSE THE BOOK ON HIS BASKETBALL CAREER.
ARE YOU SAYING THAT I'M JUST LIKE YAZAWA?

READ THIS WAY

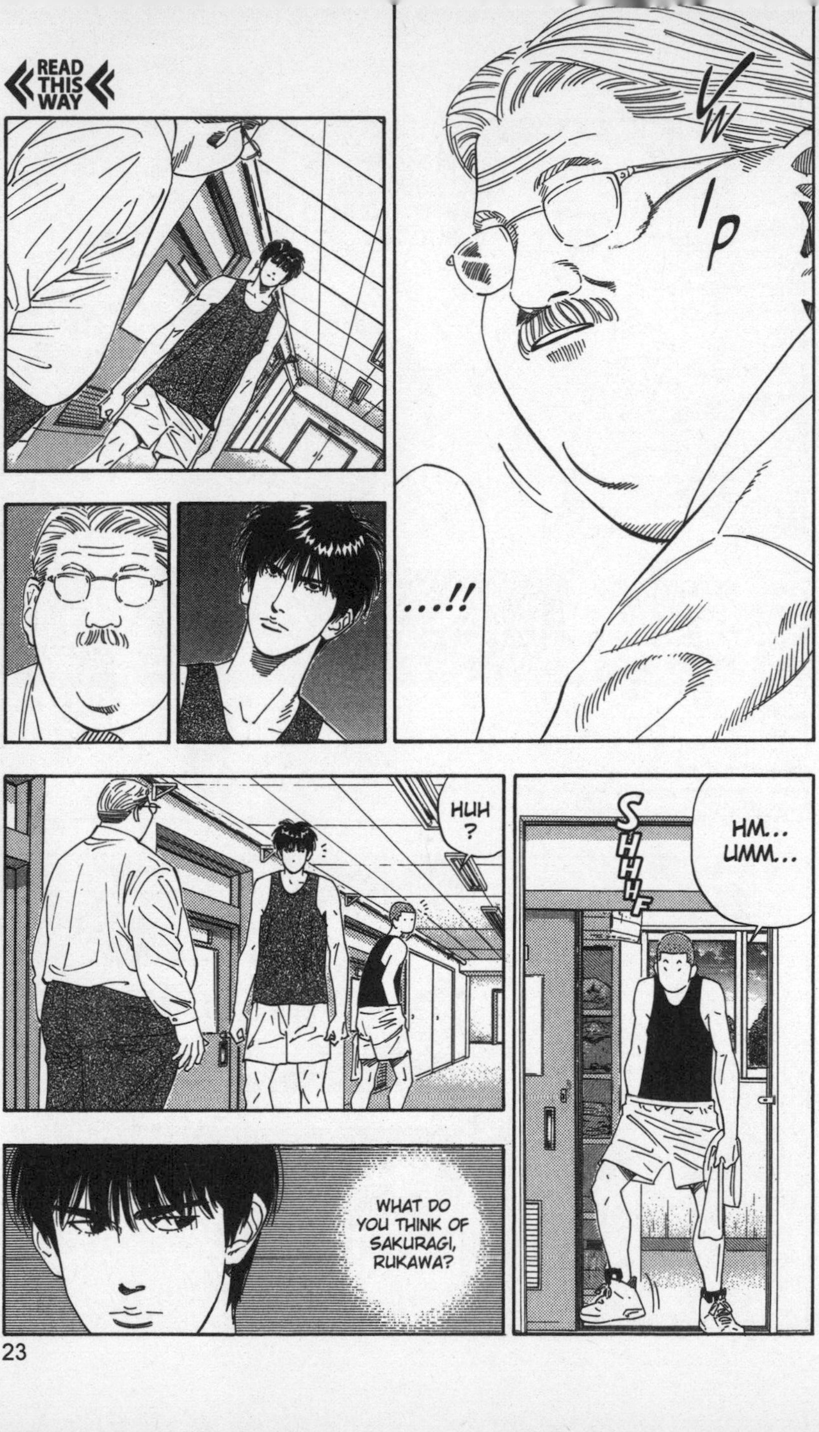

WHIP
...!!
HM... UMM...
SHHHF
HUH?
WHAT DO YOU THINK OF SAKURAGI, RUKAWA?

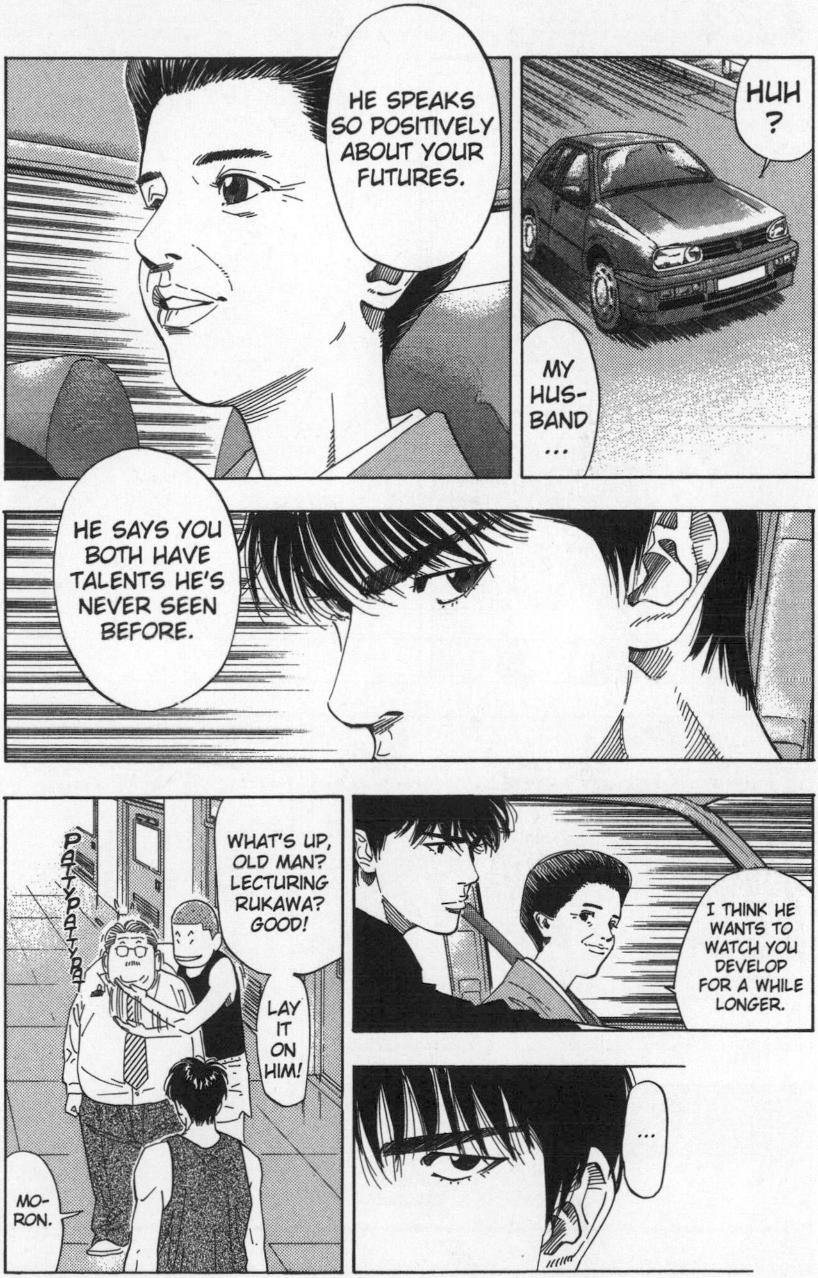
HUH ?
MY HUSBAND...
HE SPEAKS SO POSITIVELY ABOUT YOUR FUTURES.
HE SAYS YOU BOTH HAVE TALENTS HE'S NEVER SEEN BEFORE.
I THINK HE WANTS TO WATCH YOU DEVELOP FOR A WHILE LONGER.
...
WHAT'S UP, OLD MAN? LECTURING RUKAWA? GOOD!
PATTYPATTYPAT
LAY IT ON HIM!
MORON.

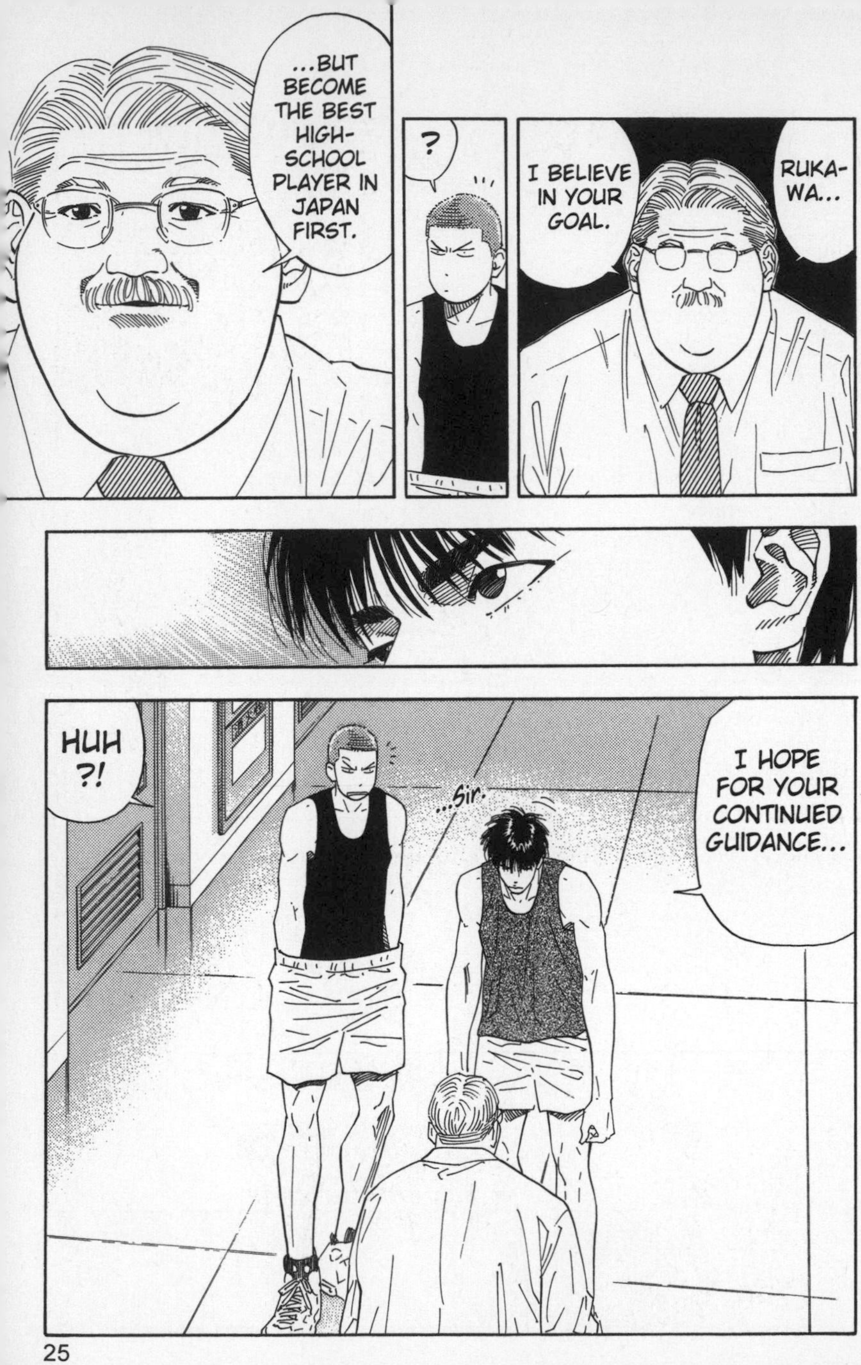
RUKA-WA...
I BELIEVE IN YOUR GOAL.
?
...BUT BECOME THE BEST HIGH-SCHOOL PLAYER IN JAPAN FIRST.
I HOPE FOR YOUR CONTINUED GUIDANCE...
...Sir.
HUH ?!

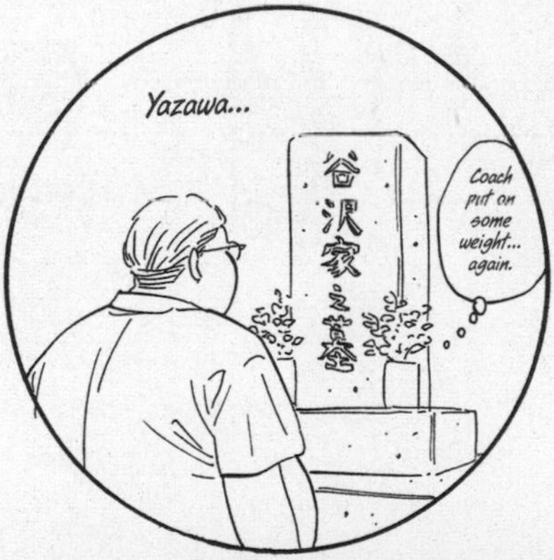
Yazawa...
谷沢家之墓
Coach put on some weight... again.

Tombstone: Yazawa

SLAM DUNK

#190 THE BEST JAPANESE HIGH SCHOOL PLAYER

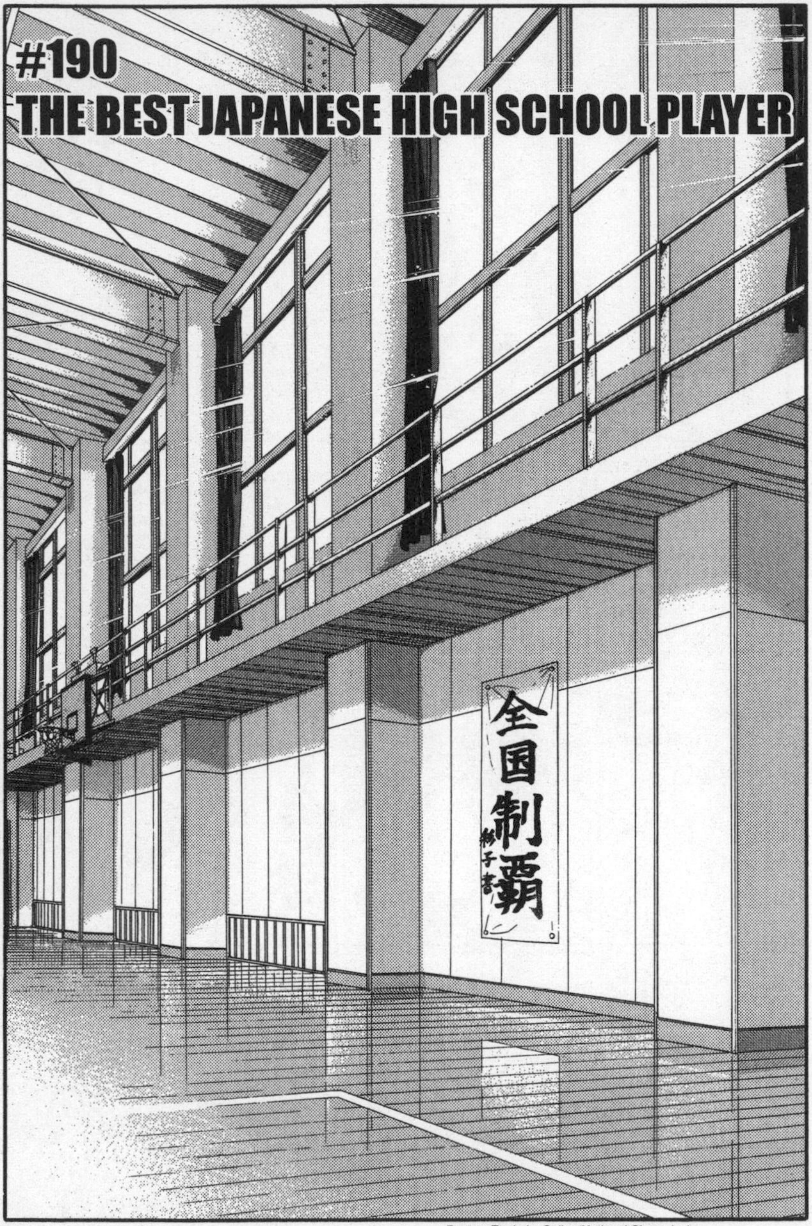
全国制覇
彩子書

Poster: *Zenkoku Seiha* (National Champion)
By Ayako

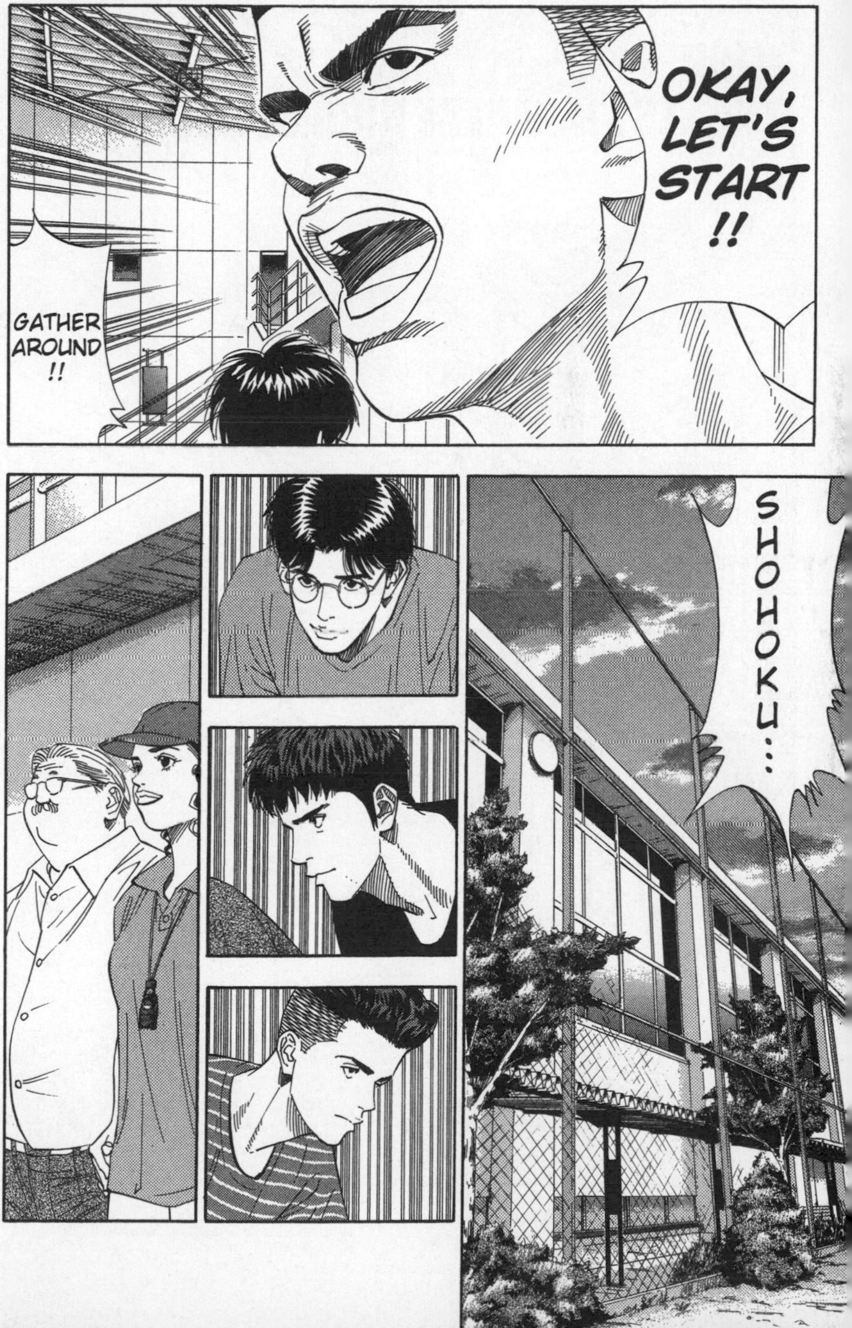
OKAY, LET'S START!!
GATHER AROUND!!
SHOHOKU...

READ THIS WAY

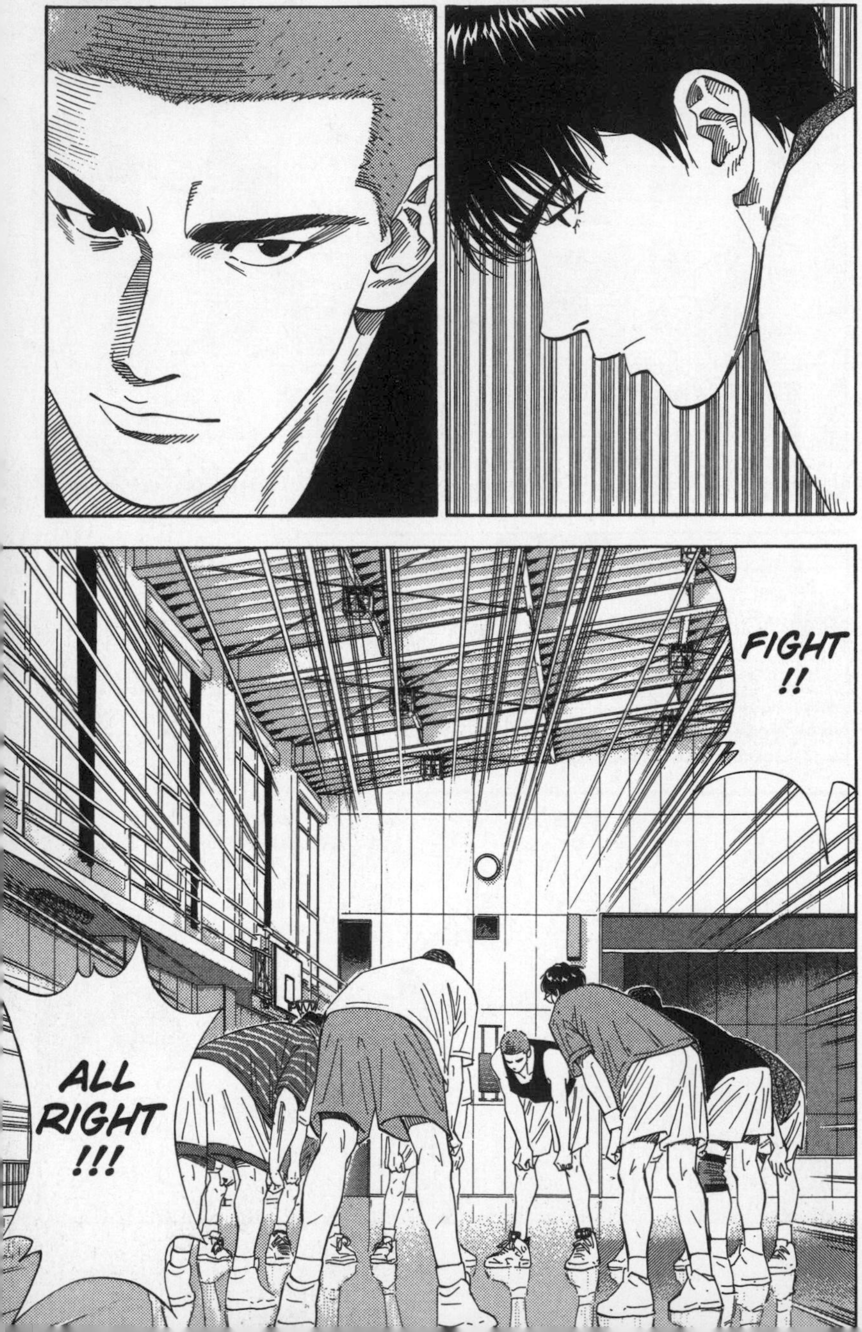
FIGHT !!
ALL RIGHT !!!

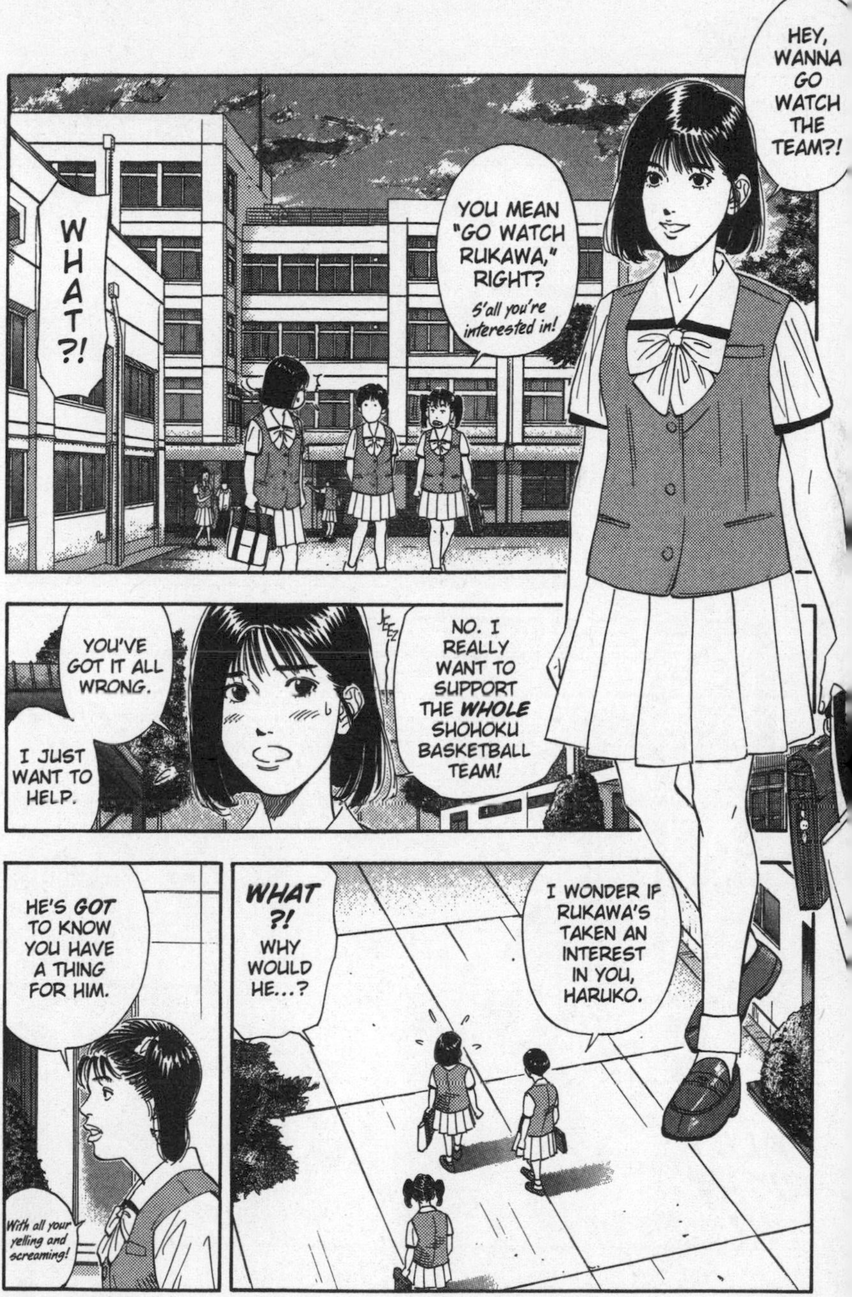
HEY, WANNA GO WATCH THE TEAM?!
YOU MEAN "GO WATCH RUKAWA," RIGHT?
S'all you're interested in!
WHAT?!
NO. I REALLY WANT TO SUPPORT THE *WHOLE* SHOHOKU BASKETBALL TEAM!
JEEZ
YOU'VE GOT IT ALL WRONG.
I JUST WANT TO HELP.
I WONDER IF RUKAWA'S TAKEN AN INTEREST IN YOU, HARUKO.
WHAT?! WHY WOULD HE...?
HE'S *GOT* TO KNOW YOU HAVE A THING FOR HIM.
With all your yelling and screaming!

READ THIS WAY

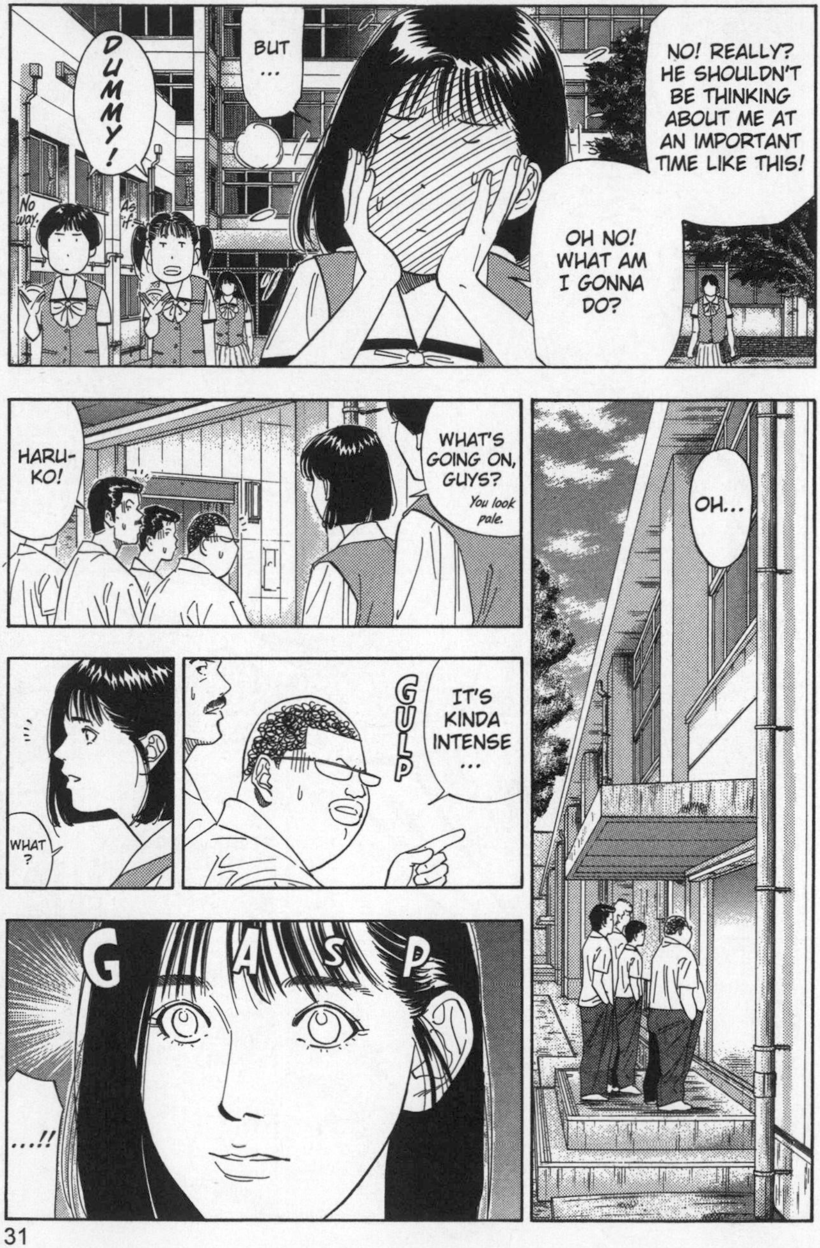
NO! REALLY? HE SHOULDN'T BE THINKING ABOUT ME AT AN IMPORTANT TIME LIKE THIS!
OH NO! WHAT AM I GONNA DO?
BUT ...
DUMMY!
As if—
No way.
OH...
WHAT'S GOING ON, GUYS?
You look pale.
HARU-KO!
GULP
IT'S KINDA INTENSE ...
WHAT?
GASP
...!!

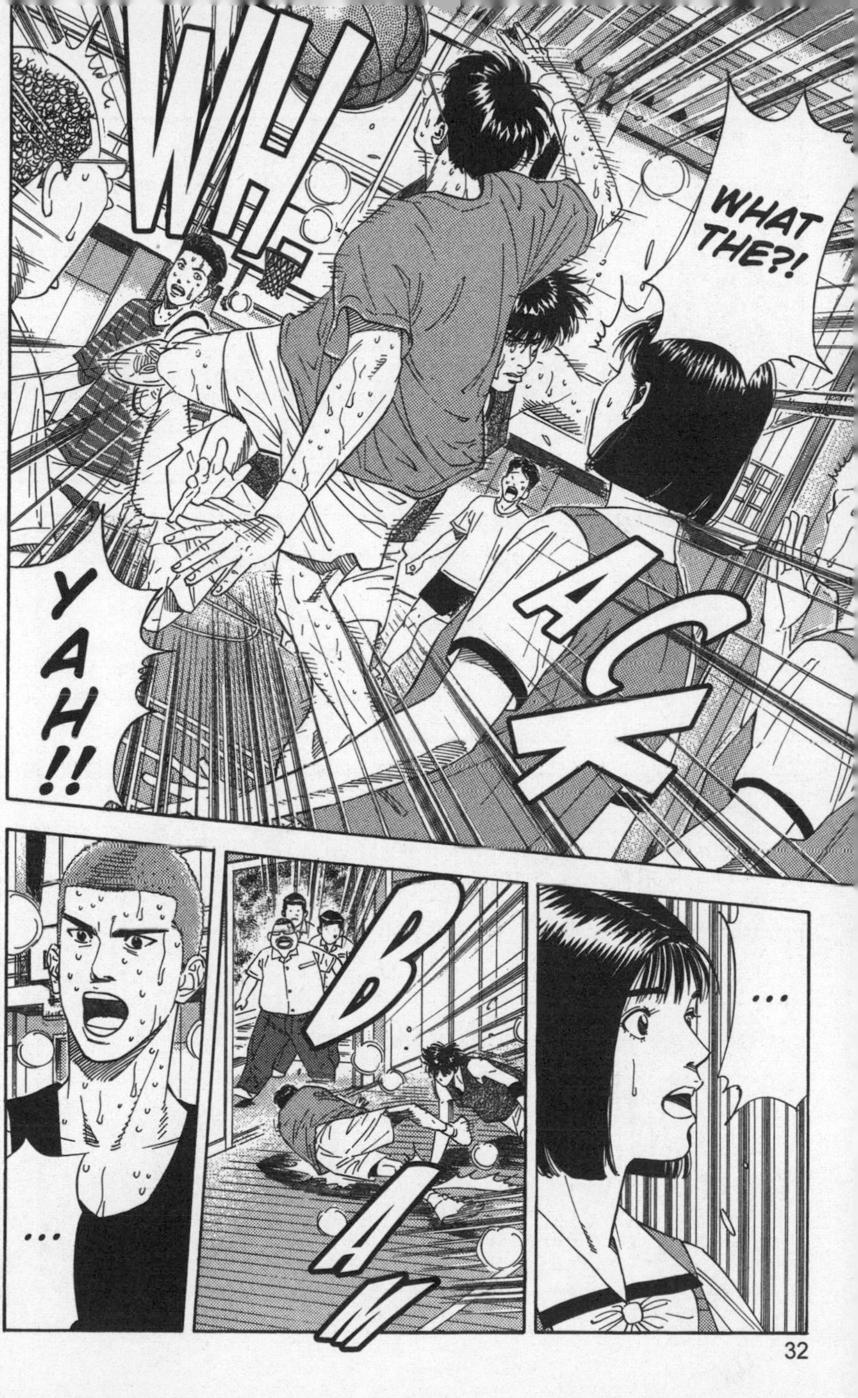
WHAT THE?!
W!!
ACK
YAH!!
...
BAM
...

READ THIS WAY

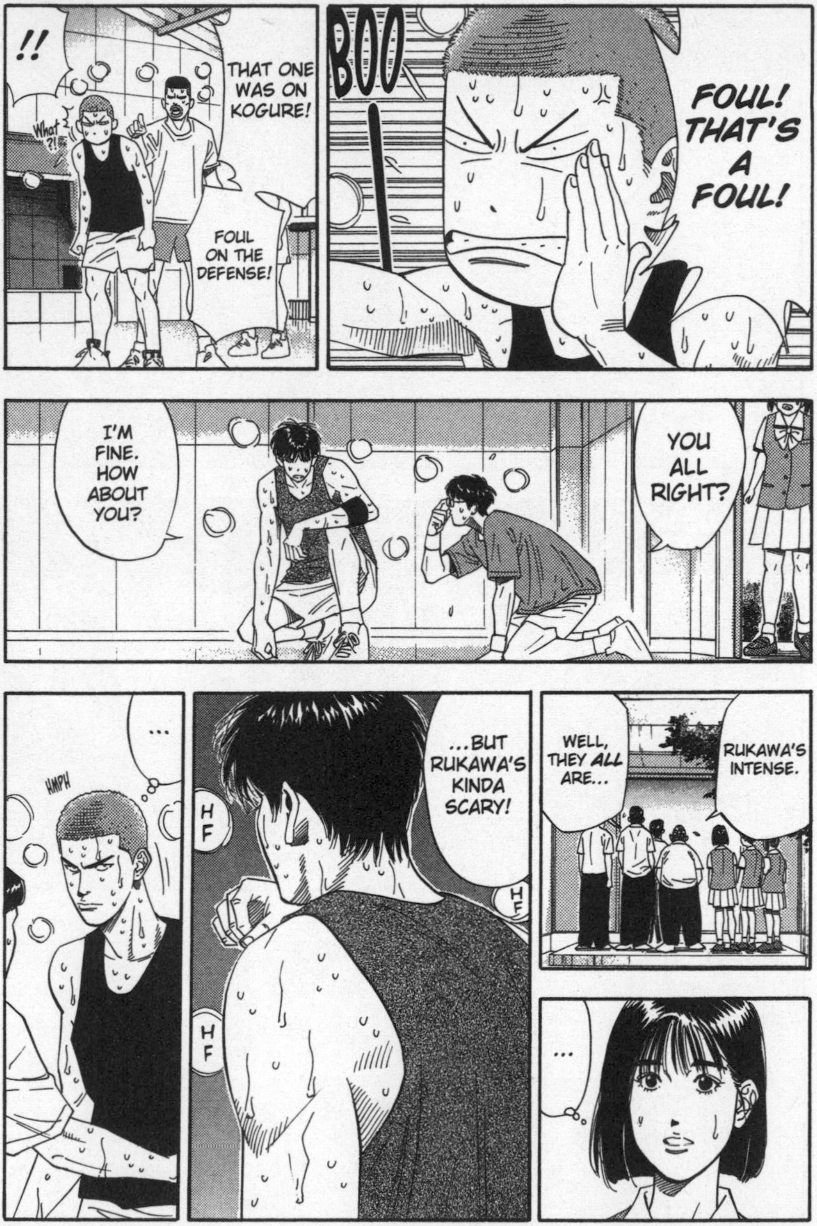

BOO
FOUL! THAT'S A FOUL!
THAT ONE WAS ON KOGURE!
!!
What?!
FOUL ON THE DEFENSE!
YOU ALL RIGHT?
I'M FINE. HOW ABOUT YOU?
RUKAWA'S INTENSE.
WELL, THEY *ALL* ARE...
...
...BUT RUKAWA'S KINDA SCARY!
HF
HF
HF
...
HMPH

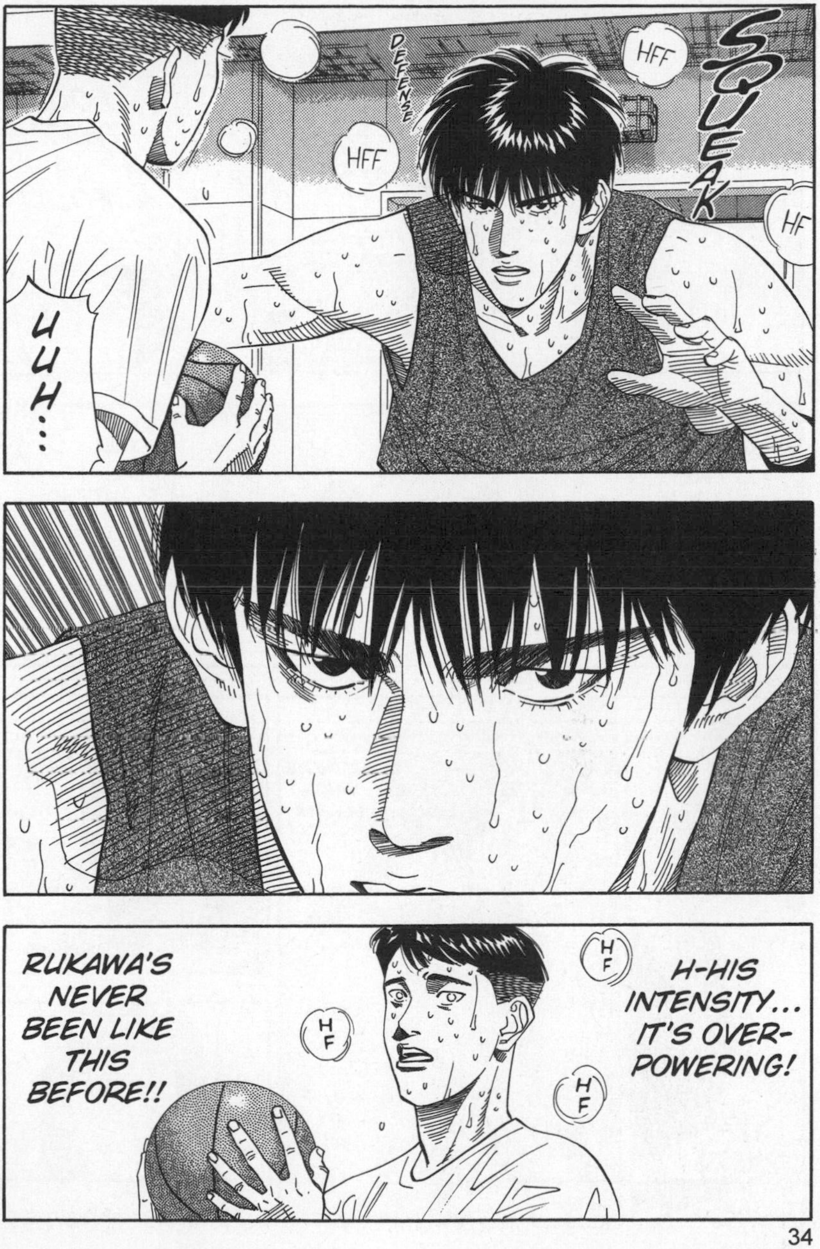
SQUEAK
HF
HFF
DEFENSE
HFF
UUH...
H-HIS INTENSITY... IT'S OVER-POWERING!
HF
HF
HF
RUKAWA'S NEVER BEEN LIKE THIS BEFORE!!

READ THIS WAY

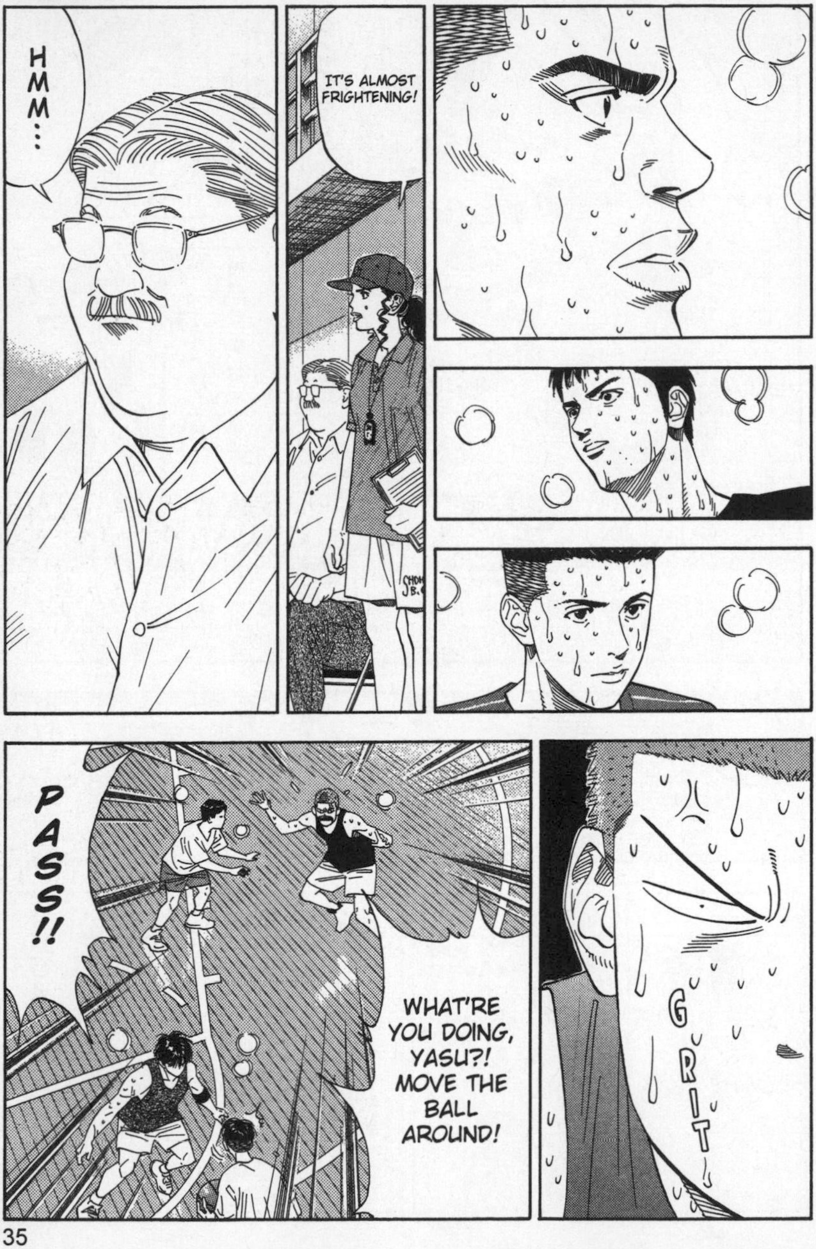
IT'S ALMOST FRIGHTENING!
HMM...
GRIT
PASS!!
WHAT'RE YOU DOING, YASU?! MOVE THE BALL AROUND!

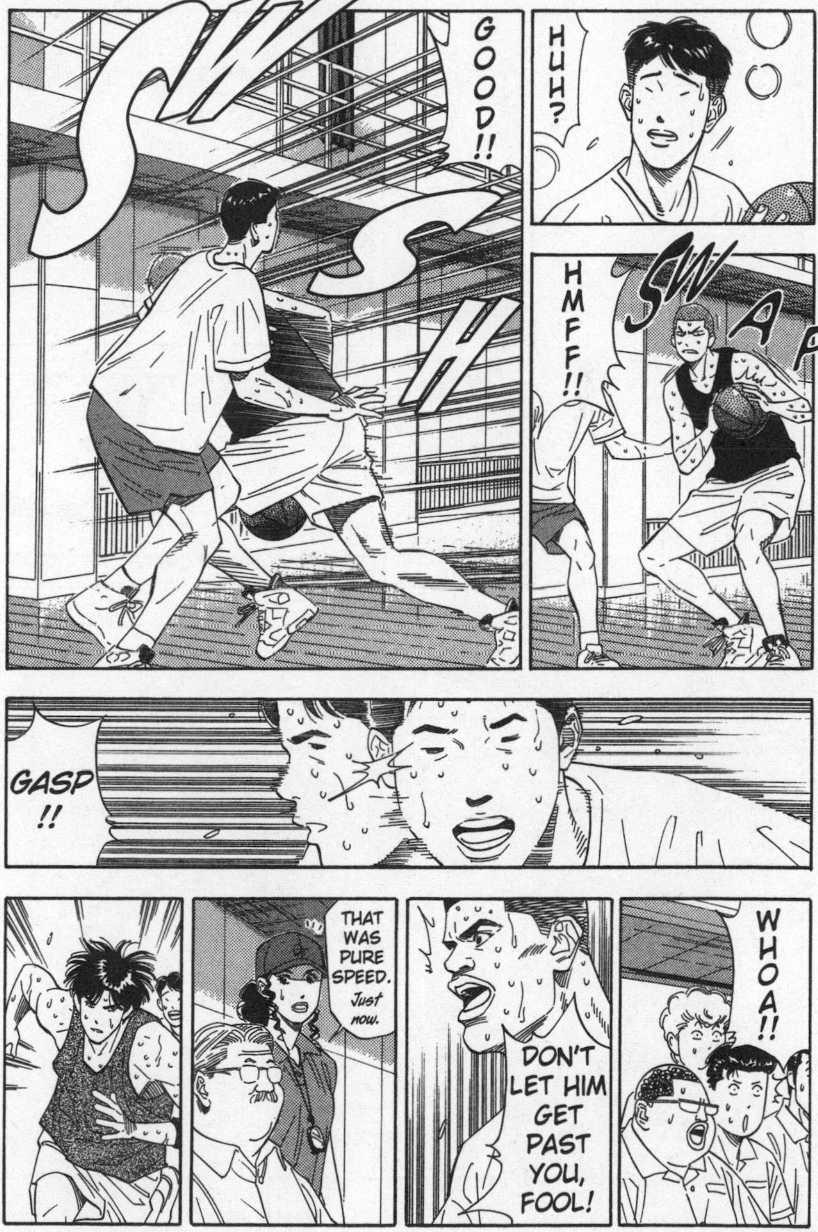
HUH?
HMFF!!
SWAP
SWSH
GOOD!!
GASP!!
WHOA!!
DON'T LET HIM GET PAST YOU, FOOL!
THAT WAS PURE SPEED. Just now.

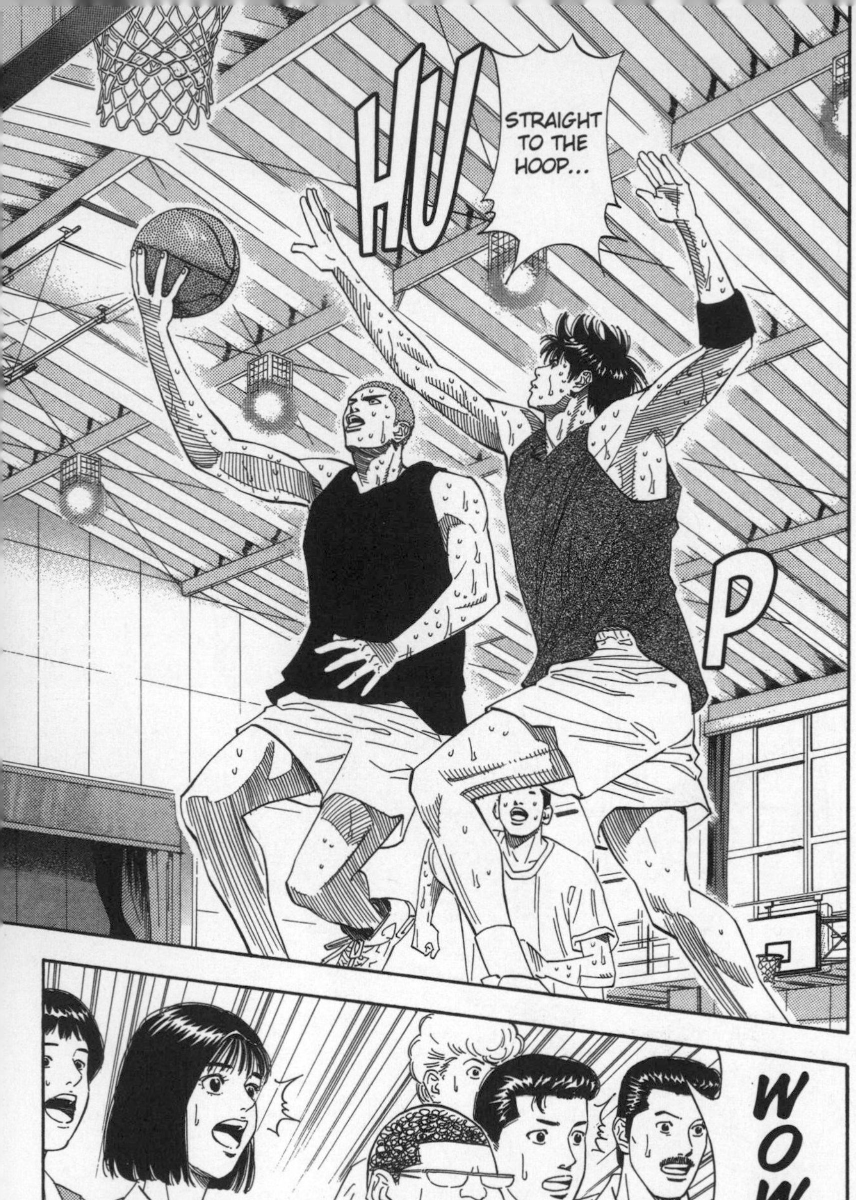
STRAIGHT TO THE HOOP...
HU
P

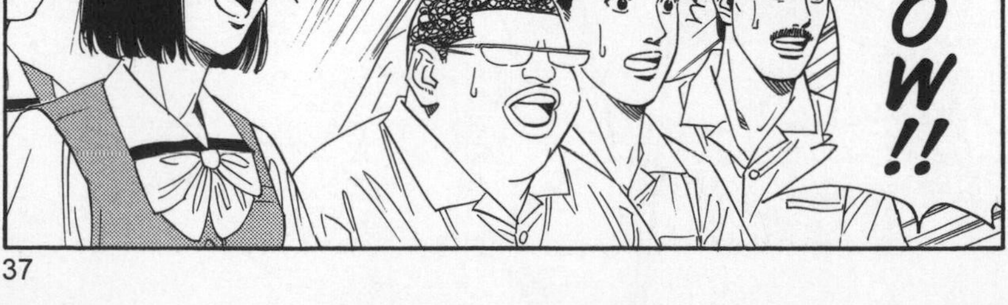
WOW!!

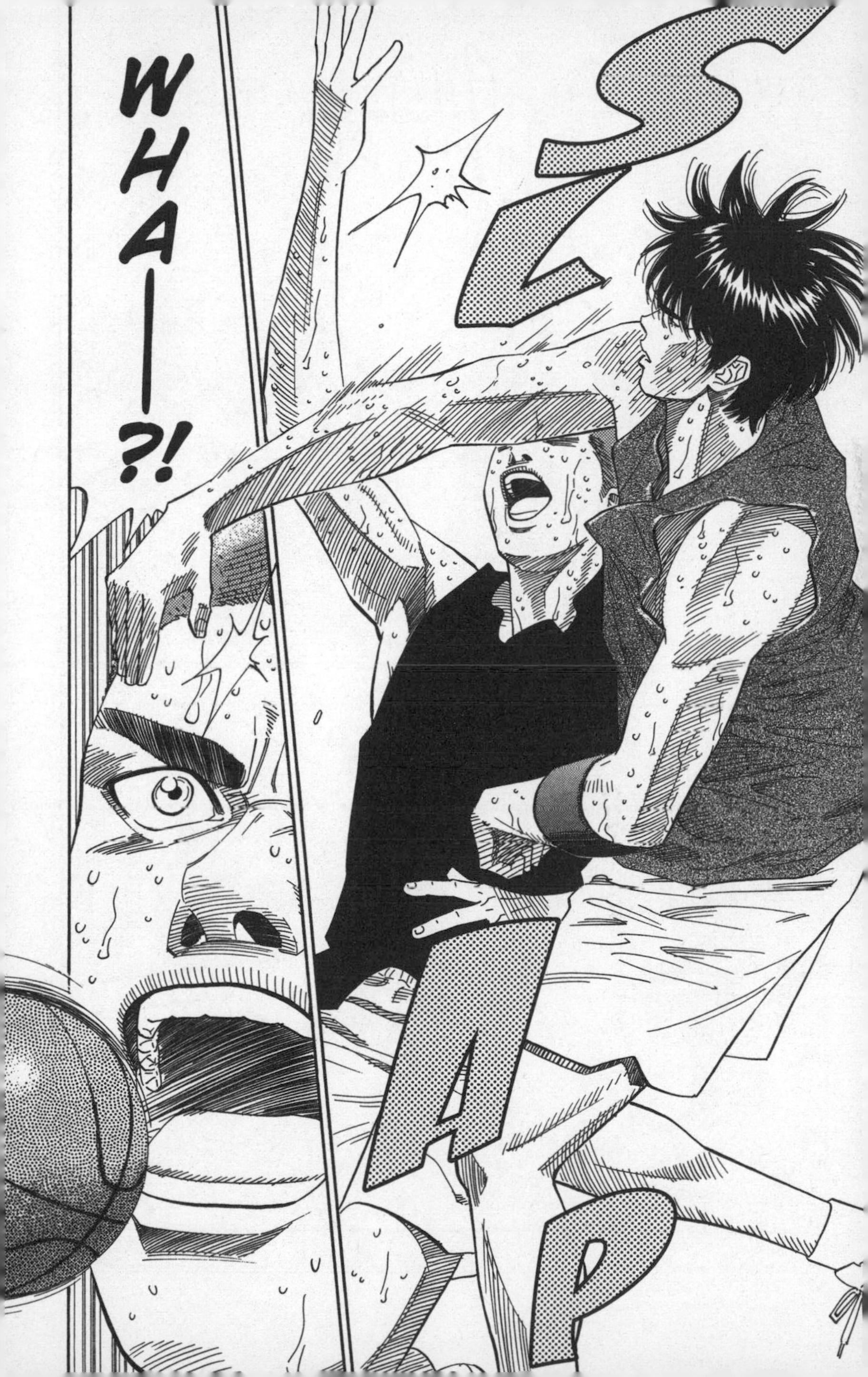
SLAP
WHA--?!

READ THIS WAY

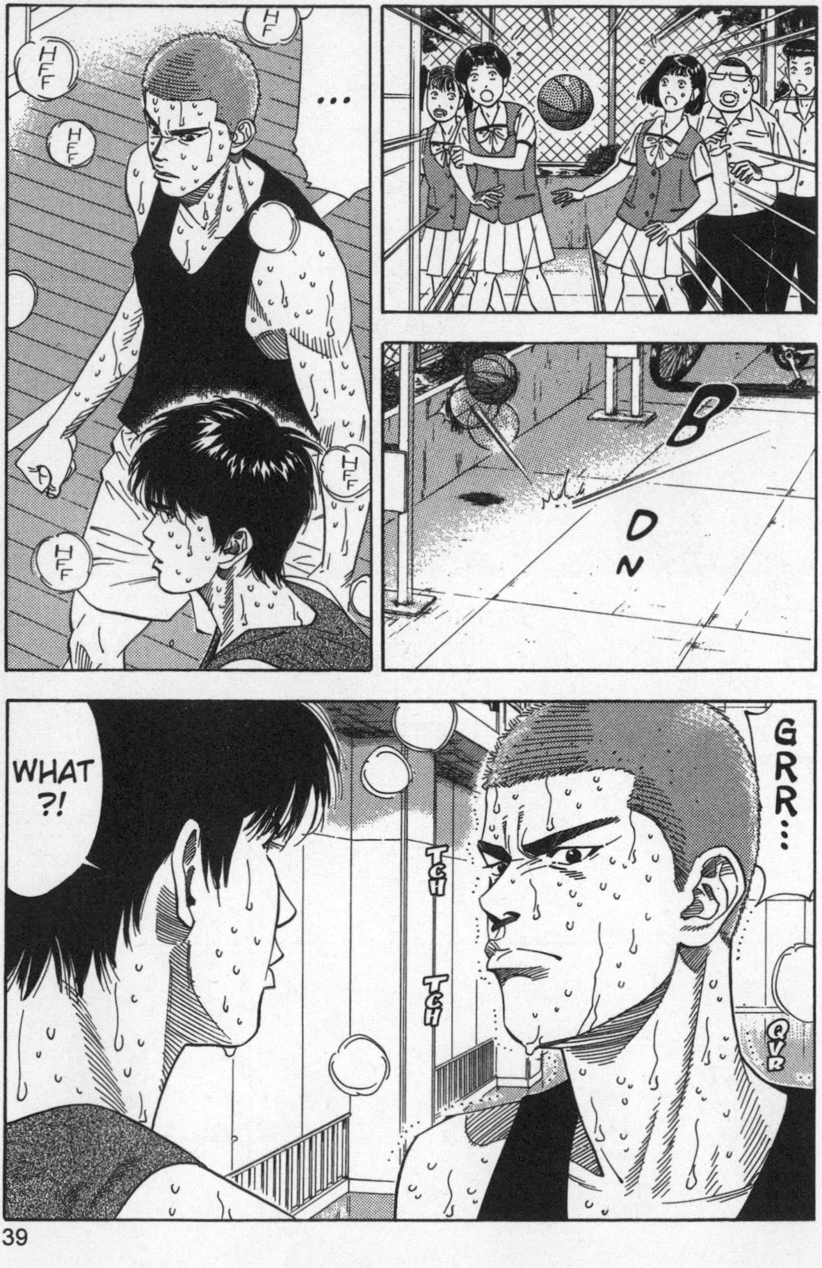
B
DON
HF
HFF
...
HFF
HFF
HFF
GRR...
QVR
TCH
TCH
WHAT ?!

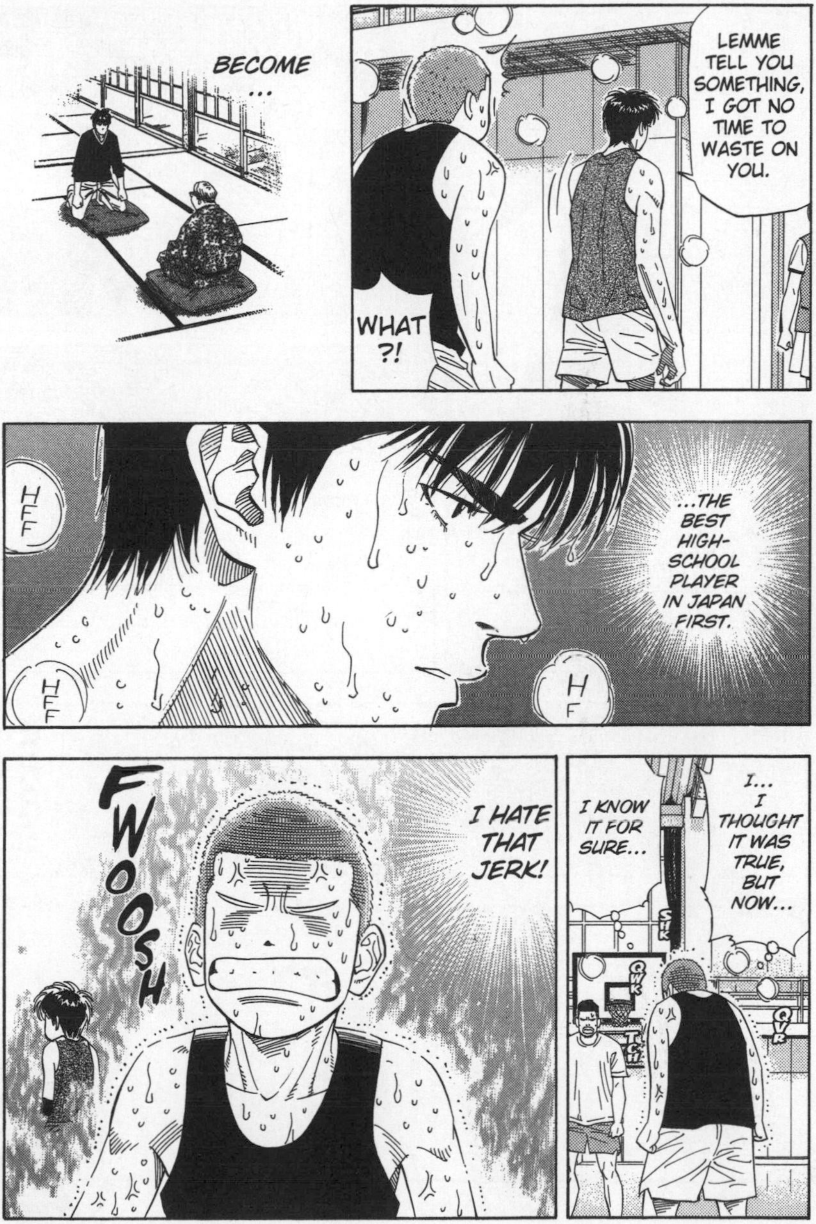
LEMME TELL YOU SOMETHING, I GOT NO TIME TO WASTE ON YOU.
WHAT ?!
BECOME ...
...THE BEST HIGH-SCHOOL PLAYER IN JAPAN FIRST.
HFF
HF
HFF
I... I THOUGHT IT WAS TRUE, BUT NOW...
I KNOW IT FOR SURE...
SHK
QVR
QWK
TCH
I HATE THAT JERK!
FWOOSH

READ THIS WAY

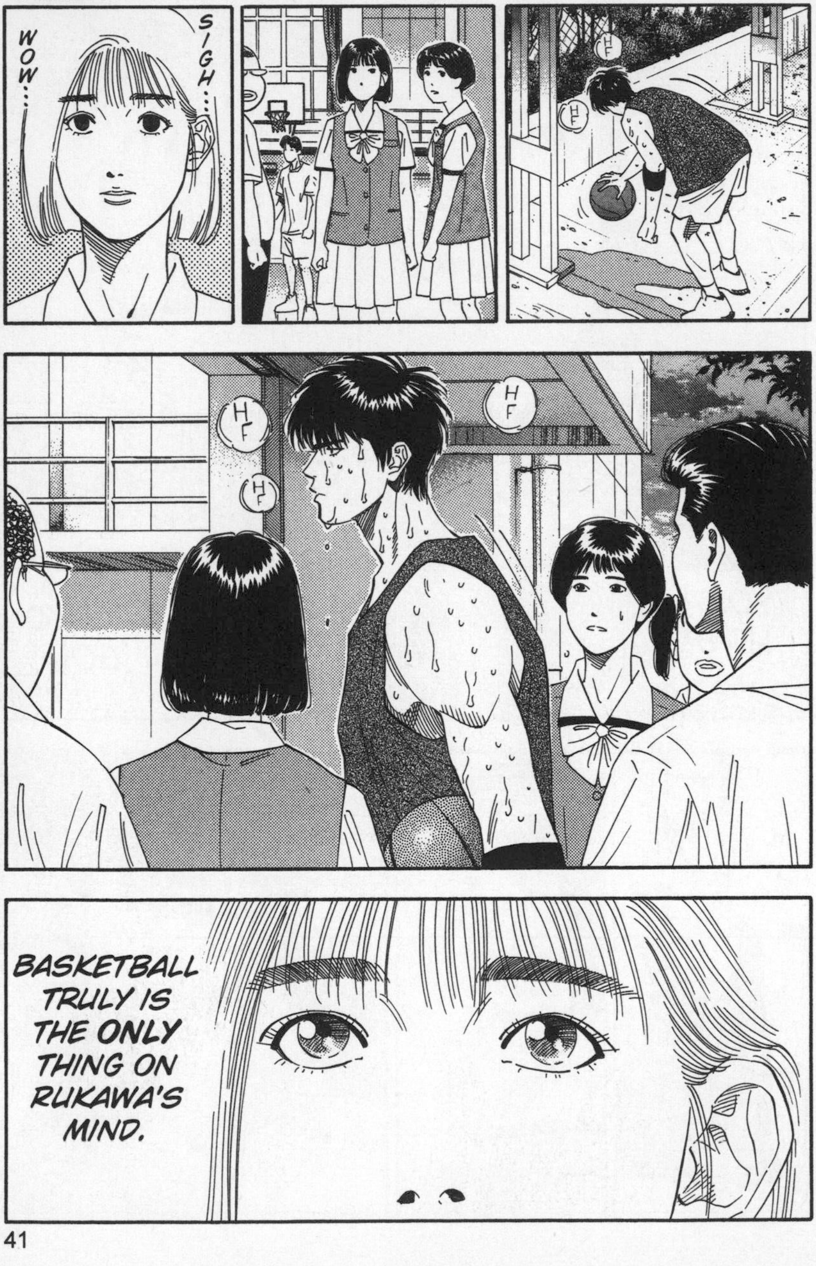

HF
HF
SIGH...
WOW...
HF
HF
HF
BASKETBALL TRULY IS THE ONLY THING ON RUKAWA'S MIND.

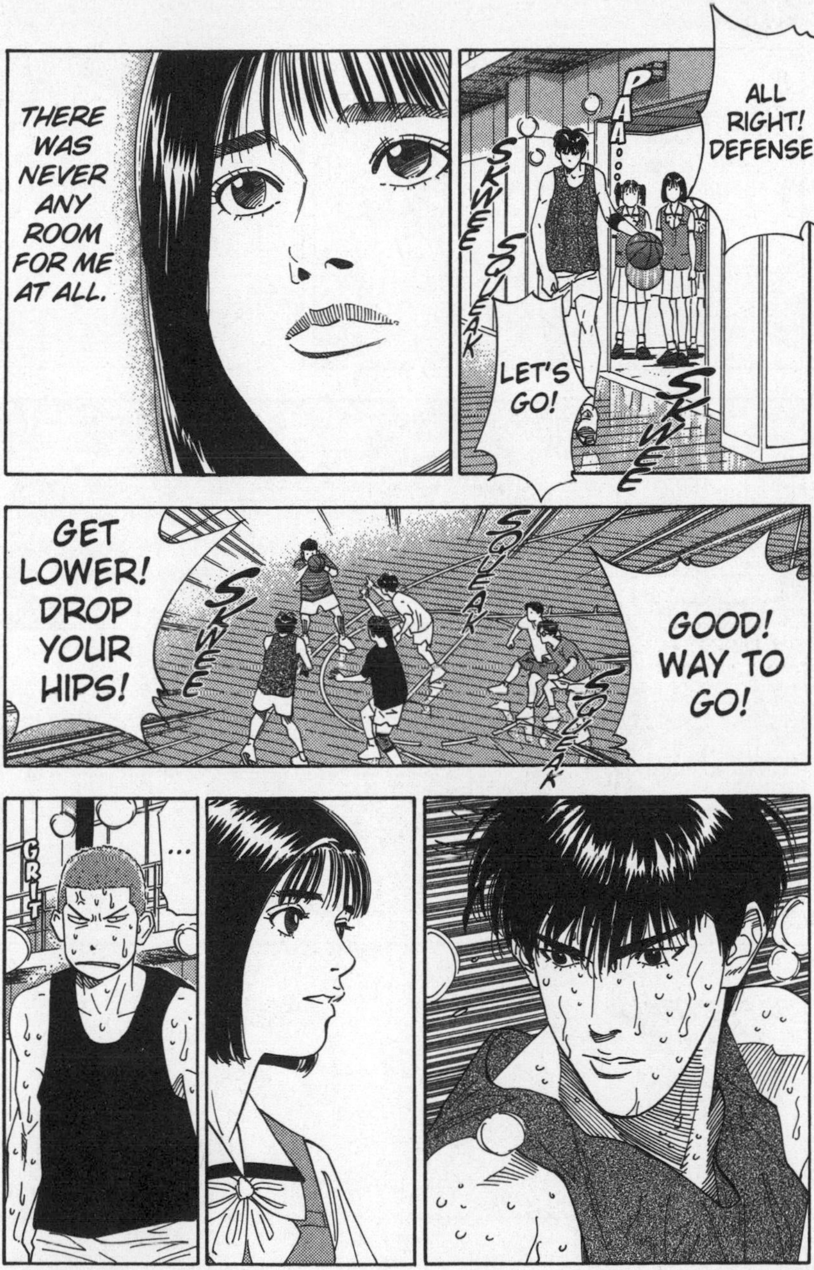
ALL RIGHT! DEFENSE!
PAAA...
SKWEE
SQUEAK
LET'S GO!
SKWEE
THERE WAS NEVER ANY ROOM FOR ME AT ALL.
GOOD! WAY TO GO!
SQUEAK
SQUEAK
SKWEE
GET LOWER! DROP YOUR HIPS!
GRIT
...

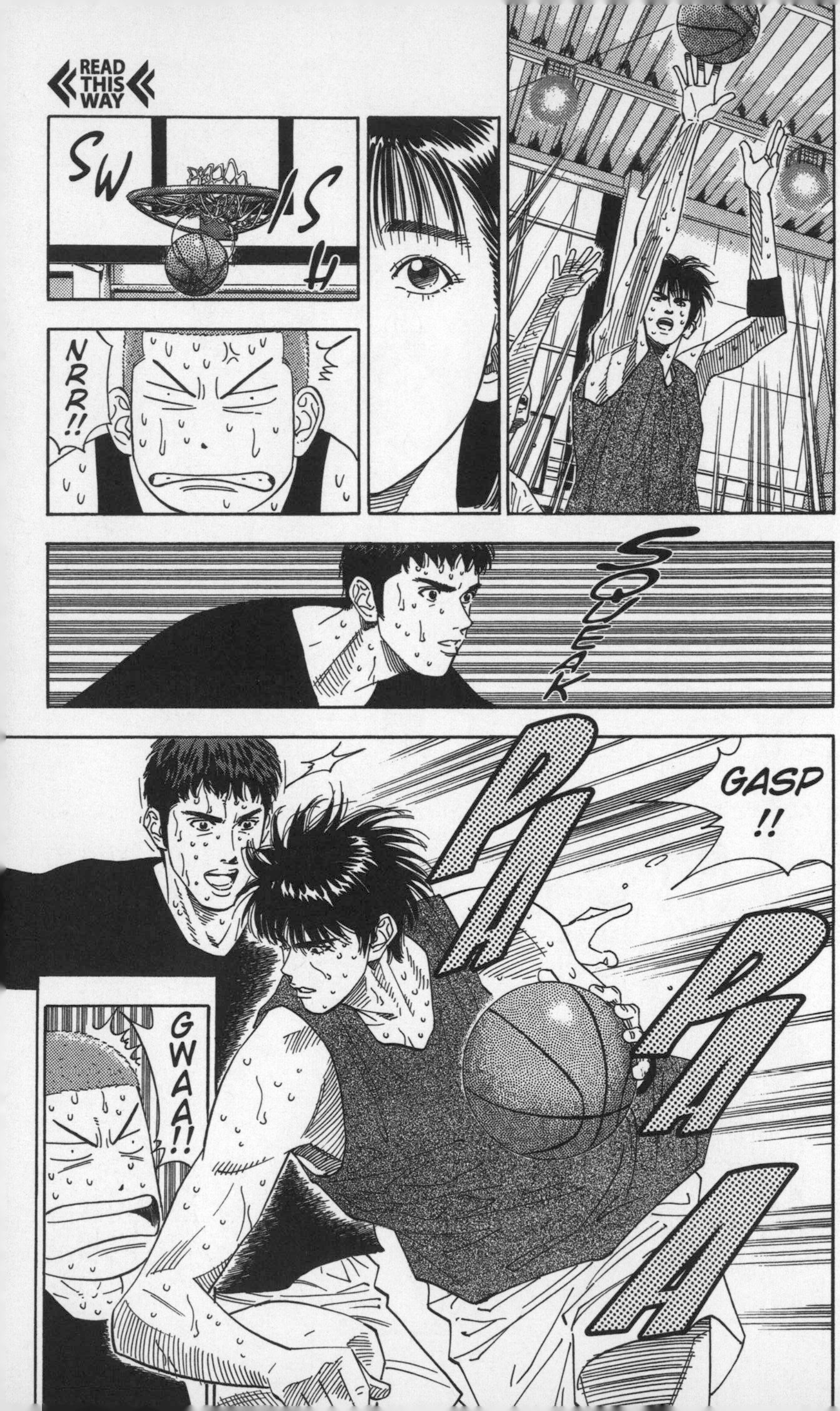
READ THIS WAY
SWISH
NRR!!
SQUEAK
GASP !!
BAAA
GWAA!!

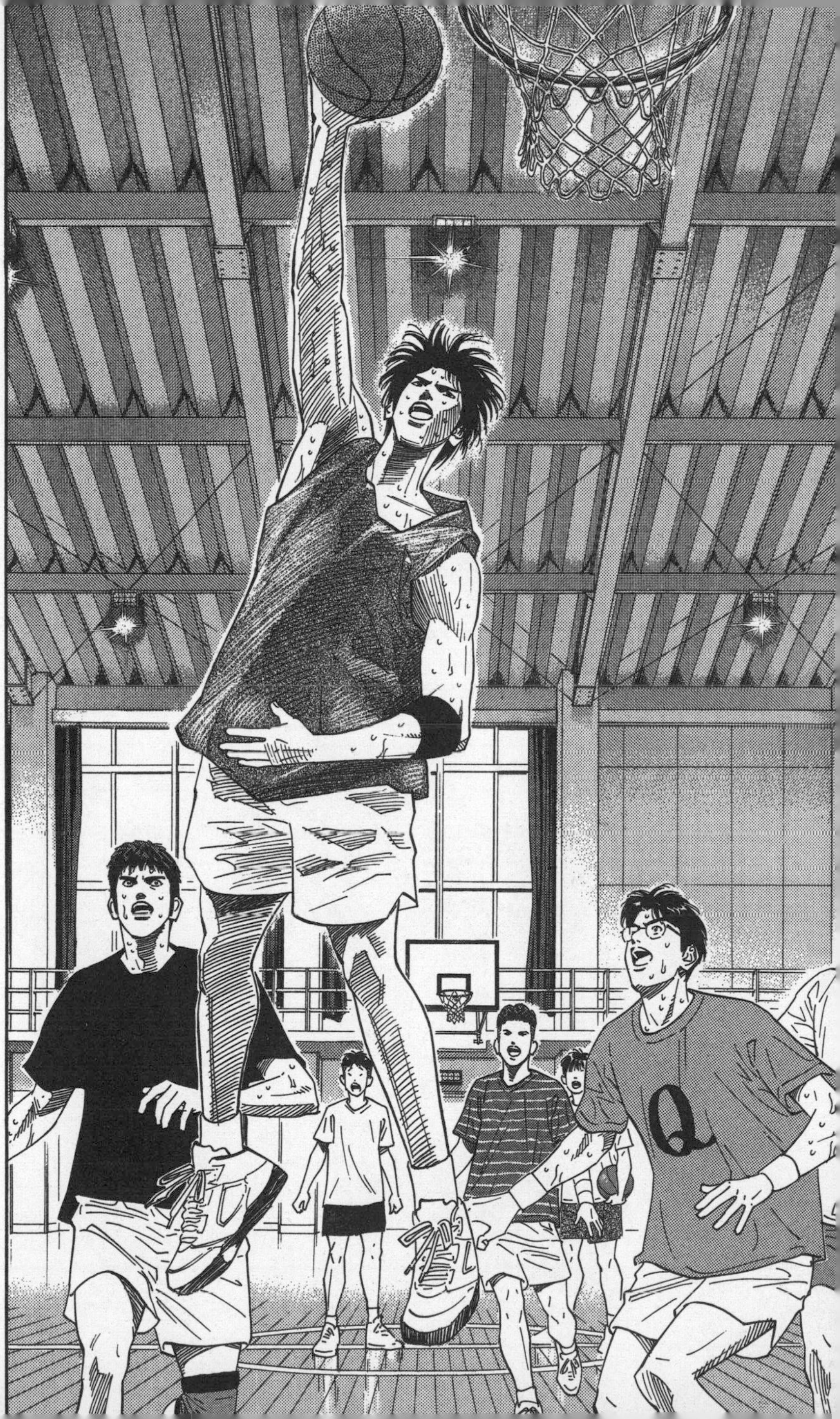

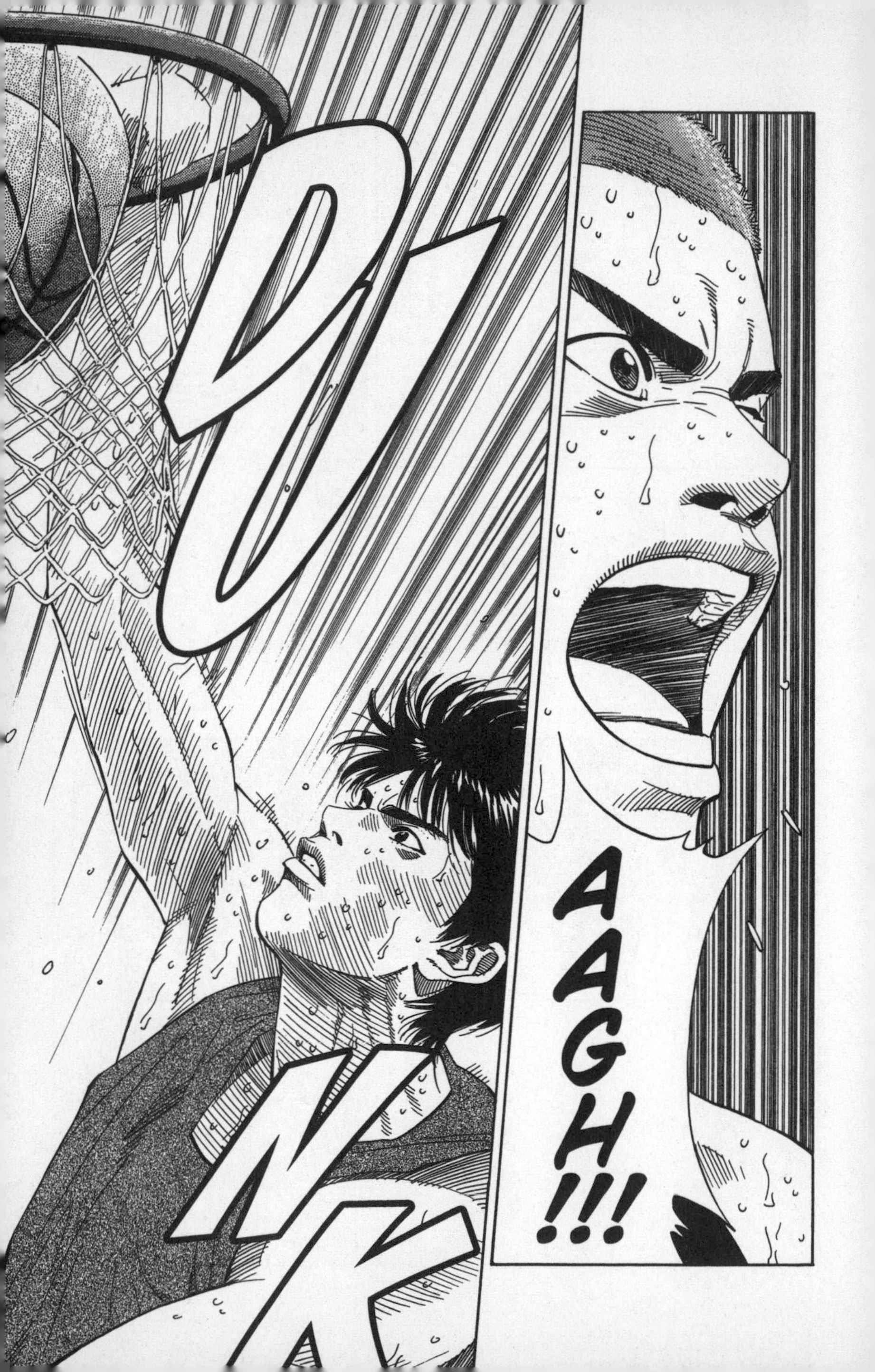
AAGH!!!
DUNK

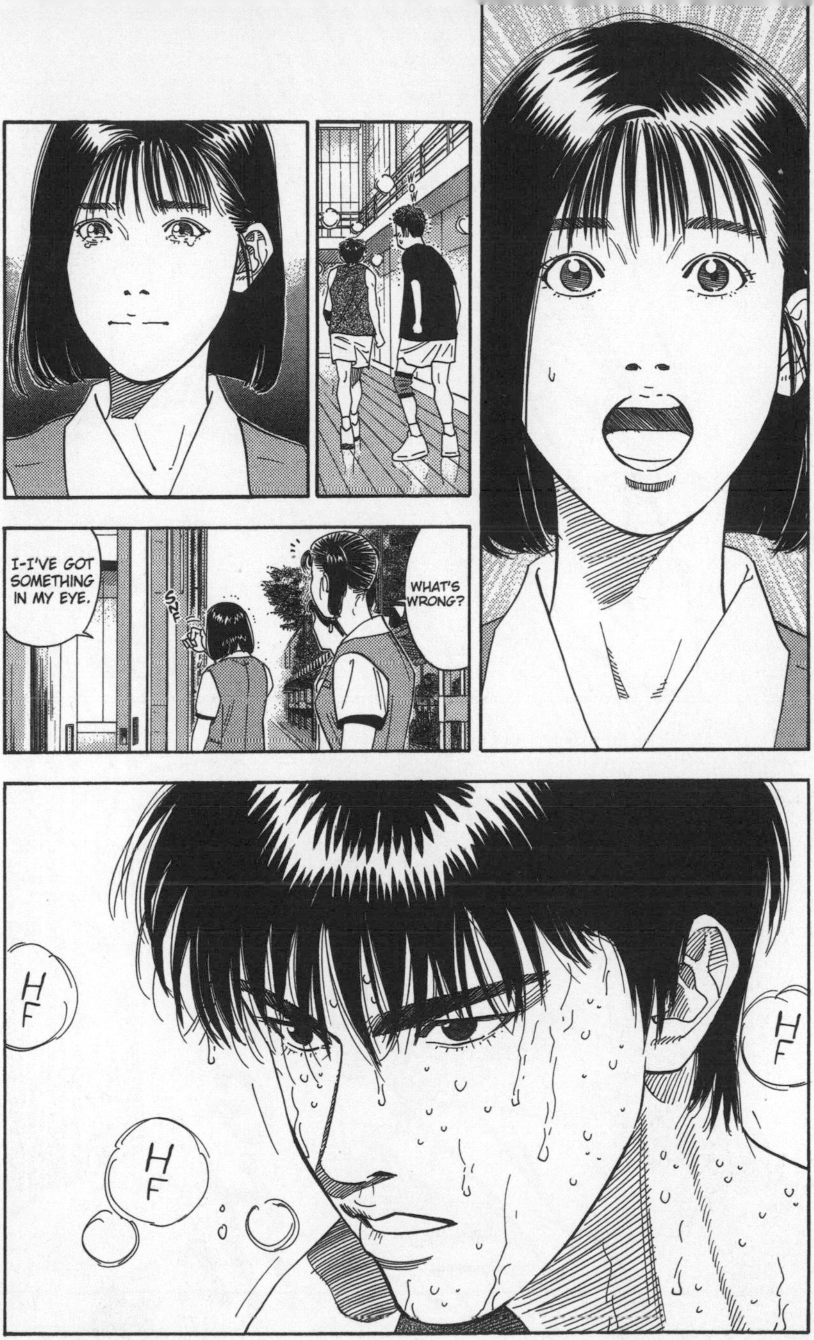
WOW
WHAT'S WRONG?
SNF
I-I'VE GOT SOMETHING IN MY EYE.
HF
HF
HF

READ THIS WAY

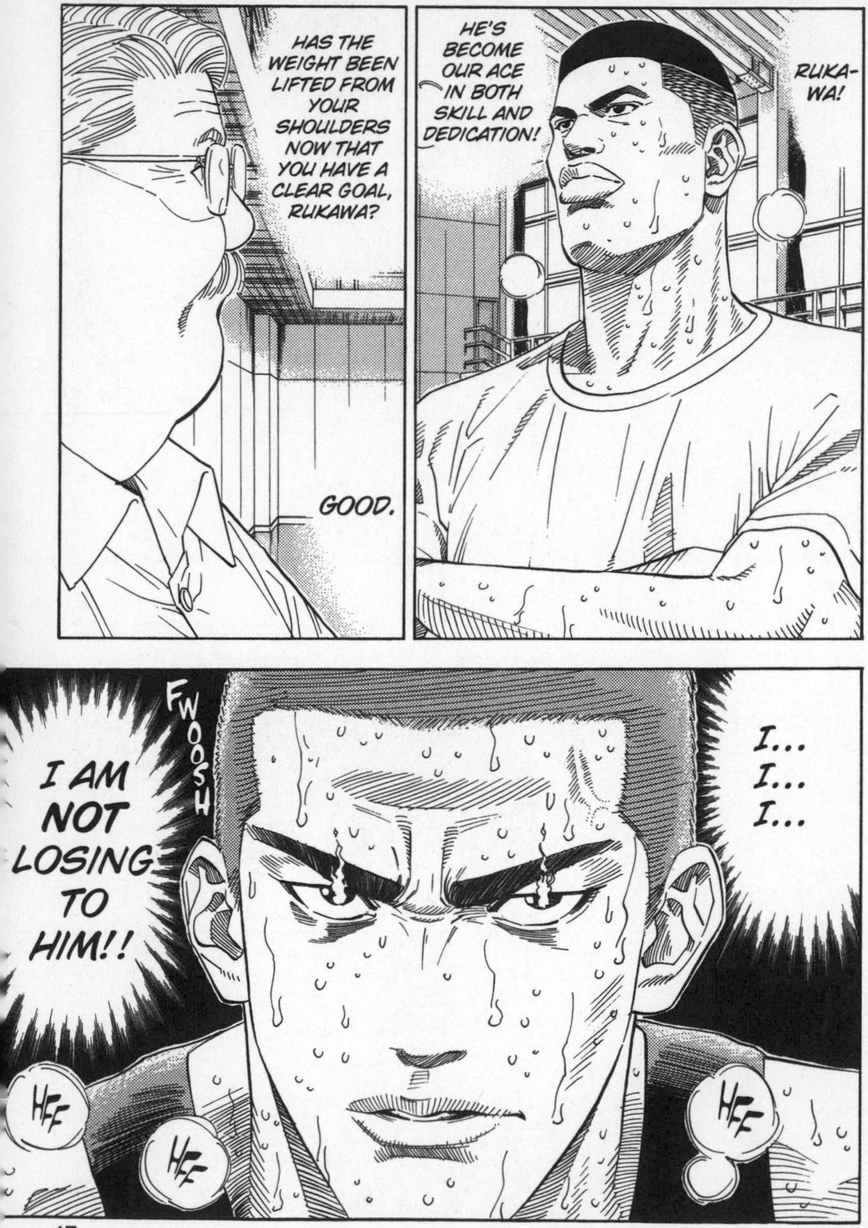
RUKA-WA!
HE'S BECOME OUR ACE IN BOTH SKILL AND DEDICATION!
HAS THE WEIGHT BEEN LIFTED FROM YOUR SHOULDERS NOW THAT YOU HAVE A CLEAR GOAL, RUKAWA?
GOOD.
I... I... I...
FWOOSH
I AM NOT LOSING TO HIM!!
HFF
HFF
HFF

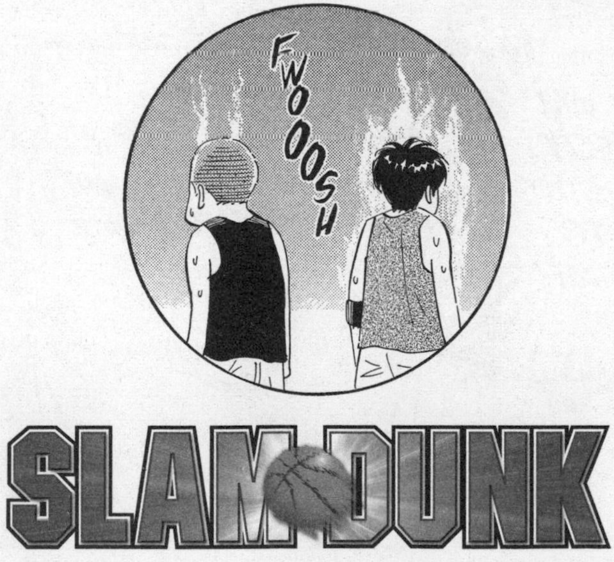
FWOOOSH

SLAM DUNK

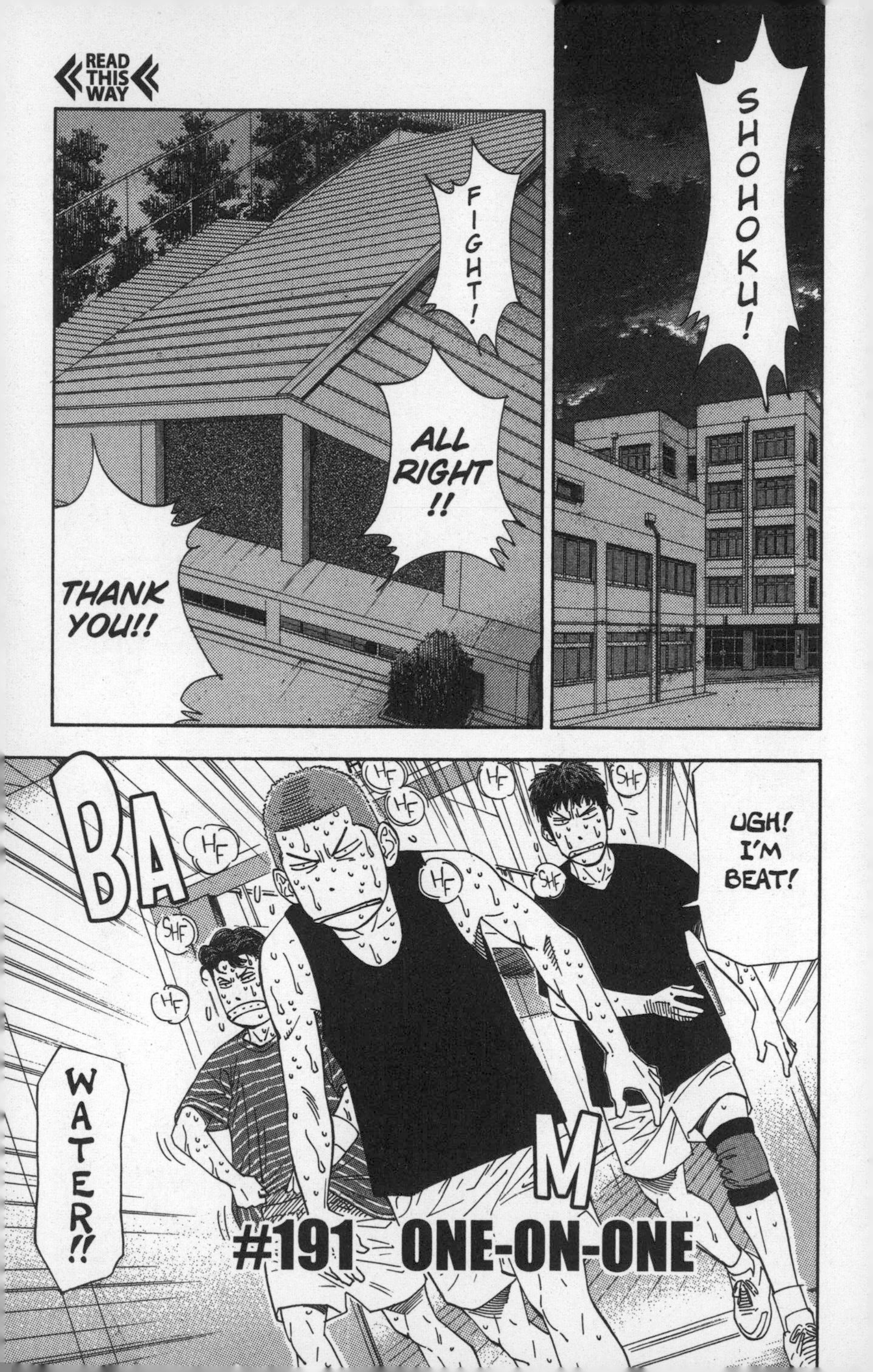
READ THIS WAY
SHOHOKU!
FIGHT!
ALL RIGHT!!
THANK YOU!!
UGH! I'M BEAT!
SHF
HF
HF
HF
HF
SHF
BA
HF
SHF
HF
WATER!!
M
#191 ONE-ON-ONE

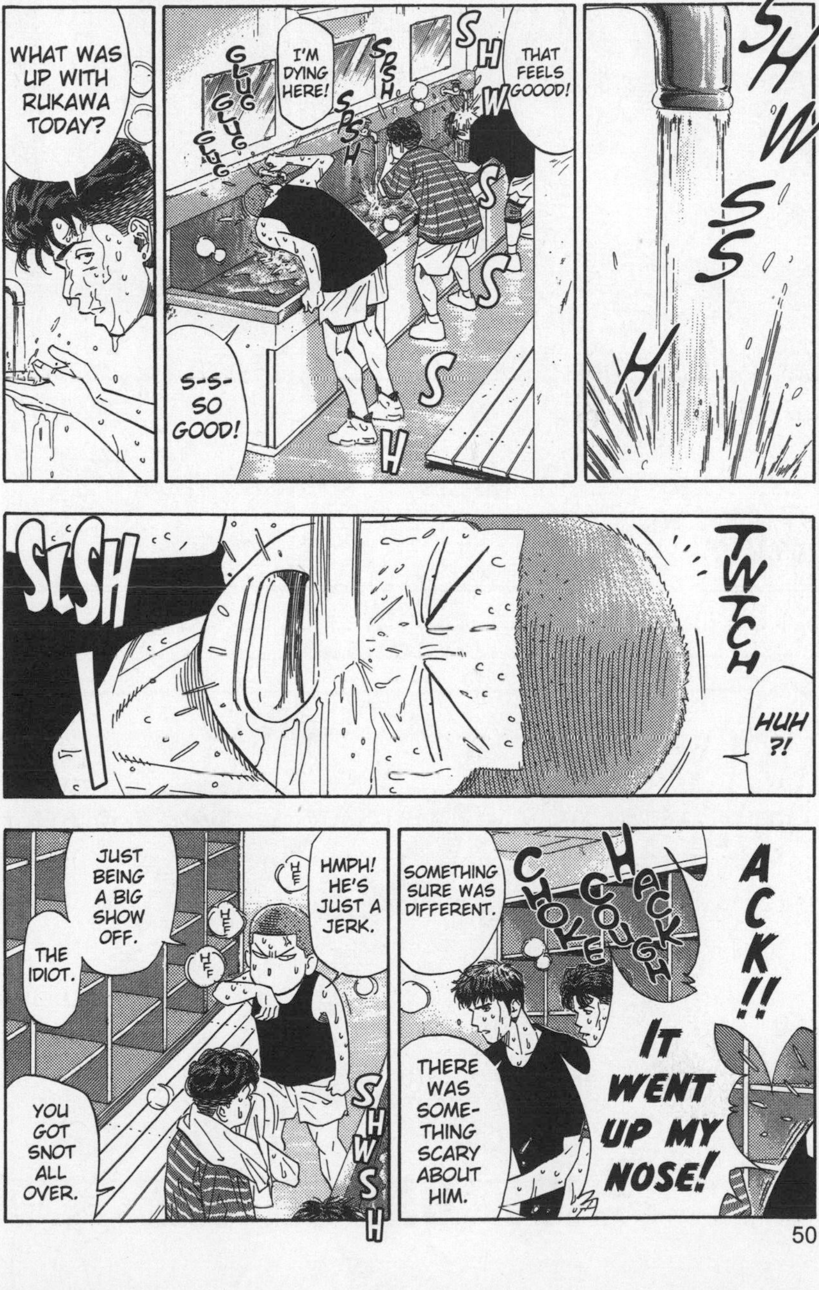
SHWSSH
THAT FEELS GOOOD!
SHWSSH
I'M DYING HERE!
SPSH SPSH
GLUG GLUG GLUG GLUG
S-S-SO GOOD!
WHAT WAS UP WITH RUKAWA TODAY?
HUH?!
TWTCH
SLSH
ACK!!
HACK COUGH CHOKE
IT WENT UP MY NOSE!
SOMETHING SURE WAS DIFFERENT.
THERE WAS SOME-THING SCARY ABOUT HIM.
HMPH! HE'S JUST A JERK.
HF HF HF
JUST BEING A BIG SHOW OFF.
THE IDIOT.
YOU GOT SNOT ALL OVER.
SHWSSH

READ THIS WAY

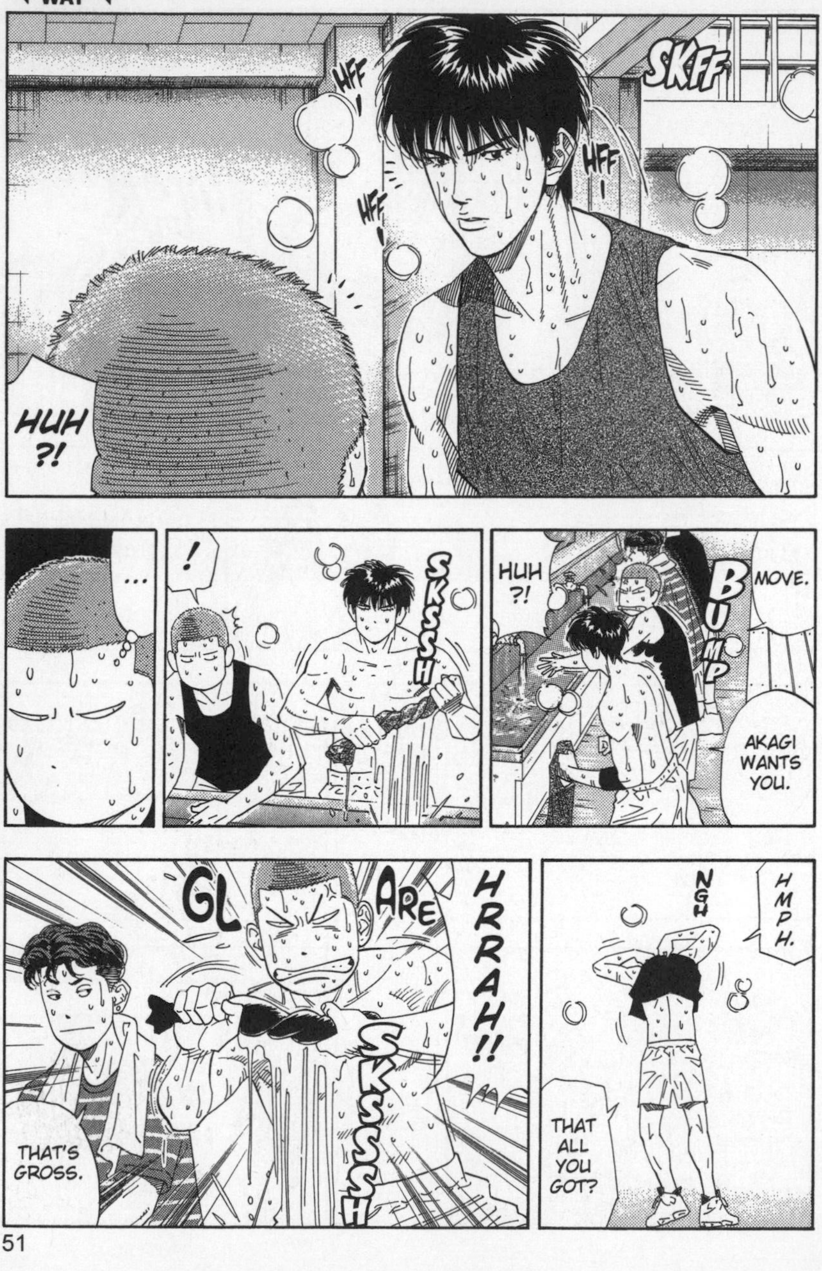

SKFF
HFF!
HFF!
HFF!
HUH?!
MOVE.
BUMP
HUH?!
AKAGI WANTS YOU.
SKSSH
!
...
HMPH.
NGH
THAT ALL YOU GOT?
HRRAH!!
GLARE
SKSSSH
THAT'S GROSS.

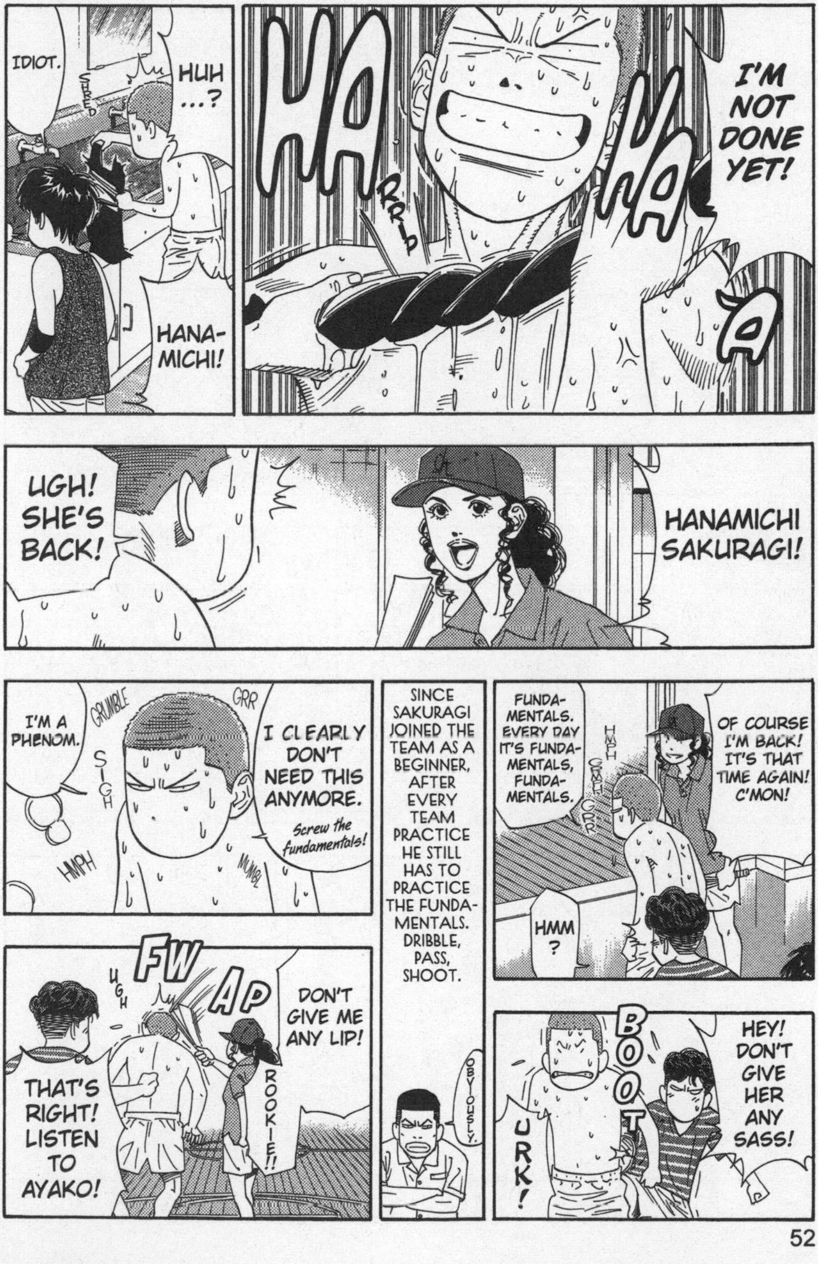
HA
HA
HA
I'M NOT DONE YET!
RRRIP
HUH ...?
HANA-MICHI!
SHRED
IDIOT.
HANAMICHI SAKURAGI!
UGH! SHE'S BACK!
OF COURSE I'M BACK! IT'S THAT TIME AGAIN! C'MON!
HMPH
GRR
FUNDA-MENTALS. EVERY DAY IT'S FUNDA-MENTALS, FUNDA-MENTALS.
HMM ?
HEY! DON'T GIVE HER ANY SASS!
BOOT
URK!
SINCE SAKURAGI JOINED THE TEAM AS A BEGINNER, AFTER EVERY TEAM PRACTICE HE STILL HAS TO PRACTICE THE FUNDA-MENTALS. DRIBBLE, PASS, SHOOT.
OBVIOUSLY.
GRR
I CLEARLY DON'T NEED THIS ANYMORE.
Screw the fundamentals!
MUMBL
GRUMBLE
SIGH
I'M A PHENOM.
HMPH
DON'T GIVE ME ANY LIP!
ROOKIE!!
FWAP
UGH
THAT'S RIGHT! LISTEN TO AYAKO!

READ THIS WAY

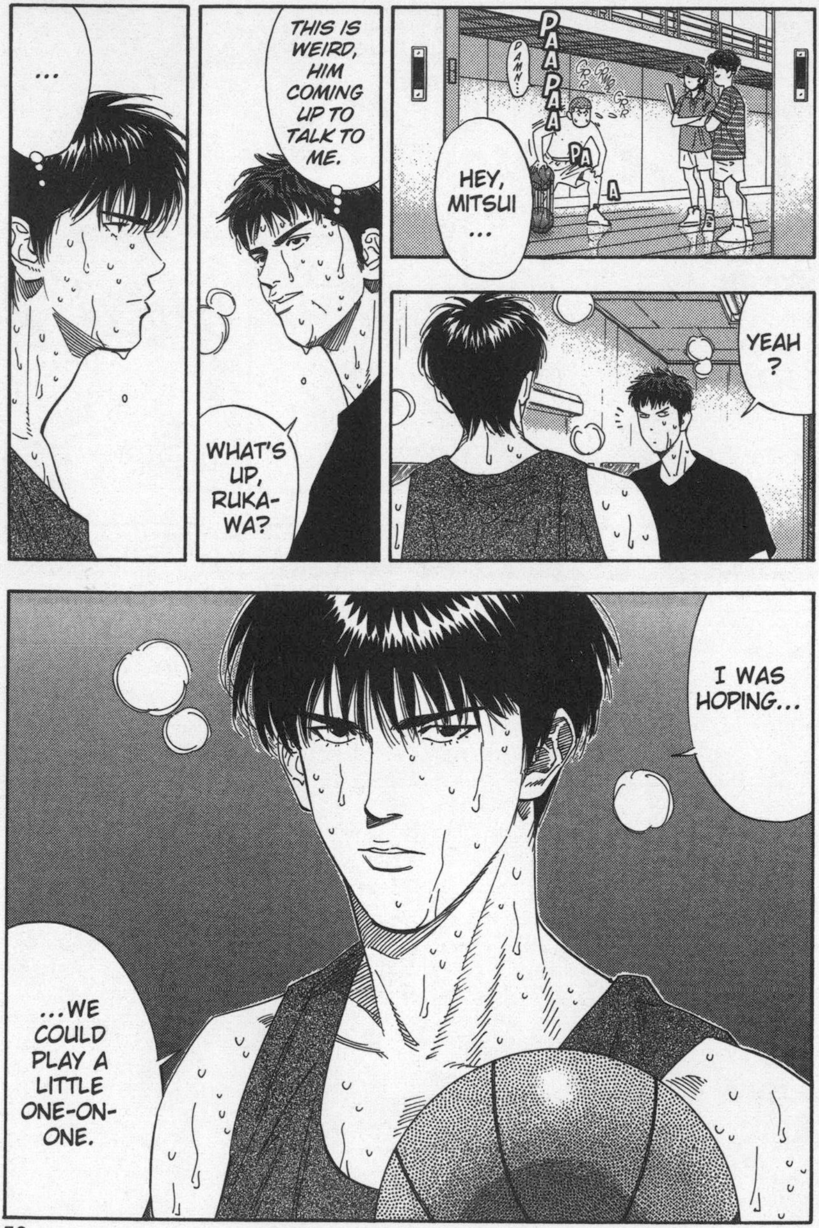
DAMN...
HEY, MITSUI ...
YEAH?
THIS IS WEIRD, HIM COMING UP TO TALK TO ME.
WHAT'S UP, RUKAWA?
...
I WAS HOPING...
...WE COULD PLAY A LITTLE ONE-ON-ONE.

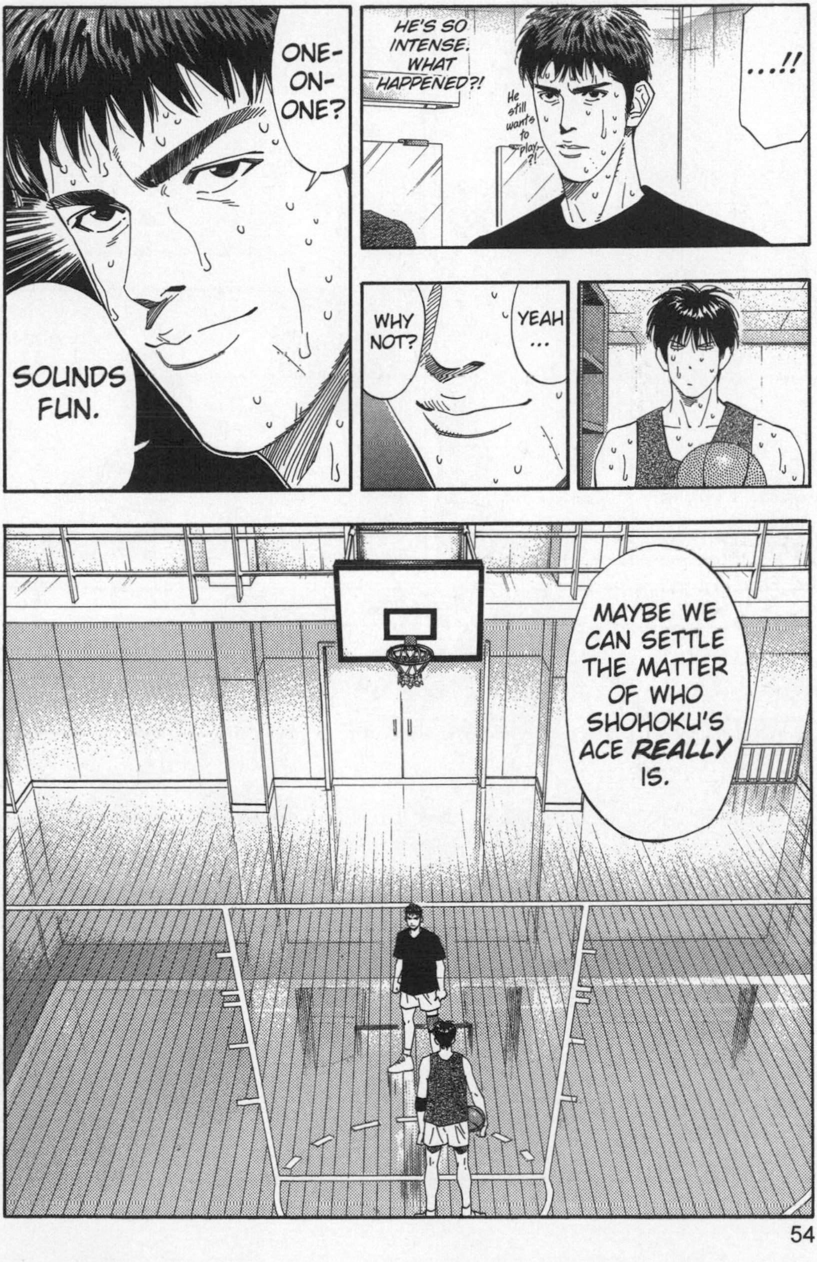
...!!
HE'S SO INTENSE. WHAT HAPPENED?!
He still wants to play?!
YEAH...
WHY NOT?
ONE-ON-ONE?
SOUNDS FUN.
MAYBE WE CAN SETTLE THE MATTER OF WHO SHOHOKU'S ACE *REALLY* IS.

READ THIS WAY

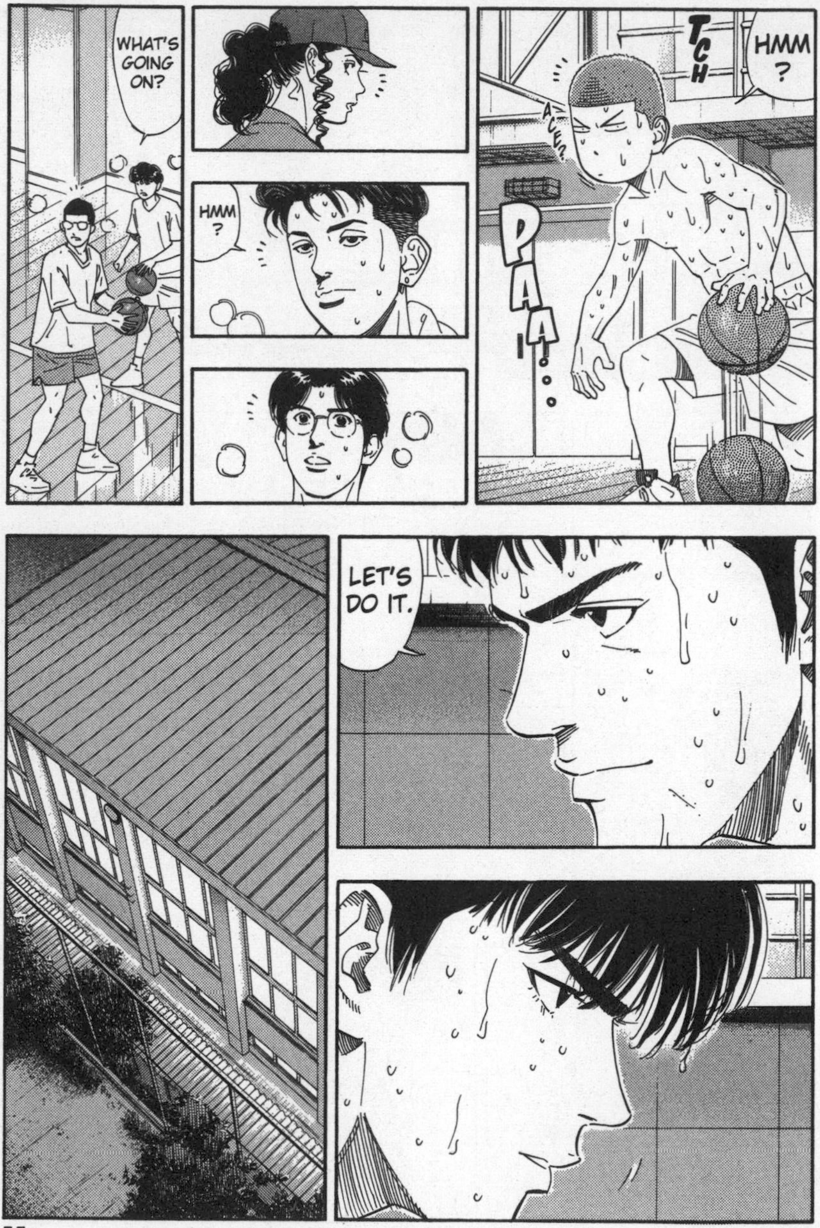

HMM?
TCH
ACE?
PAA!...
HMM?
WHAT'S GOING ON?
LET'S DO IT.

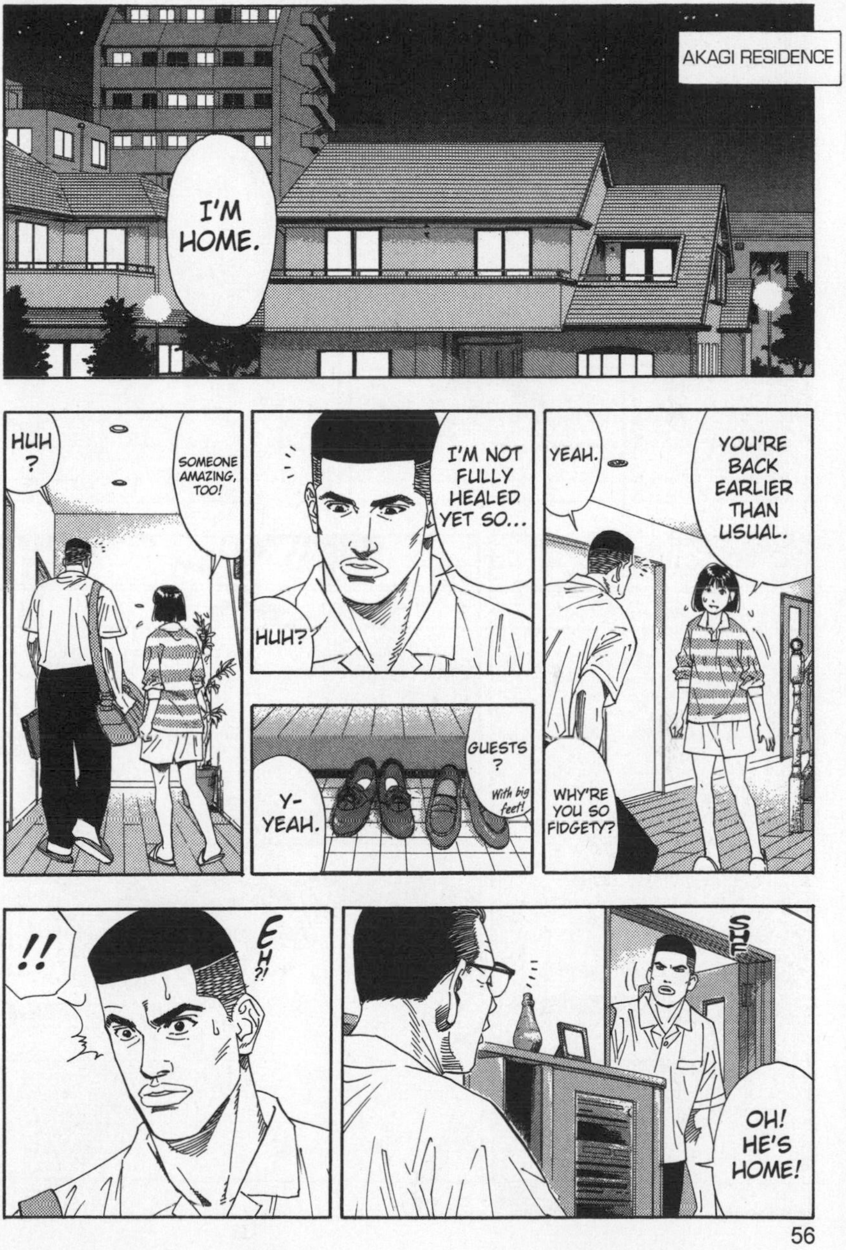
AKAGI RESIDENCE
I'M HOME.
YOU'RE BACK EARLIER THAN USUAL.
YEAH.
WHY'RE YOU SO FIDGETY?
I'M NOT FULLY HEALED YET SO...
HUH?
GUESTS?
With big feet!
Y-YEAH.
SOMEONE AMAZING, TOO!
HUH?
SHF
OH! HE'S HOME!
EH?!
!!

READ THIS WAY

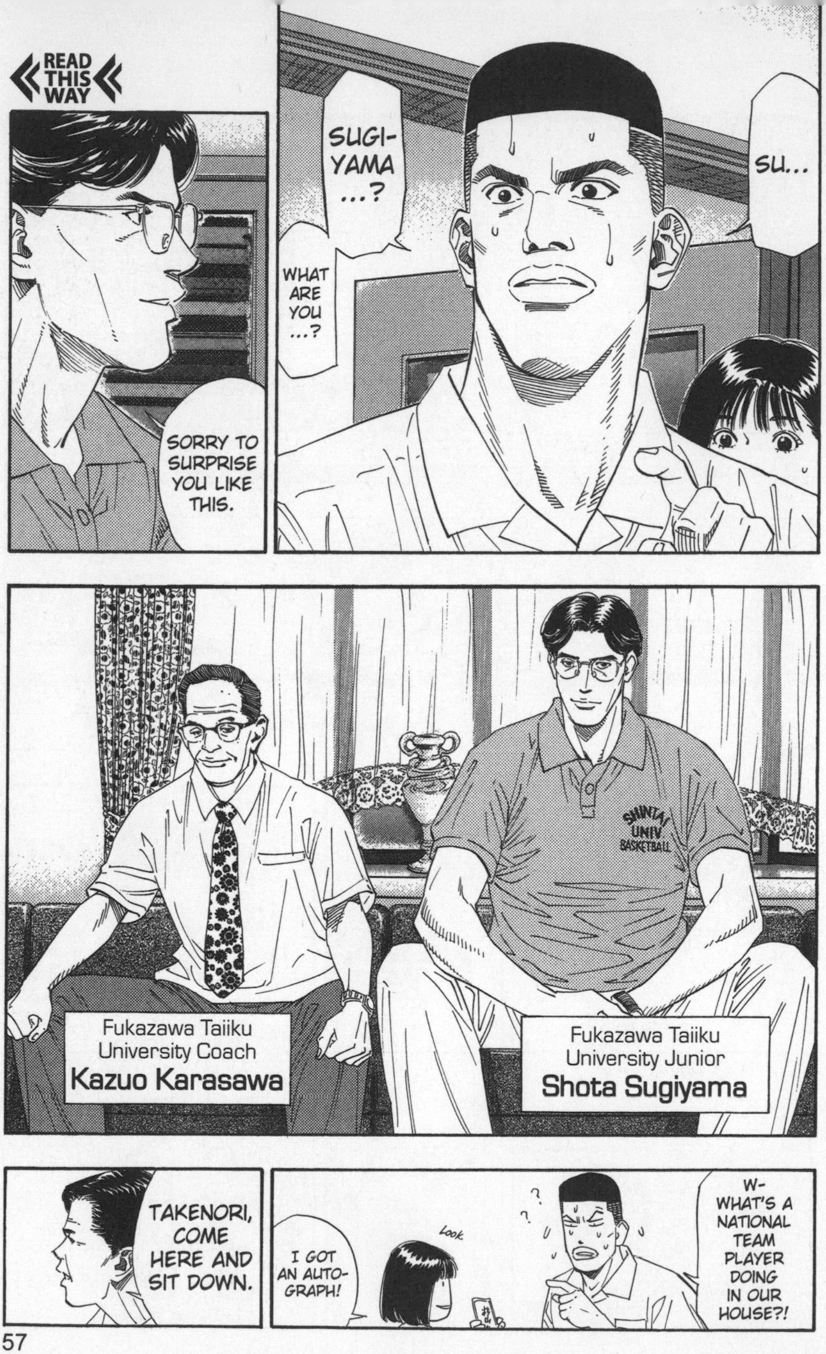
SU...
SUGI-YAMA ...?
WHAT ARE YOU ...?
SORRY TO SURPRISE YOU LIKE THIS.
Fukazawa Taiiku University Junior Shota Sugiyama
Fukazawa Taiiku University Coach Kazuo Karasawa
W-WHAT'S A NATIONAL TEAM PLAYER DOING IN OUR HOUSE?!
Look
I GOT AN AUTO-GRAPH!
TAKENORI, COME HERE AND SIT DOWN.

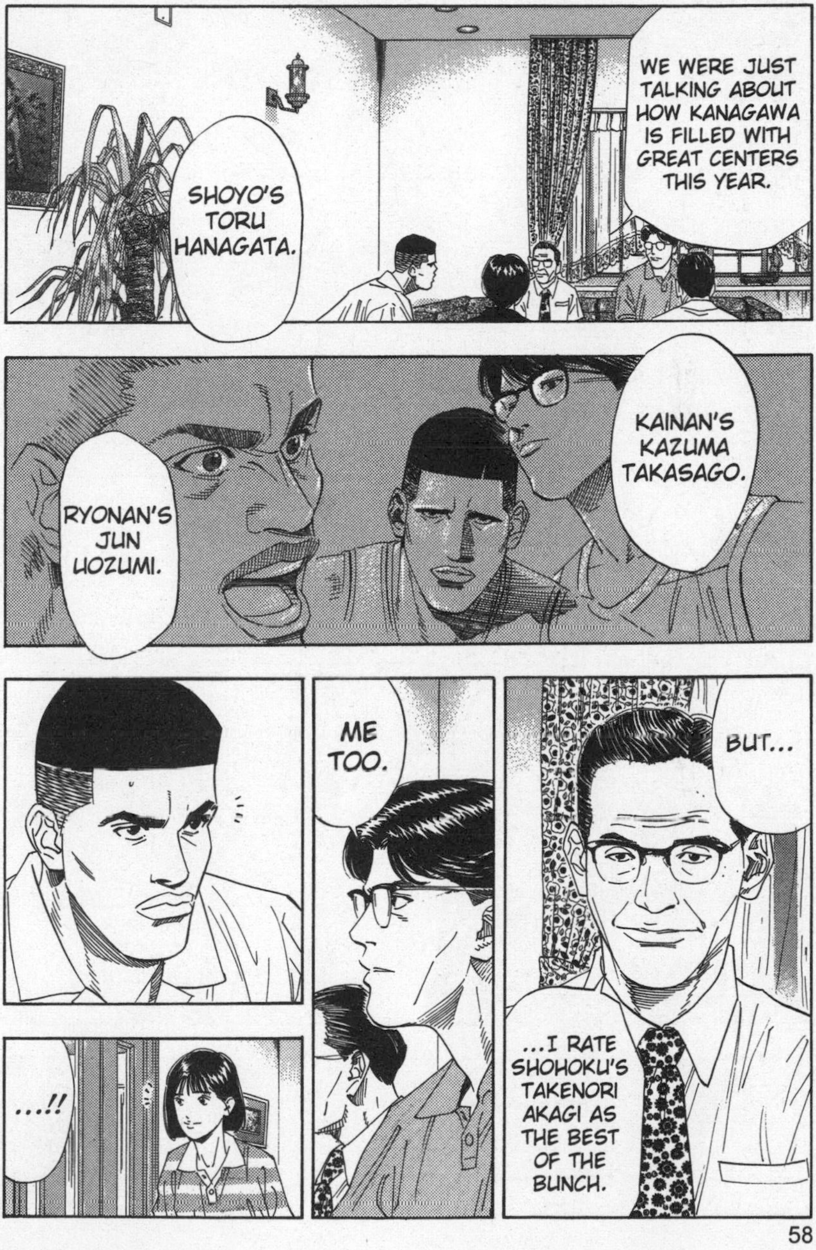
WE WERE JUST TALKING ABOUT HOW KANAGAWA IS FILLED WITH GREAT CENTERS THIS YEAR.
SHOYO'S TORU HANAGATA.
KAINAN'S KAZUMA TAKASAGO.
RYONAN'S JUN UOZUMI.
BUT...
...I RATE SHOHOKU'S TAKENORI AKAGI AS THE BEST OF THE BUNCH.
ME TOO.
...!!

READ THIS WAY

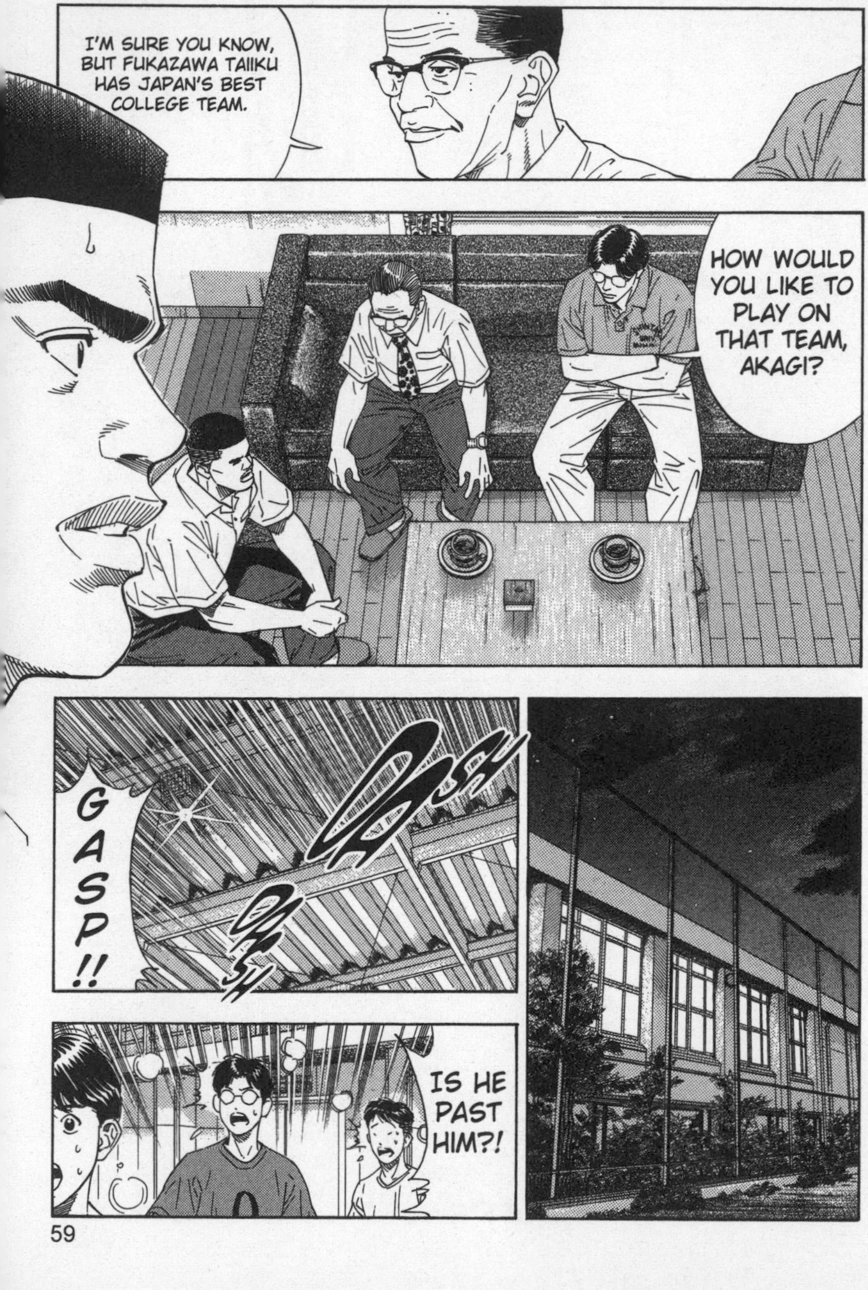
I'M SURE YOU KNOW, BUT FUKAZAWA TAIIKU HAS JAPAN'S BEST COLLEGE TEAM.
HOW WOULD YOU LIKE TO PLAY ON THAT TEAM, AKAGI?
GASP!!
IS HE PAST HIM?!

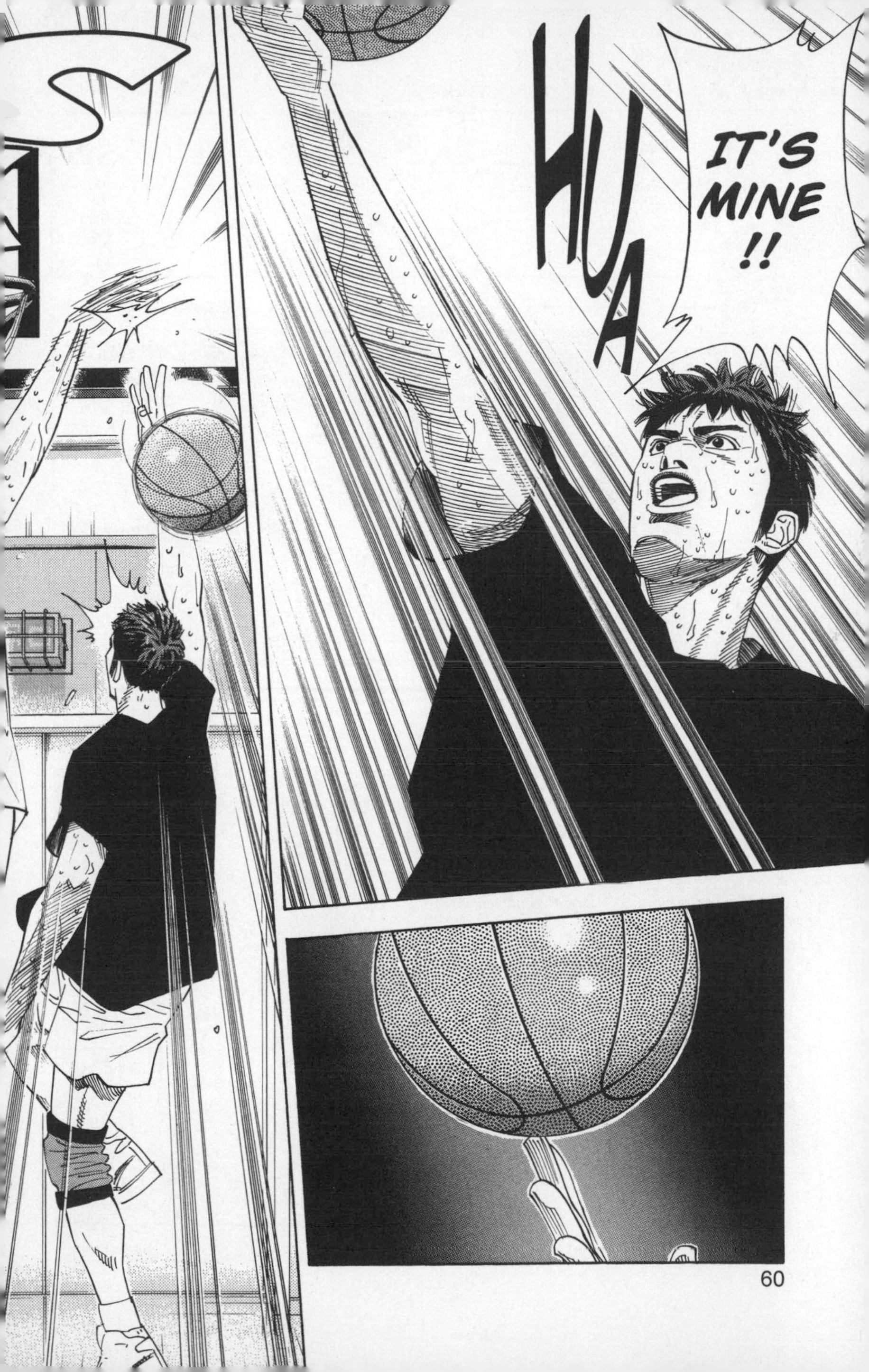
IT'S MINE !!
HUA

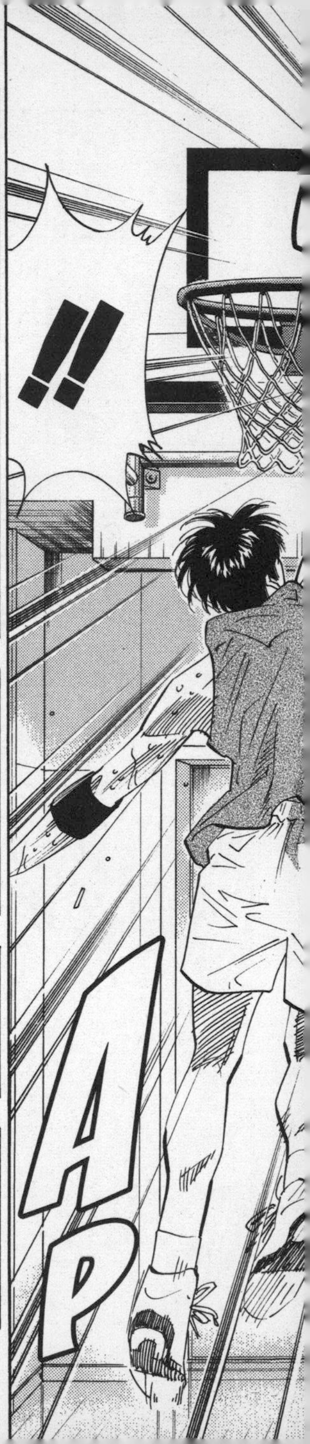
!!
AP

READ THIS WAY

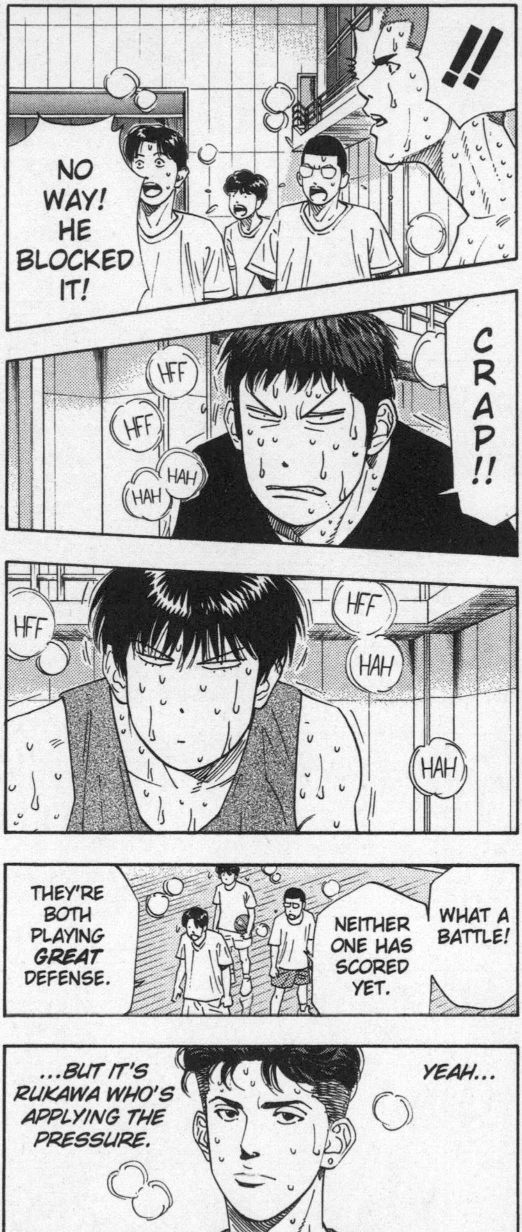
!!
NO WAY! HE BLOCKED IT!
CRAP!!
HFF
HFF
HAH
HAH
HFF
HFF
HAH
HAH
WHAT A BATTLE!
NEITHER ONE HAS SCORED YET.
THEY'RE BOTH PLAYING *GREAT* DEFENSE.
YEAH...
...BUT IT'S RUKAWA WHO'S APPLYING THE PRESSURE.

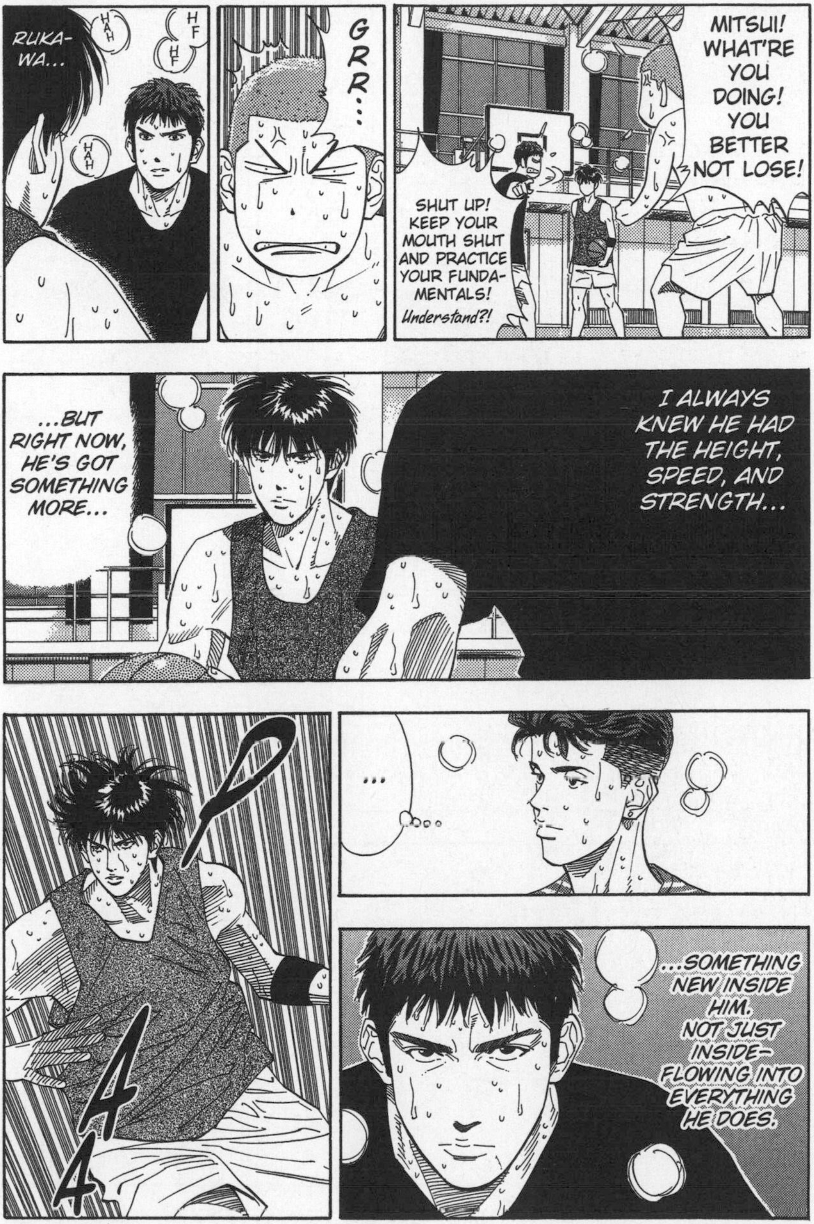
MITSUI! WHAT'RE YOU DOING! YOU BETTER NOT LOSE!
SHUT UP! KEEP YOUR MOUTH SHUT AND PRACTICE YOUR FUNDA-MENTALS!
Understand?!
GRR...
RUKA-WA...
HAH
HF
HF
HAH
I ALWAYS KNEW HE HAD THE HEIGHT, SPEED, AND STRENGTH...
...BUT RIGHT NOW, HE'S GOT SOMETHING MORE...
...
...SOMETHING NEW INSIDE HIM. NOT JUST INSIDE— FLOWING INTO EVERYTHING HE DOES.

READ THIS WAY

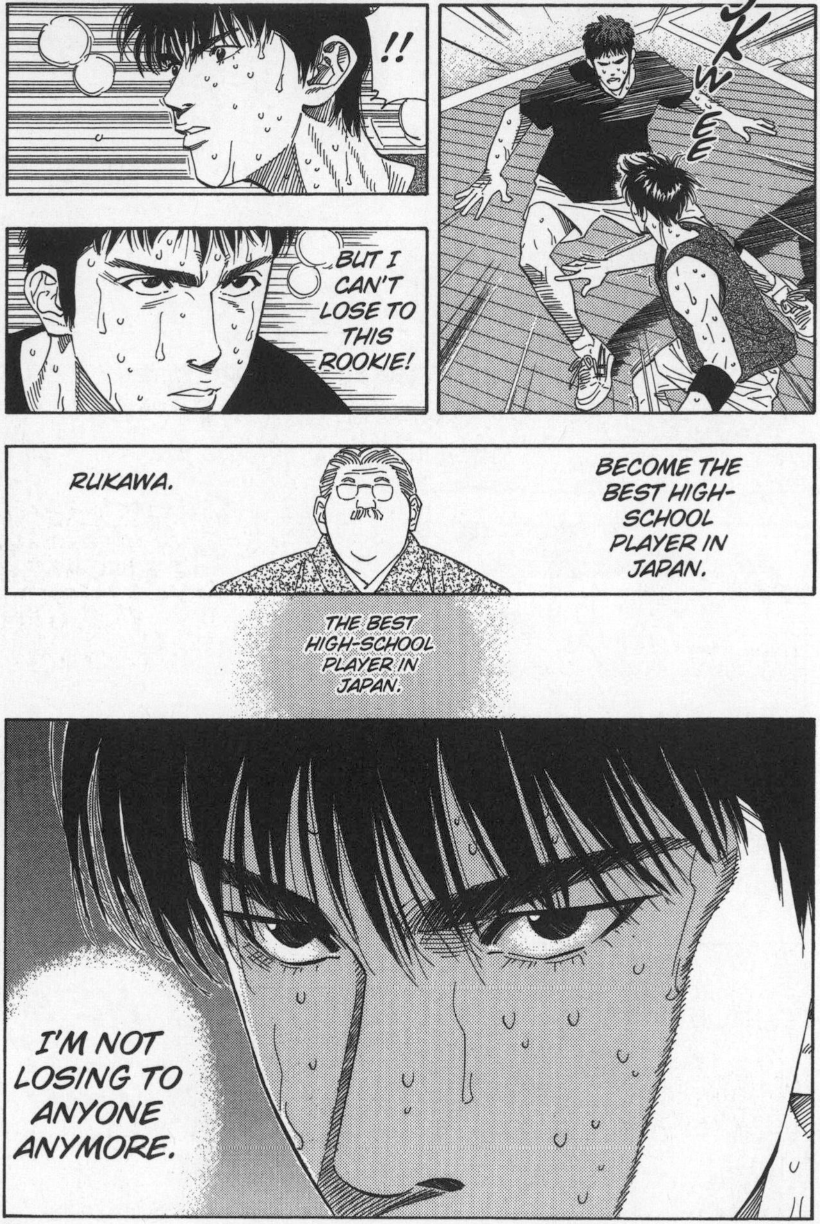
SKWEE
!!
BUT I CAN'T LOSE TO THIS ROOKIE!
BECOME THE BEST HIGH-SCHOOL PLAYER IN JAPAN.
RUKAWA.
THE BEST HIGH-SCHOOL PLAYER IN JAPAN.
I'M NOT LOSING TO ANYONE ANYMORE.

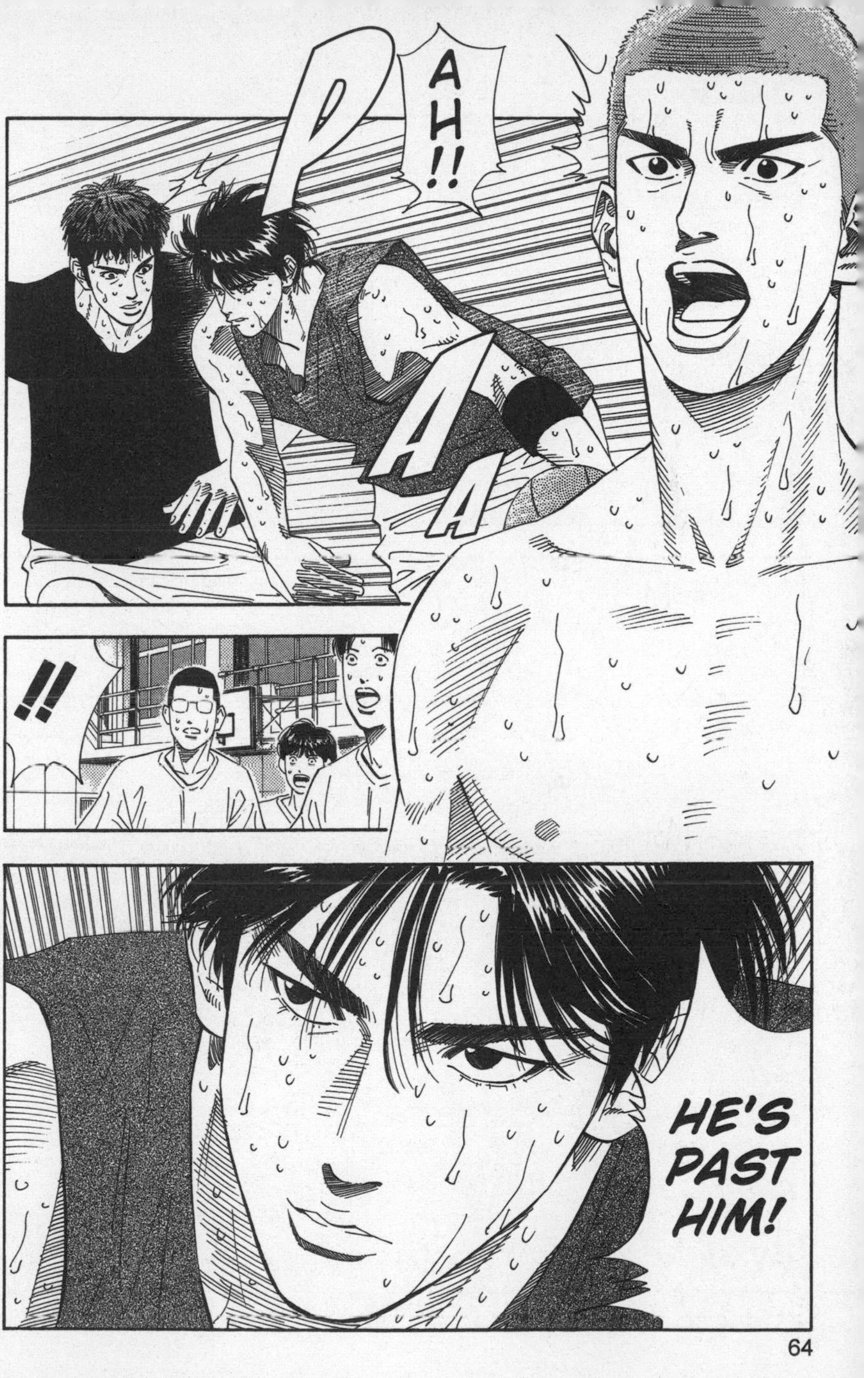
PAH!!
AAA
!!
HE'S PAST HIM!

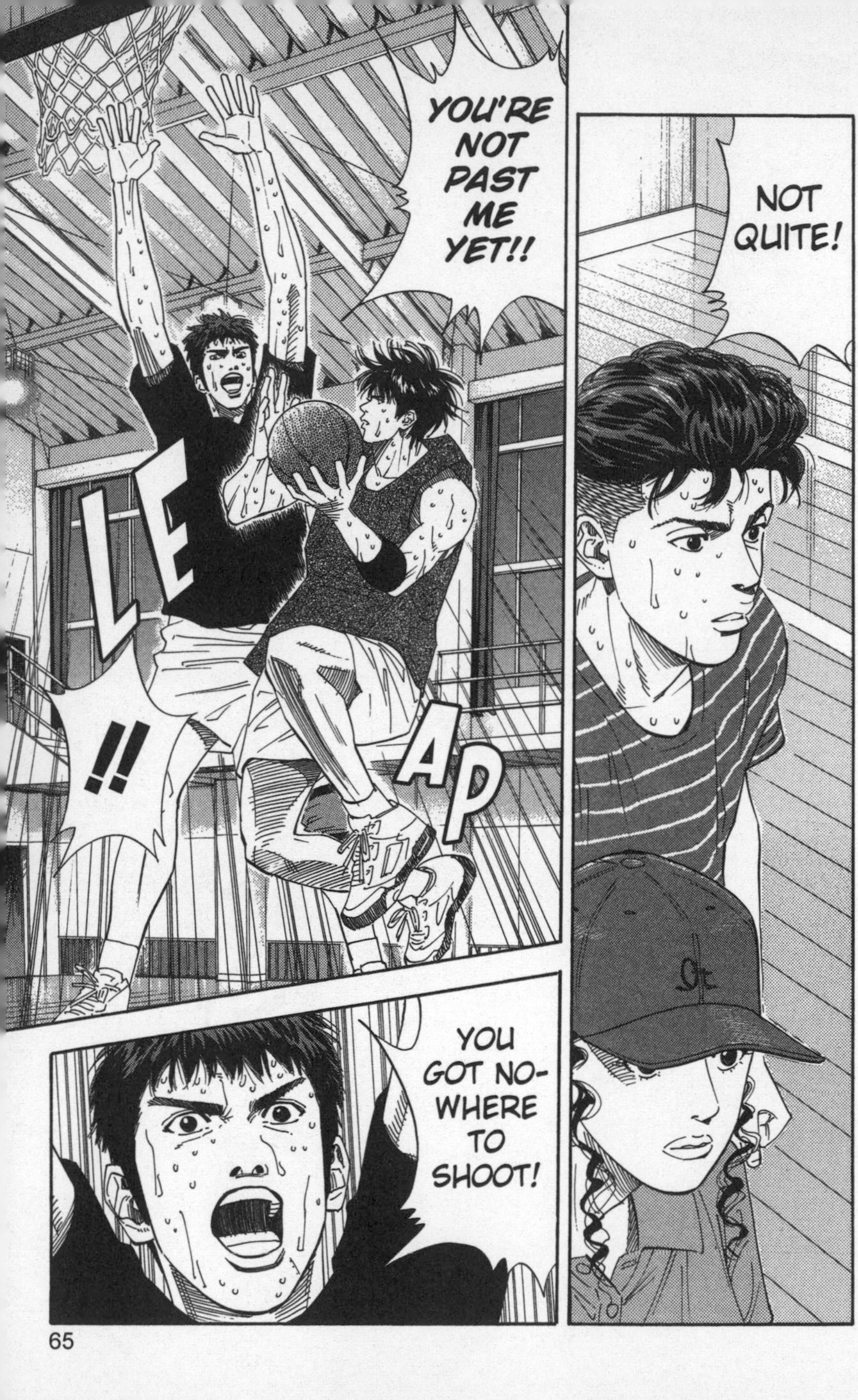
NOT QUITE!
YOU'RE NOT PAST ME YET!!
LE
AP
!!
YOU GOT NO-WHERE TO SHOOT!

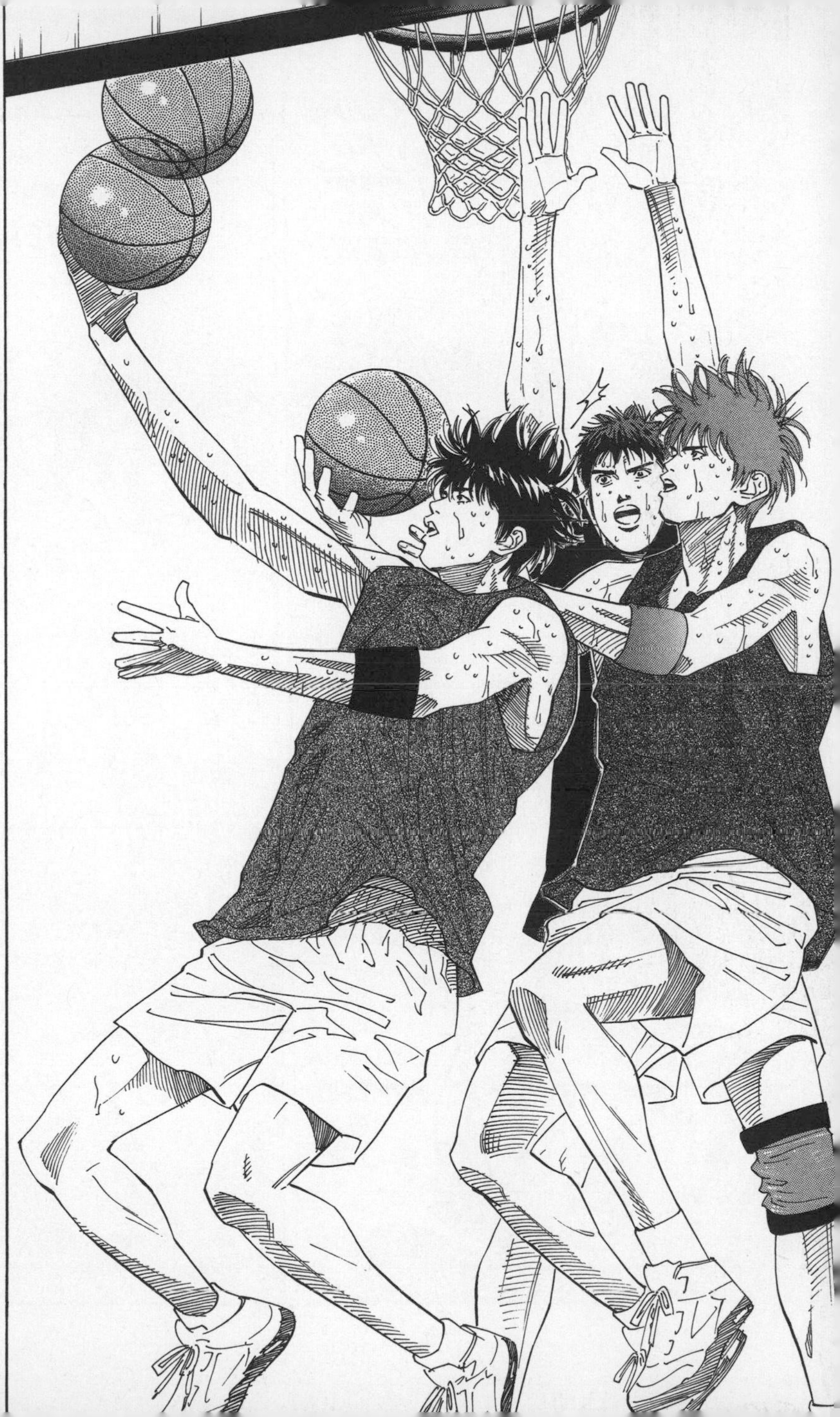

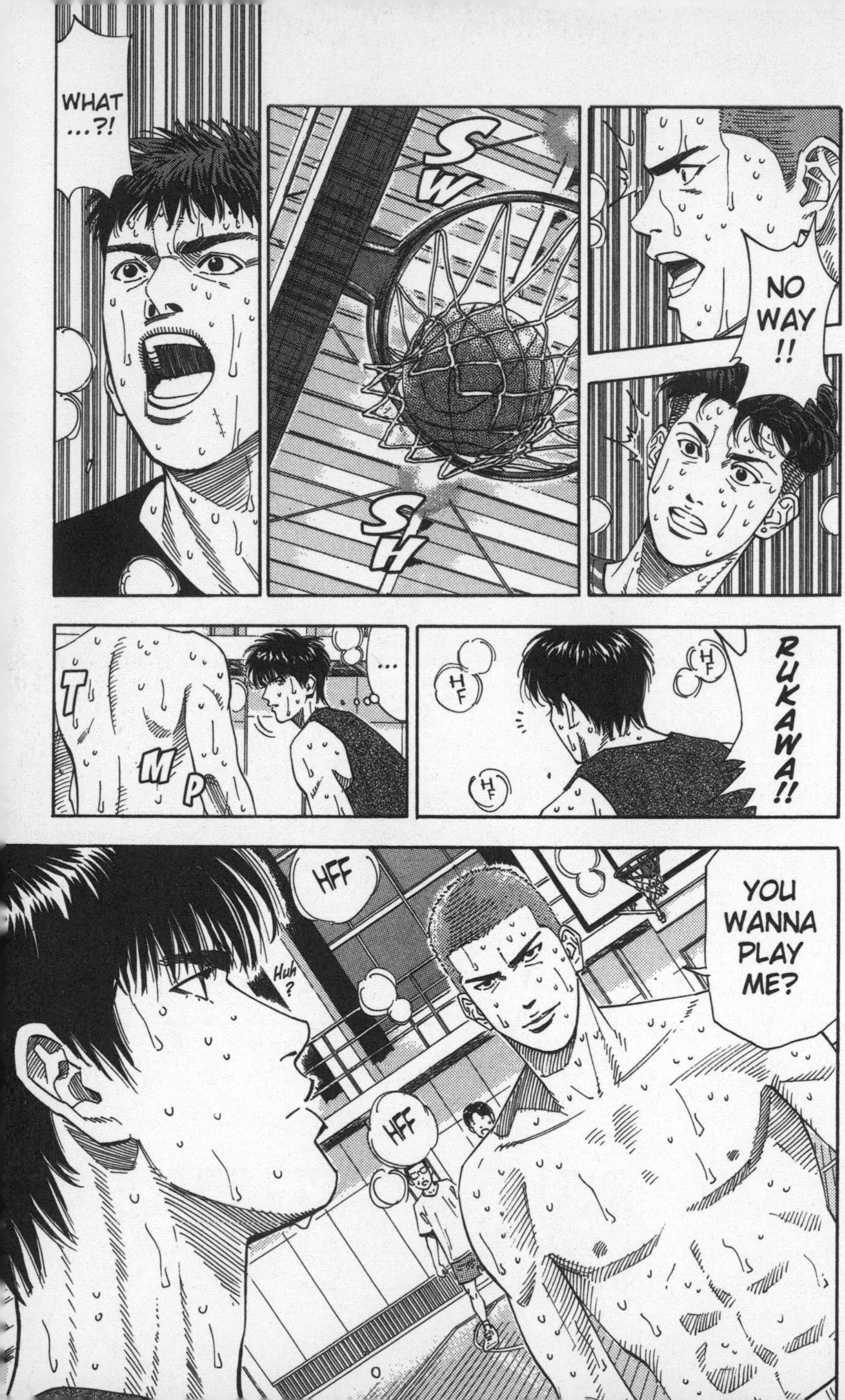
NO WAY !!
SW
SH
WHAT ...?!
RUKAWA!!
HF
HF
HF
...
TMP
YOU WANNA PLAY ME?
HFF
Huh?
HFF

Are you ready?
HEH HEH HEH HEH
Huh?

SLAM DUNK

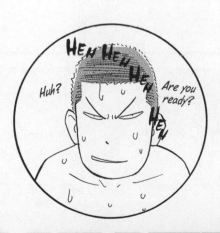

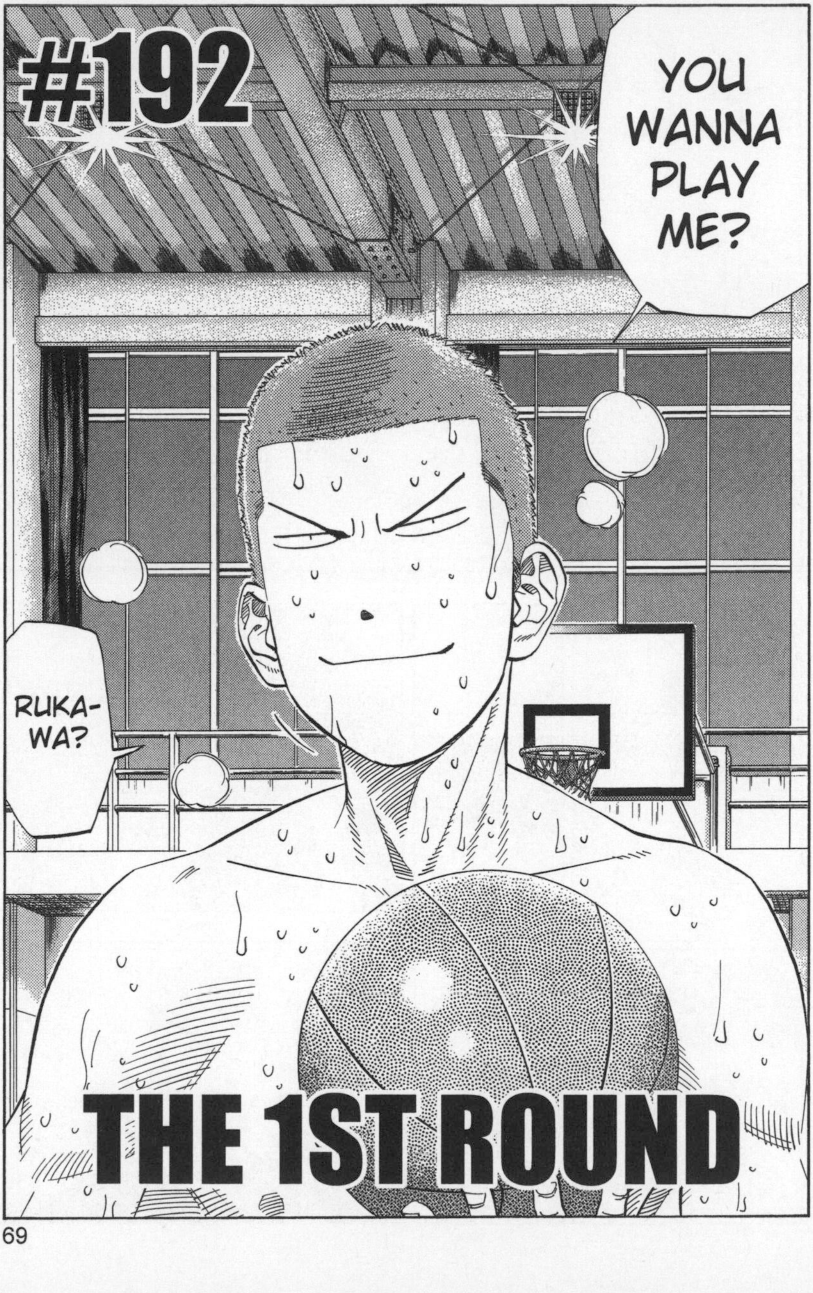
#192
YOU WANNA PLAY ME?
RUKA-WA?
THE 1ST ROUND

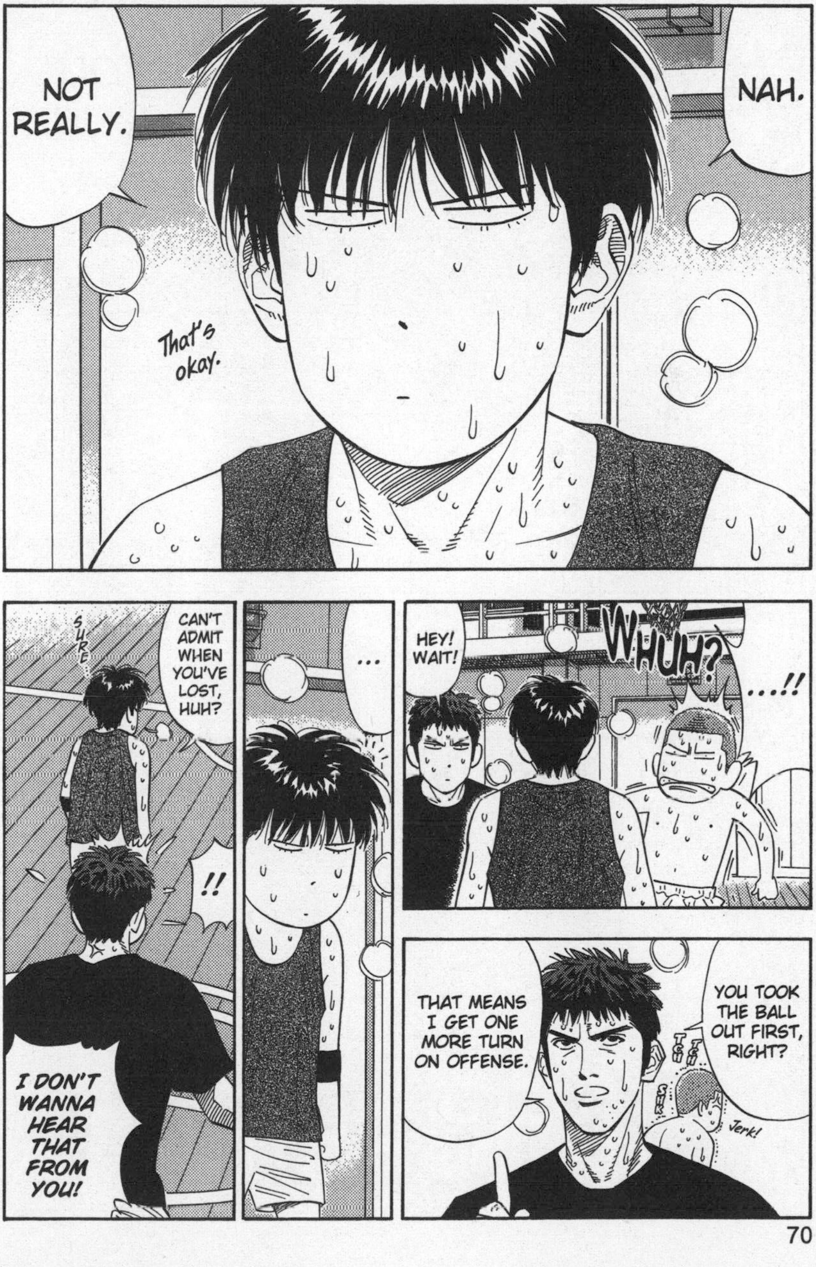
NAH.
NOT REALLY.
That's okay.
...!!
WHUH?
HEY! WAIT!
YOU TOOK THE BALL OUT FIRST, RIGHT?
Jerk!
THAT MEANS I GET ONE MORE TURN ON OFFENSE.
...
CAN'T ADMIT WHEN YOU'VE LOST, HUH?
SURE
!!
I DON'T WANNA HEAR THAT FROM YOU!

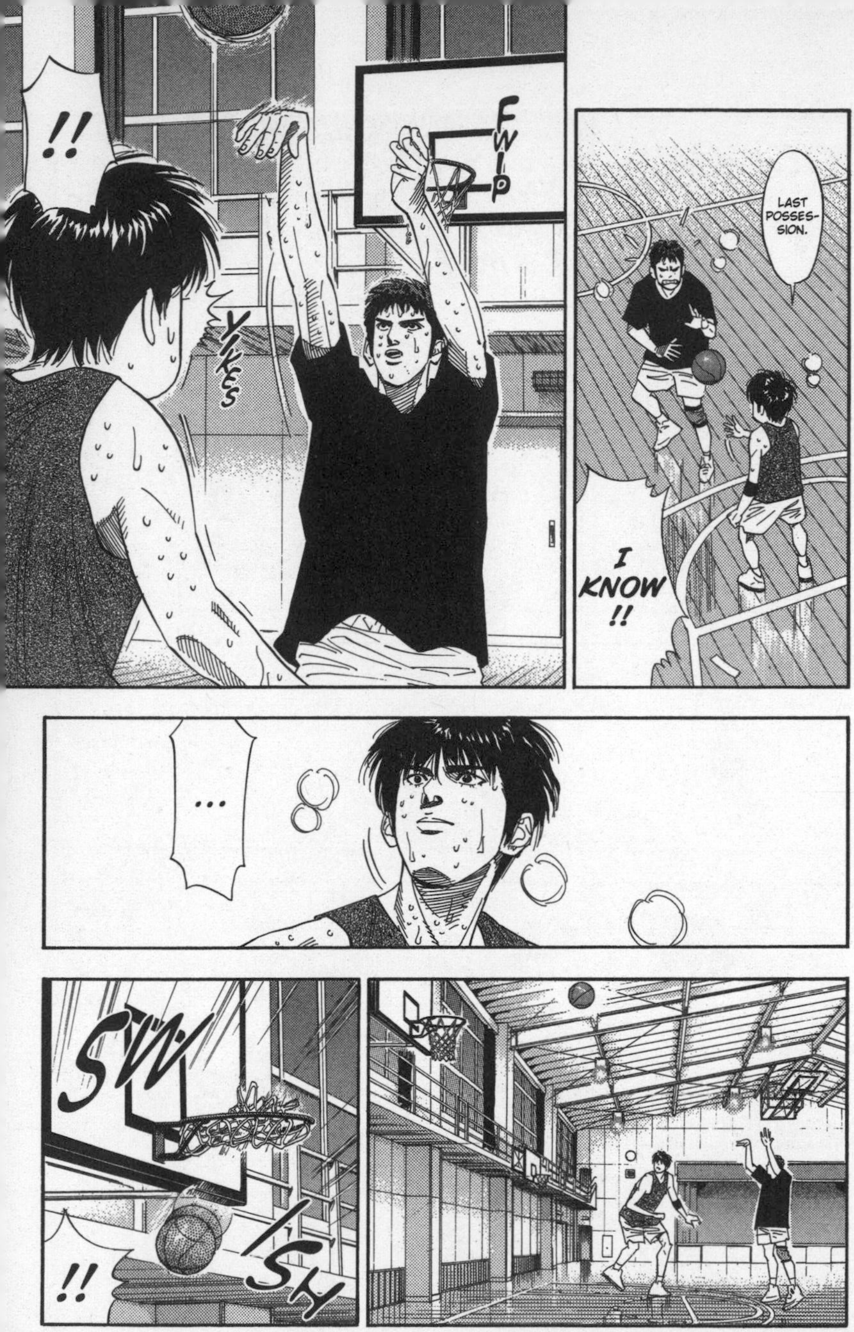
LAST POSSES-SION.
I KNOW !!
!!
FWIP
YIKES
...
SWISH
!!

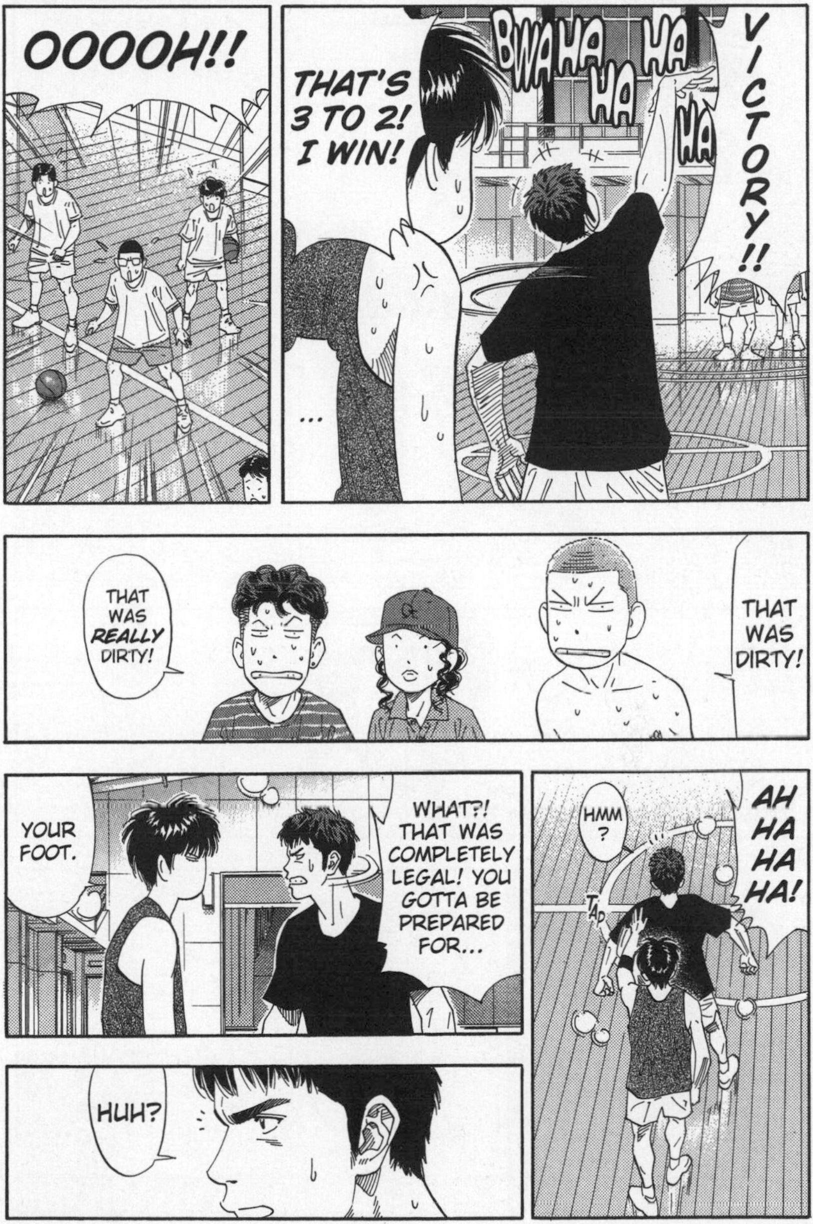
VICTORY!!
BWAHA HA HA HA
THAT'S 3 TO 2! I WIN!
...
OOOOH!!
THAT WAS DIRTY!
THAT WAS REALLY DIRTY!
AH HA HA HA!
HMM?
TAP
WHAT?! THAT WAS COMPLETELY LEGAL! YOU GOTTA BE PREPARED FOR...
YOUR FOOT.
HUH?

READ THIS WAY

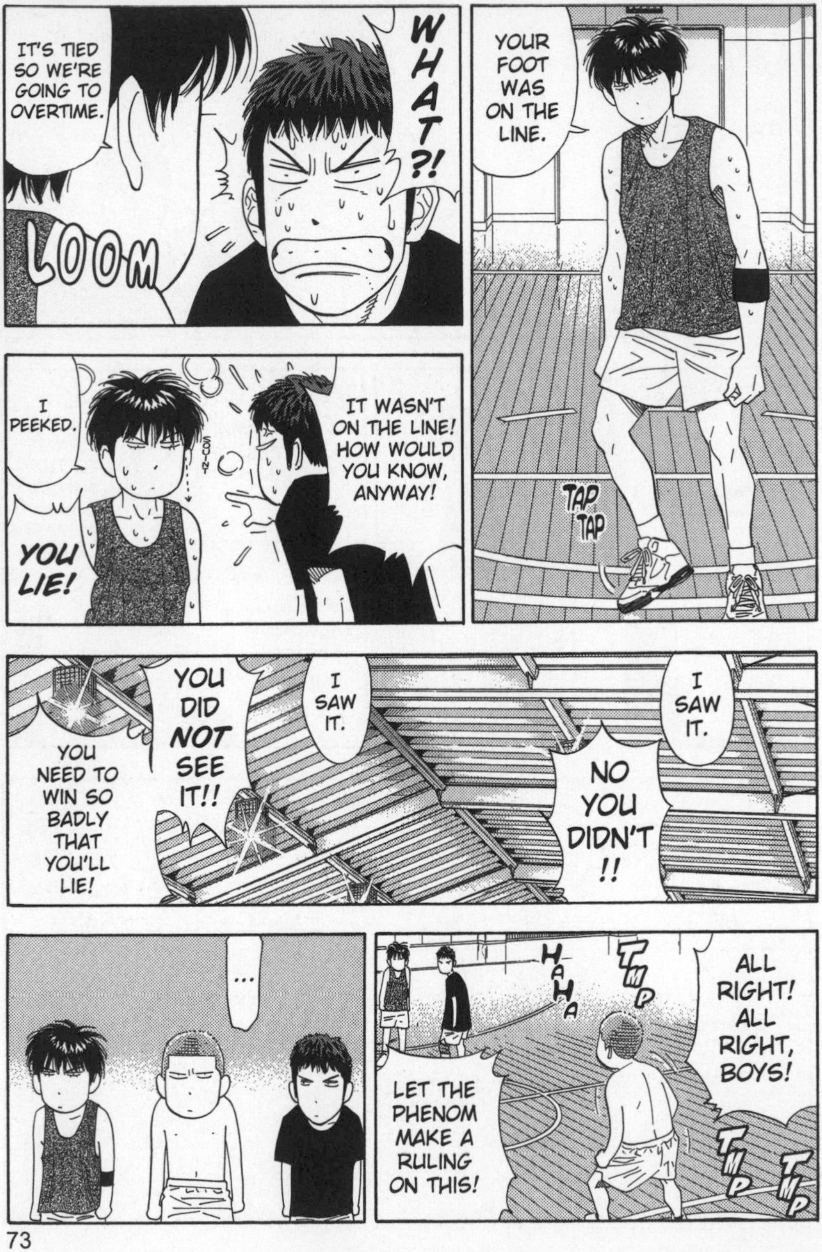
YOUR FOOT WAS ON THE LINE.
TAP TAP
WHAT?!
IT'S TIED SO WE'RE GOING TO OVERTIME.
LOOM
IT WASN'T ON THE LINE! HOW WOULD YOU KNOW, ANYWAY!
SQUINT
I PEEKED.
YOU LIE!
I SAW IT.
NO YOU DIDN'T!!
I SAW IT.
YOU DID NOT SEE IT!!
YOU NEED TO WIN SO BADLY THAT YOU'LL LIE!
TMP
HAHAHA
ALL RIGHT! ALL RIGHT, BOYS!
LET THE PHENOM MAKE A RULING ON THIS!
TMP TMP
...

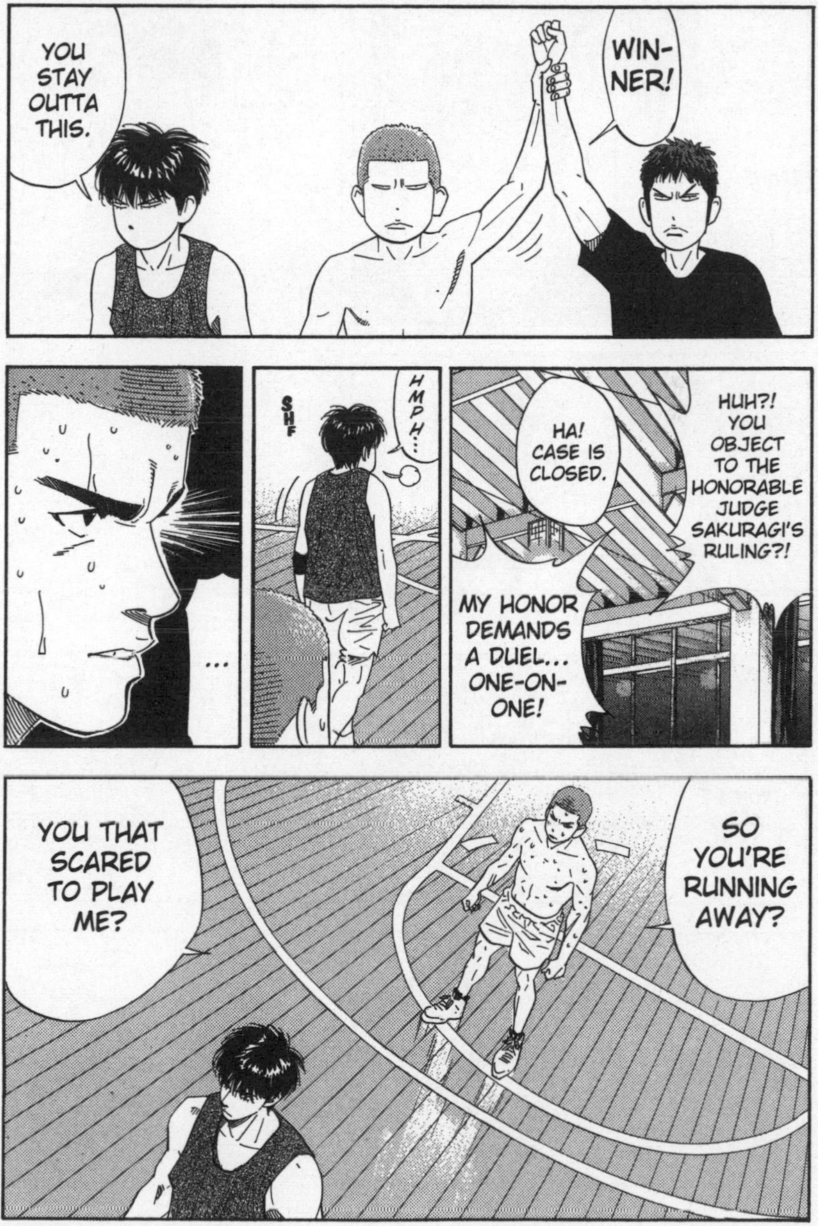
WIN-NER!
YOU STAY OUTTA THIS.
HUH?! YOU OBJECT TO THE HONORABLE JUDGE SAKURAGI'S RULING?!
HA! CASE IS CLOSED.
MY HONOR DEMANDS A DUEL... ONE-ON-ONE!
HMPH...
SHF
...
SO YOU'RE RUNNING AWAY?
YOU THAT SCARED TO PLAY ME?

READ THIS WAY

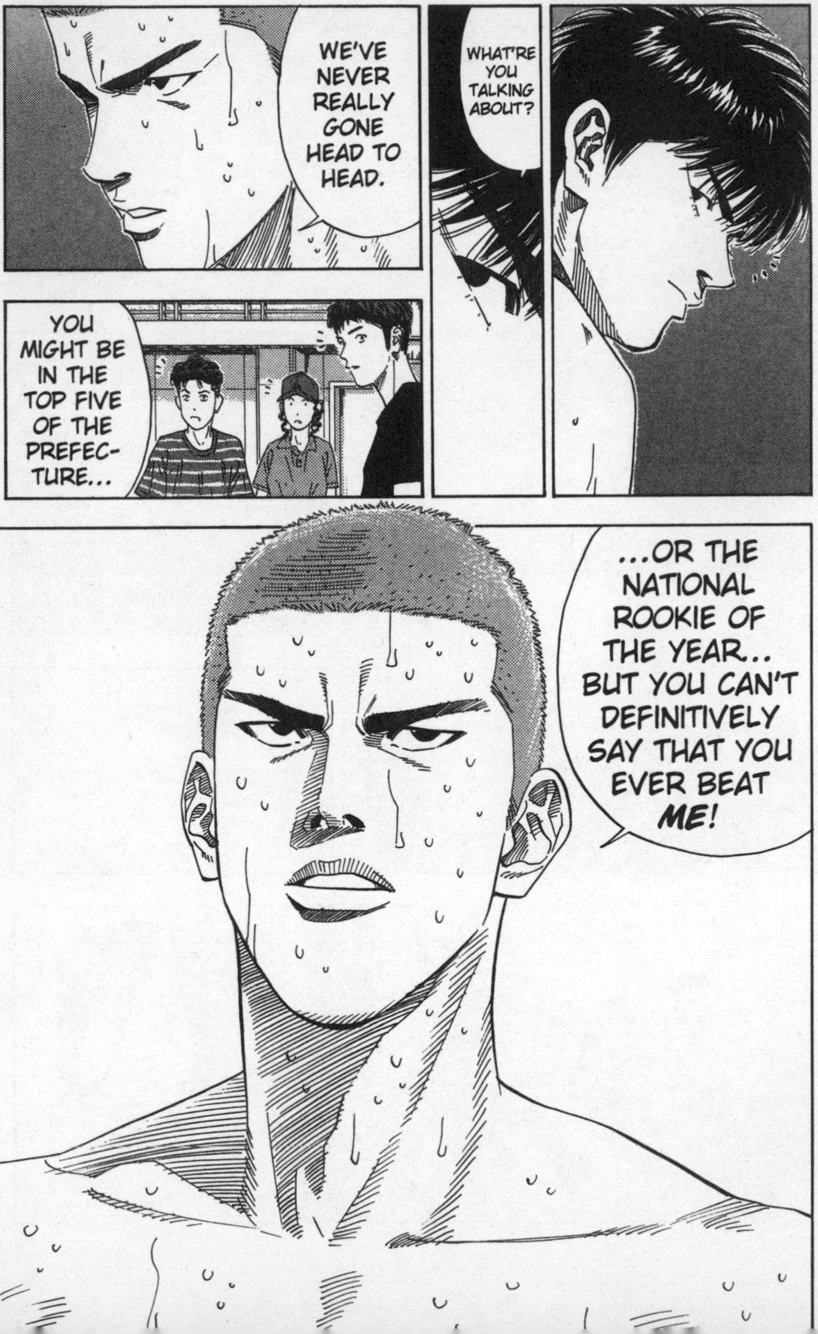
WHAT'RE YOU TALKING ABOUT?
WE'VE NEVER REALLY GONE HEAD TO HEAD.
YOU MIGHT BE IN THE TOP FIVE OF THE PREFEC-TURE...
...OR THE NATIONAL ROOKIE OF THE YEAR... BUT YOU CAN'T DEFINITIVELY SAY THAT YOU EVER BEAT ME!

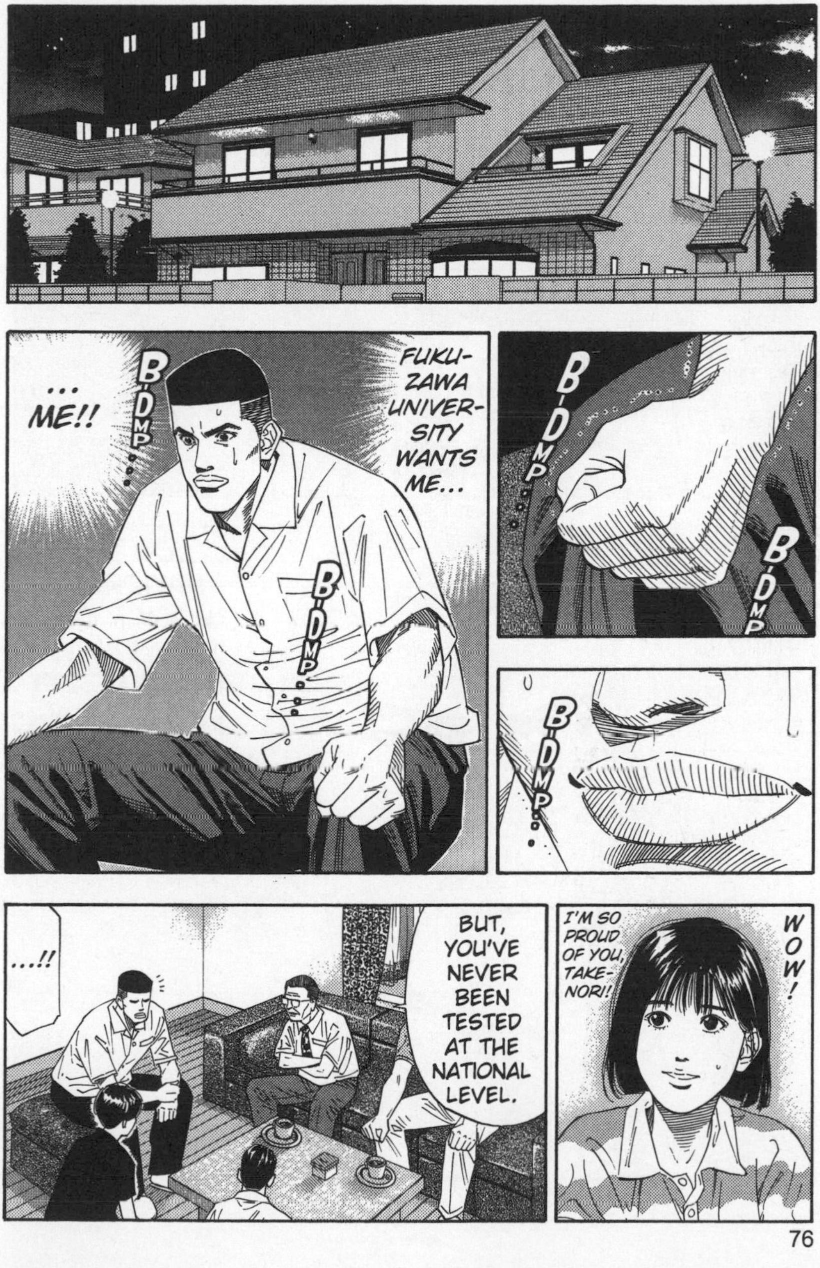
B-DMP
B-DMP
B-DMP
FUKU-ZAWA UNIVER-SITY WANTS ME...
B-DMP
... ME!!
B-DMP
WOW!
I'M SO PROUD OF YOU, TAKE-NORI!!
BUT, YOU'VE NEVER BEEN TESTED AT THE NATIONAL LEVEL.
...!!

READ THIS WAY

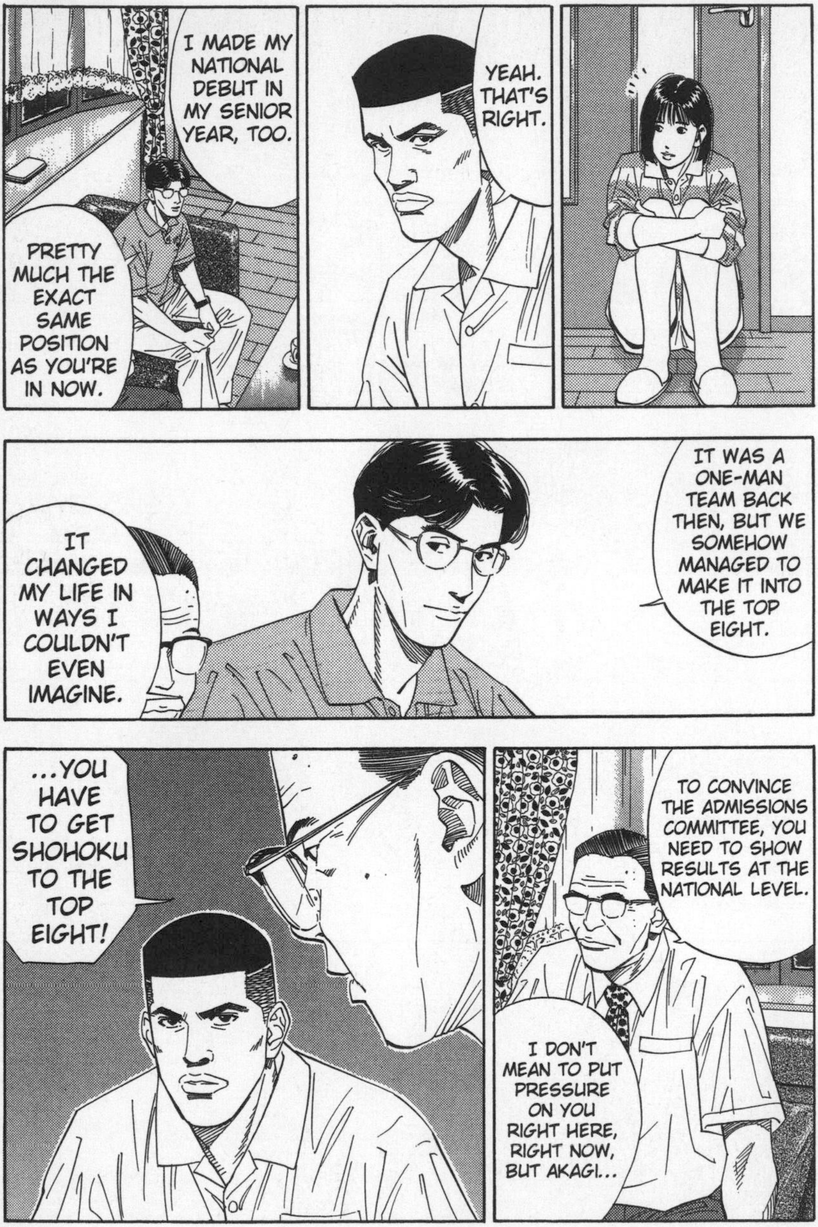
YEAH. THAT'S RIGHT.
I MADE MY NATIONAL DEBUT IN MY SENIOR YEAR, TOO.
PRETTY MUCH THE EXACT SAME POSITION AS YOU'RE IN NOW.
IT WAS A ONE-MAN TEAM BACK THEN, BUT WE SOMEHOW MANAGED TO MAKE IT INTO THE TOP EIGHT.
IT CHANGED MY LIFE IN WAYS I COULDN'T EVEN IMAGINE.
TO CONVINCE THE ADMISSIONS COMMITTEE, YOU NEED TO SHOW RESULTS AT THE NATIONAL LEVEL.
I DON'T MEAN TO PUT PRESSURE ON YOU RIGHT HERE, RIGHT NOW, BUT AKAGI...
...YOU HAVE TO GET SHOHOKU TO THE TOP EIGHT!

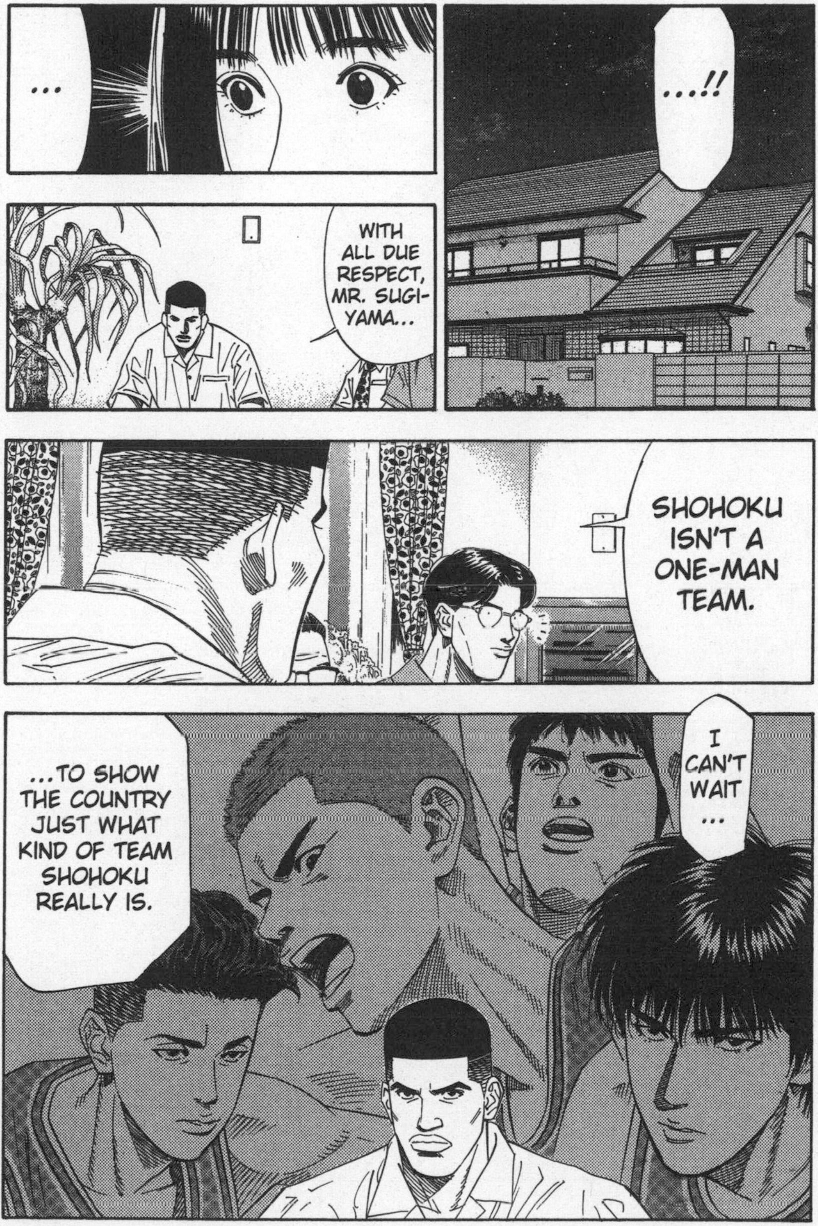
...!!
...
WITH ALL DUE RESPECT, MR. SUGI-YAMA...
SHOHOKU ISN'T A ONE-MAN TEAM.
I CAN'T WAIT...
...TO SHOW THE COUNTRY JUST WHAT KIND OF TEAM SHOHOKU REALLY IS.

READ THIS WAY

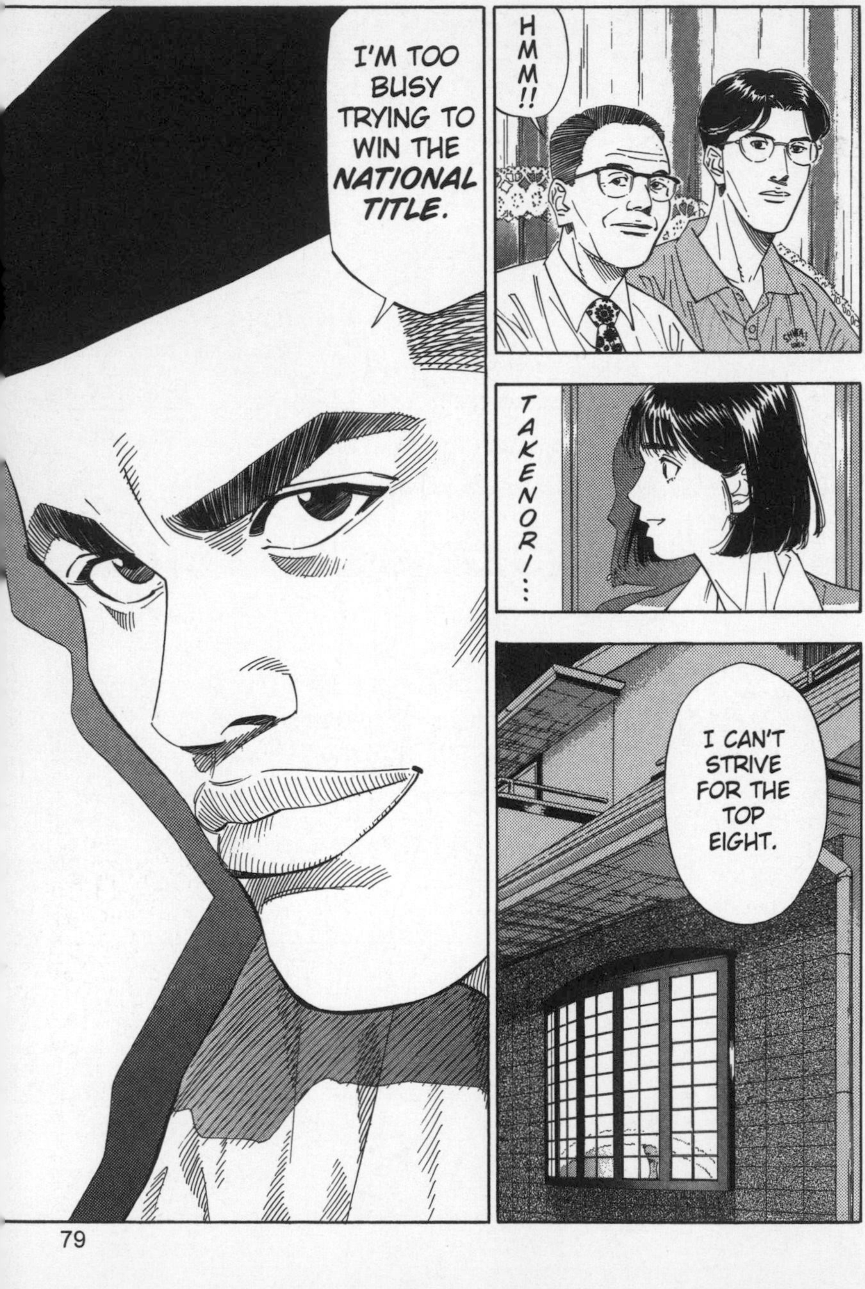
HMM!!
TAKENORI...
I CAN'T STRIVE FOR THE TOP EIGHT.
I'M TOO BUSY TRYING TO WIN THE NATIONAL TITLE.

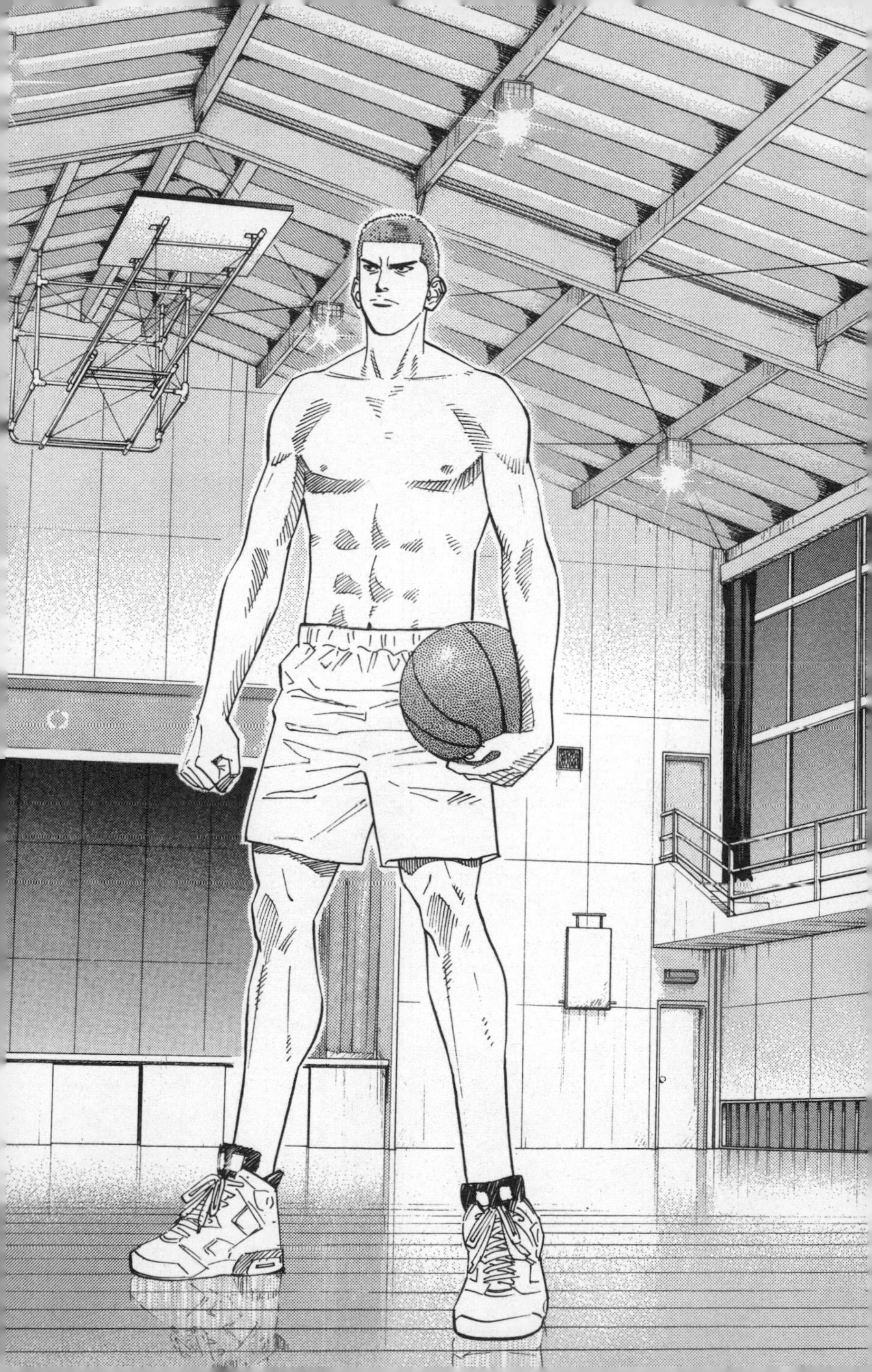

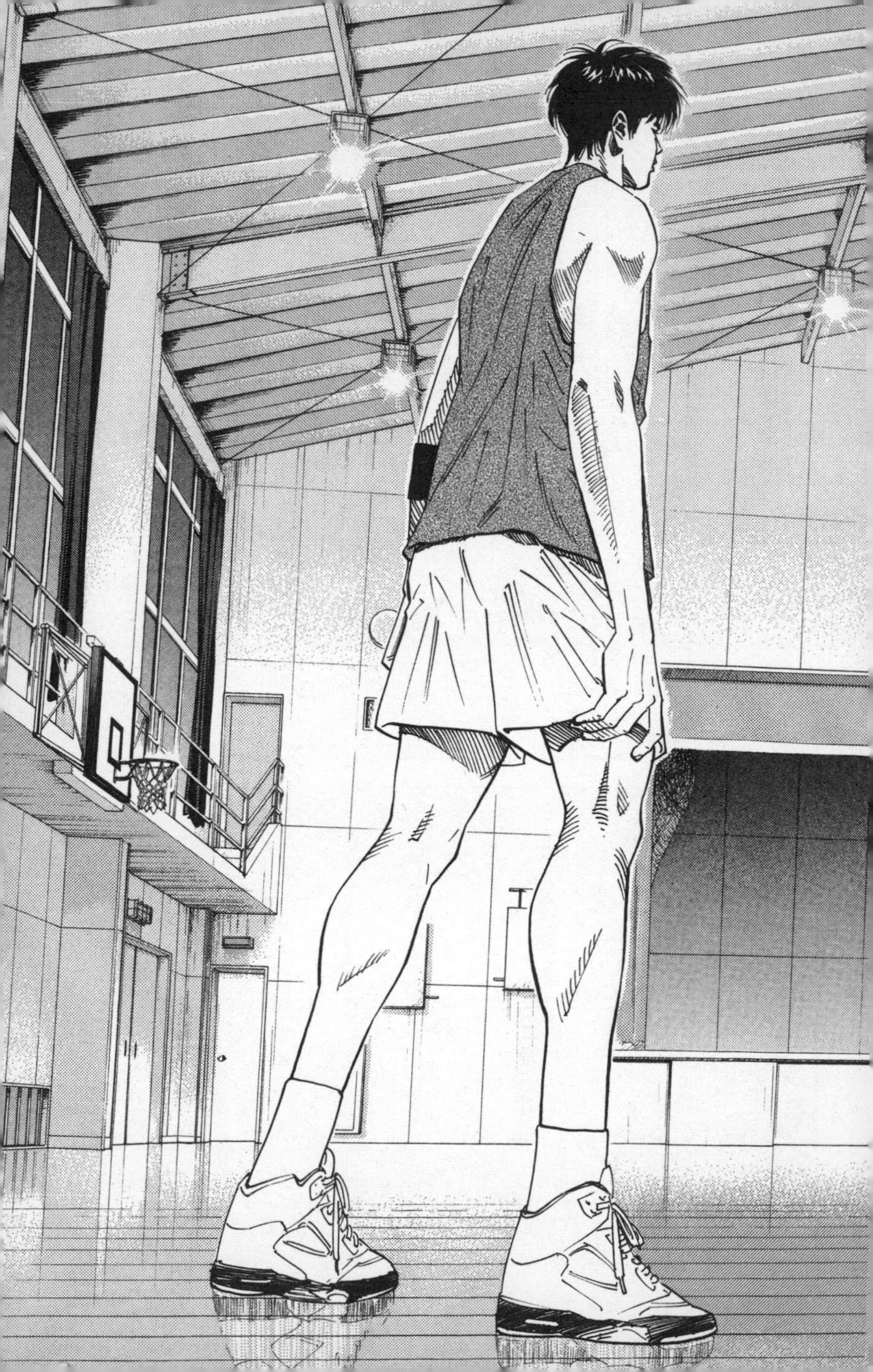

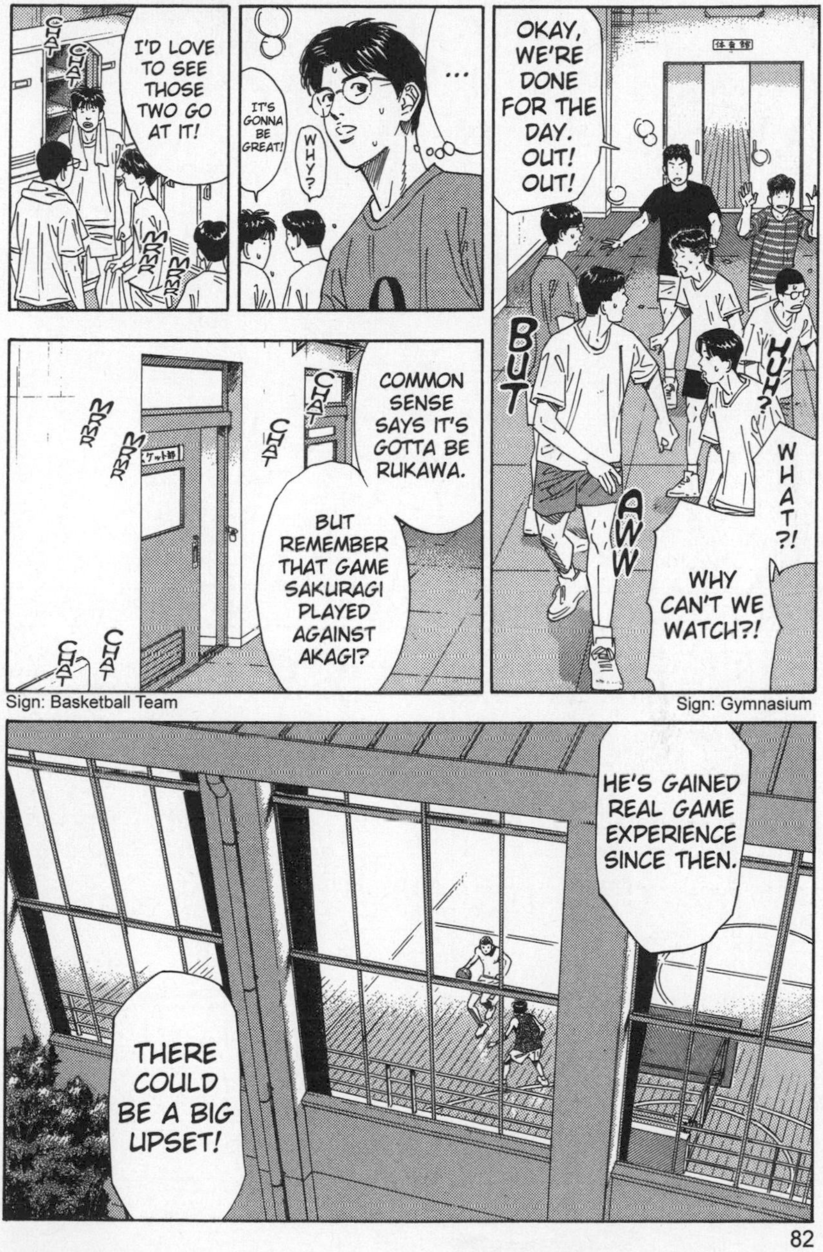
OKAY, WE'RE DONE FOR THE DAY. OUT! OUT!
HUH?
WHAT?!
BUT
WHY CAN'T WE WATCH?!
AWW
...
IT'S GONNA BE GREAT!
WHY?
I'D LOVE TO SEE THOSE TWO GO AT IT!
CHAT CHAT
MRMR MRMR
COMMON SENSE SAYS IT'S GOTTA BE RUKAWA.
CHAT CHAT
BUT REMEMBER THAT GAME SAKURAGI PLAYED AGAINST AKAGI?
MRMR MRMR
CHAT CHAT
HE'S GAINED REAL GAME EXPERIENCE SINCE THEN.
THERE COULD BE A BIG UPSET!

Sign: Gymnasium

Sign: Basketball Team

READ THIS WAY

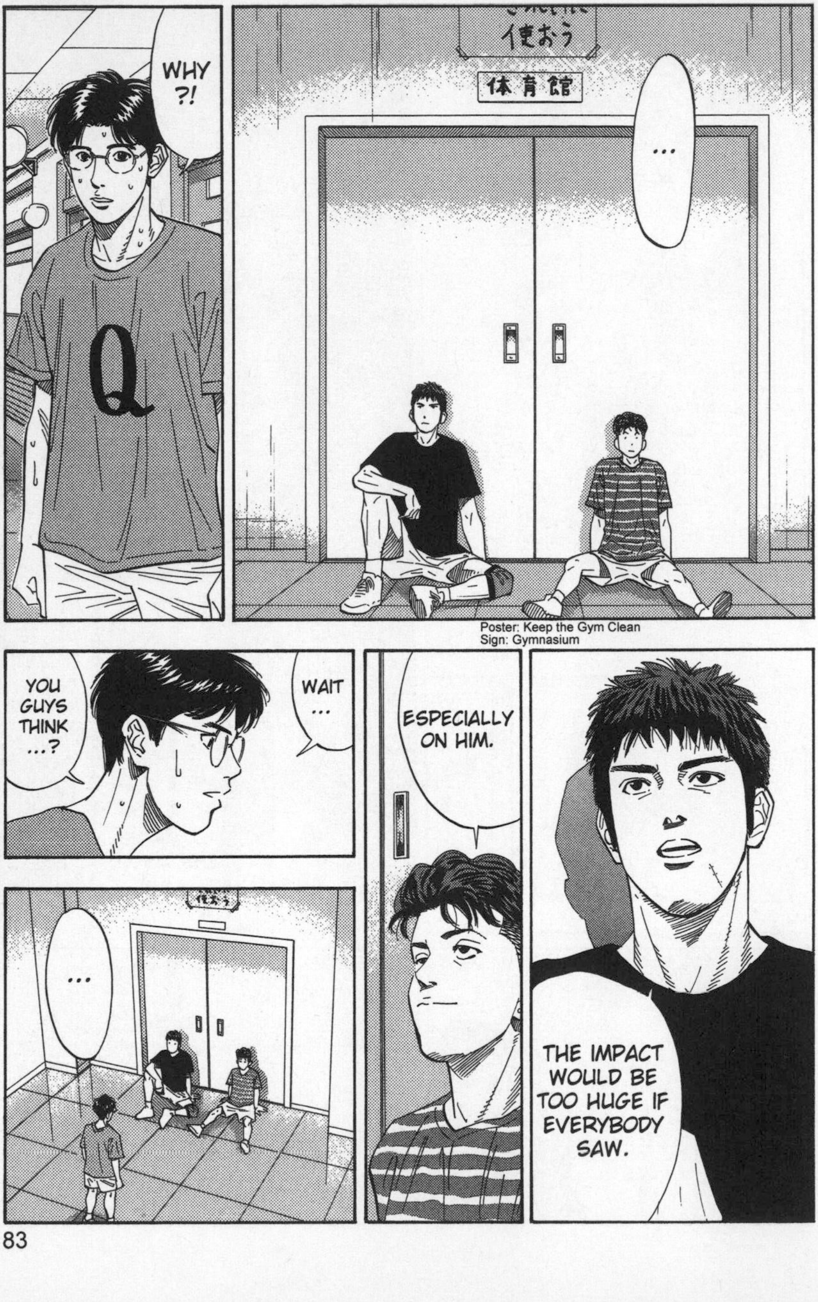
...
WHY ?!
THE IMPACT WOULD BE TOO HUGE IF EVERYBODY SAW.
ESPECIALLY ON HIM.
WAIT ...
YOU GUYS THINK ...?
...

Poster: Keep the Gym Clean
Sign: Gymnasium

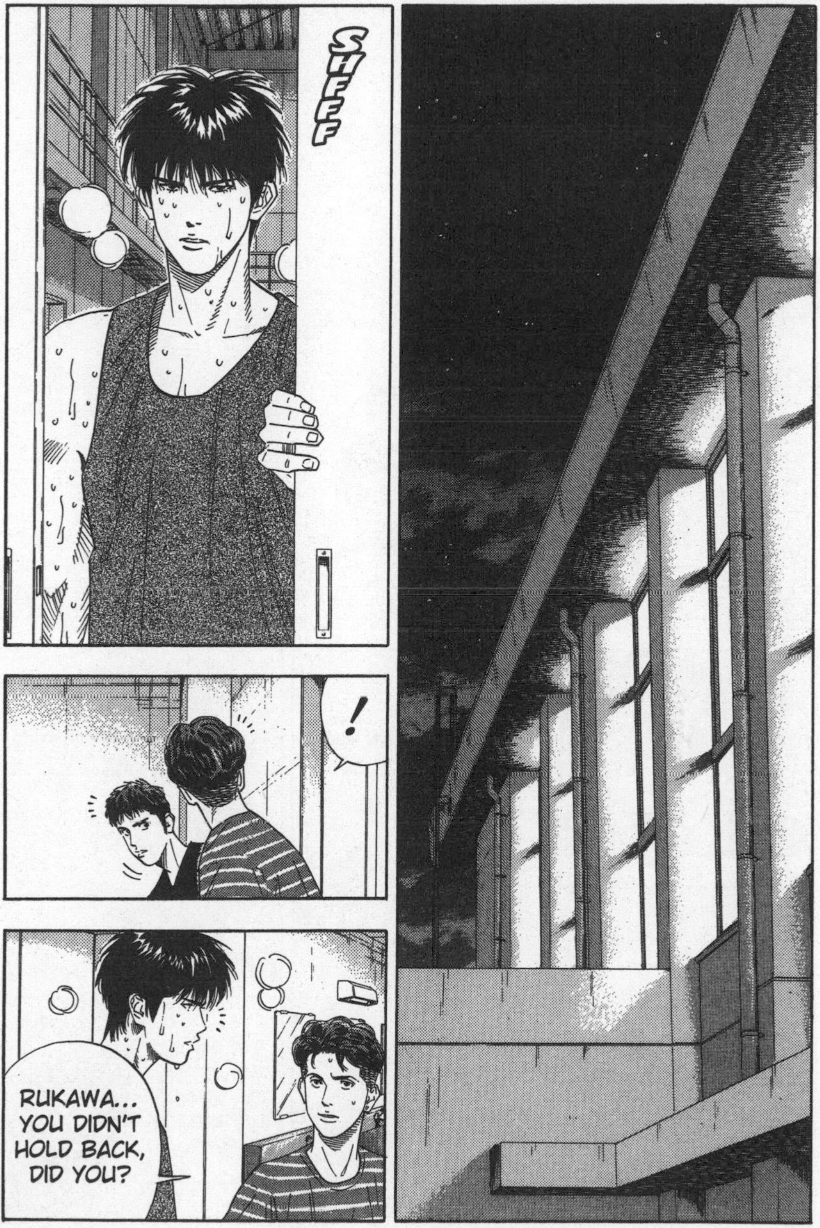
SHFFF
!
RUKAWA... YOU DIDN'T HOLD BACK, DID YOU?

READ THIS WAY

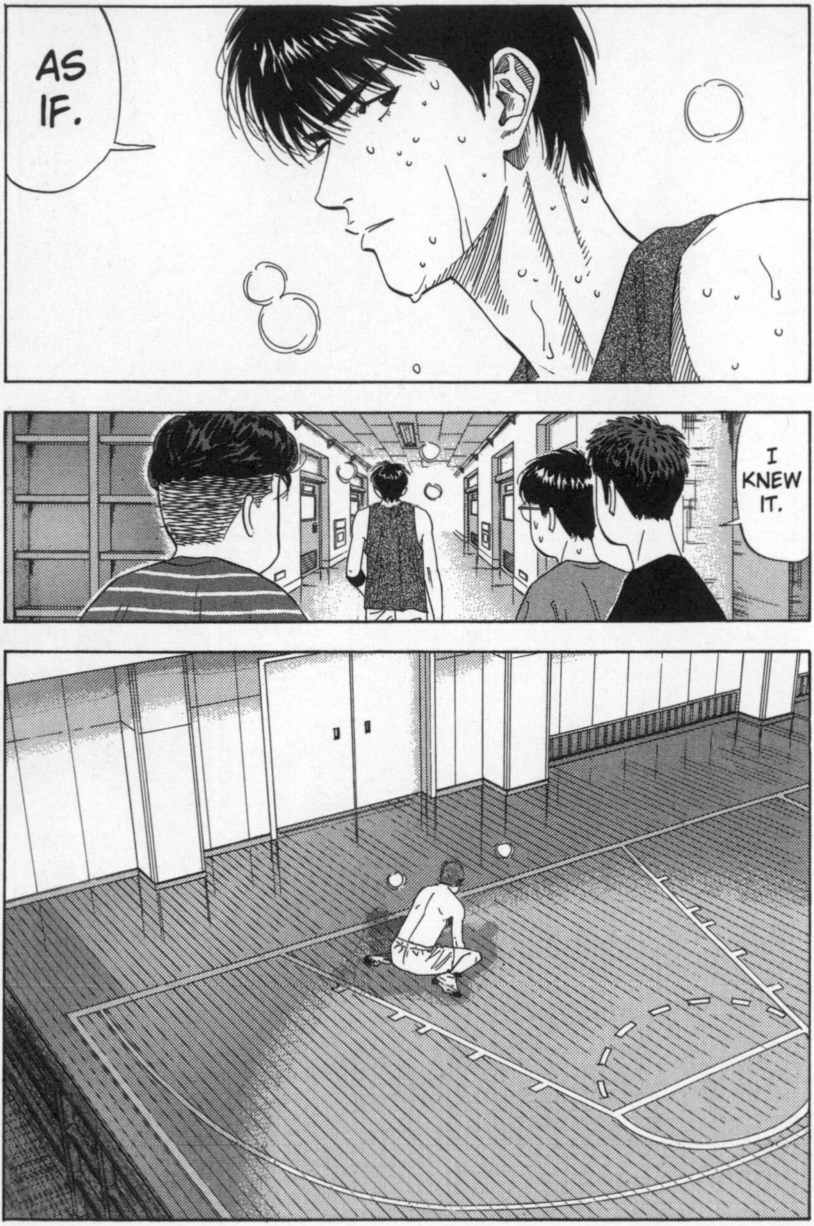
AS IF.
I KNEW IT.

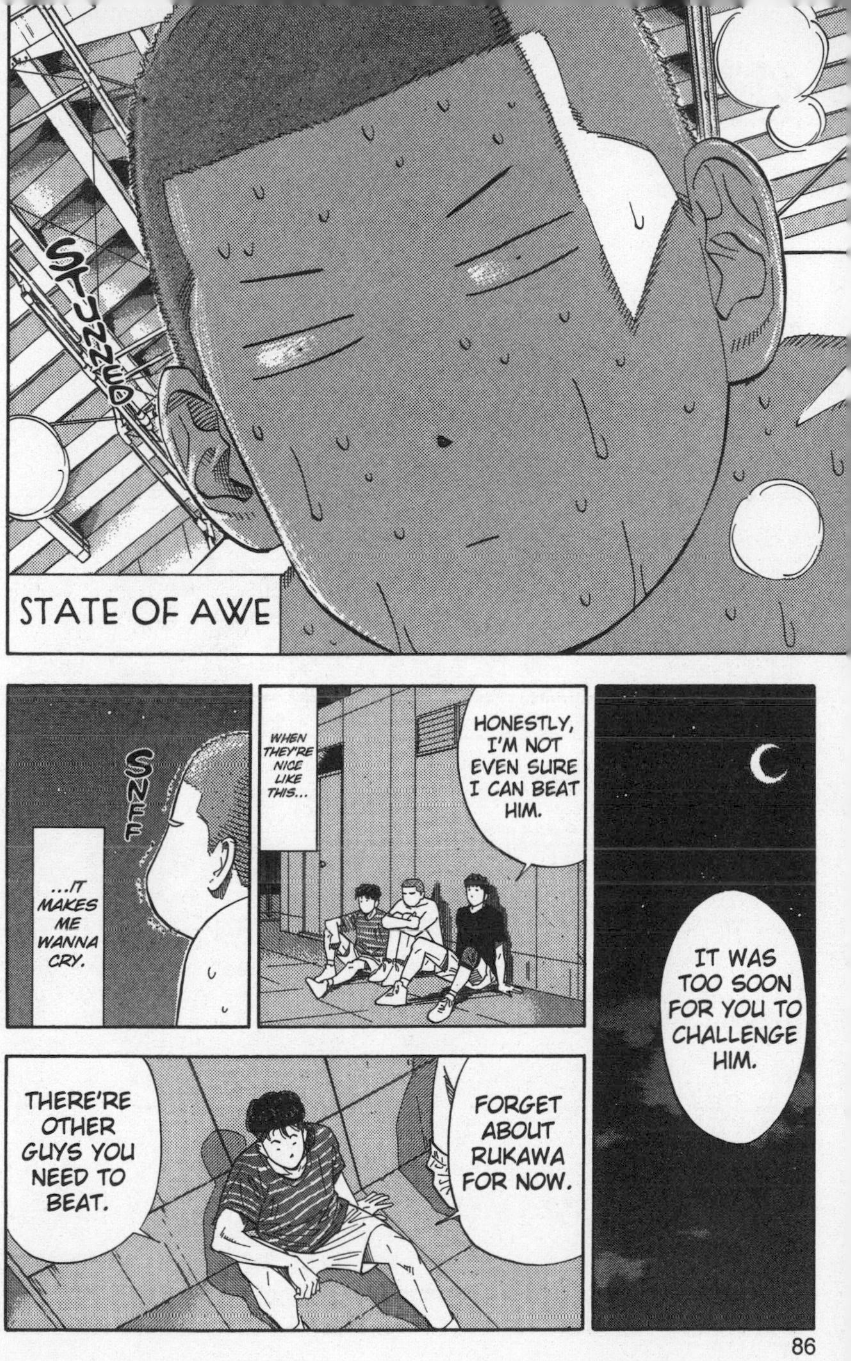
STUNNED
STATE OF AWE
IT WAS TOO SOON FOR YOU TO CHALLENGE HIM.
HONESTLY, I'M NOT EVEN SURE I CAN BEAT HIM.
WHEN THEY'RE NICE LIKE THIS...
SNFF
...IT MAKES ME WANNA CRY.
FORGET ABOUT RUKAWA FOR NOW.
THERE'RE OTHER GUYS YOU NEED TO BEAT.

READ THIS WAY

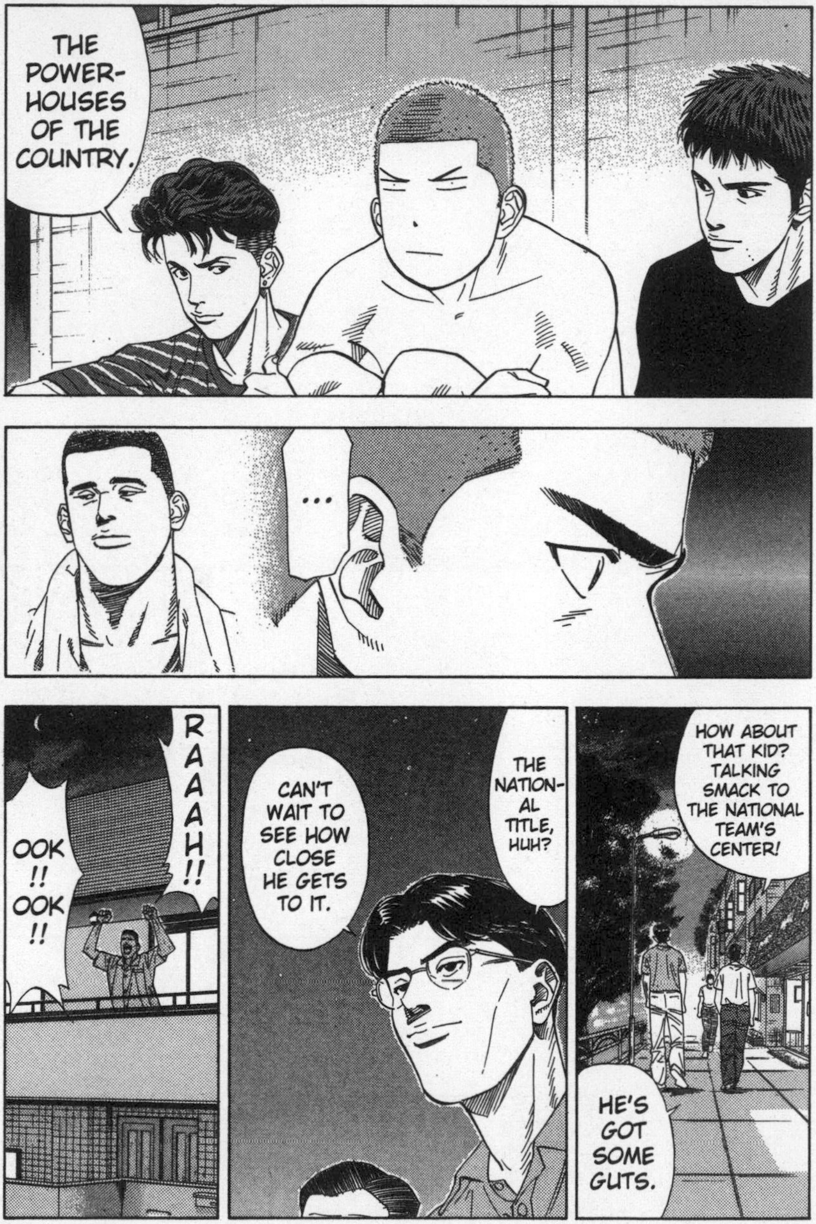
THE POWER-HOUSES OF THE COUNTRY.
...
HOW ABOUT THAT KID? TALKING SMACK TO THE NATIONAL TEAM'S CENTER!
HE'S GOT SOME GUTS.
THE NATION-AL TITLE, HUH?
CAN'T WAIT TO SEE HOW CLOSE HE GETS TO IT.
RAAAAH!!
OOK!! OOK!!

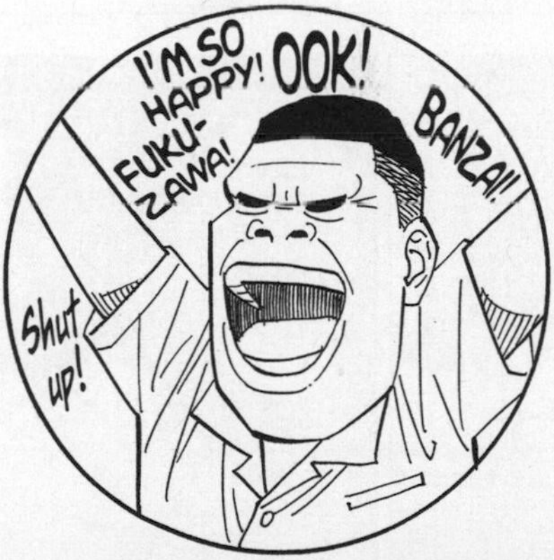
BANZAI!!
OOK!
I'M SO HAPPY! FUKU-ZAWA!
Shut up!

SLAM DUNK

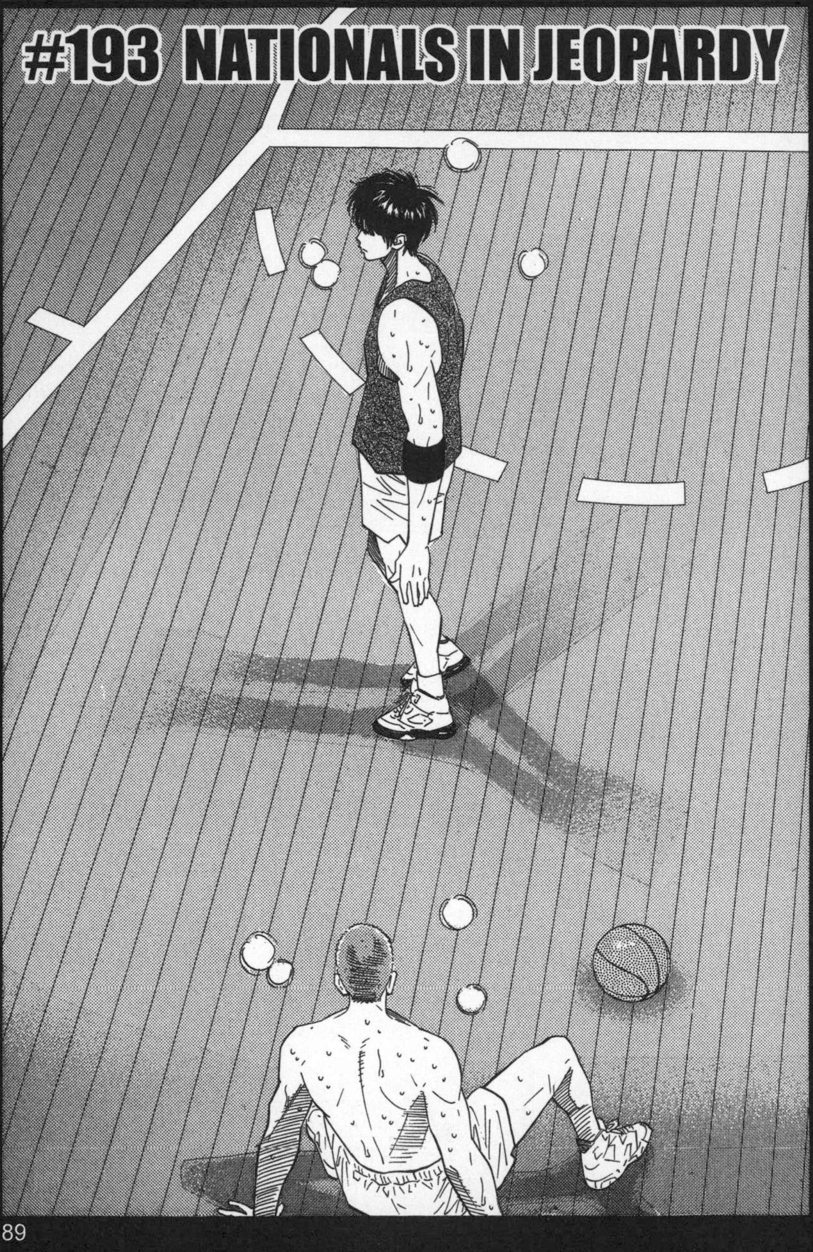
#193 NATIONALS IN JEOPARDY

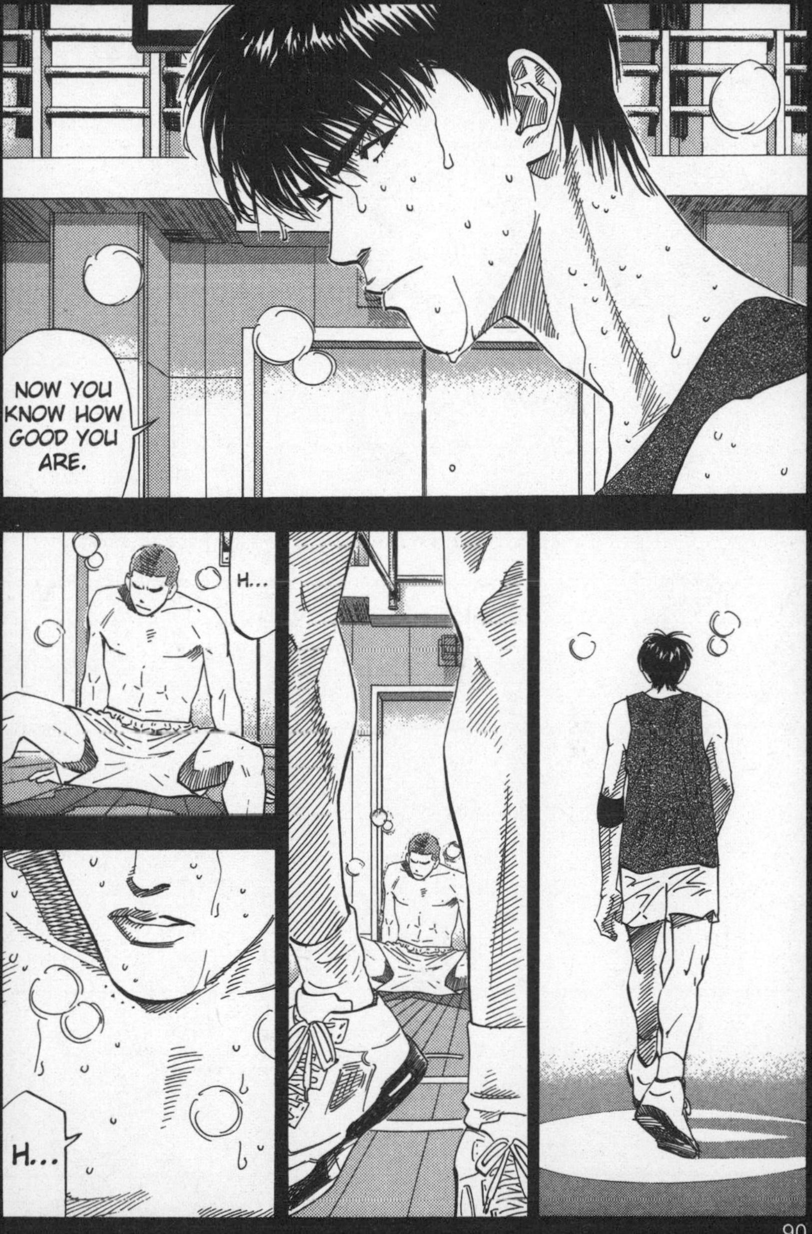
NOW YOU KNOW HOW GOOD YOU ARE.
H...
H...

READ THIS WAY

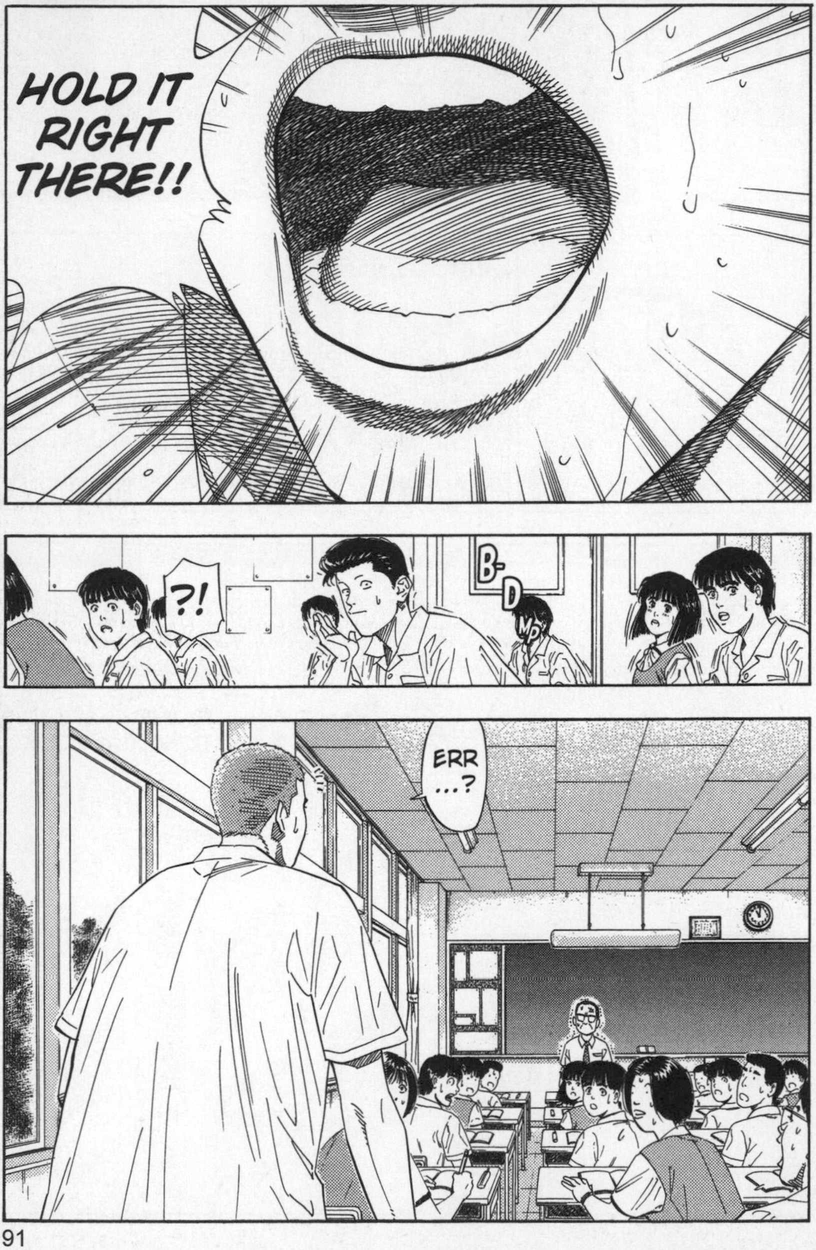
HOLD IT RIGHT THERE!!
B-DMP
?!
ERR ...?

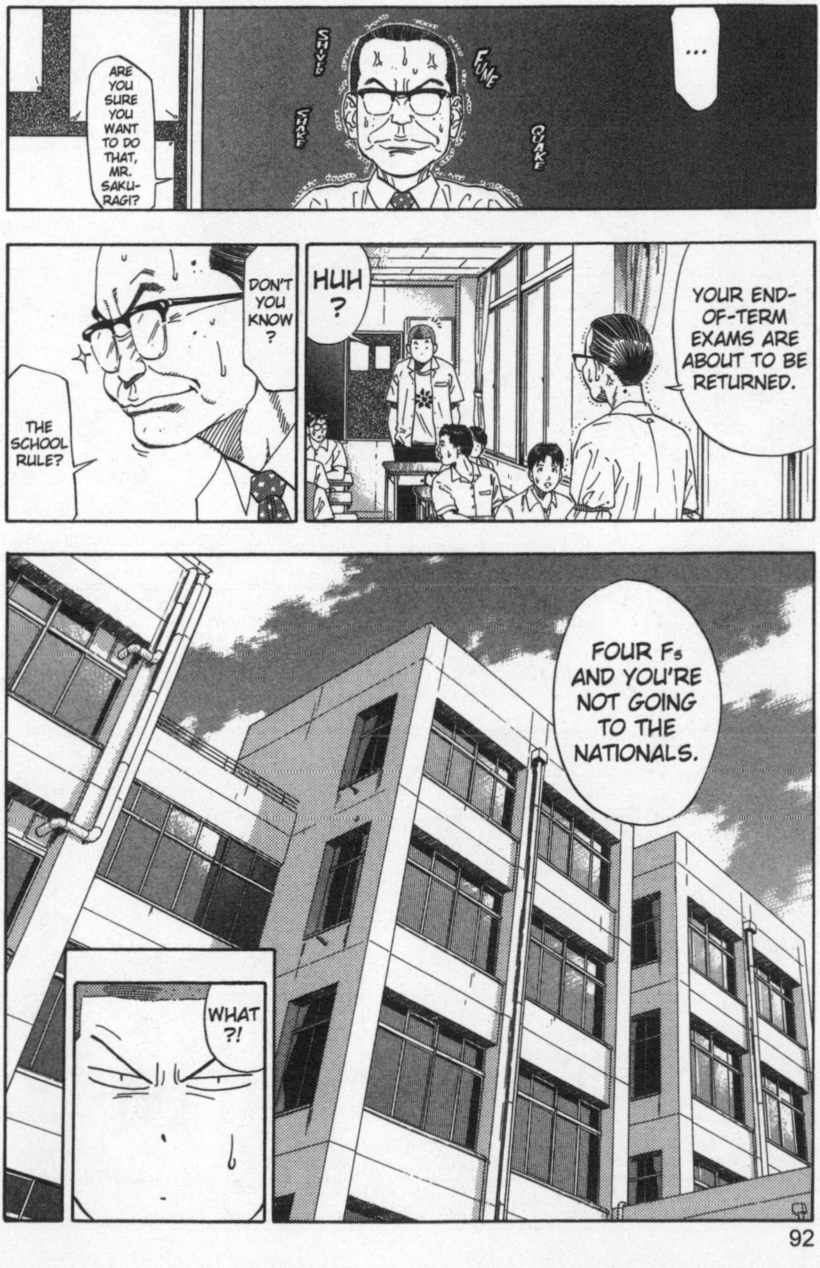
...
FUME
SHIVER
QUAKE
SHAKE
ARE YOU SURE YOU WANT TO DO THAT, MR. SAKURAGI?
YOUR END-OF-TERM EXAMS ARE ABOUT TO BE RETURNED.
HUH?
DON'T YOU KNOW?
THE SCHOOL RULE?
FOUR Fs AND YOU'RE NOT GOING TO THE NATIONALS.
WHAT?!

READ THIS WAY

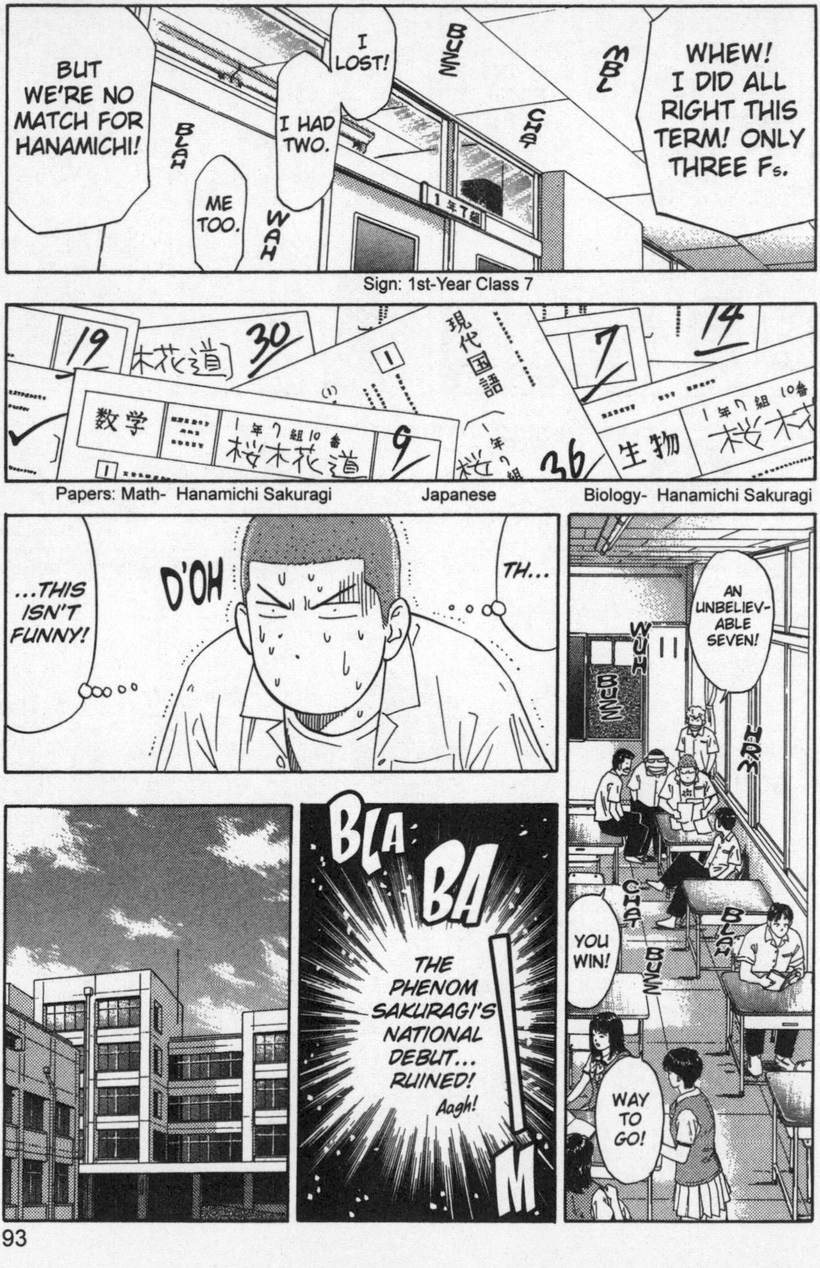
WHEW! I DID ALL RIGHT THIS TERM! ONLY THREE Fs.
MBL
CHAT
BUZZ
I LOST!
I HAD TWO.
WAH
ME TOO.
BLAH
BUT WE'RE NO MATCH FOR HANAMICHI!
Sign: 1st-Year Class 7
14
7
生物
36
現代国語
9
数学
1年7組10番 桜木花道
30
19
Papers: Math- Hanamichi Sakuragi Japanese Biology- Hanamichi Sakuragi
AN UNBELIEVABLE SEVEN!
WUH
BUZZ
HRM
CHAT
BLAH
YOU WIN!
BUZZ
WAY TO GO!
TH...
D'OH
...THIS ISN'T FUNNY!
BLA BA M
THE PHENOM SAKURAGI'S NATIONAL DEBUT... RUINED!
Aagh!

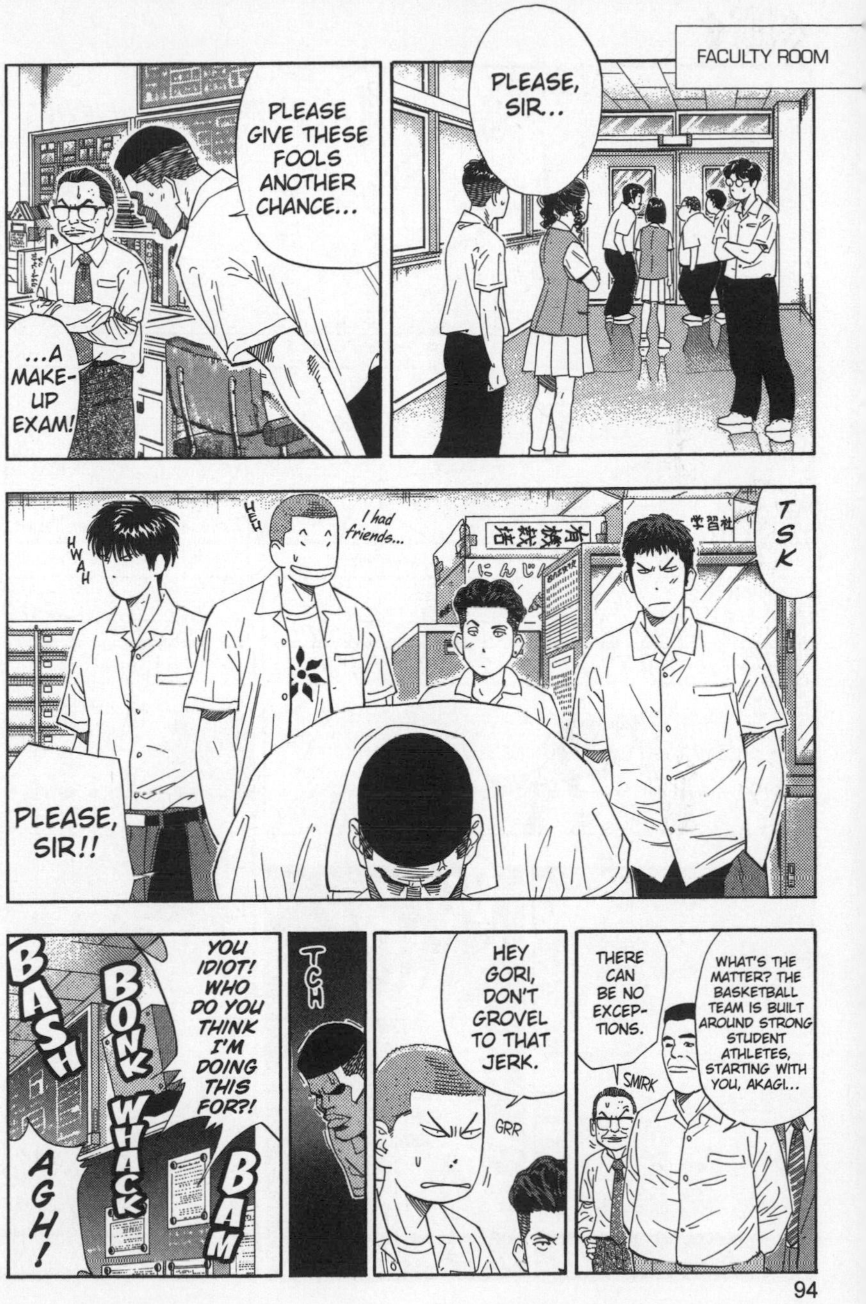
FACULTY ROOM
PLEASE, SIR...
PLEASE GIVE THESE FOOLS ANOTHER CHANCE...
...A MAKE-UP EXAM!
TSK
学習社
I had friends...
HEH
HWAH
PLEASE, SIR!!
WHAT'S THE MATTER? THE BASKETBALL TEAM IS BUILT AROUND STRONG STUDENT ATHLETES, STARTING WITH YOU, AKAGI...
THERE CAN BE NO EXCEPTIONS.
SMIRK
HEY GORI, DON'T GROVEL TO THAT JERK.
GRR
TCH
YOU IDIOT! WHO DO YOU THINK I'M DOING THIS FOR?!
BAM
BONK
WHACK
BASH
AGH!

READ THIS WAY

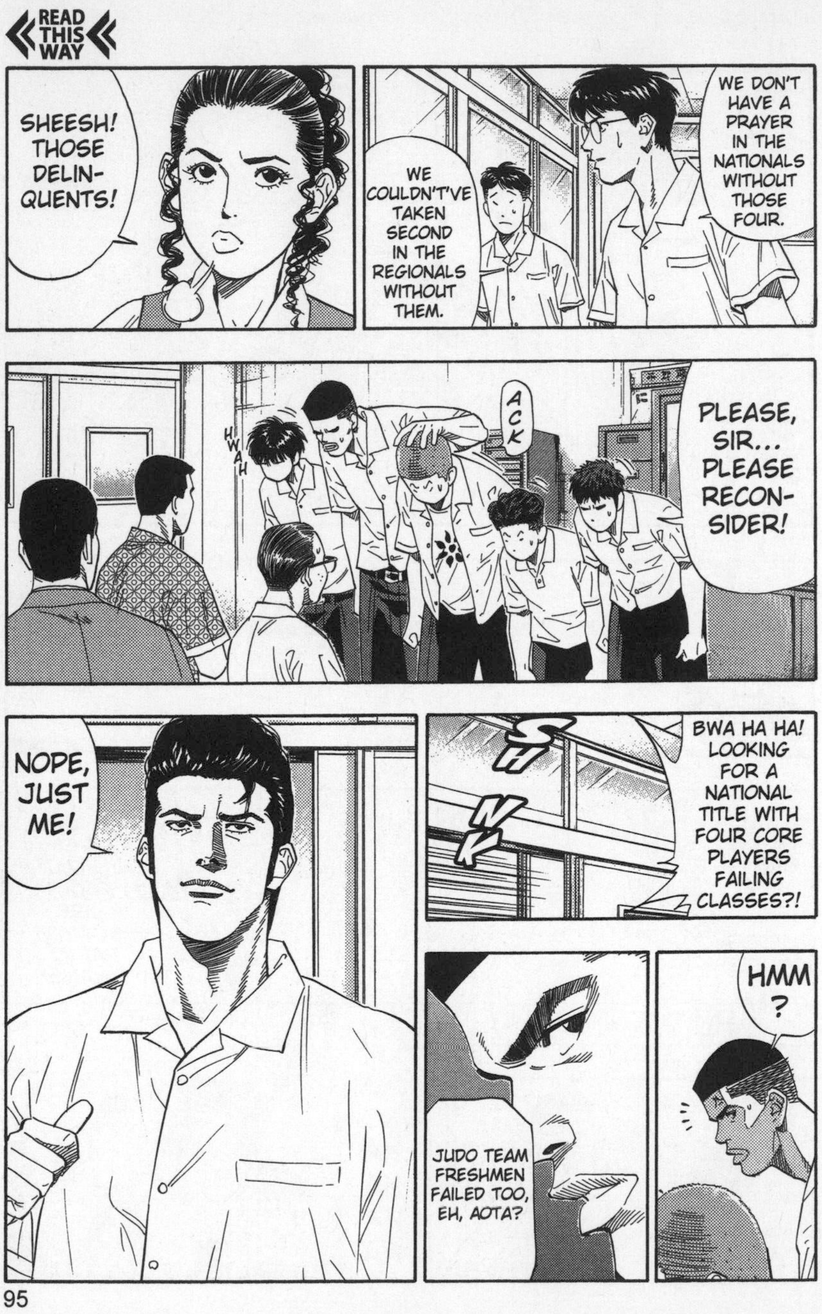
WE DON'T HAVE A PRAYER IN THE NATIONALS WITHOUT THOSE FOUR.
WE COULDN'T'VE TAKEN SECOND IN THE REGIONALS WITHOUT THEM.
SHEESH! THOSE DELIN-QUENTS!
PLEASE, SIR... PLEASE RECON-SIDER!
ACK
HWAH
SHNK
BWA HA HA! LOOKING FOR A NATIONAL TITLE WITH FOUR CORE PLAYERS FAILING CLASSES?!
HMM?
JUDO TEAM FRESHMEN FAILED TOO, EH, AOTA?
NOPE, JUST ME!

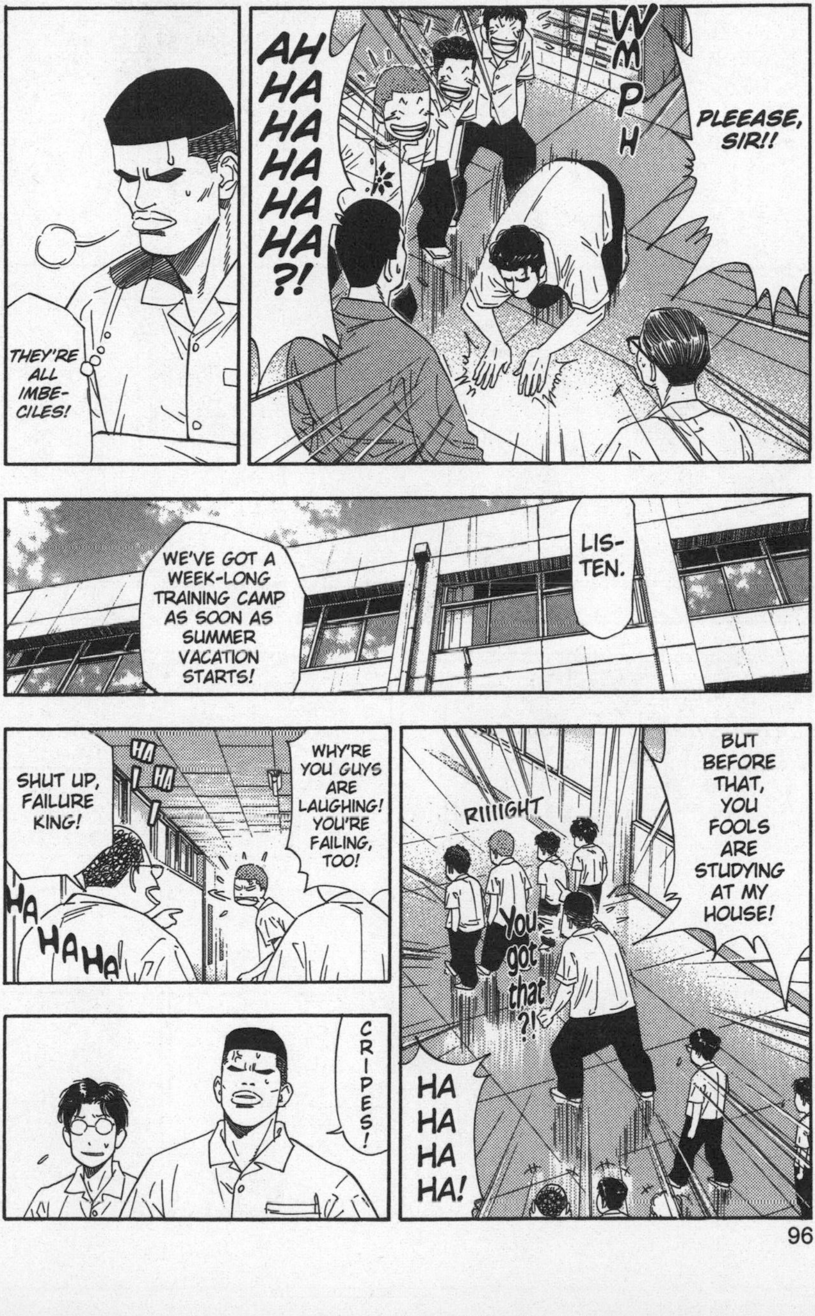
WMPH
PLEEASE, SIR!!
AH HA HA HA HA HA HA ?!
THEY'RE ALL IMBECILES!
LISTEN.
WE'VE GOT A WEEK-LONG TRAINING CAMP AS SOON AS SUMMER VACATION STARTS!
BUT BEFORE THAT, YOU FOOLS ARE STUDYING AT MY HOUSE!
RIIIIGHT
You got that ?!
HA HA HA HA!
WHY'RE YOU GUYS ARE LAUGHING! YOU'RE FAILING, TOO!
HA HA
SHUT UP, FAILURE KING!
HA HA HA
CRIPES!

READ THIS WAY

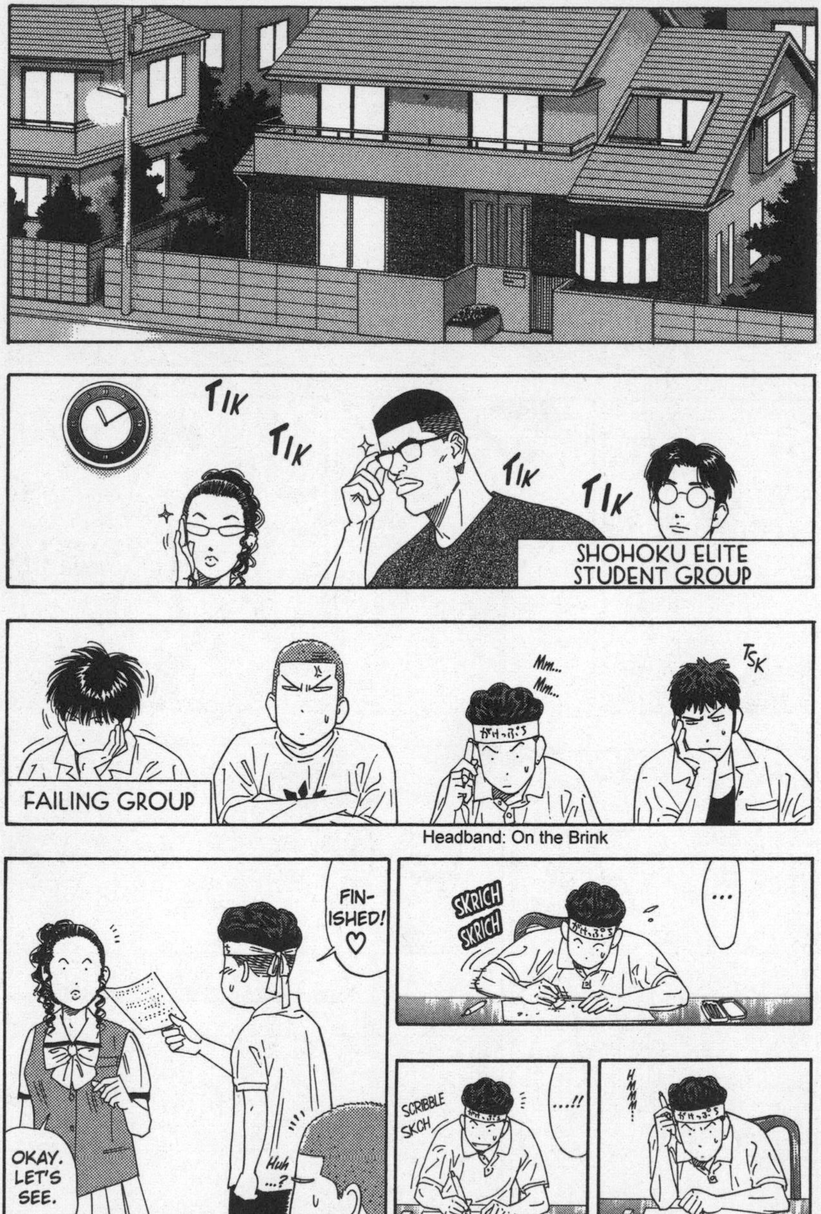
TIK
TIK
TIK
TIK
SHOHOKU ELITE STUDENT GROUP
TSK
Mm... Mm...
FAILING GROUP
Headband: On the Brink
...
SKRICH SKRICH
HMMM...
....!!
SCRIBBLE SKCH
FIN-ISHED! ♡
Huh ...?
OKAY. LET'S SEE.

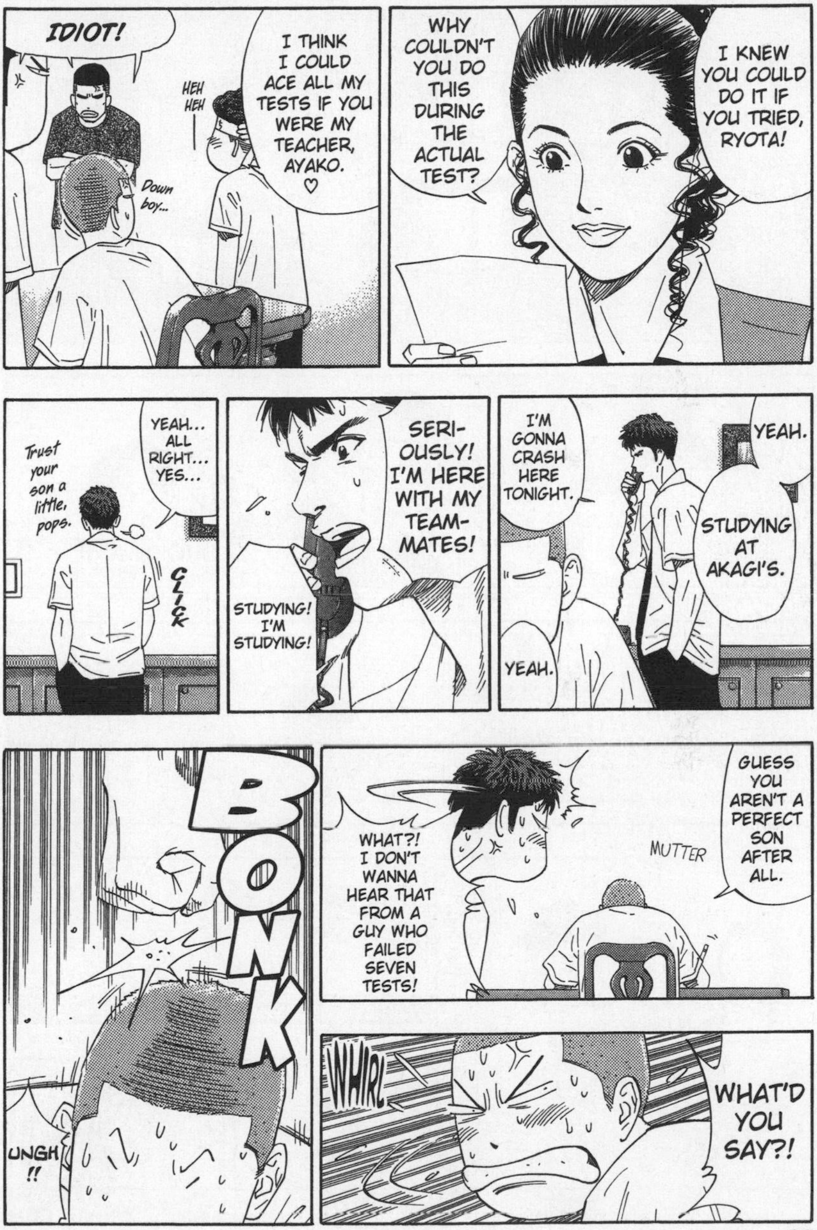
I KNEW YOU COULD DO IT IF YOU TRIED, RYOTA!
WHY COULDN'T YOU DO THIS DURING THE ACTUAL TEST?
I THINK I COULD ACE ALL MY TESTS IF YOU WERE MY TEACHER, AYAKO. ♡
HEH HEH
IDIOT!
Down boy...
YEAH.
STUDYING AT AKAGI'S.
I'M GONNA CRASH HERE TONIGHT.
YEAH.
SERI-OUSLY! I'M HERE WITH MY TEAM-MATES!
STUDYING! I'M STUDYING!
YEAH... ALL RIGHT... YES...
CLICK
Trust your son a little, pops.
GUESS YOU AREN'T A PERFECT SON AFTER ALL.
MUTTER
WHAT?! I DON'T WANNA HEAR THAT FROM A GUY WHO FAILED SEVEN TESTS!
WHAT'D YOU SAY?!
WHIRL
BONK
UNGH !!

...

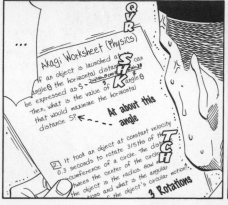

Akagi Worksheet (Physics)

If an object is launched at angle θ the horizontal distance can be expressed as $S = \frac{2v^2 \sin\theta\cos\theta}{g}$

Then, what is the value of angle θ that would maximize the horizontal distance S?

At about this angle

2. It took an object at constant velocity 0.3 seconds to rotate 3/5ths of the circumference of a circle. The distance between the center of the circle and the object is the radius. How many rotations and what is the angular velocity of the object's circular motion?

3 Rotations

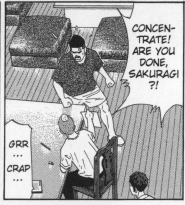

CONCENTRATE! ARE YOU DONE, SAKURAGI?!

GRR... CRAP...

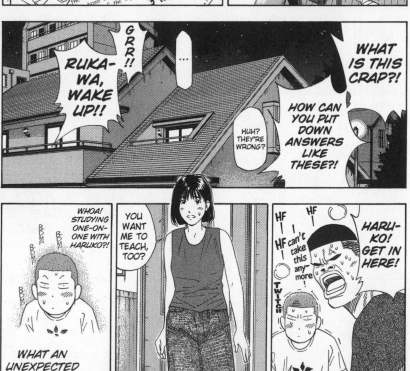

GRR!!

RUKAWA, WAKE UP!!

...

WHAT IS THIS CRAP?!

HUH? THEY'RE WRONG?

HOW CAN YOU PUT DOWN ANSWERS LIKE THESE?!

WHOA! STUDYING ONE-ON-ONE WITH HARUKO?!

B·DMP B·DMP B·DMP B·DMP

WHAT AN UNEXPECTED BONUS!

YOU WANT ME TO TEACH, TOO?

HF HF HF

I can't take this anymore

TWITCH

HARUKO! GET IN HERE!

!!

99

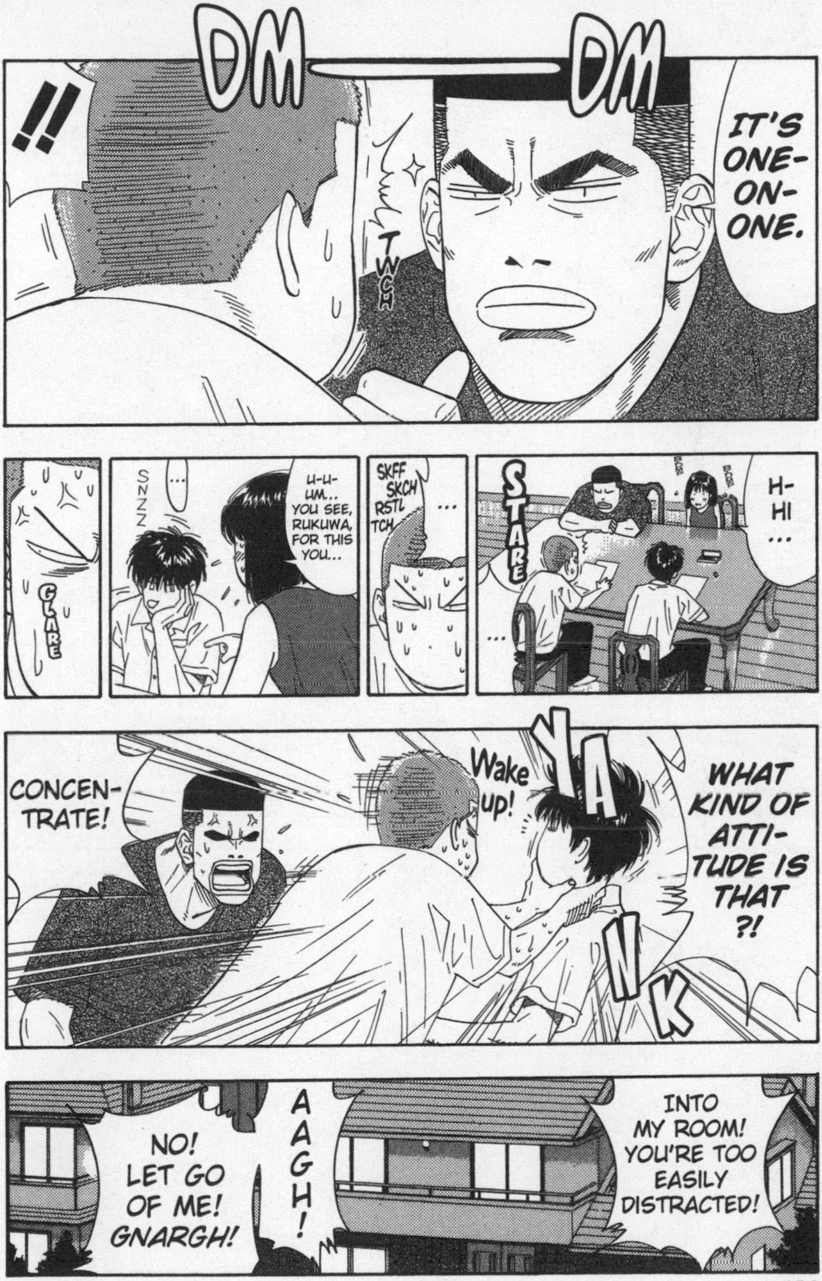
DM DM
IT'S ONE-ON-ONE.
TWCH
!!
H-HI...
STARE
...
...
SKFF SKCH RSTL TCH
U-U-UM... YOU SEE, RUKUWA, FOR THIS YOU...
...
SNZZ
GLARE
WHAT KIND OF ATTITUDE IS THAT?!
YANK
Wake up!
CONCENTRATE!
INTO MY ROOM! YOU'RE TOO EASILY DISTRACTED!
AAGH!
NO! LET GO OF ME! GNARGH!

READ THIS WAY

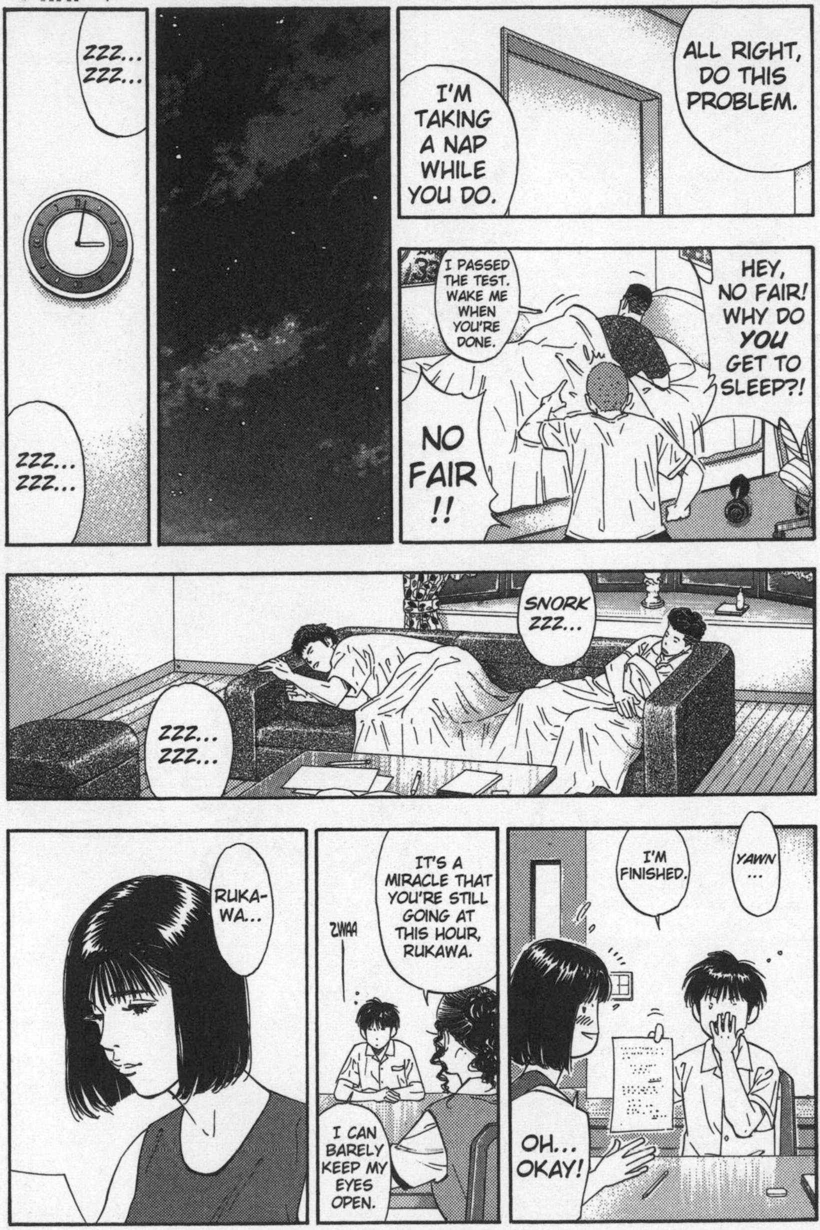
ALL RIGHT, DO THIS PROBLEM.
I'M TAKING A NAP WHILE YOU DO.
HEY, NO FAIR! WHY DO YOU GET TO SLEEP?!
I PASSED THE TEST. WAKE ME WHEN YOU'RE DONE.
NO FAIR!!
ZZZ... ZZZ...
ZZZ... ZZZ...
SNORK ZZZ...
ZZZ... ZZZ...
YAWN...
I'M FINISHED.
OH... OKAY!
IT'S A MIRACLE THAT YOU'RE STILL GOING AT THIS HOUR, RUKAWA.
ZWAA
I CAN BARELY KEEP MY EYES OPEN.
RUKA-WA...

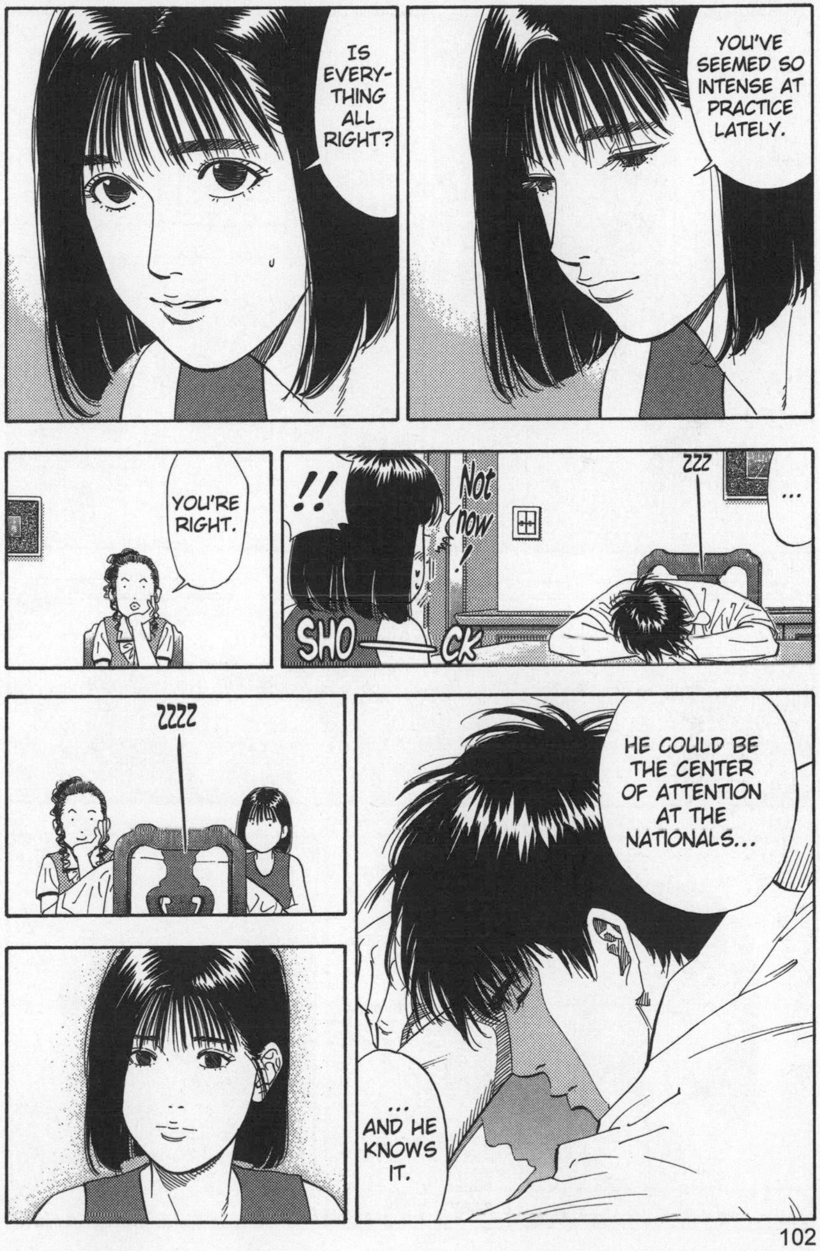
YOU'VE SEEMED SO INTENSE AT PRACTICE LATELY.
IS EVERY-THING ALL RIGHT?
...
ZZZ
Not now!
!!
SHOCK
YOU'RE RIGHT.
HE COULD BE THE CENTER OF ATTENTION AT THE NATIONALS...
... AND HE KNOWS IT.
ZZZZ

READ THIS WAY

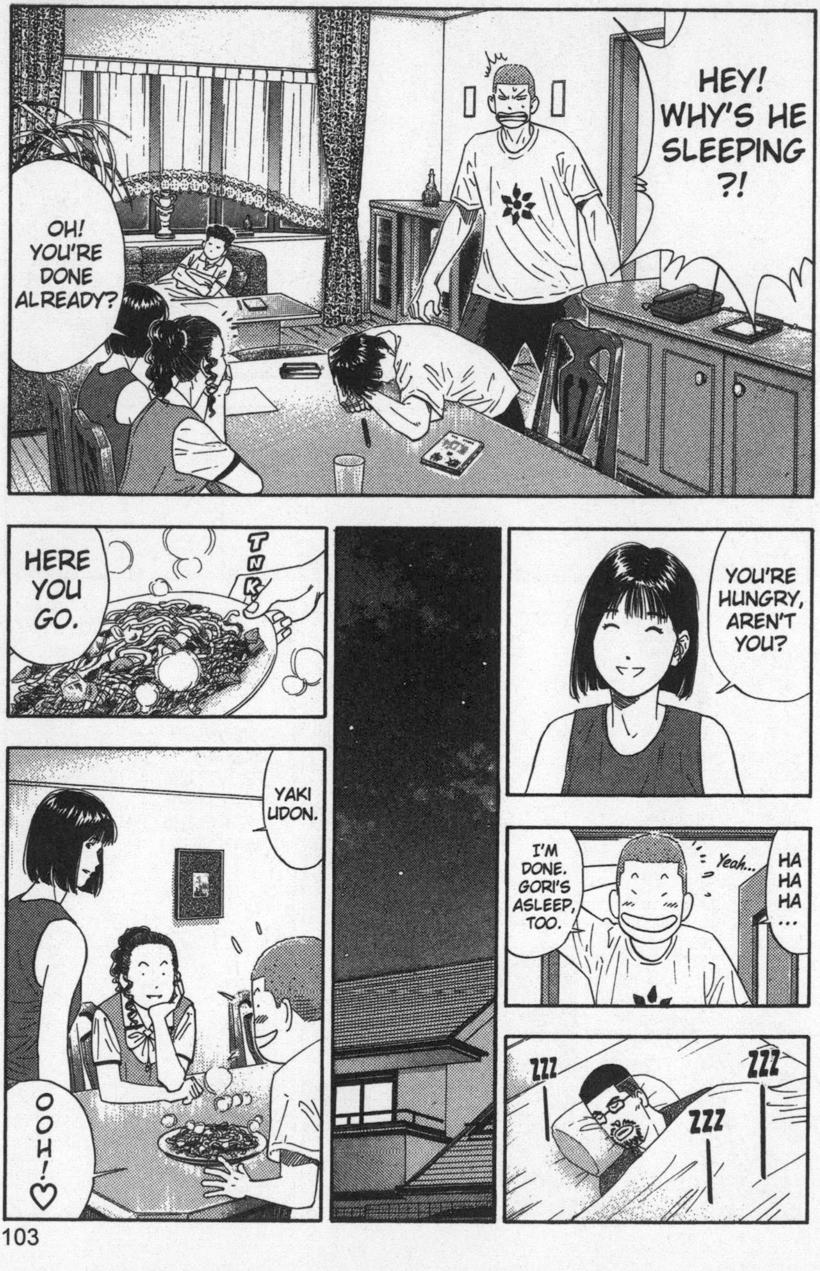
HEY! WHY'S HE SLEEPING ?!
OH! YOU'RE DONE ALREADY?
YOU'RE HUNGRY, AREN'T YOU?
I'M DONE. GORI'S ASLEEP, TOO.
Yeah...
HA HA HA ...
ZZZ
ZZZ
ZZZ
HERE YOU GO.
TNK
YAKI UDON.
OOOH!♡

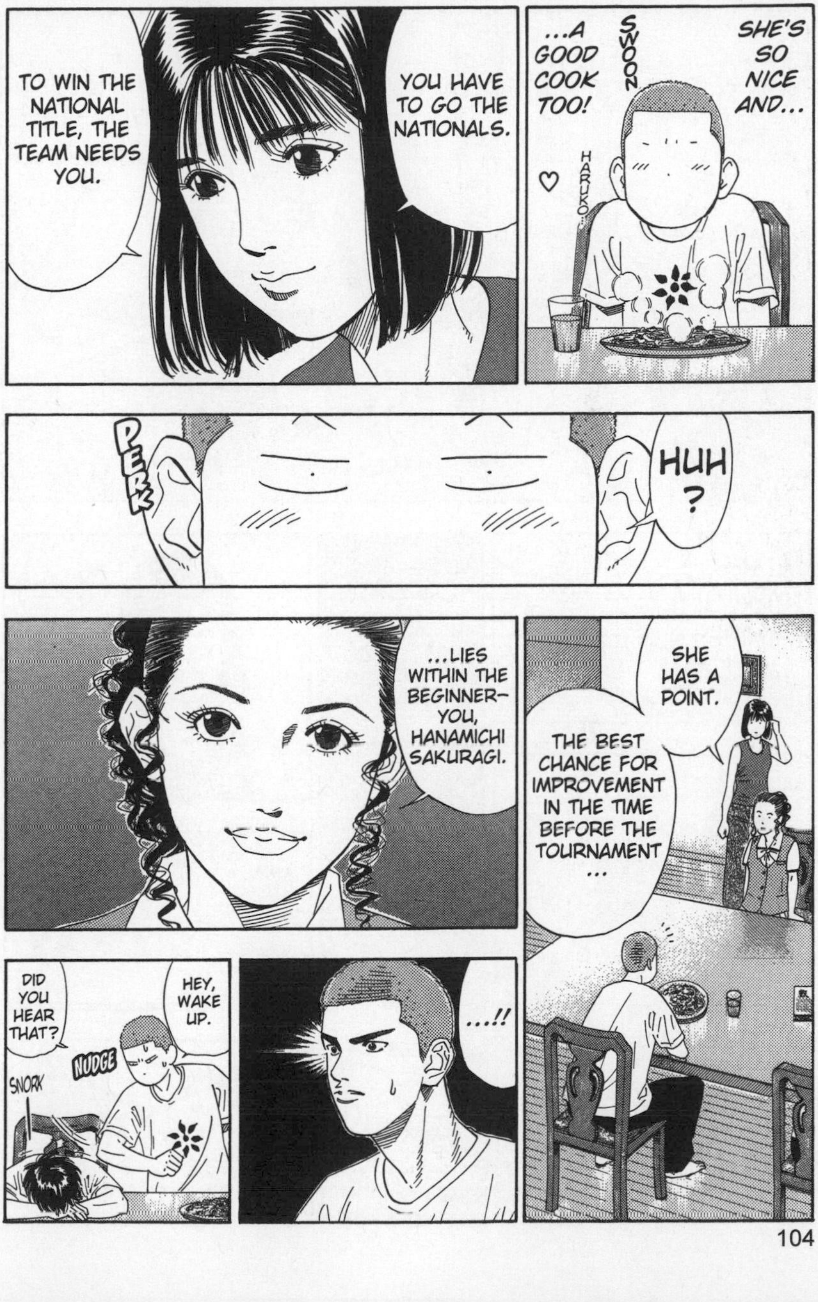
SHE'S SO NICE AND...
SWOON
...A GOOD COOK TOO!
HARUKO...
♡
YOU HAVE TO GO THE NATIONALS.
TO WIN THE NATIONAL TITLE, THE TEAM NEEDS YOU.
HUH ?
PERK
SHE HAS A POINT.
THE BEST CHANCE FOR IMPROVEMENT IN THE TIME BEFORE THE TOURNAMENT ...
...LIES WITHIN THE BEGINNER— YOU, HANAMICHI SAKURAGI.
...!!
HEY, WAKE UP.
DID YOU HEAR THAT?
NUDGE
SNORK

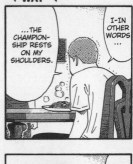

READ THIS WAY

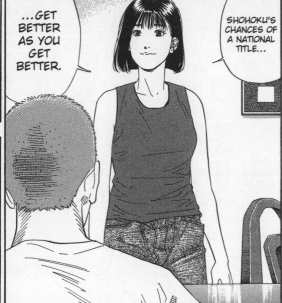

SHOHOKU'S CHANCES OF A NATIONAL TITLE...
...GET BETTER AS YOU GET BETTER.
I-IN OTHER WORDS...
...THE CHAMPIONSHIP RESTS ON MY SHOULDERS.
UH-HUH.
I KNEW IT!
GLOW

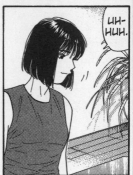

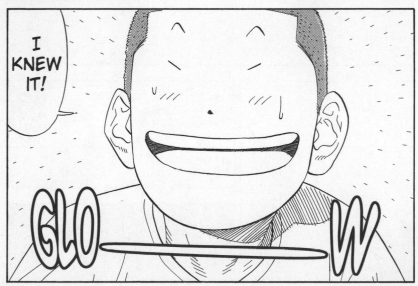

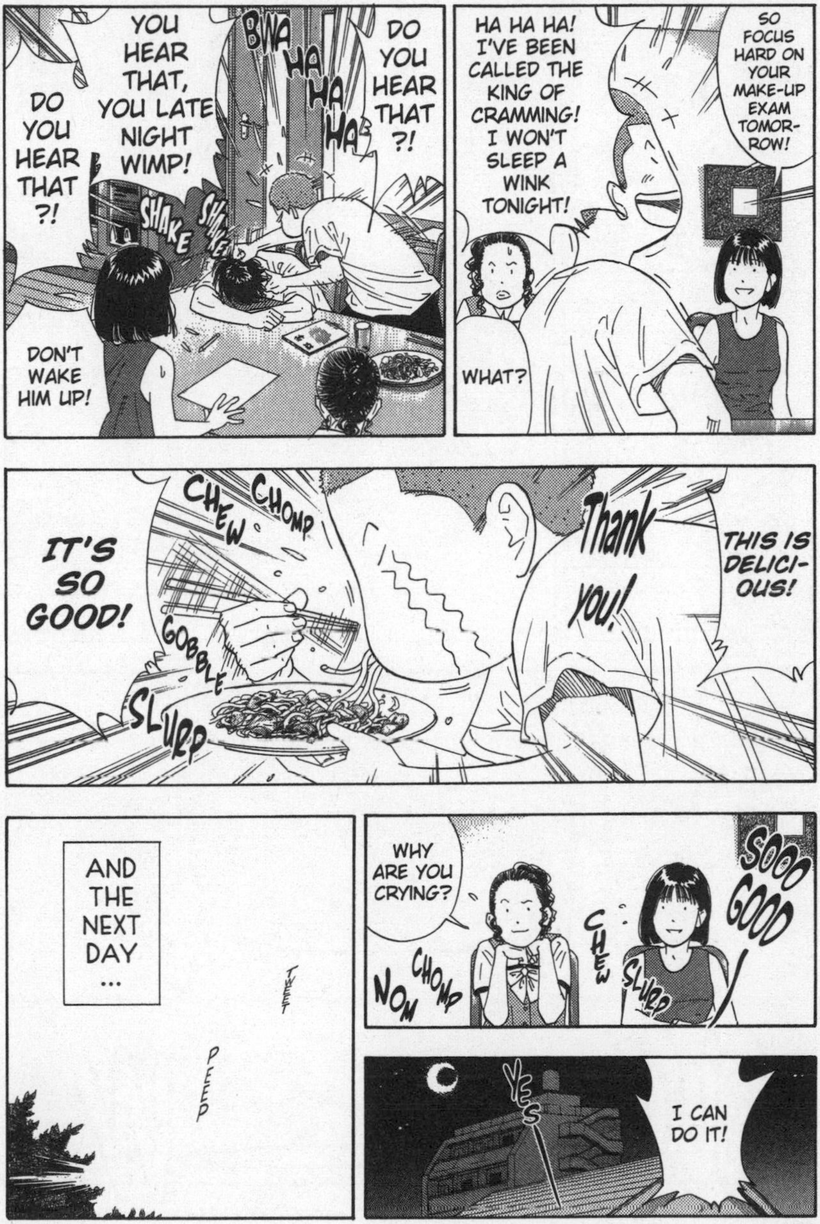
SO FOCUS HARD ON YOUR MAKE-UP EXAM TOMORROW!
HA HA HA! I'VE BEEN CALLED THE KING OF CRAMMING! I WON'T SLEEP A WINK TONIGHT!
WHAT?
DO YOU HEAR THAT ?!
BWAHAHAHA
YOU HEAR THAT, YOU LATE NIGHT WIMP!
DO YOU HEAR THAT ?!
SHAKE
SHAKE
DON'T WAKE HIM UP!
THIS IS DELICIOUS!
Thank you!
CHOMP
CHEW
IT'S SO GOOD!
GOBBLE
SLURP
SOOO GOOD
WHY ARE YOU CRYING?
CHEW
SLURP
CHOMP
NOM
I CAN DO IT!
YES
AND THE NEXT DAY ...
TWEET
PEEP

READ THIS WAY

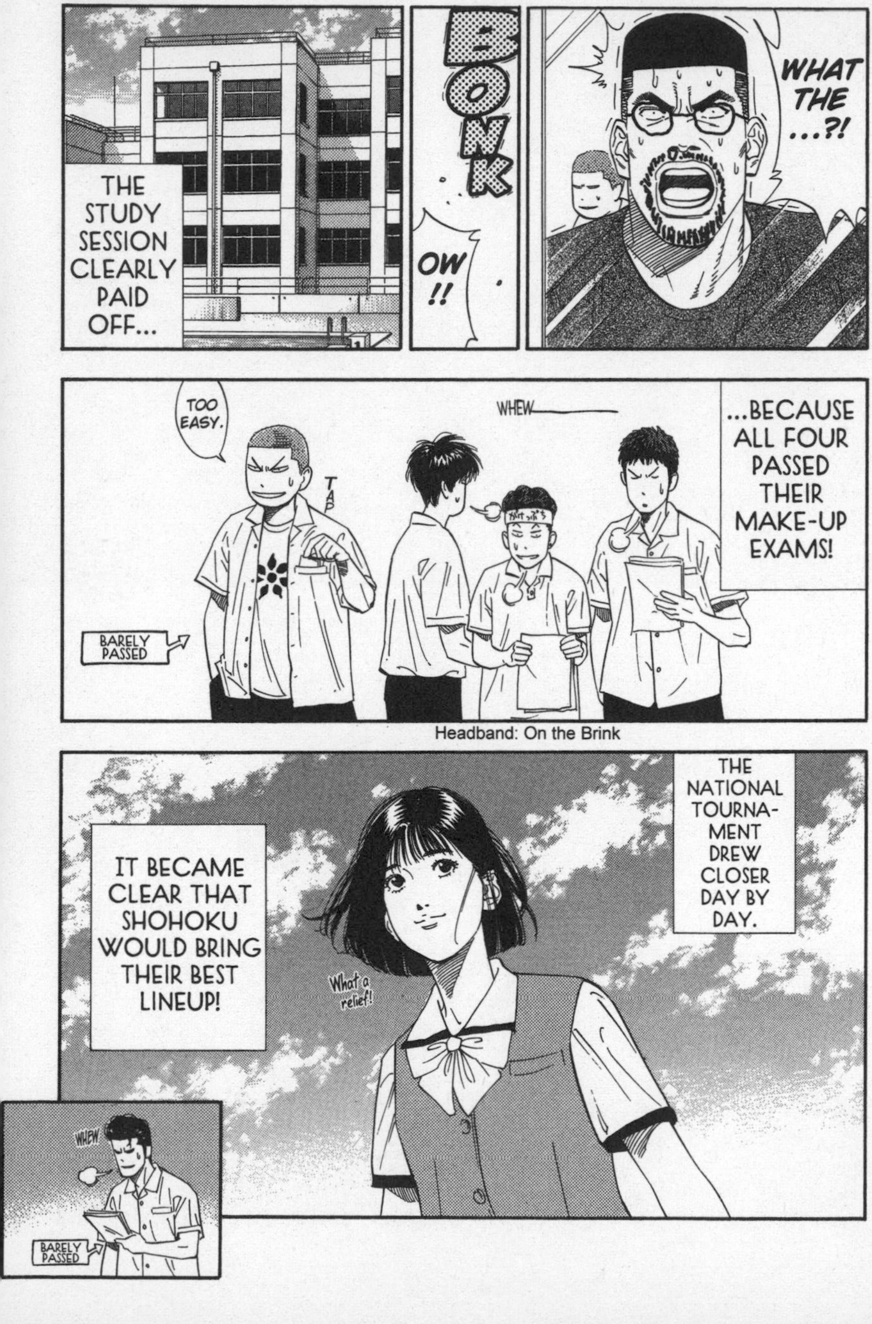
WHAT THE ...?!
BONK
OW !!
THE STUDY SESSION CLEARLY PAID OFF...
...BECAUSE ALL FOUR PASSED THEIR MAKE-UP EXAMS!
WHEW
TOO EASY.
TAP
BARELY PASSED
Headband: On the Brink
THE NATIONAL TOURNA-MENT DREW CLOSER DAY BY DAY.
IT BECAME CLEAR THAT SHOHOKU WOULD BRING THEIR BEST LINEUP!
What a relief!
WHEW
BARELY PASSED

R-Rukawa sat on this chair...
Note: Reserved for Haruko

SLAM DUNK

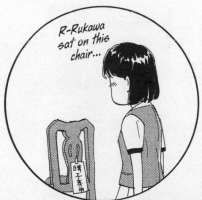

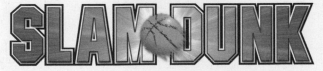

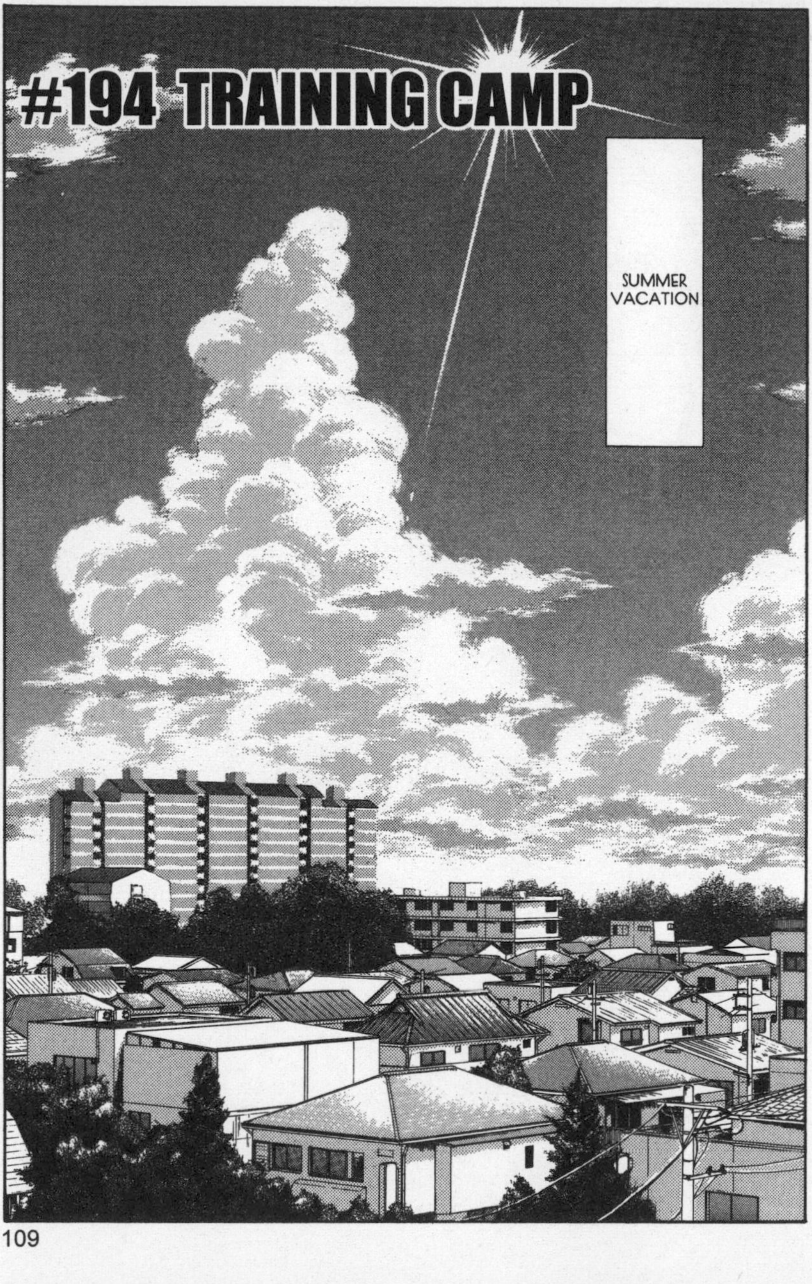
#194 TRAINING CAMP
SUMMER VACATION

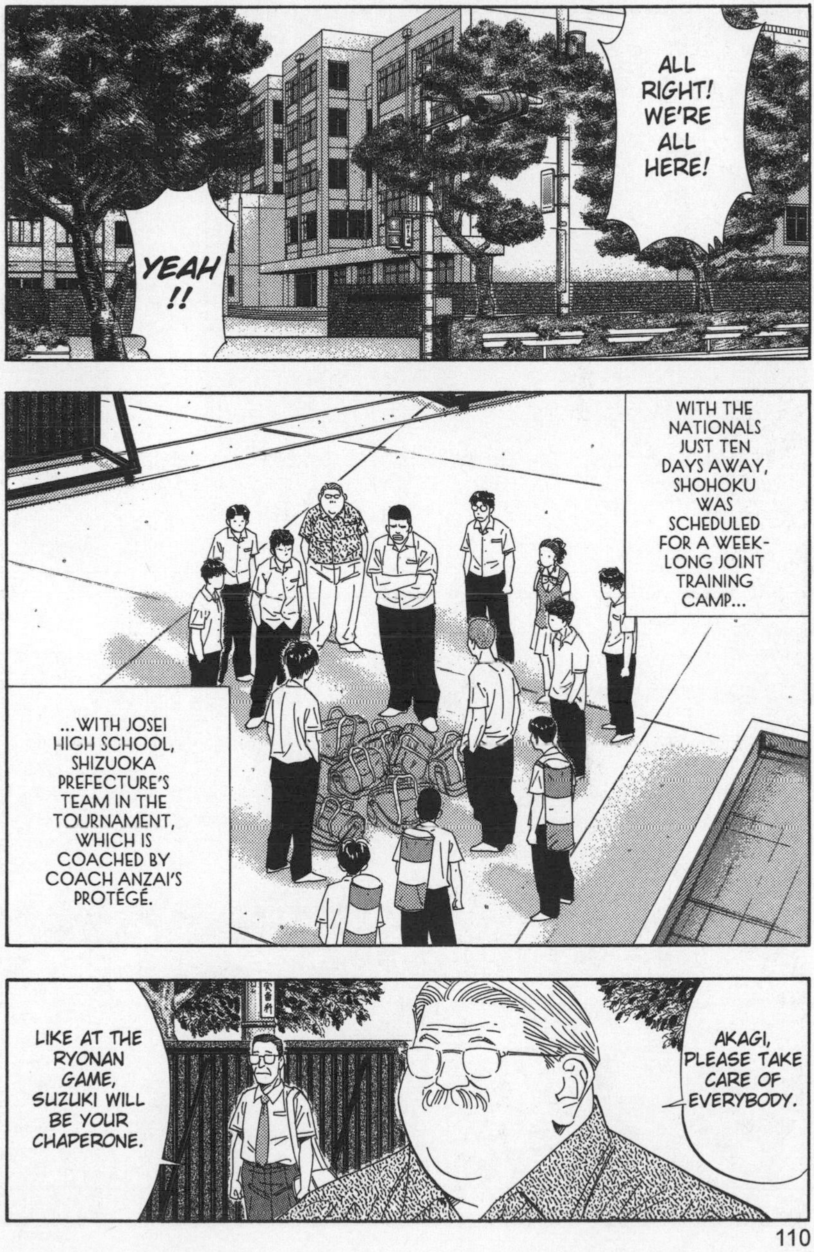
ALL RIGHT! WE'RE ALL HERE!
YEAH!!
WITH THE NATIONALS JUST TEN DAYS AWAY, SHOHOKU WAS SCHEDULED FOR A WEEK-LONG JOINT TRAINING CAMP...
...WITH JOSEI HIGH SCHOOL, SHIZUOKA PREFECTURE'S TEAM IN THE TOURNAMENT, WHICH IS COACHED BY COACH ANZAI'S PROTÉGÉ.
AKAGI, PLEASE TAKE CARE OF EVERYBODY.
LIKE AT THE RYONAN GAME, SUZUKI WILL BE YOUR CHAPERONE.

READ THIS WAY

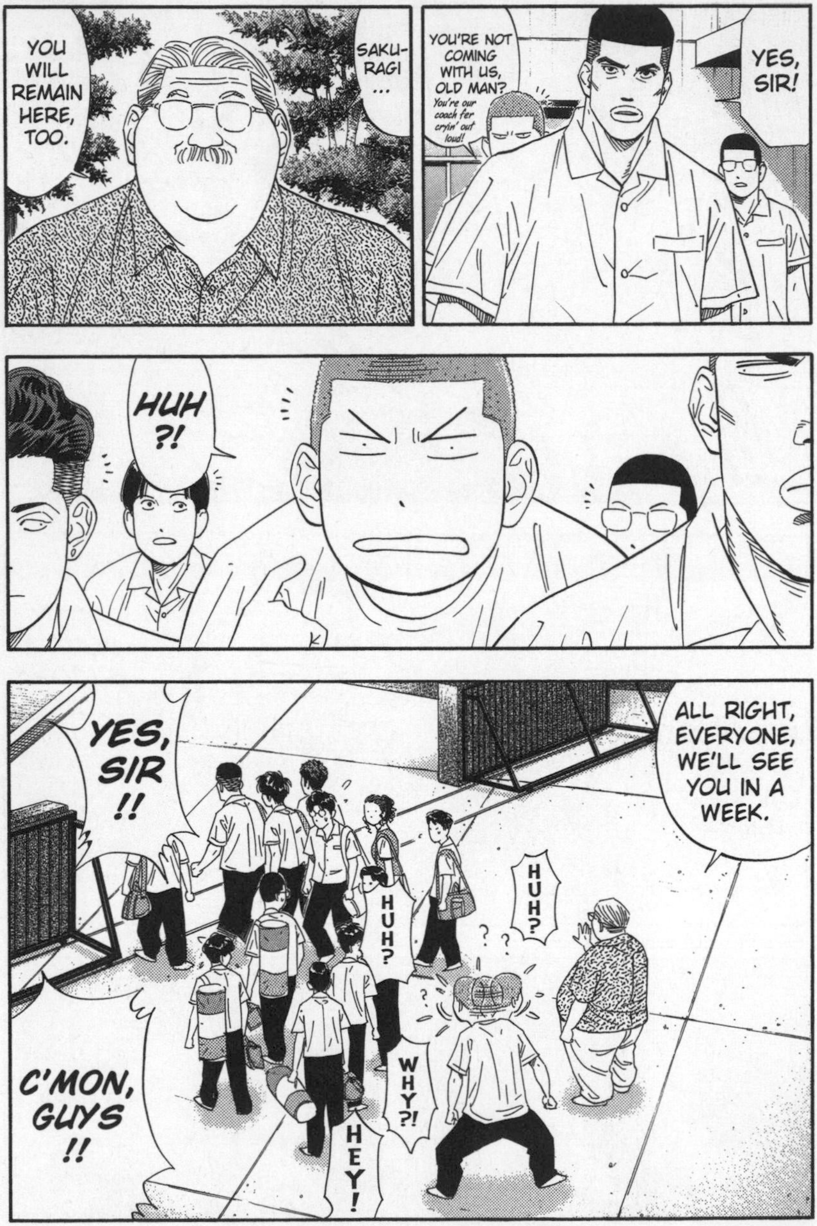
YES, SIR!
YOU'RE NOT COMING WITH US, OLD MAN?
You're our coach fer cryin' out loud!
SAKURAGI ...
YOU WILL REMAIN HERE, TOO.
HUH ?!
ALL RIGHT, EVERYONE, WE'LL SEE YOU IN A WEEK.
HUH?
YES, SIR !!
HUH?
WHY ?!
HEY!
C'MON, GUYS !!

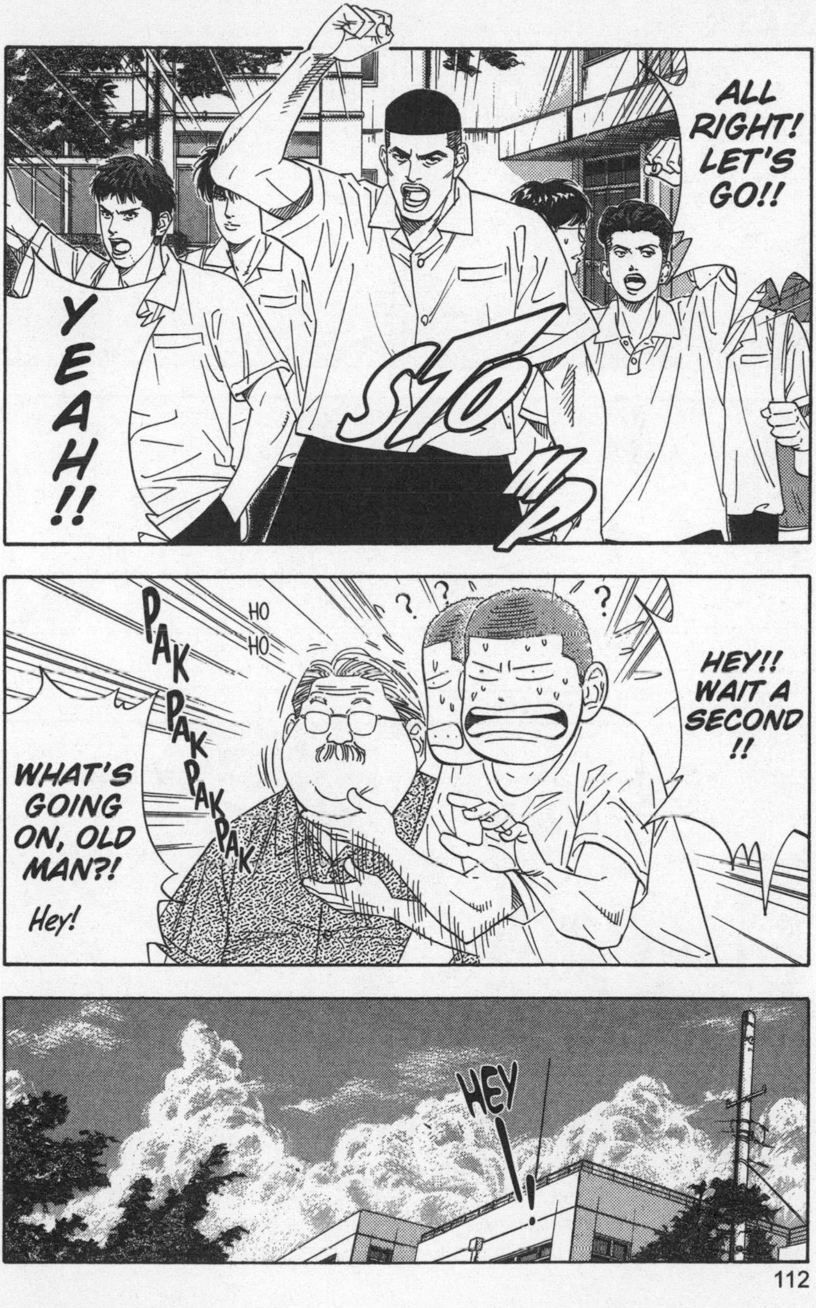
ALL RIGHT! LET'S GO!!
STOMP
YEAH!!
HEY!! WAIT A SECOND!!
HO HO
PAK PAK PAK PAK
WHAT'S GOING ON, OLD MAN?!
Hey!
HEY!

READ THIS WAY

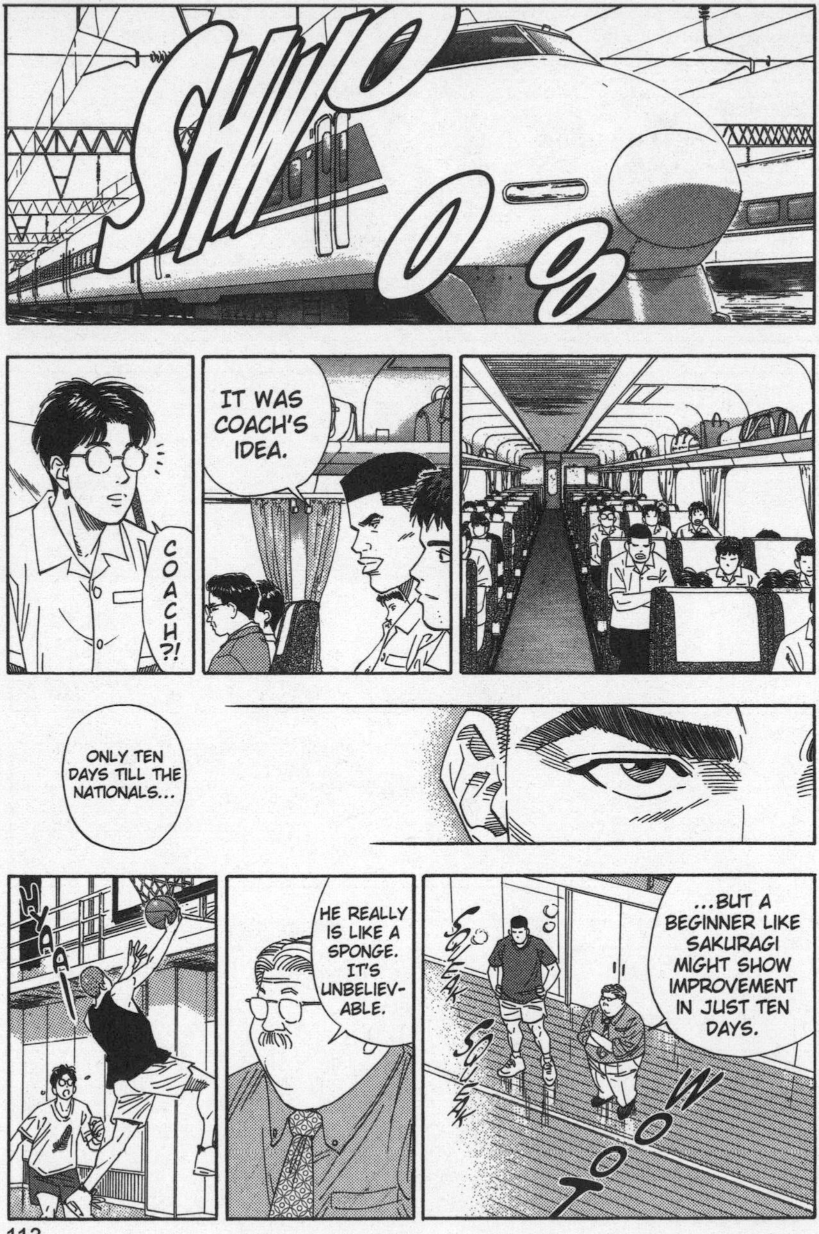
SHWOOOO
IT WAS COACH'S IDEA.
COACH?!
ONLY TEN DAYS TILL THE NATIONALS...
...BUT A BEGINNER LIKE SAKURAGI MIGHT SHOW IMPROVEMENT IN JUST TEN DAYS.
SQUEAK
SQUEAK
WOOOT
HE REALLY IS LIKE A SPONGE. IT'S UNBELIEV-ABLE.
HYA!

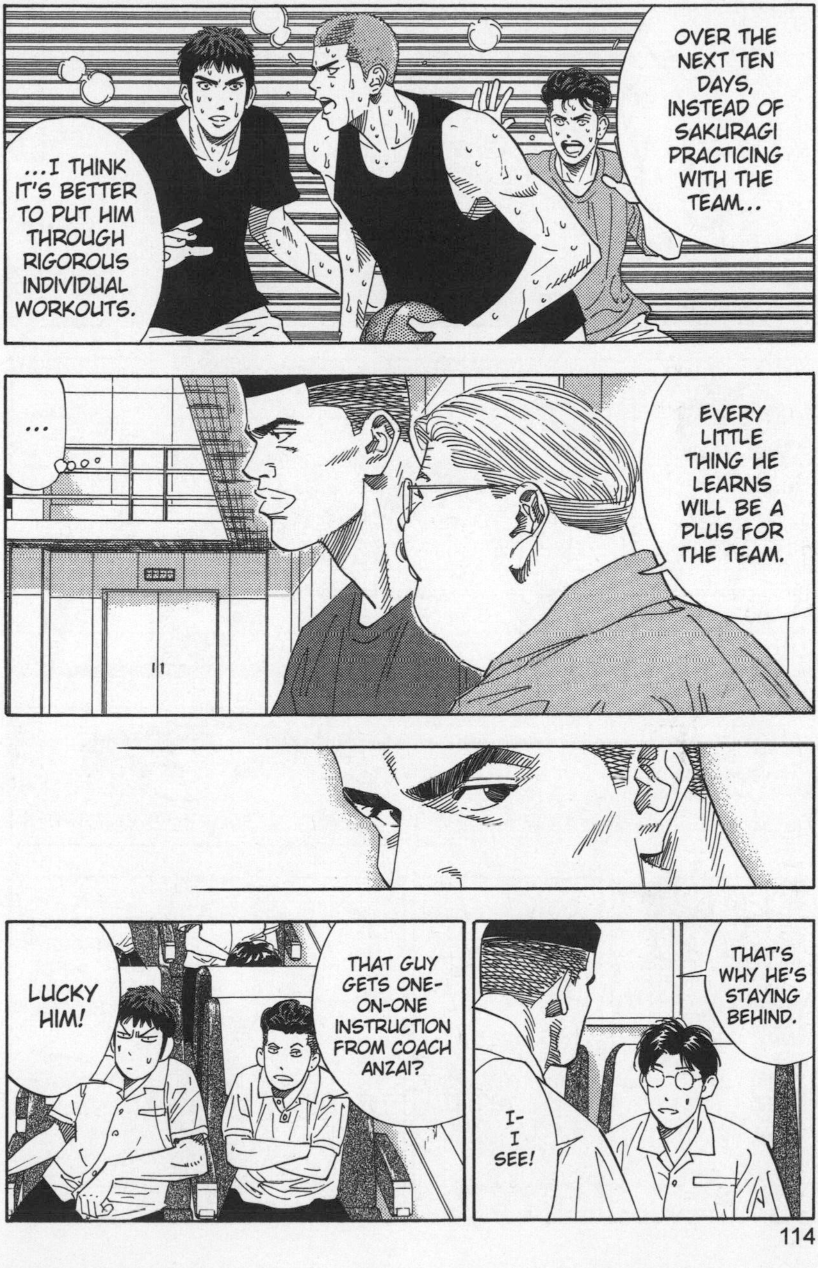
OVER THE NEXT TEN DAYS, INSTEAD OF SAKURAGI PRACTICING WITH THE TEAM...
...I THINK IT'S BETTER TO PUT HIM THROUGH RIGOROUS INDIVIDUAL WORKOUTS.
EVERY LITTLE THING HE LEARNS WILL BE A PLUS FOR THE TEAM.
...
THAT'S WHY HE'S STAYING BEHIND.
I- I SEE!
THAT GUY GETS ONE-ON-ONE INSTRUCTION FROM COACH ANZAI?
LUCKY HIM!

READ THIS WAY

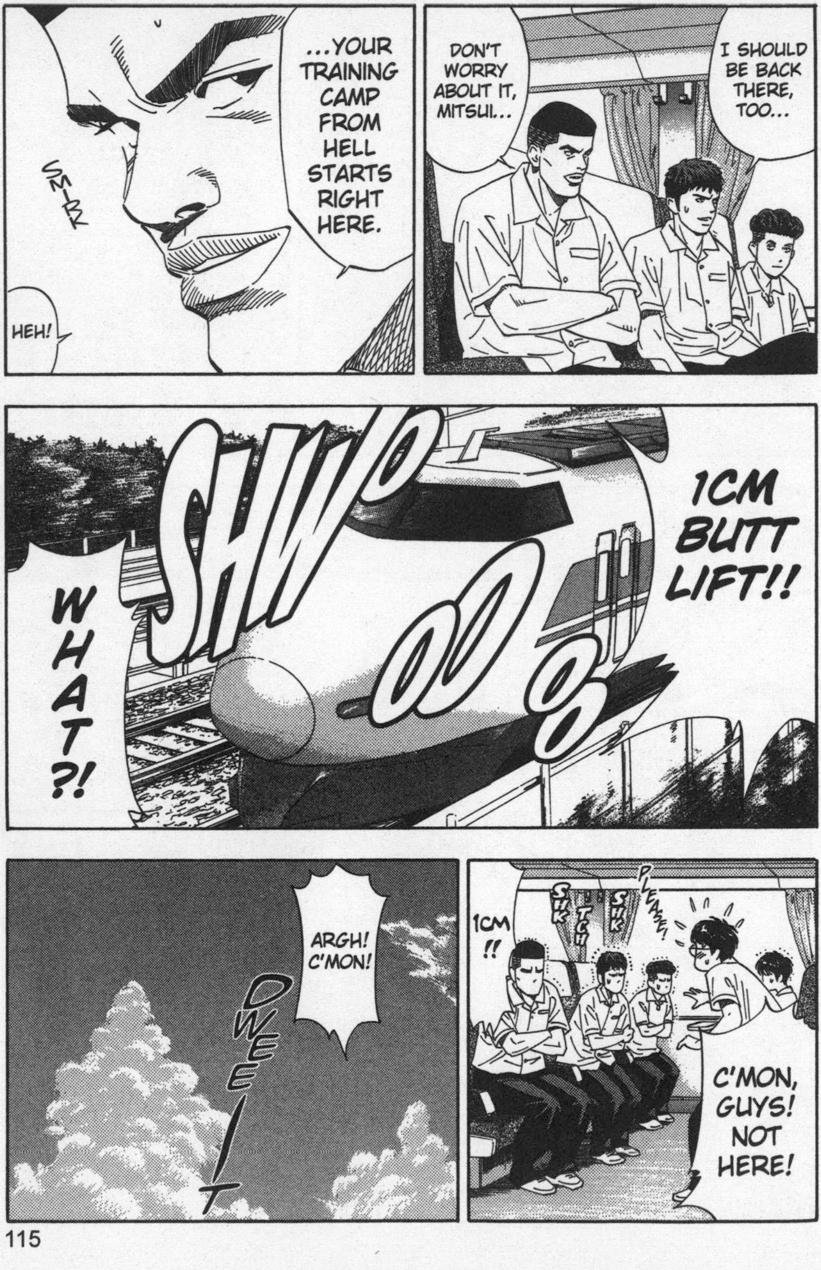

I SHOULD BE BACK THERE, TOO...
DON'T WORRY ABOUT IT, MITSUI...
...YOUR TRAINING CAMP FROM HELL STARTS RIGHT HERE.
SMIRK
HEH!
1CM BUTT LIFT!!
SHWOOOO
WHAT?!
PLEASE!
SHK
TCH
SHK
1CM !!
C'MON, GUYS! NOT HERE!
ARGH! C'MON!
DWEEET

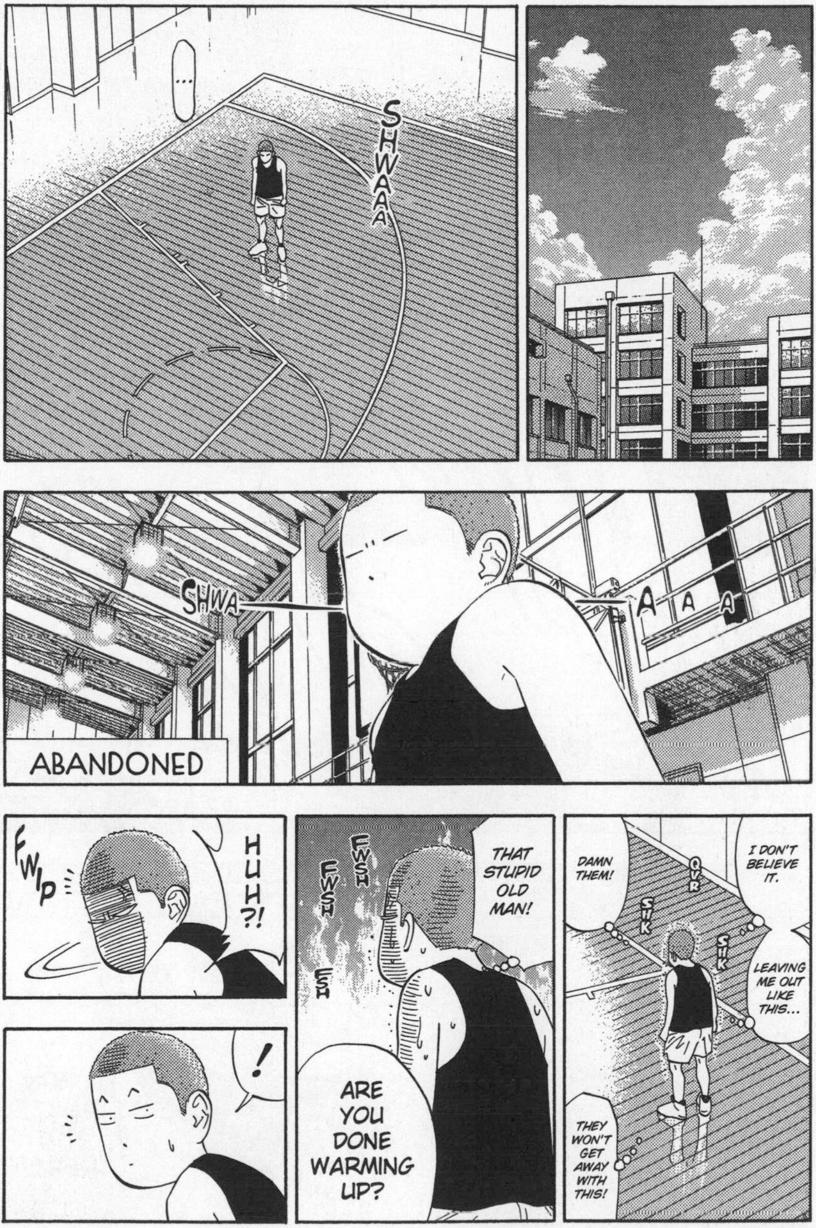
...
SHWAAAA
SHWA
AAA
ABANDONED
I DON'T BELIEVE IT.
QVR
DAMN THEM!
SHK
SHK
LEAVING ME OUT LIKE THIS...
THEY WON'T GET AWAY WITH THIS!
THAT STUPID OLD MAN!
FWSH
FWSH
FSH
ARE YOU DONE WARMING UP?
HUH?!
FWIP
!

READ THIS WAY

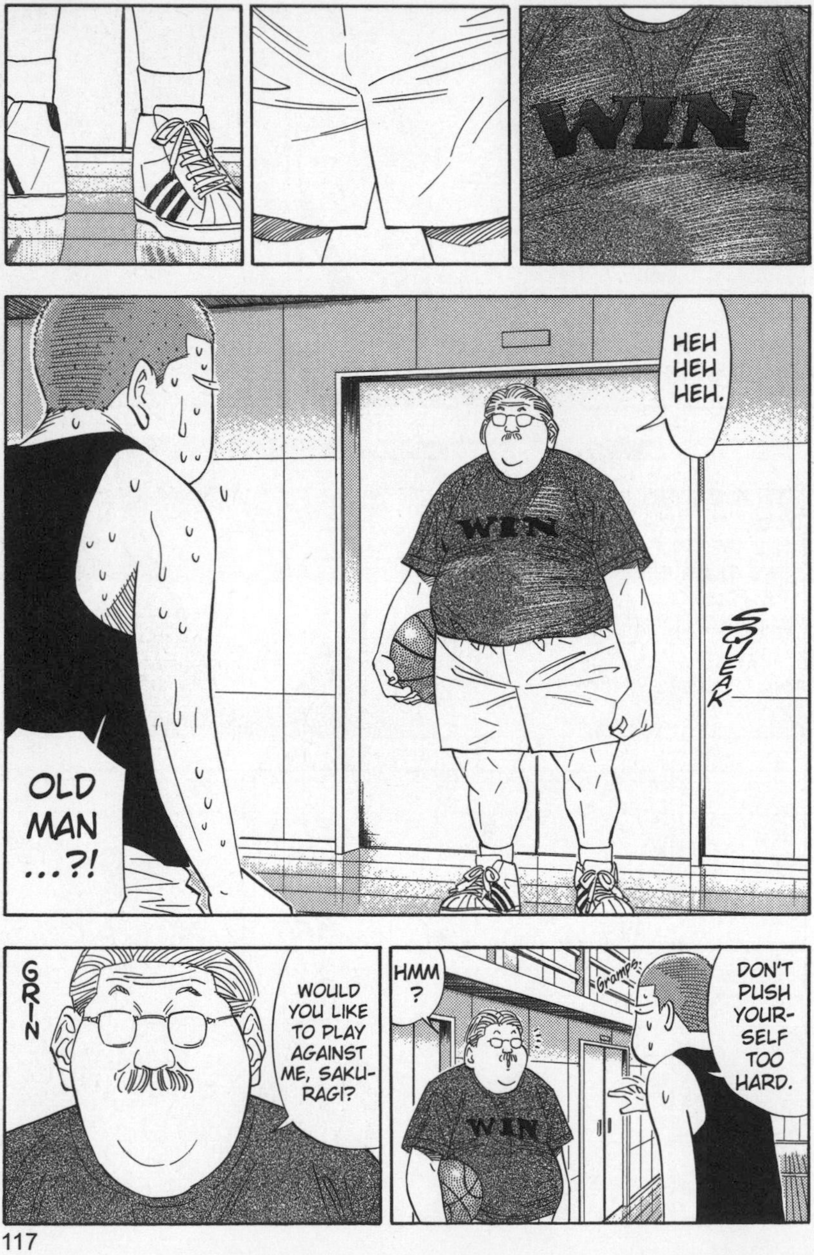
WIN
HEH HEH HEH.
WIN
SQUEAK
OLD MAN ...?!
DON'T PUSH YOUR-SELF TOO HARD.
Gramps.
HMM ?
WIN
WOULD YOU LIKE TO PLAY AGAINST ME, SAKU-RAGI?
GRIN

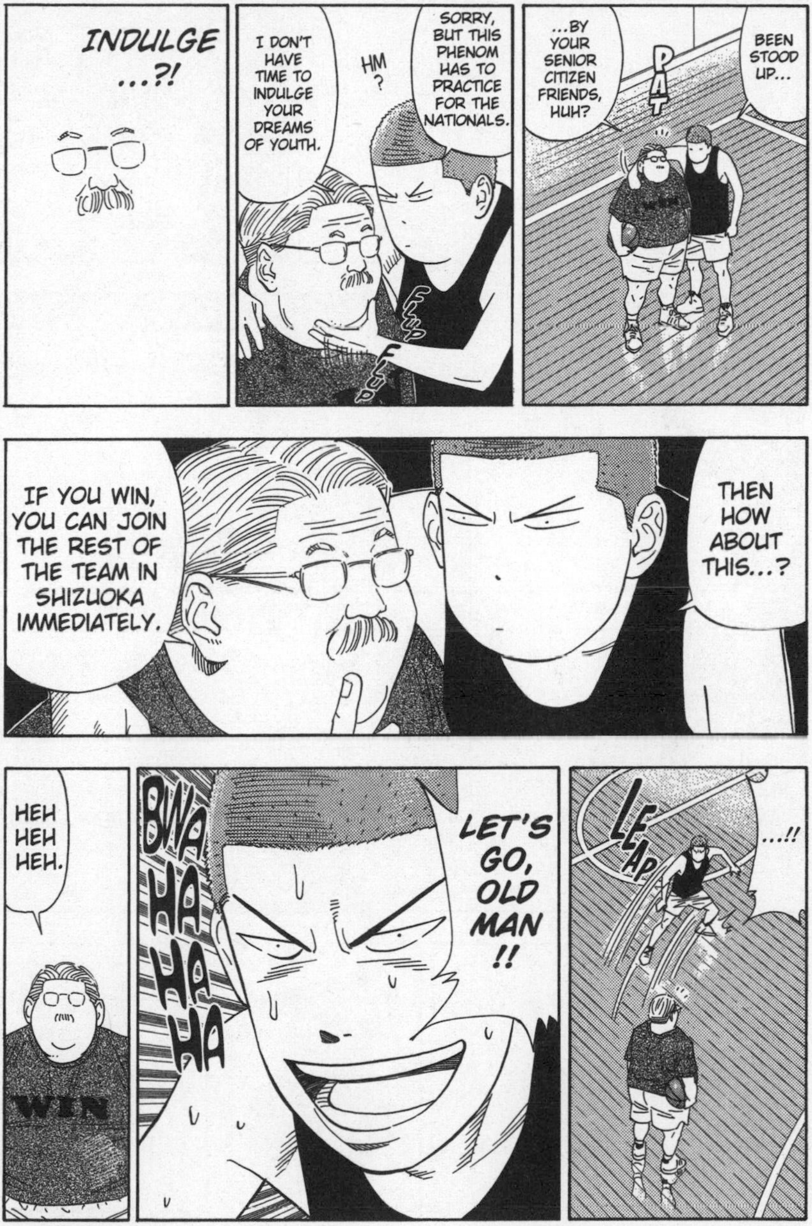
BEEN STOOD UP...
...BY YOUR SENIOR CITIZEN FRIENDS, HUH?
PAT
SORRY, BUT THIS PHENOM HAS TO PRACTICE FOR THE NATIONALS.
HM ?
I DON'T HAVE TIME TO INDULGE YOUR DREAMS OF YOUTH.
FLUP
FLUP
INDULGE ...?!
THEN HOW ABOUT THIS...?
IF YOU WIN, YOU CAN JOIN THE REST OF THE TEAM IN SHIZUOKA IMMEDIATELY.
LEAP
...!!
LET'S GO, OLD MAN!!
BWAHAHAHAHAHA
HEH HEH HEH.
WIN

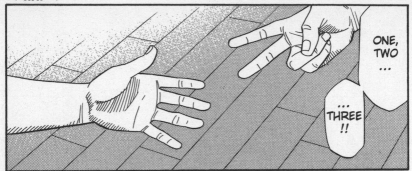

READ THIS WAY

ONE, TWO ...
... THREE !!
SEE? I'M WINNING ALREADY!
SHOOTING CONTEST
-RULES-
MAKE TWO SHOTS FROM EACH OF THE FIVE MARKED SPOTS, FOR A TOTAL OF TEN SHOTS. WHOEVER SINKS MORE IS THE WINNER.
I GUESS I'M UP FIRST...
PAA
HEH
IT DOESN'T MATTER.

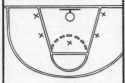

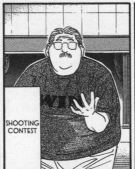

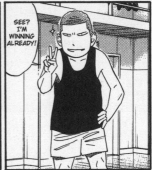

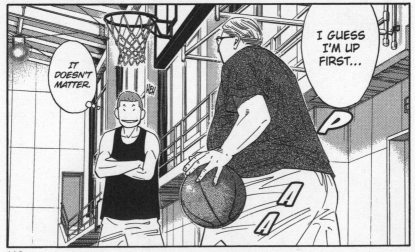

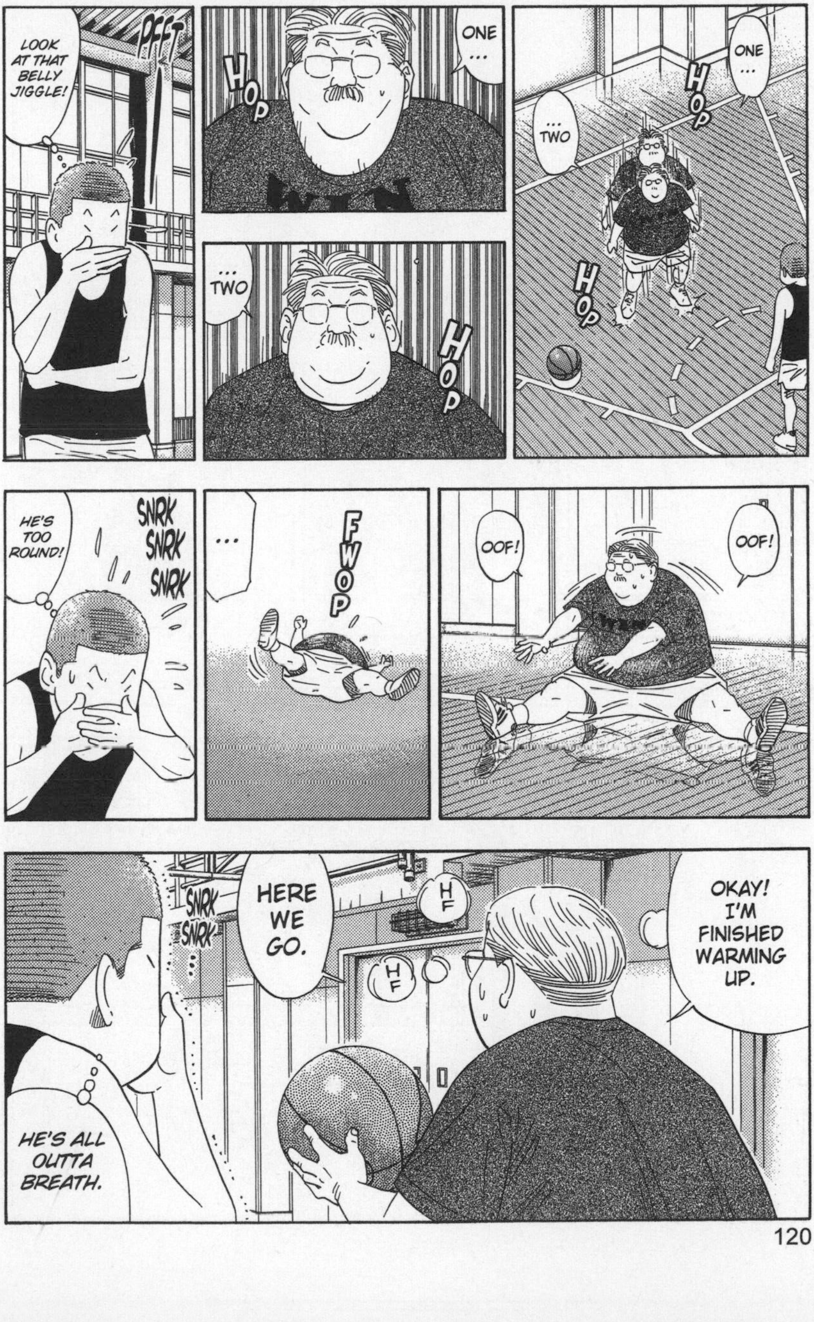
ONE...
...TWO
HOP
HOP
ONE...
HOP
...TWO
HOP
LOOK AT THAT BELLY JIGGLE!
PFFT
OOF!
OOF!
...
FWOP
HE'S TOO ROUND!
SNRK SNRK SNRK
OKAY! I'M FINISHED WARMING UP.
HF
HF
HERE WE GO.
SNRK SNRK
HE'S ALL OUTTA BREATH.

READ THIS WAY

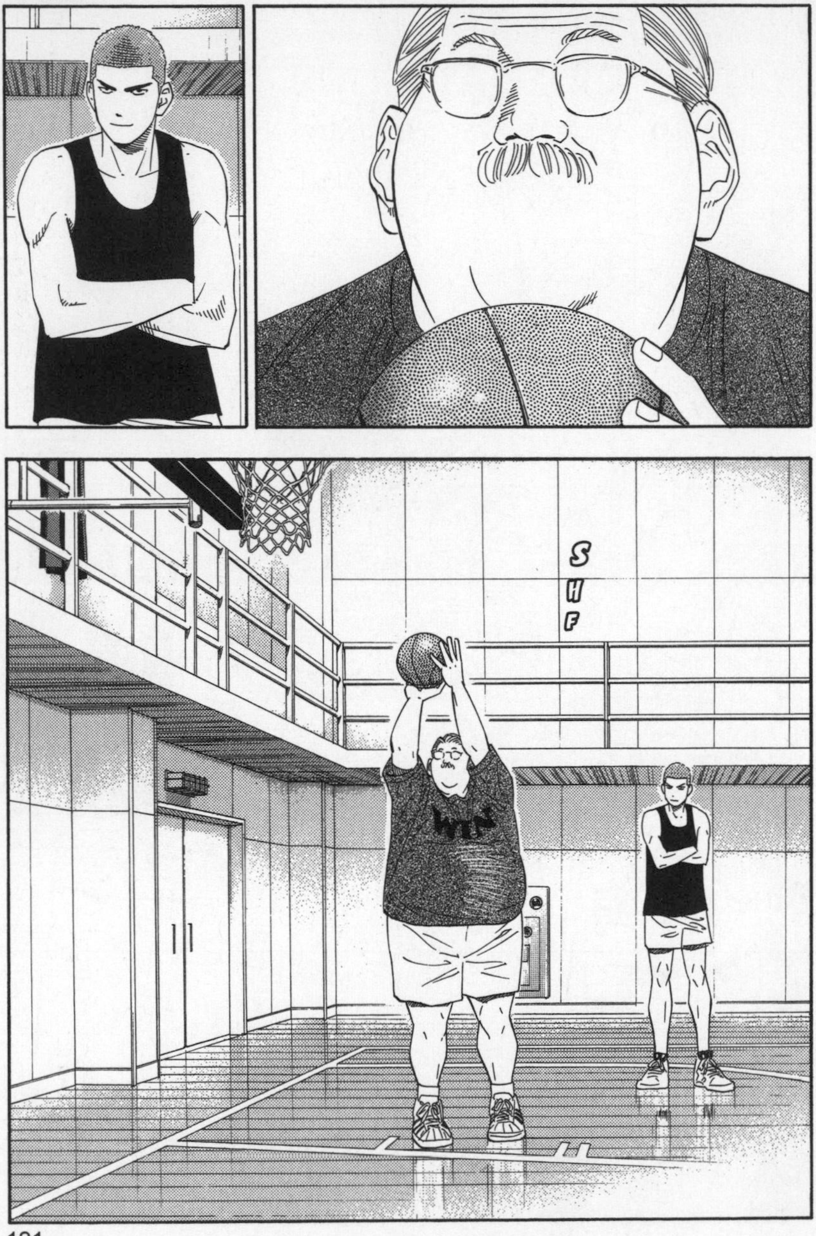
SHF

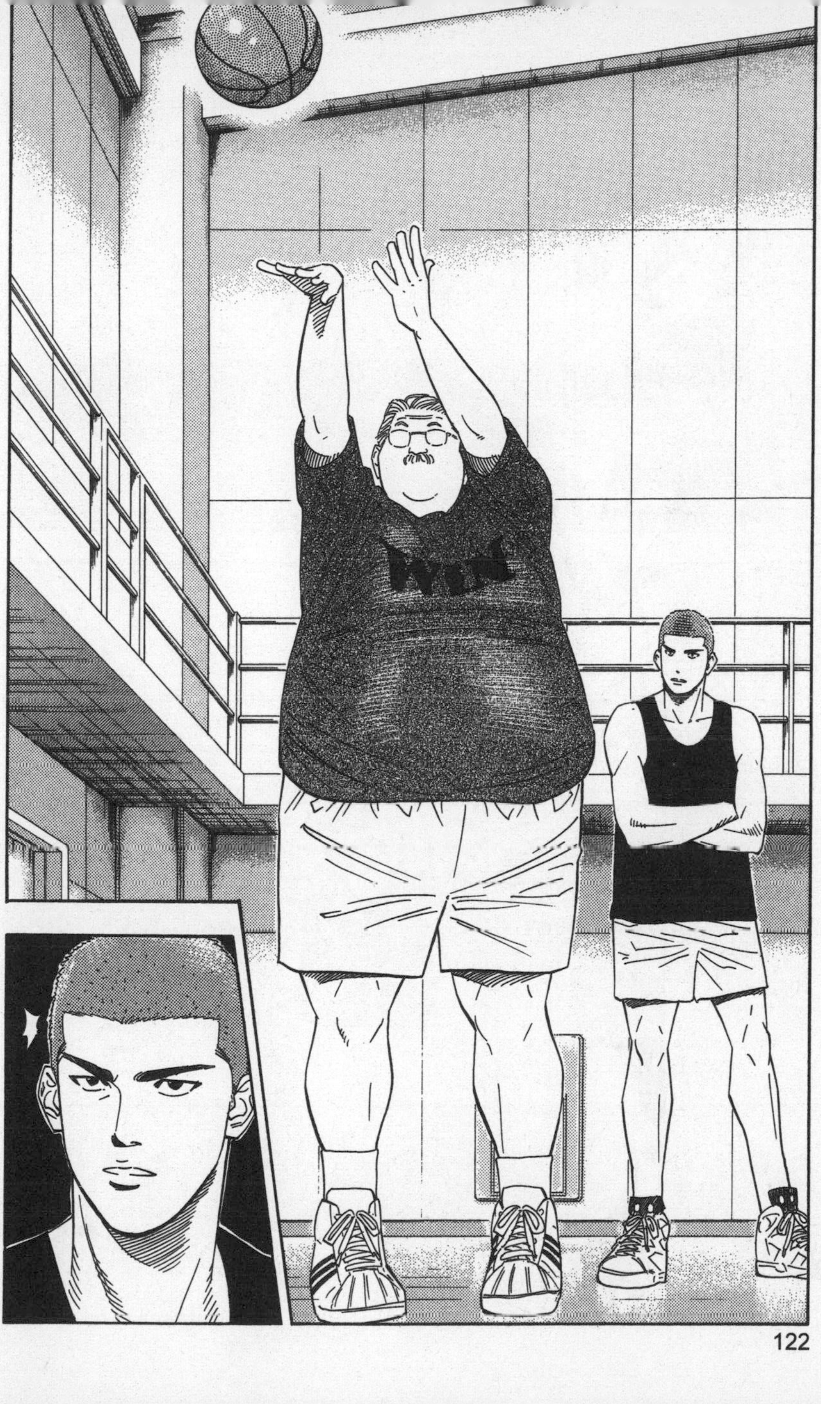

READ THIS WAY

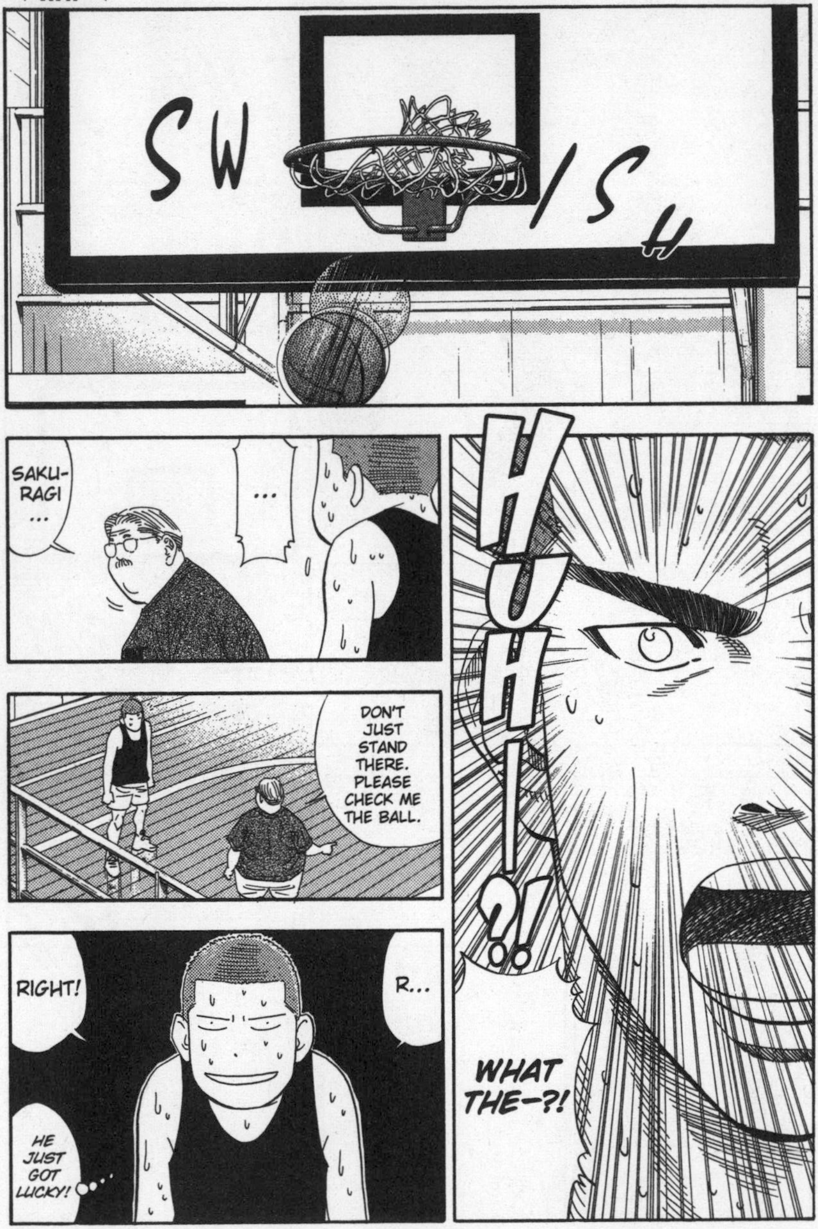

SWISH
HUH!?!
WHAT THE-?!
...
SAKURAGI...
DON'T JUST STAND THERE. PLEASE CHECK ME THE BALL.
R...
RIGHT!
HE JUST GOT LUCKY!

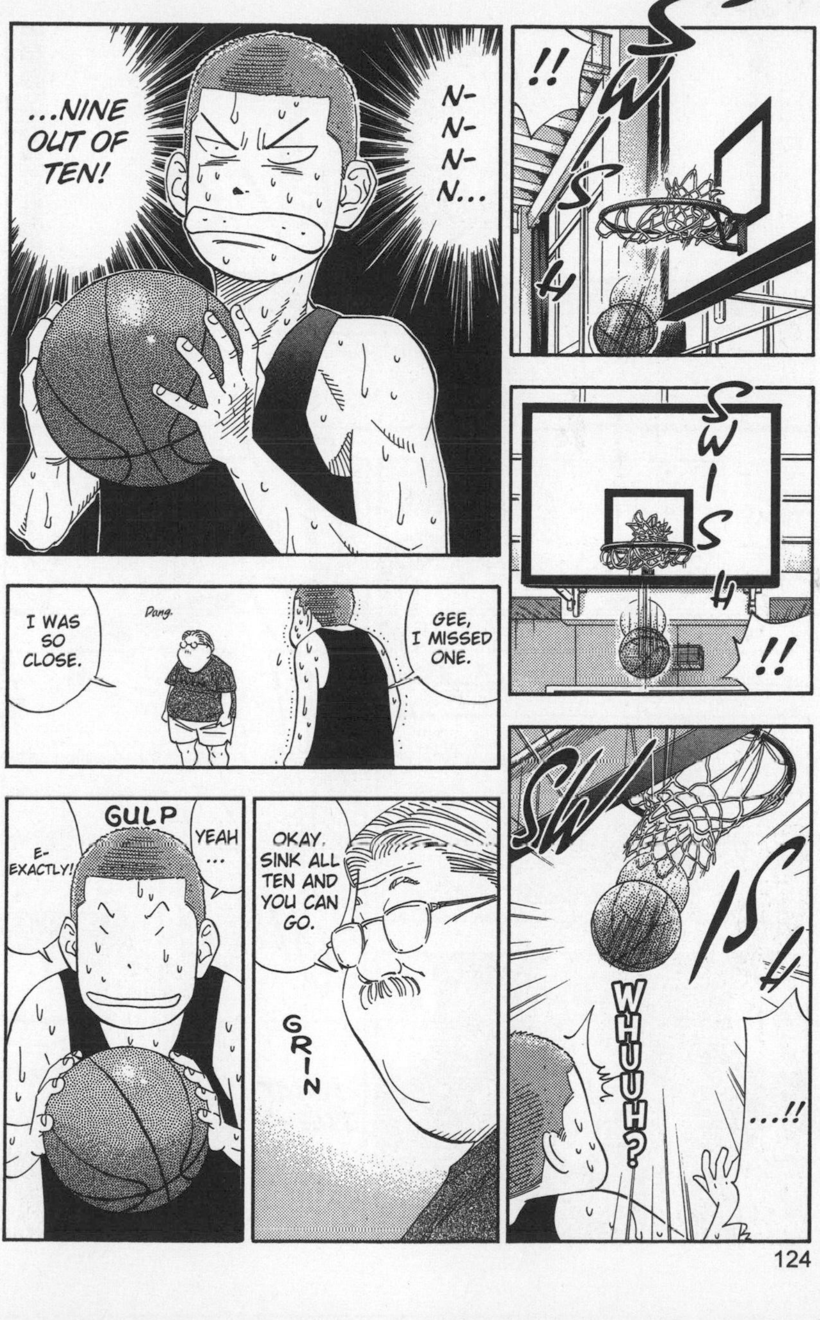
SWISH
!!
SWISH
!!
SWISH
WHUUH?
...!!
N-N-N-N...
...NINE OUT OF TEN!
GEE, I MISSED ONE.
Dang.
I WAS SO CLOSE.
OKAY, SINK ALL TEN AND YOU CAN GO.
GRIN
GULP
YEAH ...
E-EXACTLY!

READ THIS WAY

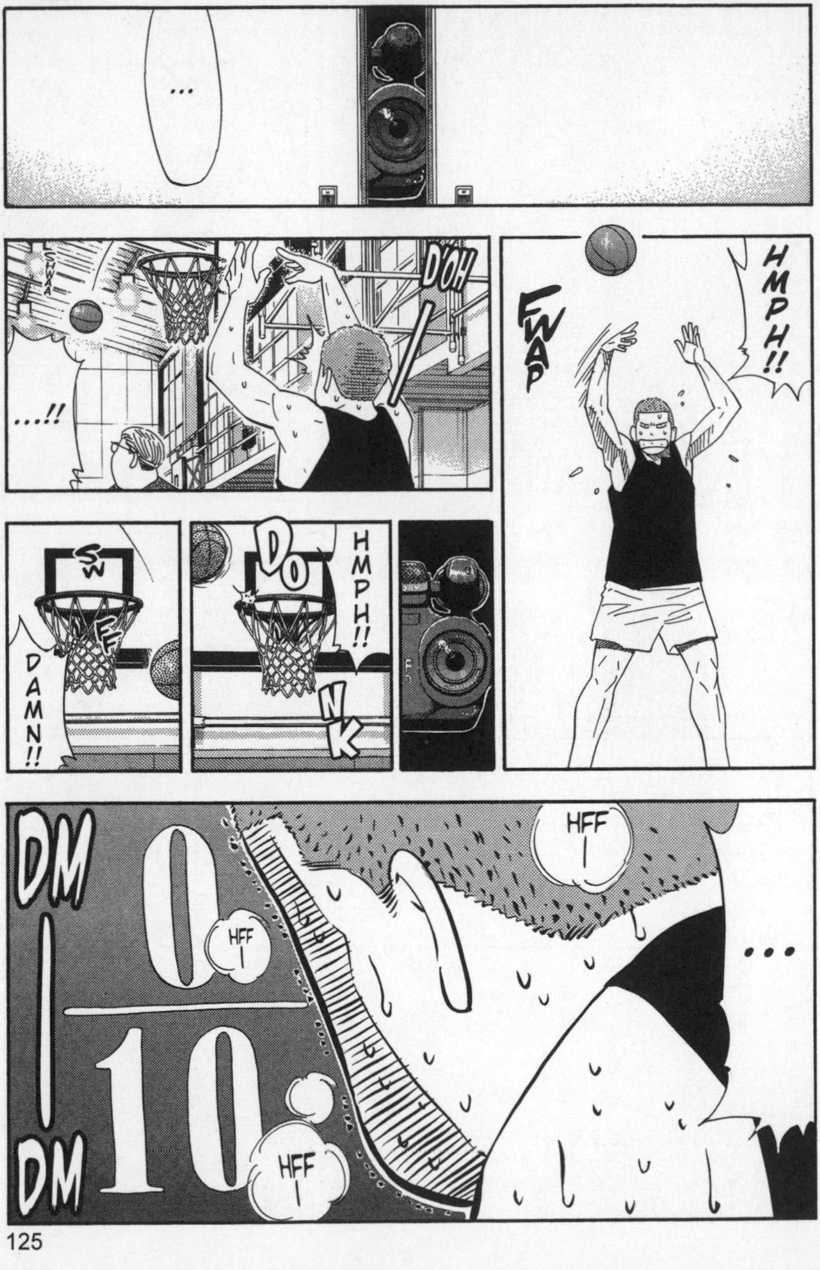

...
HMPH!!
FWAP
D'OH
SHWAA
...!!
HMPH!!
DONK
SWFF
DAMN!!
HFF
...
HFF
0
10
DM
DM
HFF

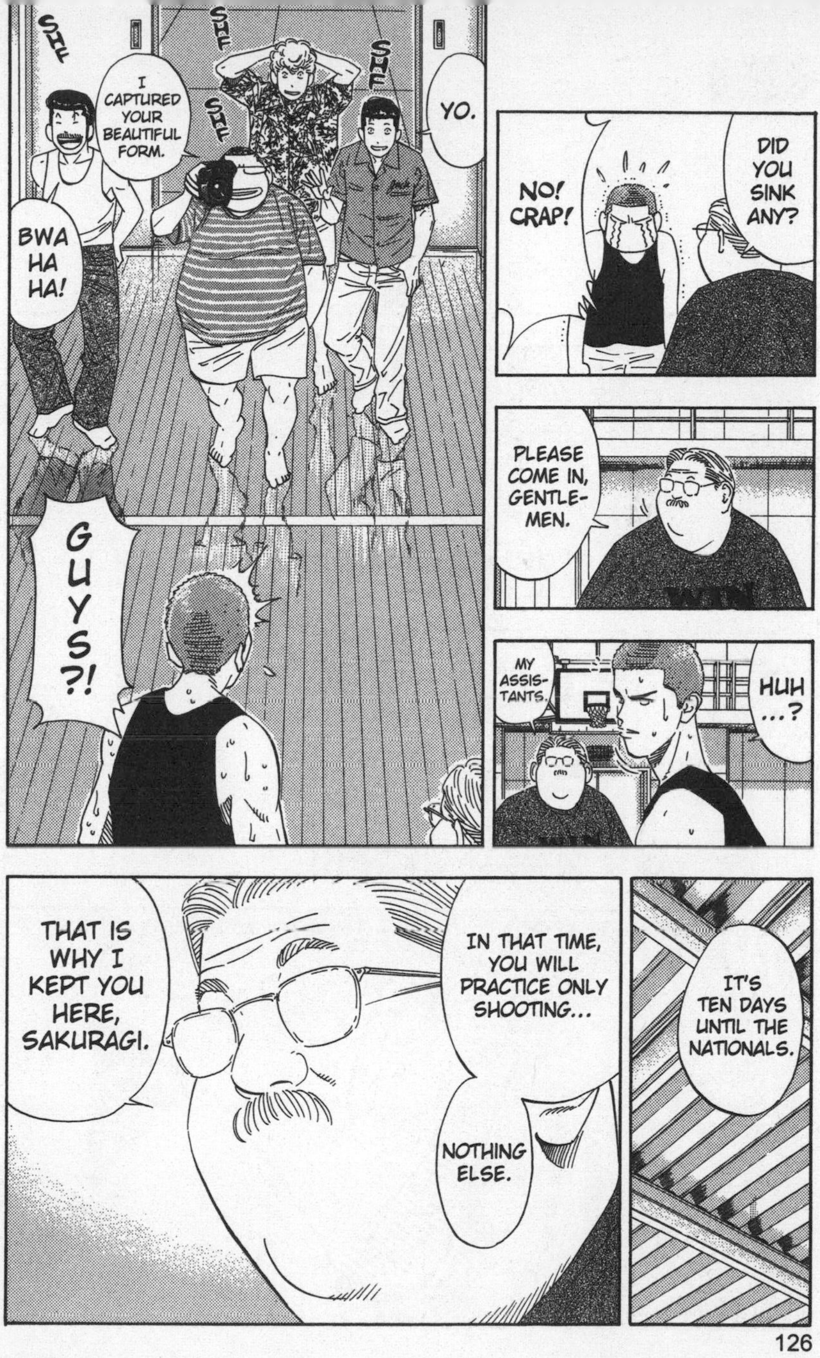
DID YOU SINK ANY?
NO! CRAP!
PLEASE COME IN, GENTLEMEN.
HUH ...?
MY ASSISTANTS.
SHF
SHF
SHF
SHF
YO.
I CAPTURED YOUR BEAUTIFUL FORM.
BWA HA HA!
GUYS?!
IT'S TEN DAYS UNTIL THE NATIONALS.
IN THAT TIME, YOU WILL PRACTICE ONLY SHOOTING...
NOTHING ELSE.
THAT IS WHY I KEPT YOU HERE, SAKURAGI.

READ THIS WAY

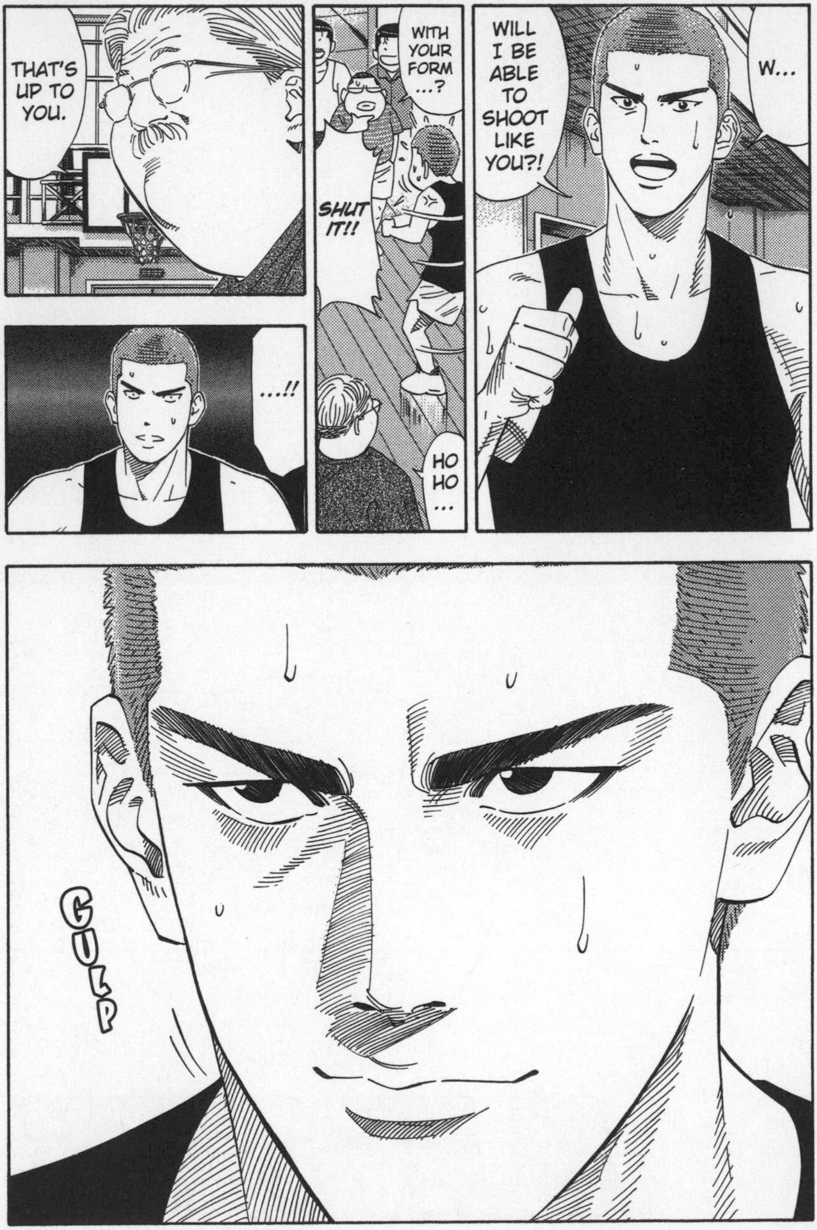
W...
WILL I BE ABLE TO SHOOT LIKE YOU?!
WITH YOUR FORM ...?
SHUT IT!!
HO HO ...
THAT'S UP TO YOU.
...!!
GULP

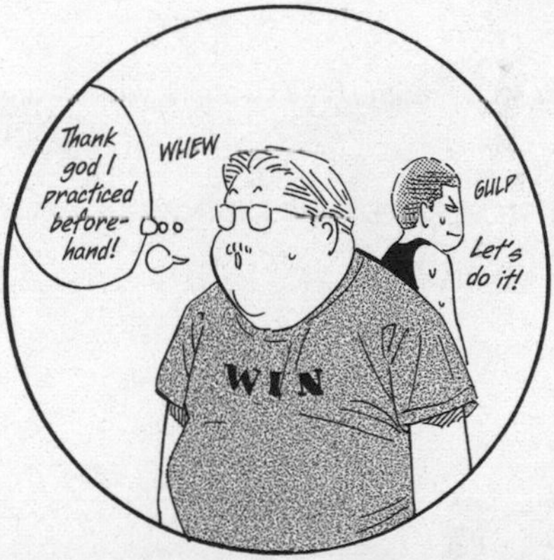
GULP
Let's do it!
WHEW
Thank god I practiced beforehand!
WIN

SLAM DUNK

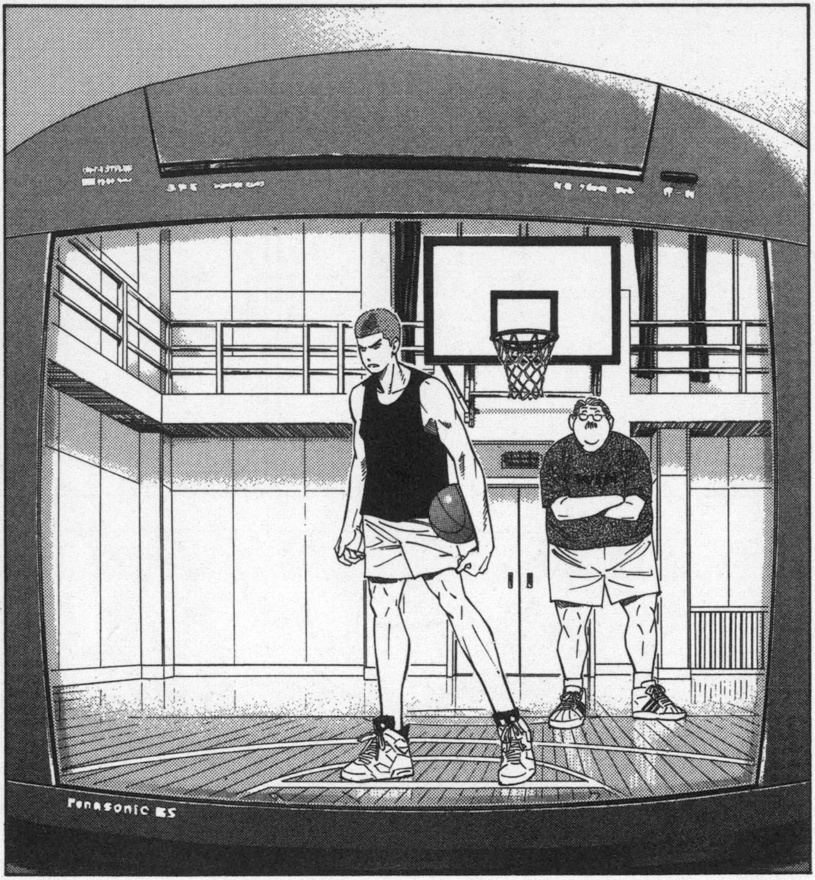

#195 TRAINING CAMP 2

HMPH!!
NO WAY!
QVR
TCH
TCH
SHK
QVR
I LOOK LIKE THAT?!
YOU SURE DO!
ARGH! NO!!

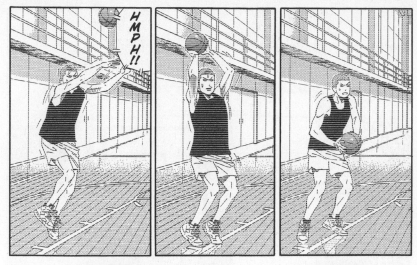

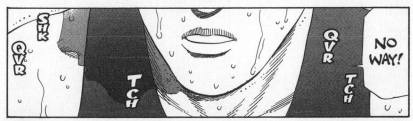

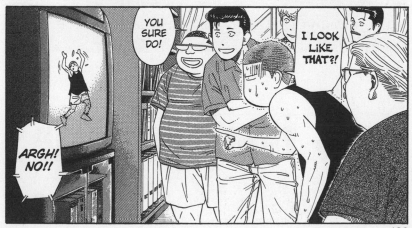

READ THIS WAY

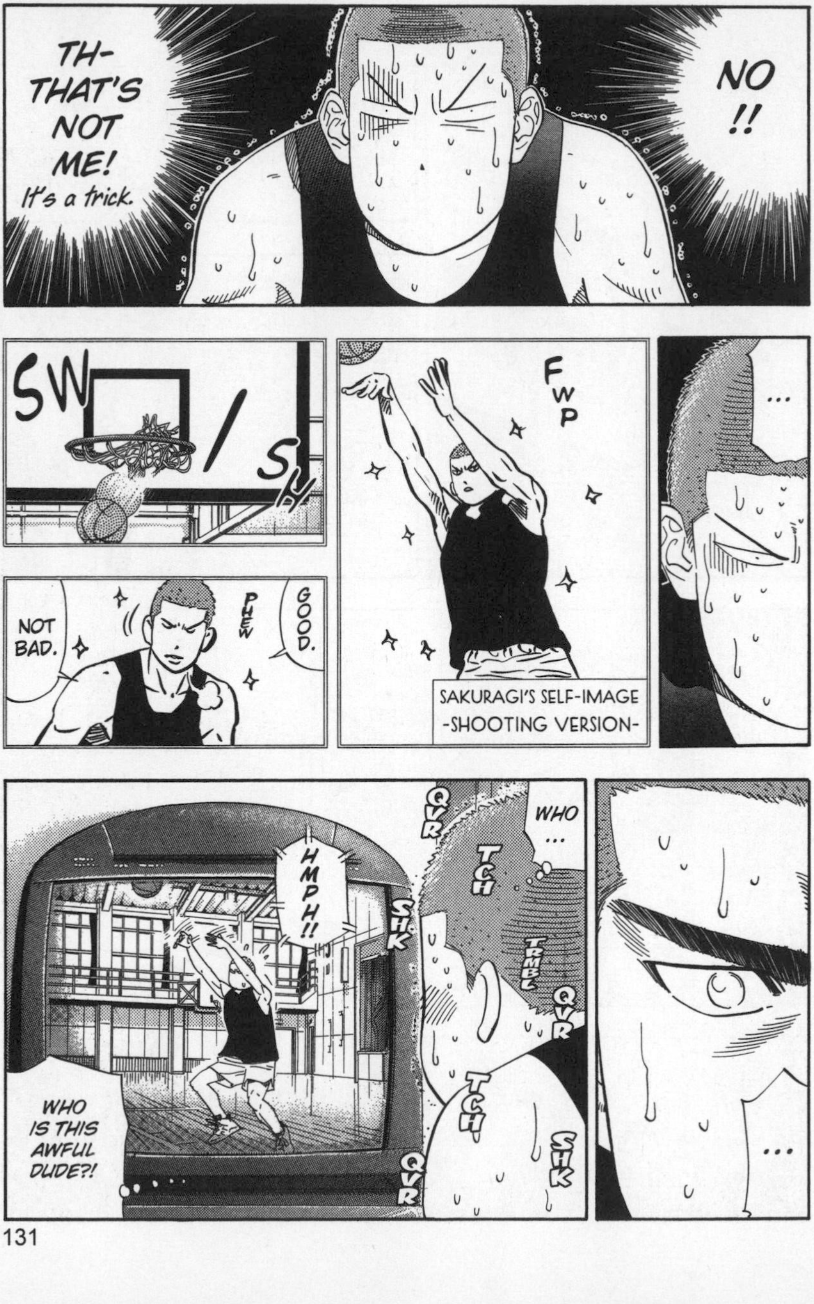
NO !!
TH- THAT'S NOT ME!
It's a trick.
...
FWP
SAKURAGI'S SELF-IMAGE -SHOOTING VERSION-
SW / SH
GOOD.
PHEW
NOT BAD.
...
WHO ...
QVR
TCH
HMPH!!
SHK
TRMBL
QVR
TCH
SHK
QVR
WHO IS THIS AWFUL DUDE?!

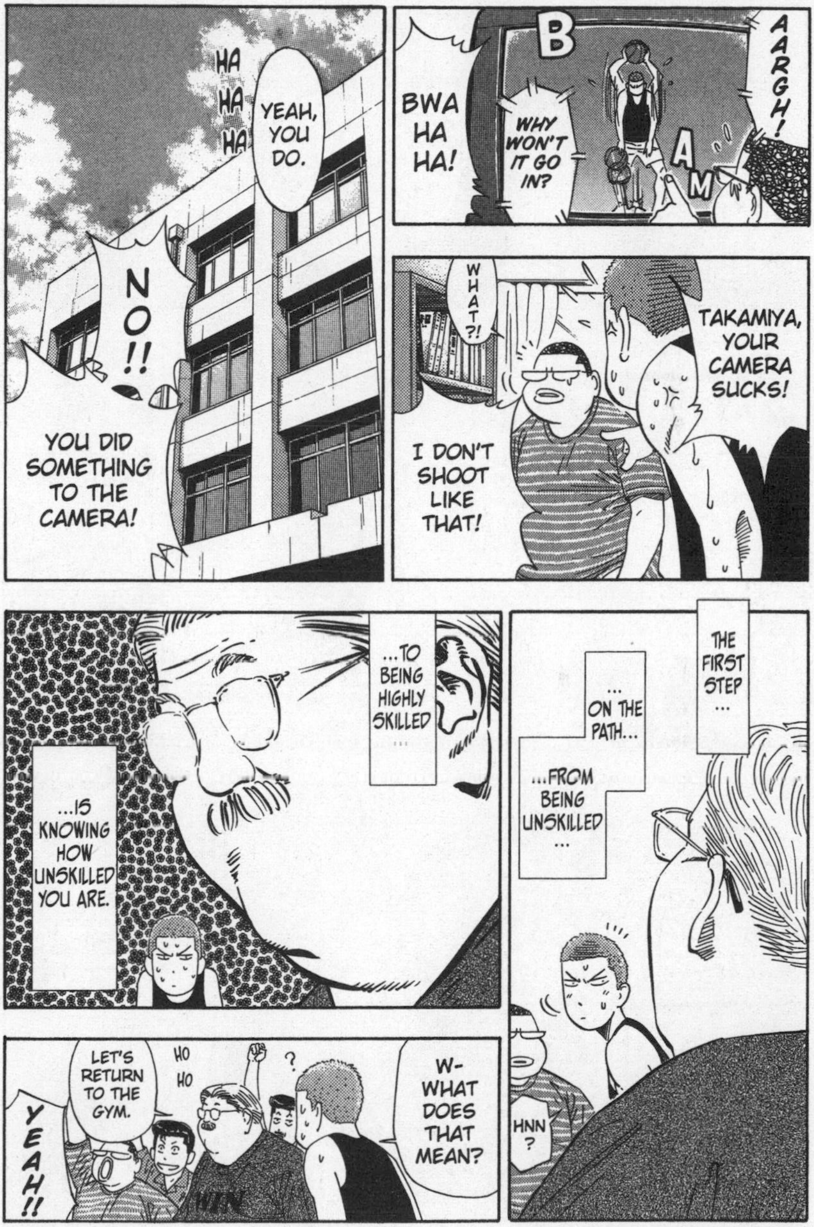
AARGH!
B
AM
WHY WON'T IT GO IN?
BWA HA HA!
TAKAMIYA, YOUR CAMERA SUCKS!
WHAT?!
I DON'T SHOOT LIKE THAT!
YEAH, YOU DO.
HA HA HA
NO!!
YOU DID SOMETHING TO THE CAMERA!
THE FIRST STEP ...
... ON THE PATH...
...FROM BEING UNSKILLED ...
HNN ?
...TO BEING HIGHLY SKILLED ...
...IS KNOWING HOW UNSKILLED YOU ARE.
W-WHAT DOES THAT MEAN?
?
HO HO
LET'S RETURN TO THE GYM.
YEAH!!

READ THIS WAY

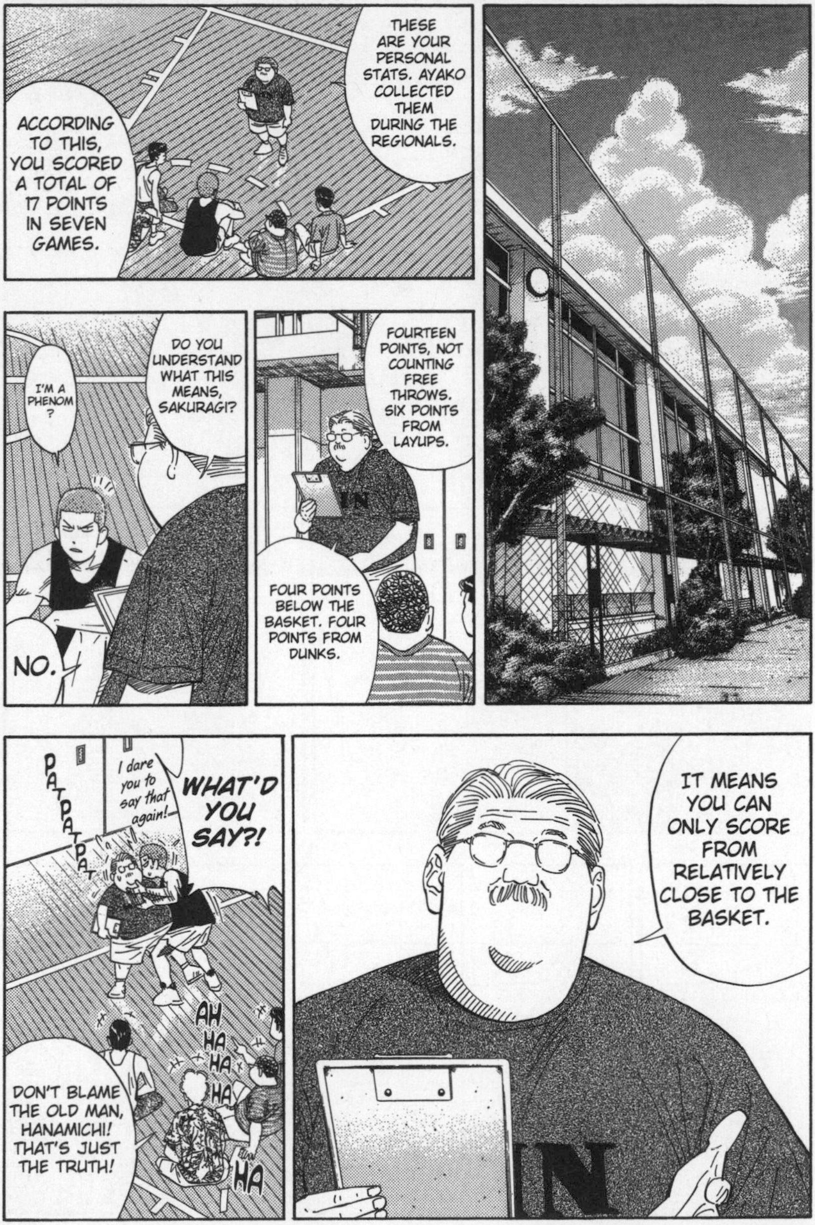
THESE ARE YOUR PERSONAL STATS. AYAKO COLLECTED THEM DURING THE REGIONALS.
ACCORDING TO THIS, YOU SCORED A TOTAL OF 17 POINTS IN SEVEN GAMES.
FOURTEEN POINTS, NOT COUNTING FREE THROWS. SIX POINTS FROM LAYUPS.
FOUR POINTS BELOW THE BASKET. FOUR POINTS FROM DUNKS.
DO YOU UNDERSTAND WHAT THIS MEANS, SAKURAGI?
I'M A PHENOM?
NO.
IT MEANS YOU CAN ONLY SCORE FROM RELATIVELY CLOSE TO THE BASKET.
WHAT'D YOU SAY?!
I dare you to say that again!
PATPATPATPAT
AH HA HA HA HA
DON'T BLAME THE OLD MAN, HANAMICHI! THAT'S JUST THE TRUTH!

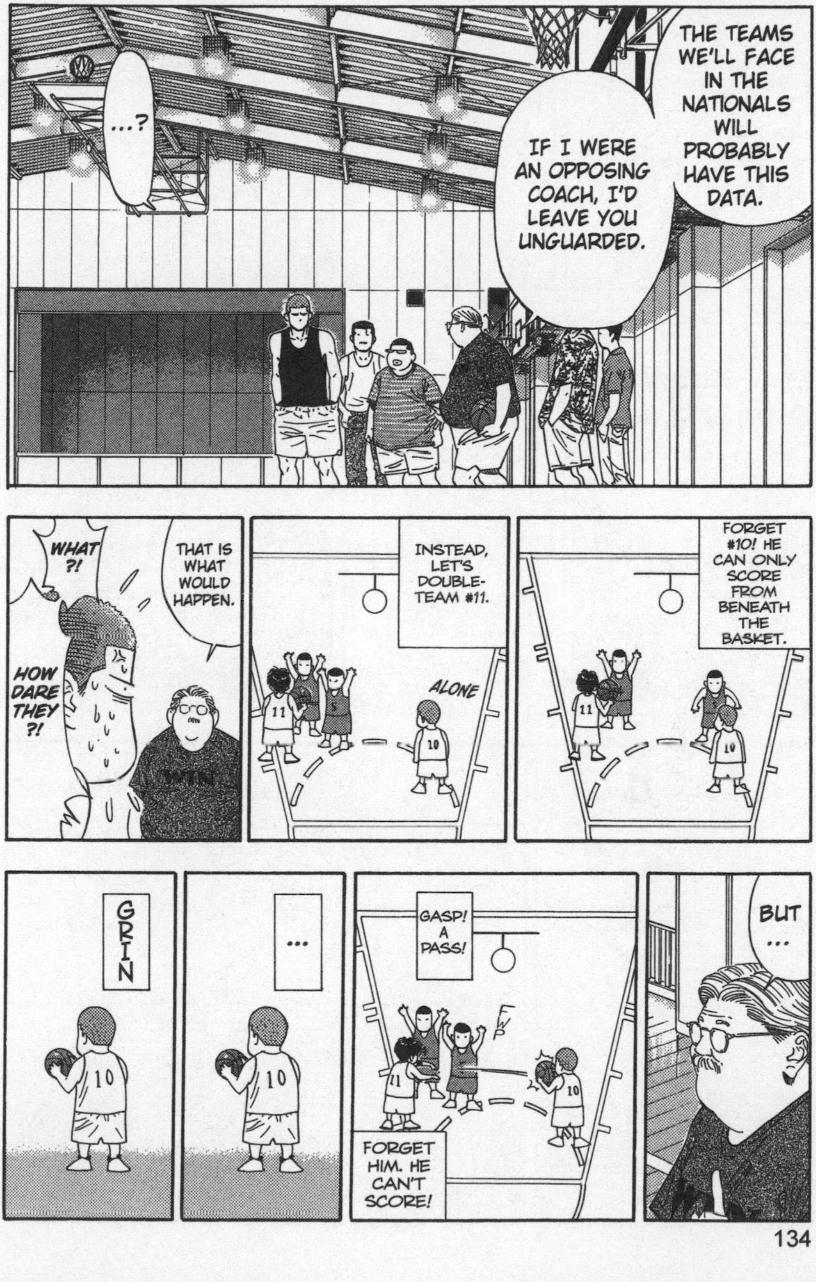
THE TEAMS WE'LL FACE IN THE NATIONALS WILL PROBABLY HAVE THIS DATA.
IF I WERE AN OPPOSING COACH, I'D LEAVE YOU UNGUARDED.
...?
FORGET #10! HE CAN ONLY SCORE FROM BENEATH THE BASKET.
INSTEAD, LET'S DOUBLE-TEAM #11.
ALONE
THAT IS WHAT WOULD HAPPEN.
WHAT?!
HOW DARE THEY?!
BUT ...
GASP! A PASS!
FWP
FORGET HIM. HE CAN'T SCORE!
...
GRIN

READ THIS WAY

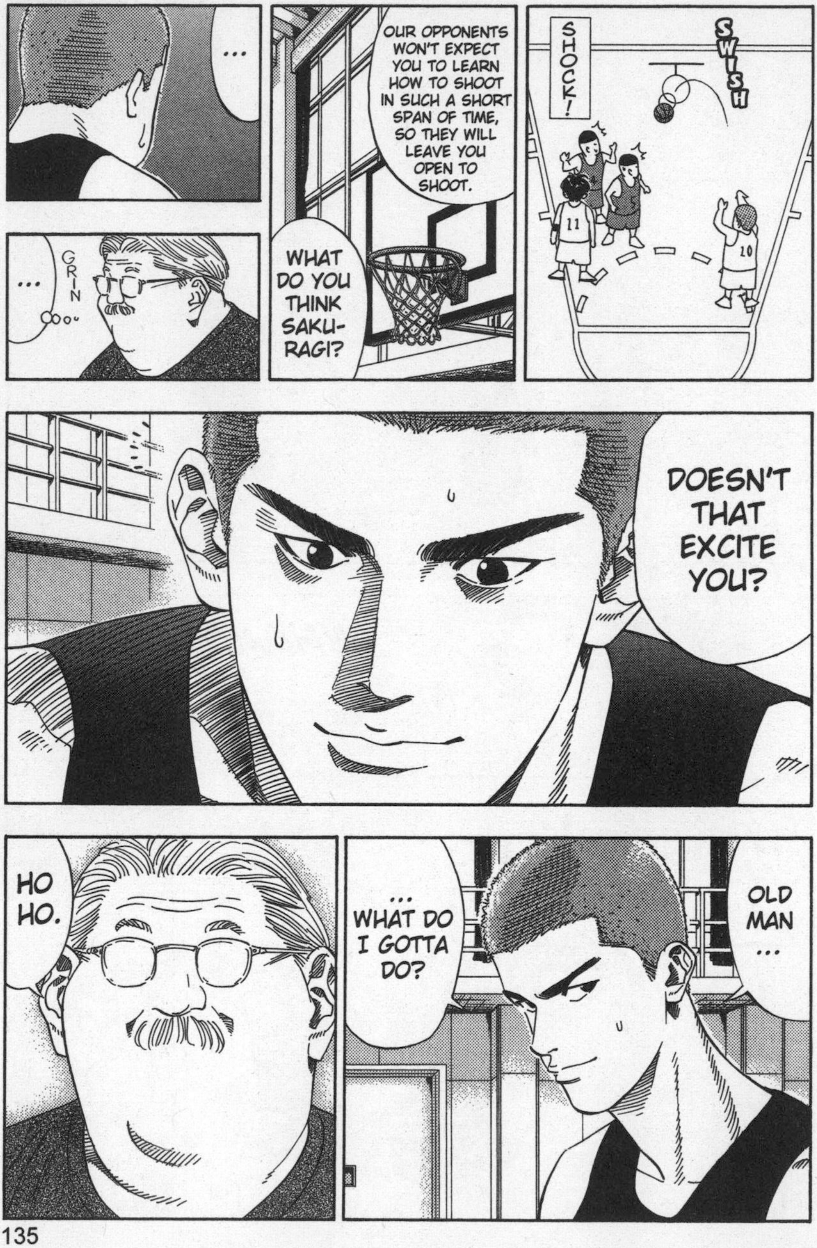

SWISH
SHOCK!
OUR OPPONENTS WON'T EXPECT YOU TO LEARN HOW TO SHOOT IN SUCH A SHORT SPAN OF TIME, SO THEY WILL LEAVE YOU OPEN TO SHOOT.
WHAT DO YOU THINK SAKURAGI?
...
GRIN
...
DOESN'T THAT EXCITE YOU?
OLD MAN ...
... WHAT DO I GOTTA DO?
HO HO.

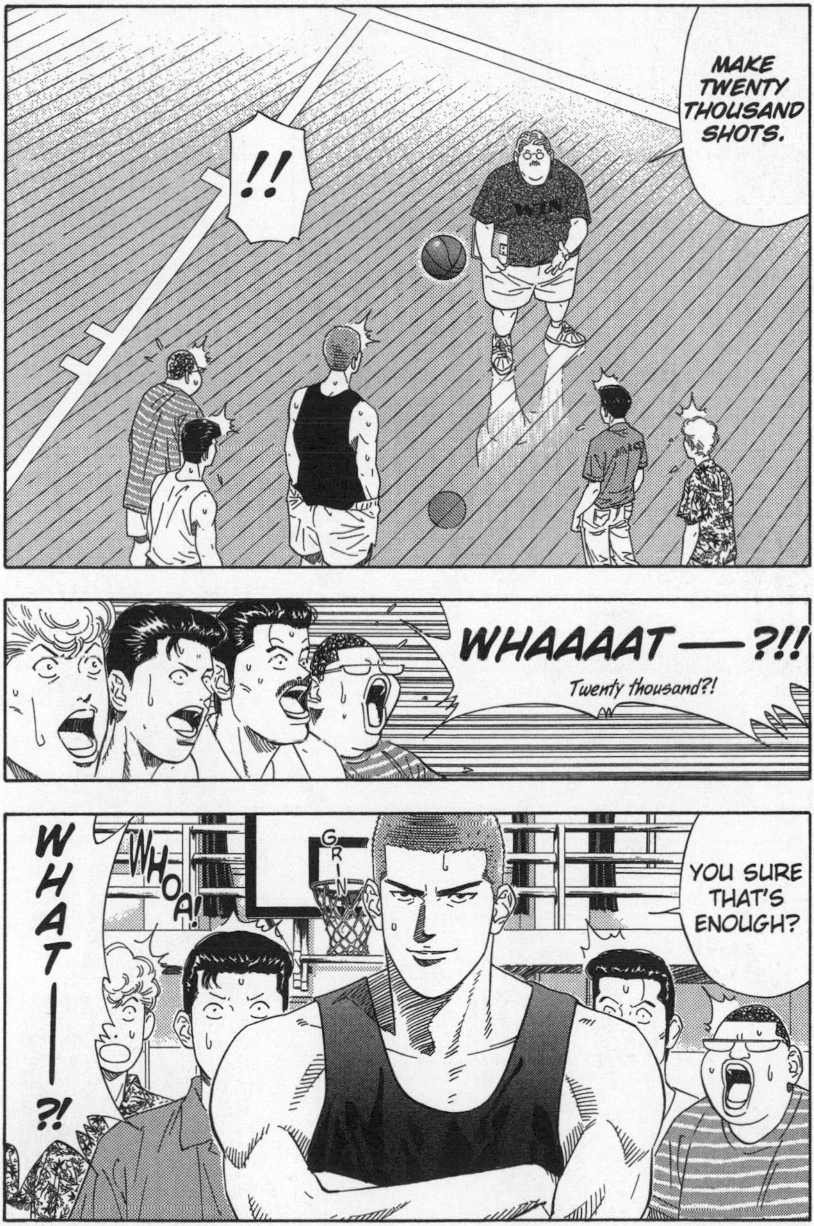
MAKE TWENTY THOUSAND SHOTS.
!!
WHAAAAT——?!!
Twenty thousand?!
YOU SURE THAT'S ENOUGH?
GRIN
WHOA!
WHAT——?!

READ THIS WAY

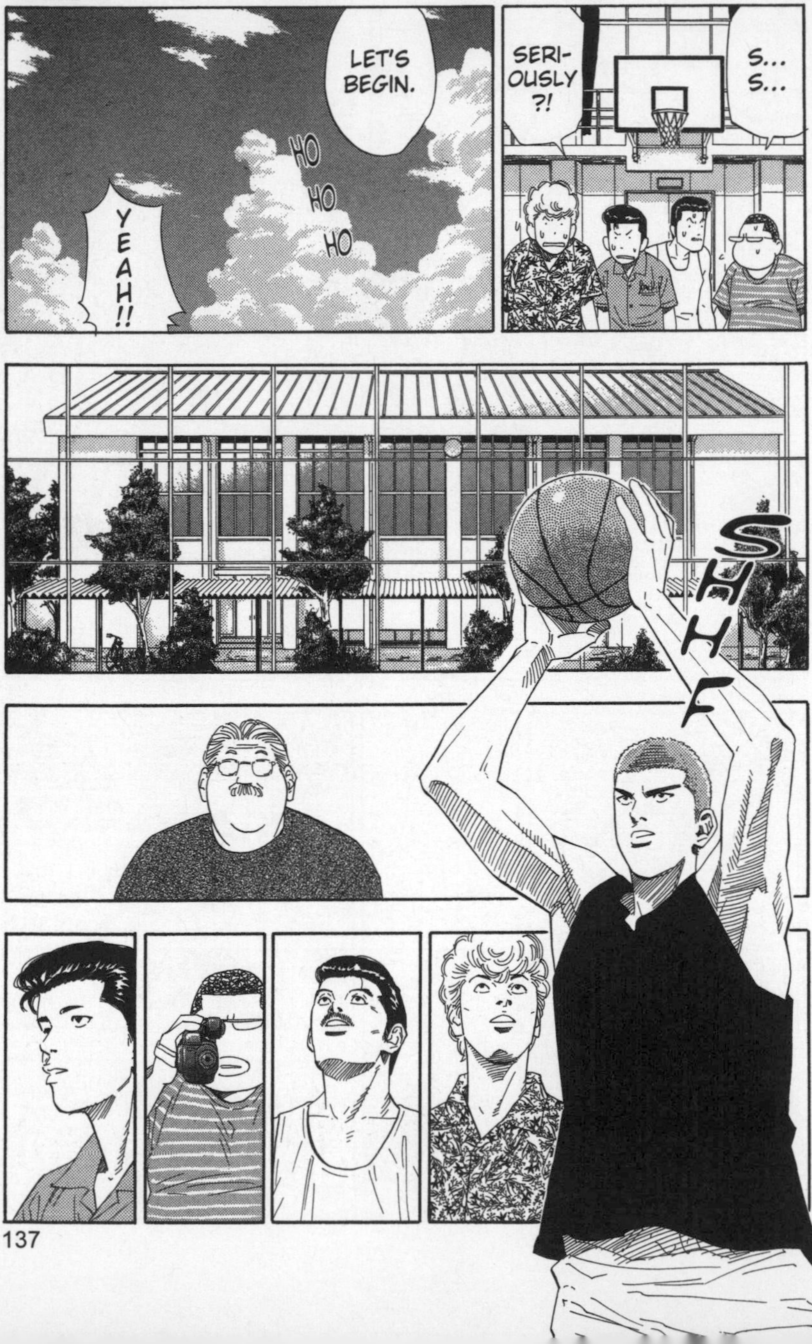
S... S...
SERI-OUSLY?!
LET'S BEGIN.
HO HO HO
YEAH!!
SHHF

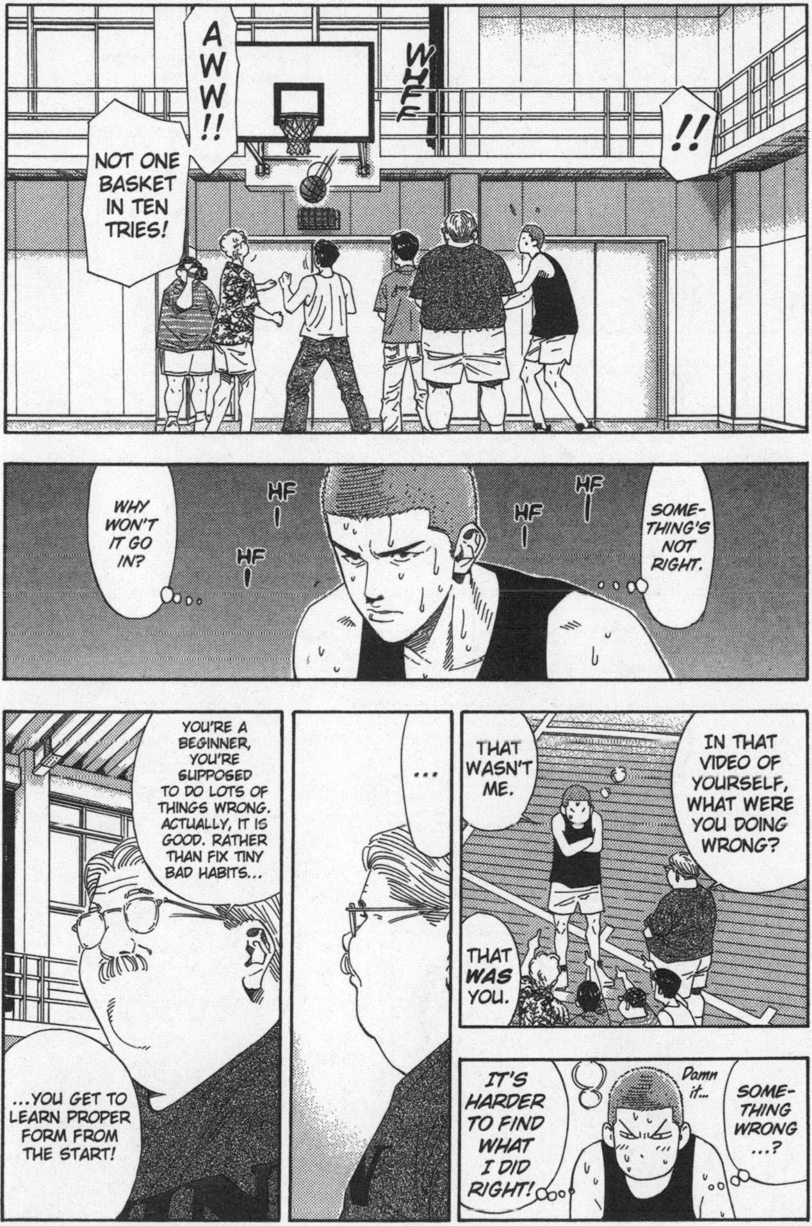
!!
WHFF
AWW!!
NOT ONE BASKET IN TEN TRIES!
SOME-THING'S NOT RIGHT.
HF
HF
HF
WHY WON'T IT GO IN?
IN THAT VIDEO OF YOURSELF, WHAT WERE YOU DOING WRONG?
THAT WASN'T ME.
THAT *WAS* YOU.
SOME-THING WRONG ...?
Damn it...
IT'S HARDER TO FIND WHAT I DID RIGHT!
...
YOU'RE A BEGINNER, YOU'RE SUPPOSED TO DO LOTS OF THINGS WRONG. ACTUALLY, IT IS GOOD. RATHER THAN FIX TINY BAD HABITS...
...YOU GET TO LEARN PROPER FORM FROM THE START!

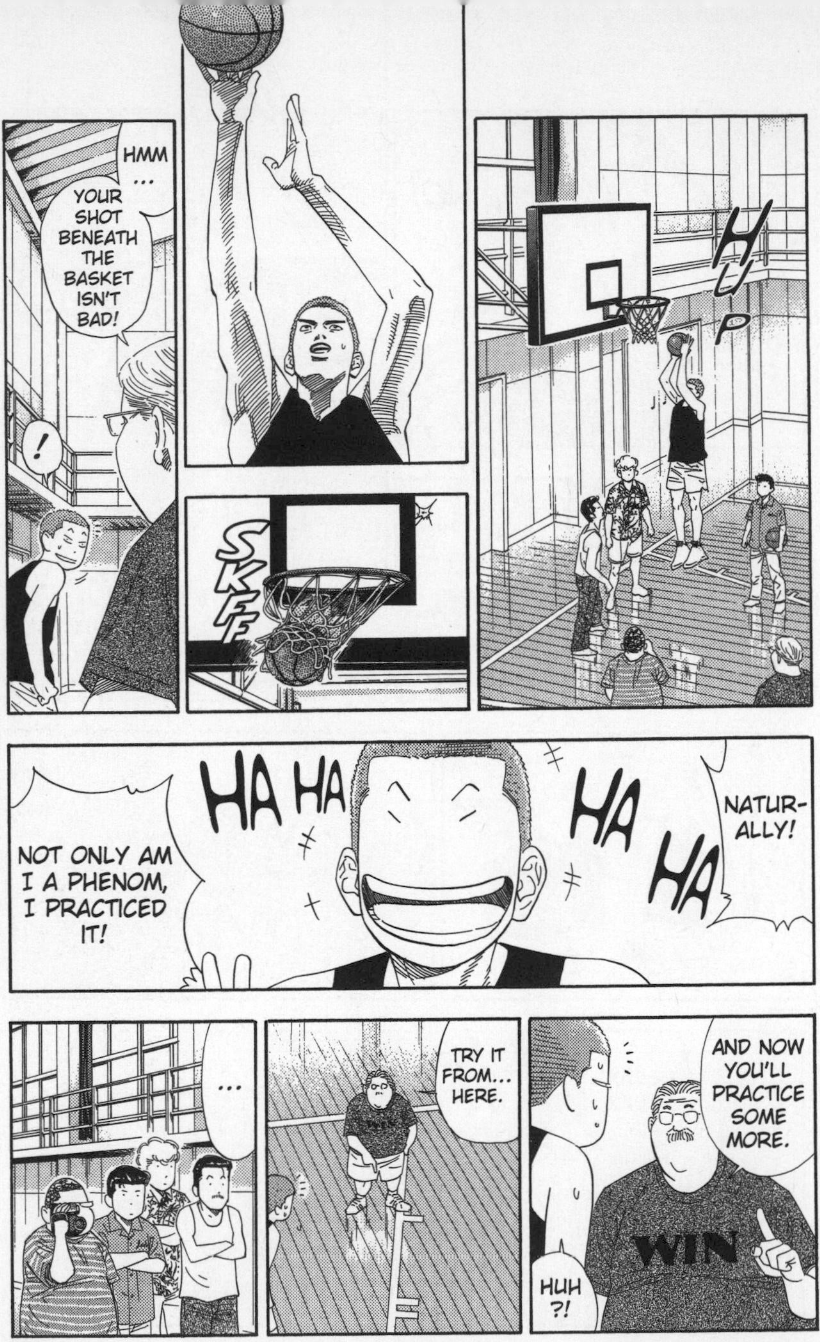
HUP
SKFF
HMM ...
YOUR SHOT BENEATH THE BASKET ISN'T BAD!
!
NATUR-ALLY!
HA HA
HA HA
NOT ONLY AM I A PHENOM, I PRACTICED IT!
AND NOW YOU'LL PRACTICE SOME MORE.
WIN
HUH ?!
TRY IT FROM... HERE.
...

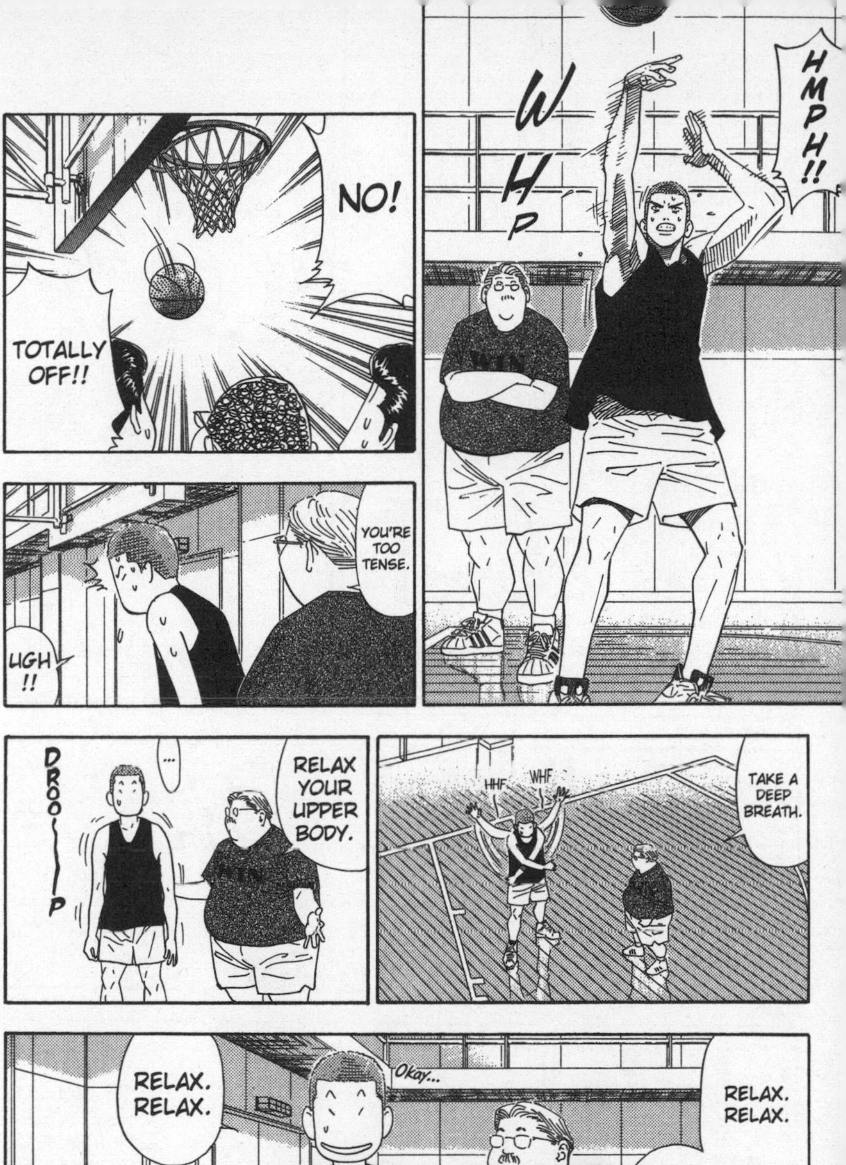
HMPH!!
WHP
NO!
TOTALLY OFF!!
YOU'RE TOO TENSE.
UGH!!
TAKE A DEEP BREATH.
WHF
HHF
RELAX YOUR UPPER BODY.
...
DROOOP
RELAX. RELAX.
SHOOTING ISN'T ABOUT STRENGTH.
Okay...
RELAX. RELAX.
THAT'S RIGHT.

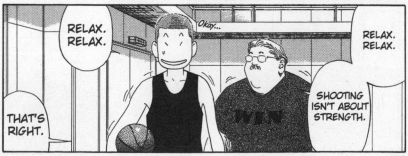

READ THIS WAY

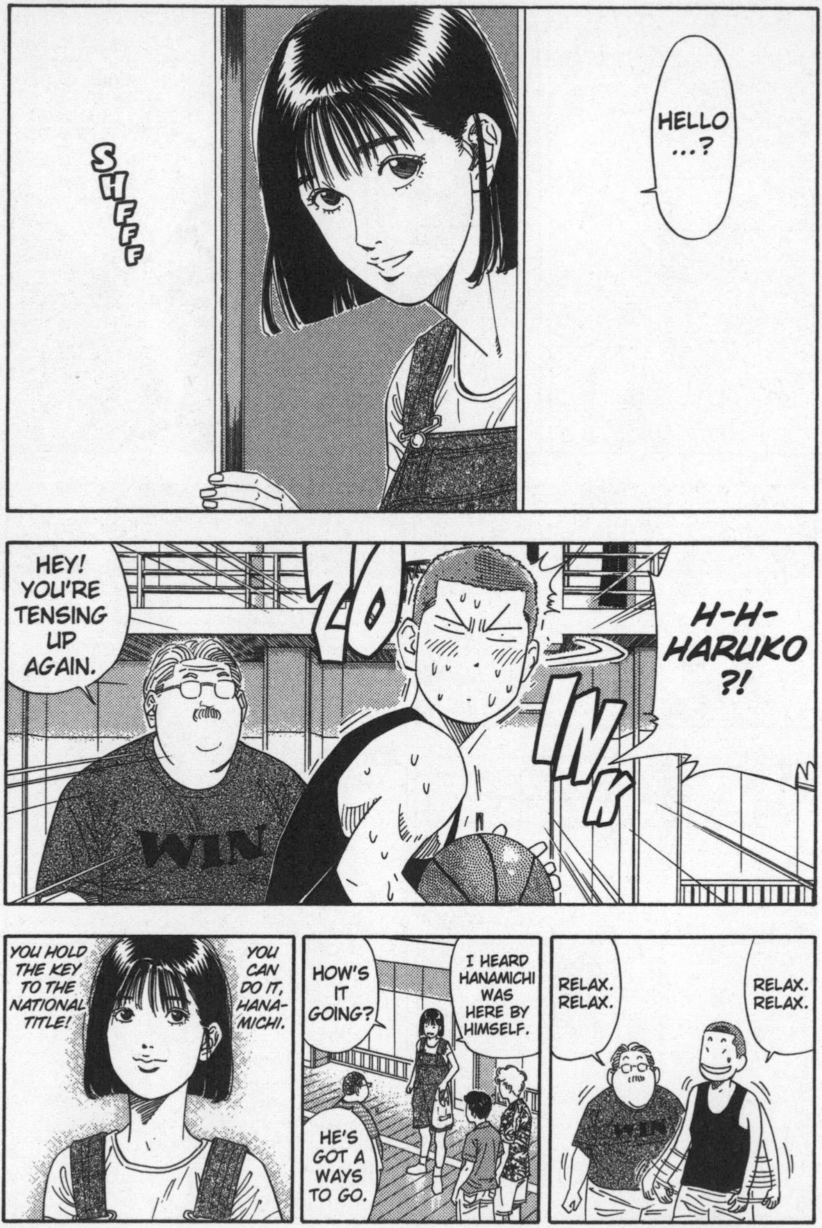

HELLO ...?
SHFFF
H-H-HARUKO ?!
ZOINK
HEY! YOU'RE TENSING UP AGAIN.
RELAX. RELAX.
RELAX. RELAX.
I HEARD HANAMICHI WAS HERE BY HIMSELF.
HOW'S IT GOING?
HE'S GOT A WAYS TO GO.
YOU CAN DO IT, HANAMICHI.
YOU HOLD THE KEY TO THE NATIONAL TITLE!

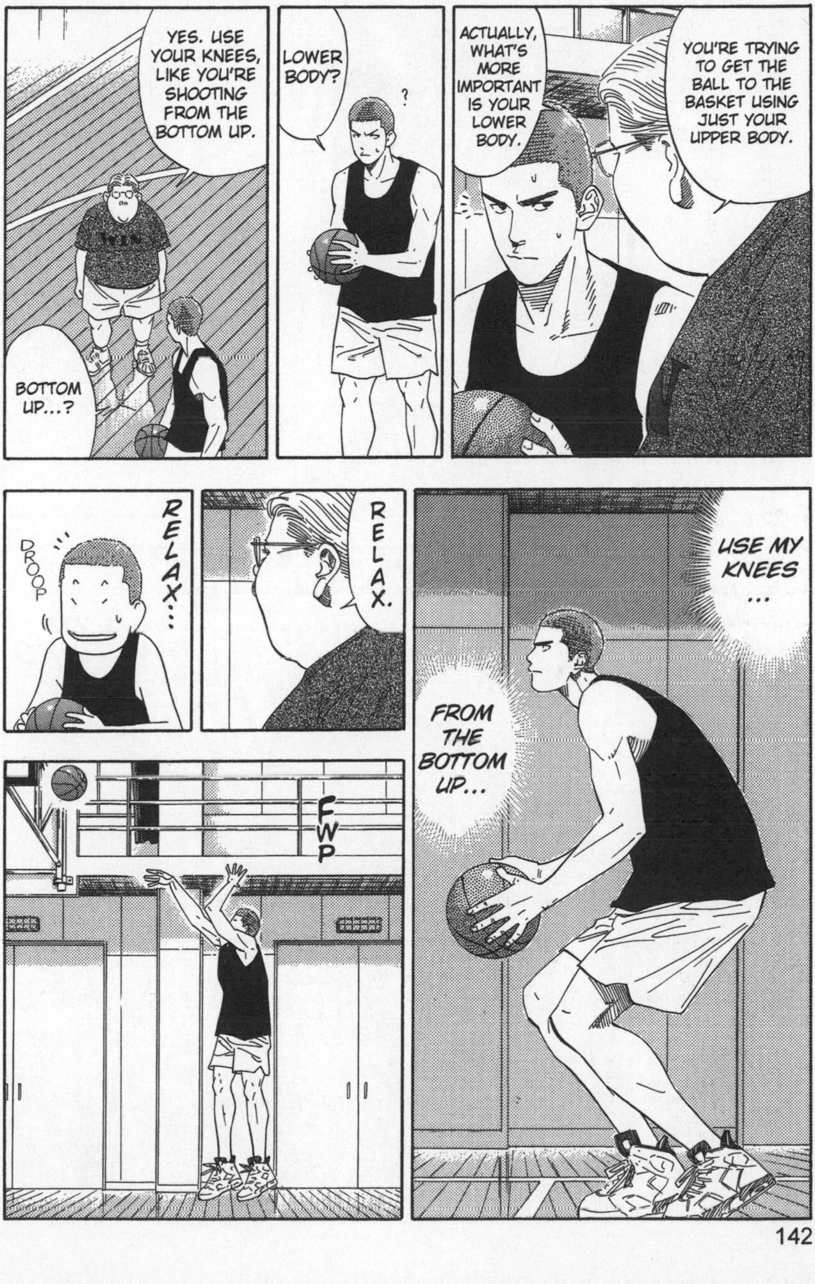
YOU'RE TRYING TO GET THE BALL TO THE BASKET USING JUST YOUR UPPER BODY.
ACTUALLY, WHAT'S MORE IMPORTANT IS YOUR LOWER BODY.
LOWER BODY?
?
YES. USE YOUR KNEES, LIKE YOU'RE SHOOTING FROM THE BOTTOM UP.
BOTTOM UP...?
RELAX.
RELAX...
DROOP
USE MY KNEES...
FROM THE BOTTOM UP...
FWP

READ THIS WAY

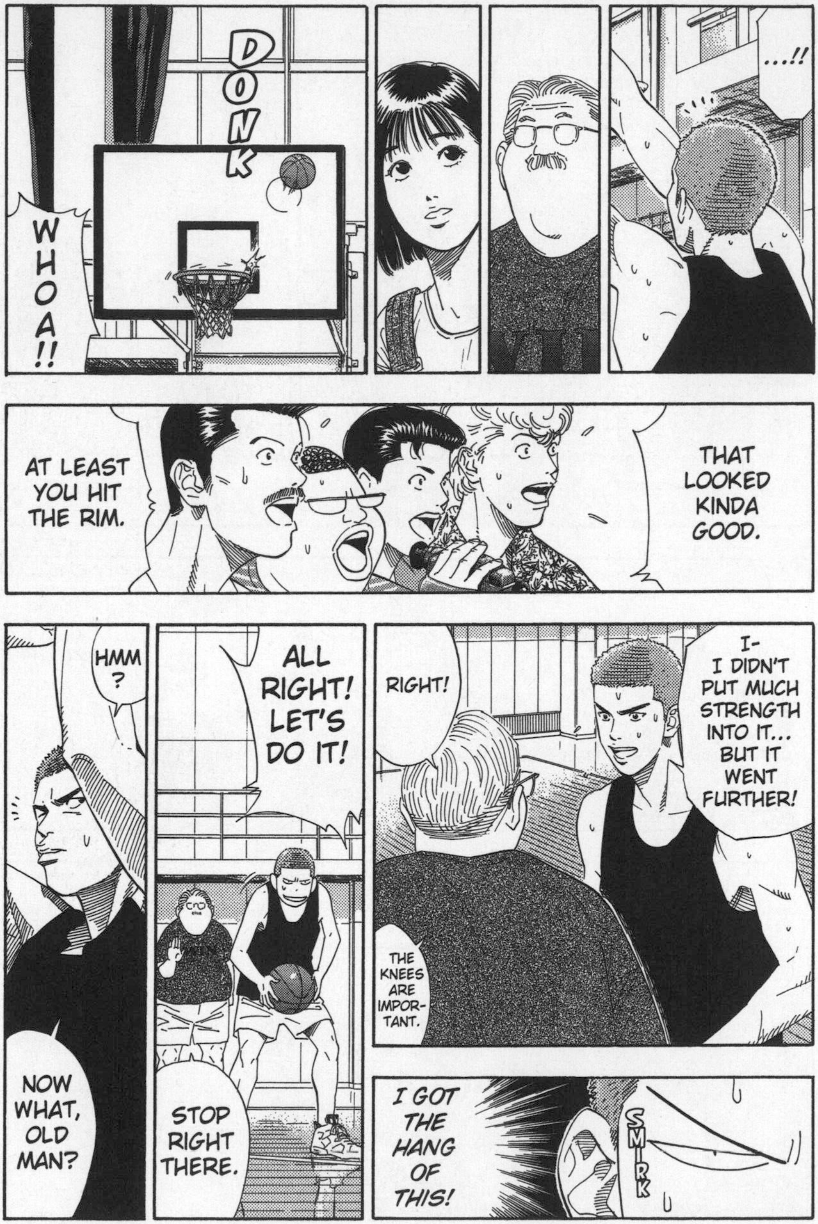
...!!
DONK
WHOA!!
THAT LOOKED KINDA GOOD.
AT LEAST YOU HIT THE RIM.
I- I DIDN'T PUT MUCH STRENGTH INTO IT... BUT IT WENT FURTHER!
RIGHT!
THE KNEES ARE IMPOR-TANT.
SMIRK
I GOT THE HANG OF THIS!
ALL RIGHT! LET'S DO IT!
STOP RIGHT THERE.
HMM?
NOW WHAT, OLD MAN?

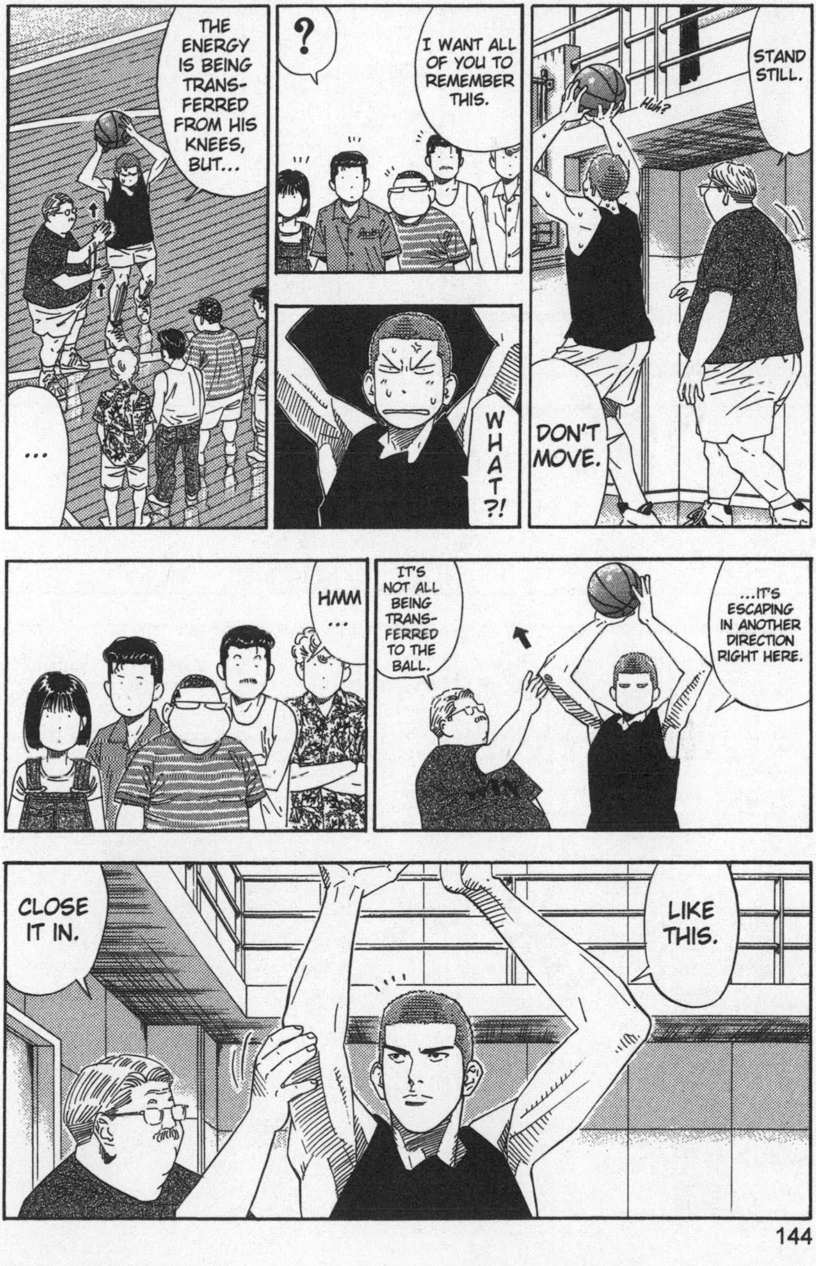
STAND STILL.
Huh?
DON'T MOVE.
?
I WANT ALL OF YOU TO REMEMBER THIS.
WHAT?!
THE ENERGY IS BEING TRANS- FERRED FROM HIS KNEES, BUT...
...
IT'S NOT ALL BEING TRANS- FERRED TO THE BALL.
...IT'S ESCAPING IN ANOTHER DIRECTION RIGHT HERE.
HMM ...
CLOSE IT IN.
LIKE THIS.

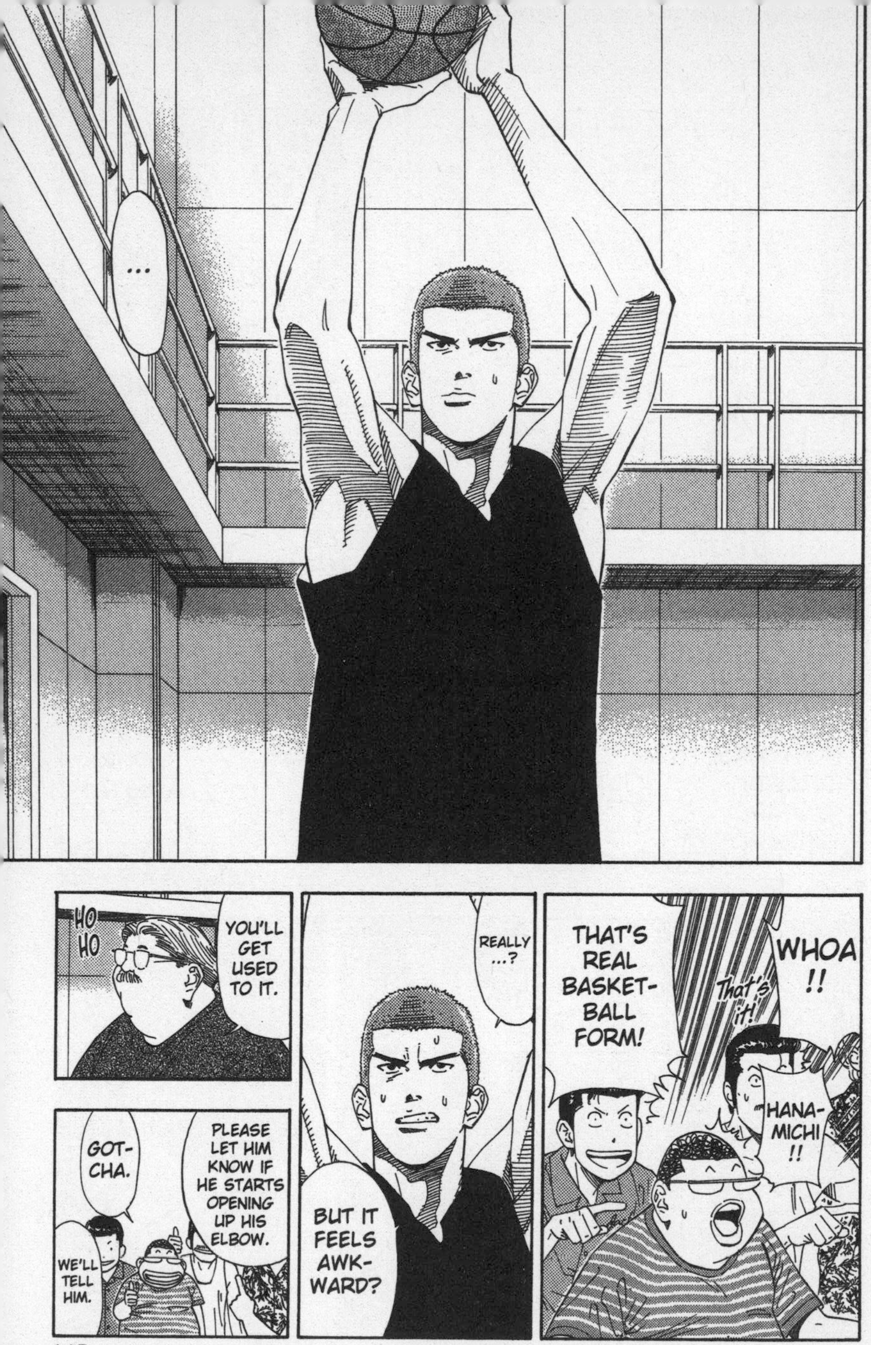
...
WHOA!!
That's it!
THAT'S REAL BASKETBALL FORM!
HANAMICHI!!
REALLY...?
BUT IT FEELS AWKWARD?
HO HO
YOU'LL GET USED TO IT.
PLEASE LET HIM KNOW IF HE STARTS OPENING UP HIS ELBOW.
GOTCHA.
WE'LL TELL HIM.

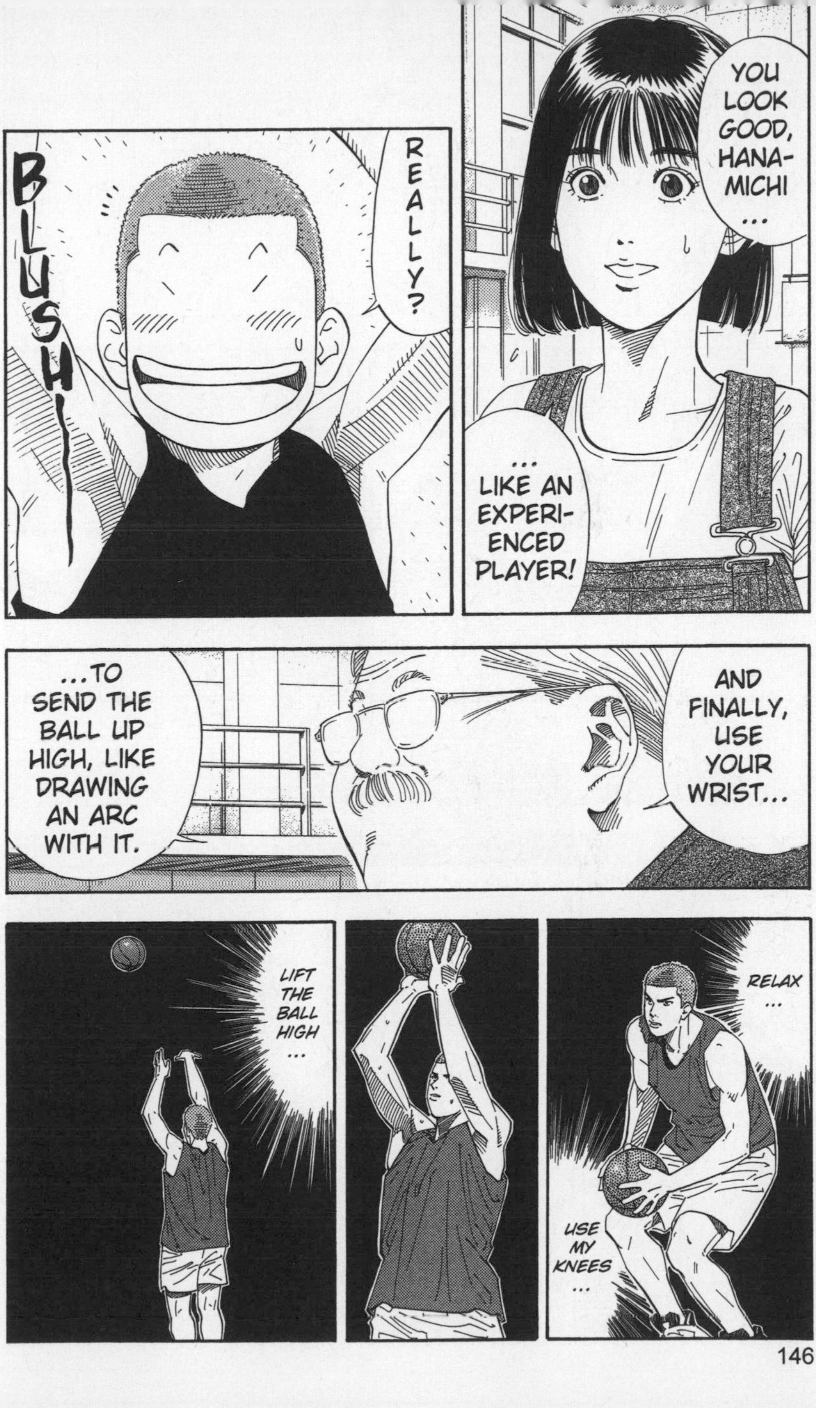
YOU LOOK GOOD, HANA-MICHI ...
... LIKE AN EXPERI-ENCED PLAYER!
REALLY?
BLUSH
AND FINALLY, USE YOUR WRIST...
...TO SEND THE BALL UP HIGH, LIKE DRAWING AN ARC WITH IT.
RELAX ...
USE MY KNEES ...
LIFT THE BALL HIGH ...

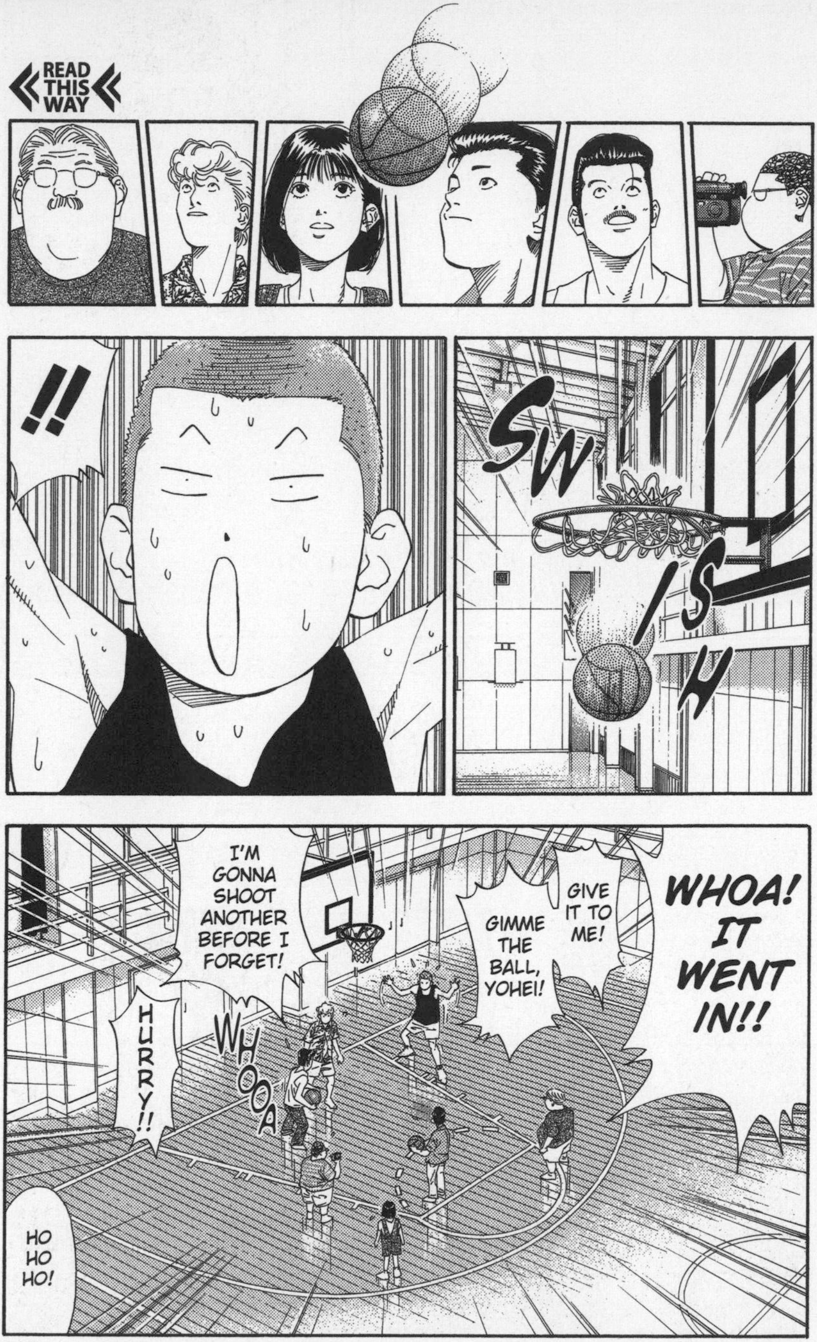
READ THIS WAY
SWISH
!!
WHOA! IT WENT IN!!
GIVE IT TO ME!
GIMME THE BALL, YOHEI!
I'M GONNA SHOOT ANOTHER BEFORE I FORGET!
WHOOA
HURRY!!
HO HO HO!

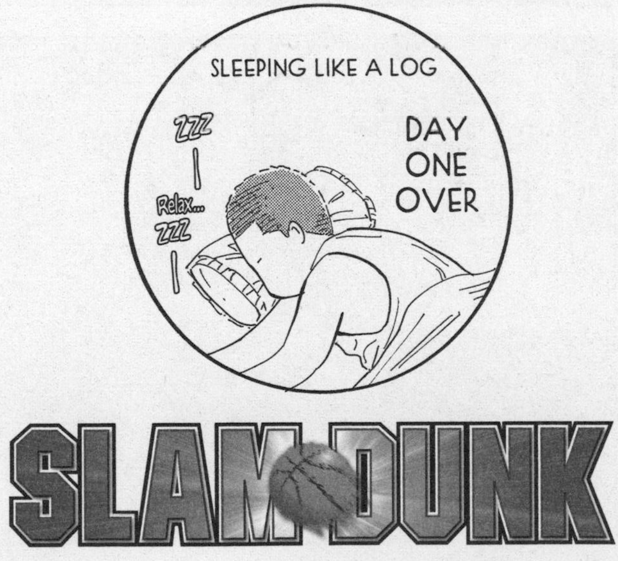
SLEEPING LIKE A LOG
DAY ONE OVER
ZZZ
Relax...
ZZZ

SLAM DUNK

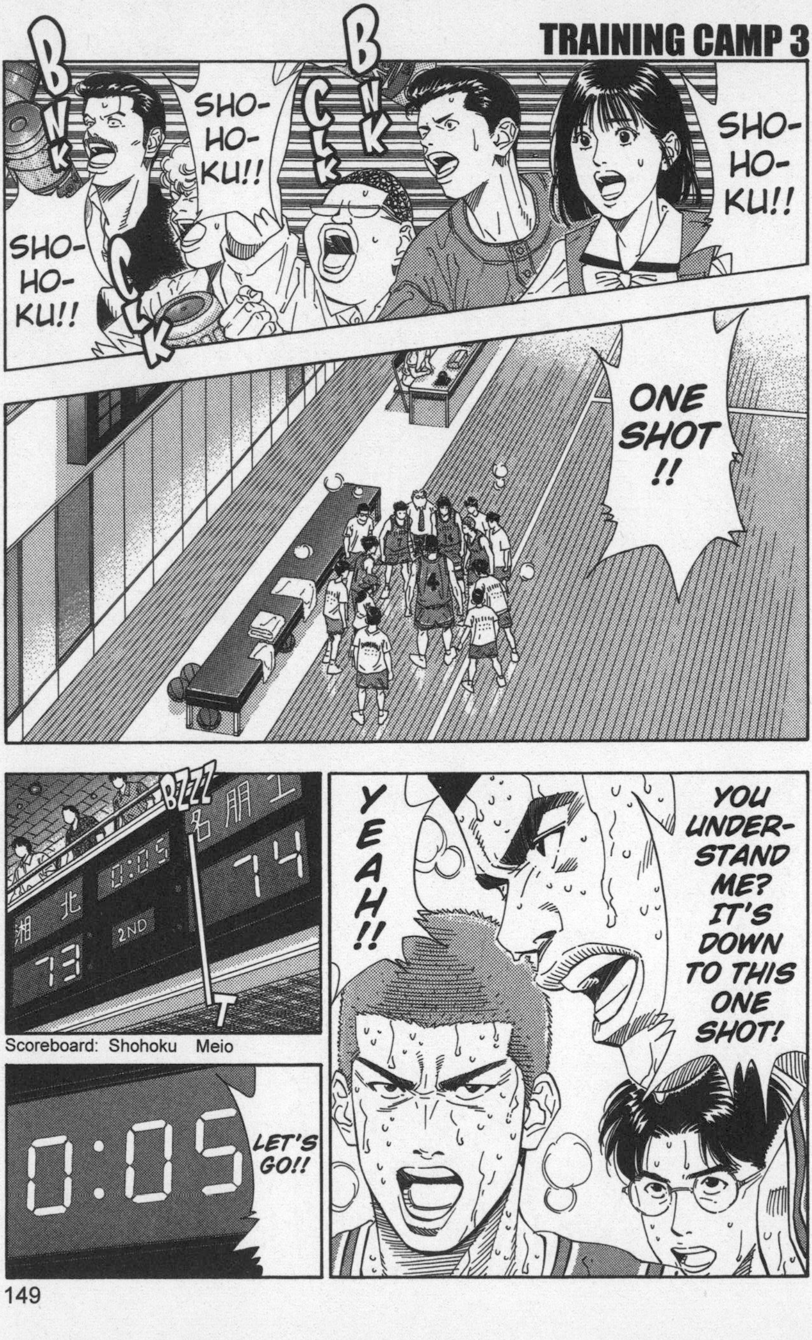
SHO-HO-KU!!
BNK
CLK
SHO-HO-KU!!
BNK
SHO-HO-KU!!
CLK
ONE SHOT!!
YOU UNDER-STAND ME? IT'S DOWN TO THIS ONE SHOT!
YEAH!!
BZZZ
名朋工
0:05
74
湘北
2ND
73
0:05
LET'S GO!!
Scoreboard: Shohoku Meio

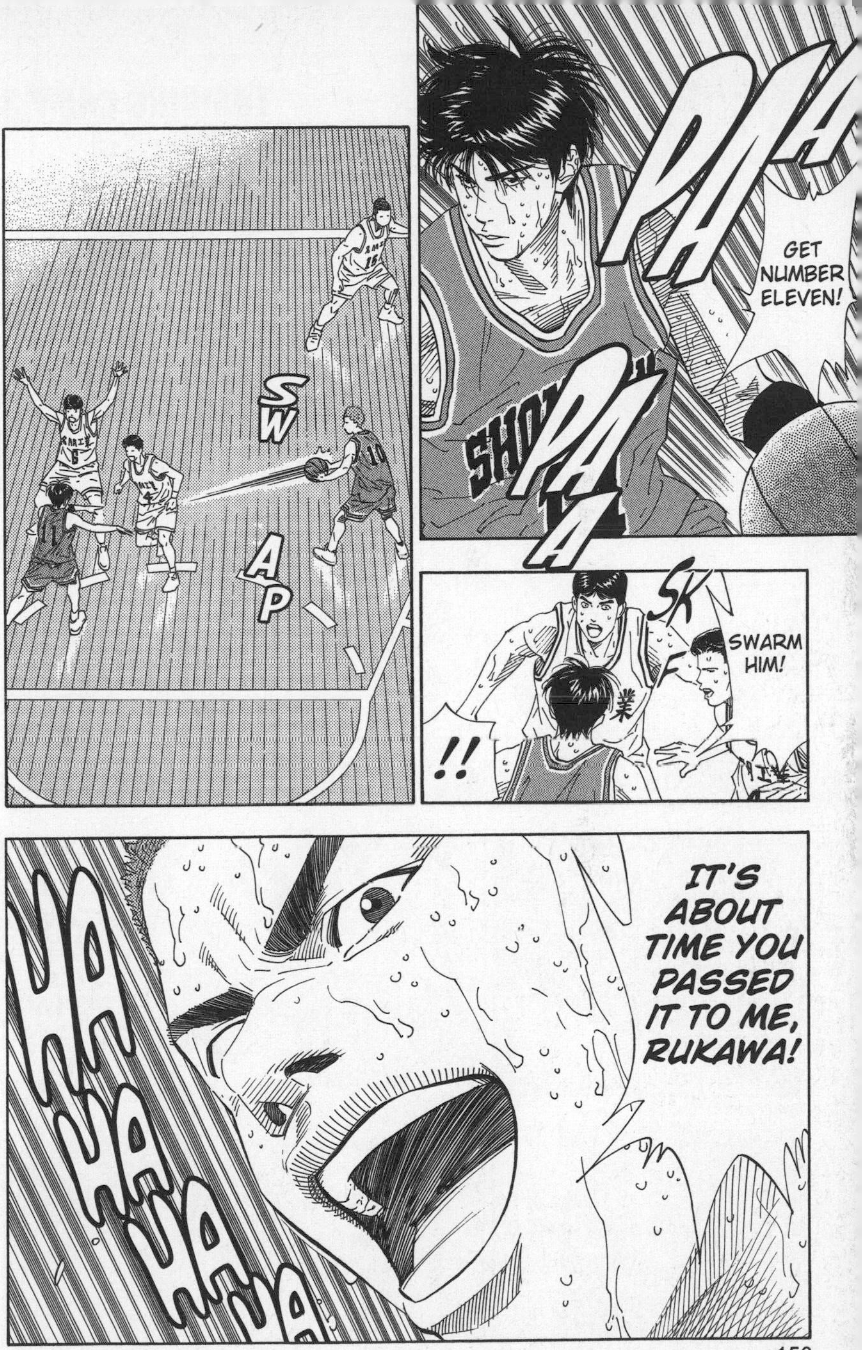
GET NUMBER ELEVEN!
SK
SWARM HIM!
!!
SW
AP
IT'S ABOUT TIME YOU PASSED IT TO ME, RUKAWA!

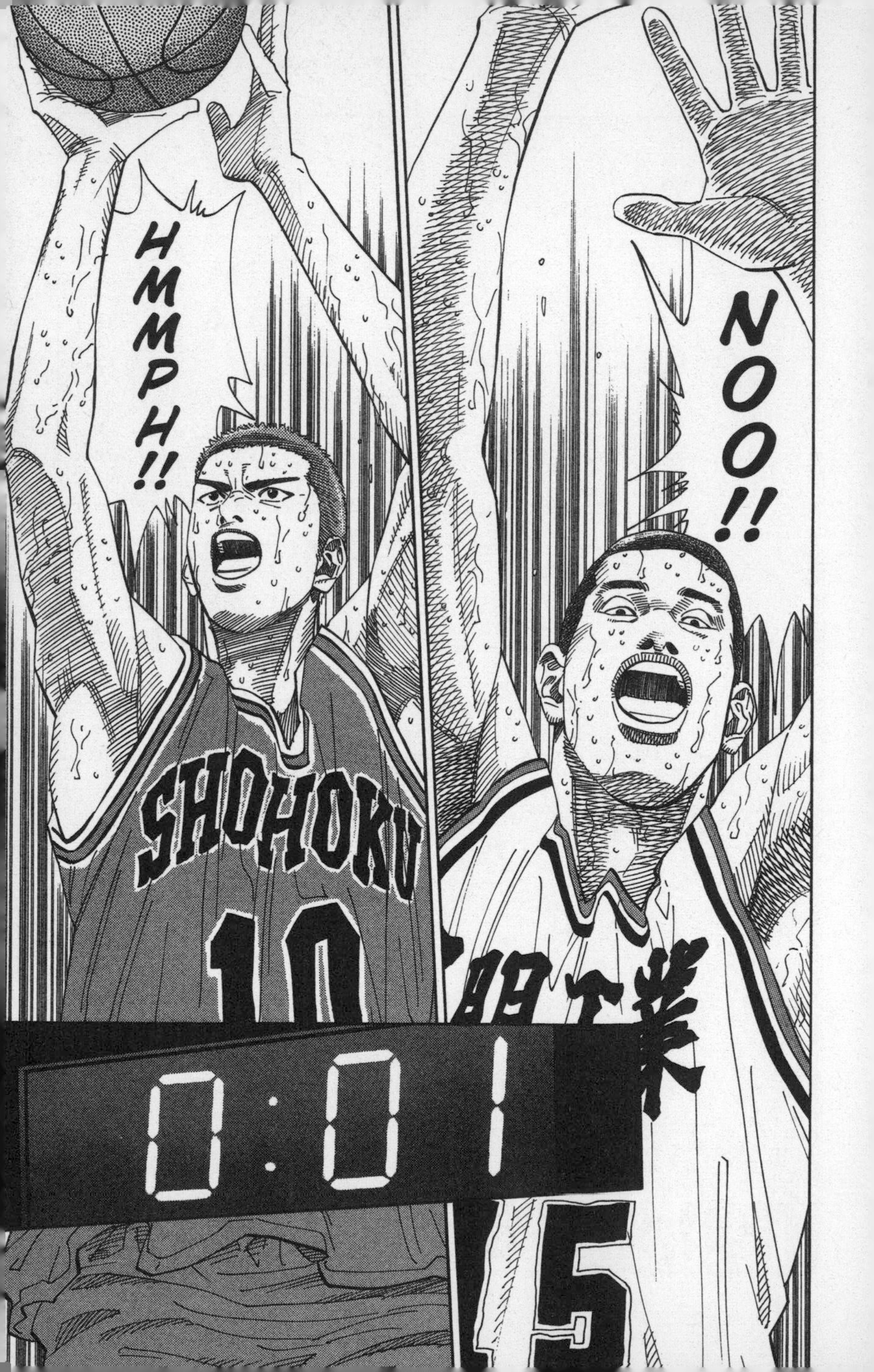
NOO!!
HMMPH!!
SHOHOKU
10
0:01
15

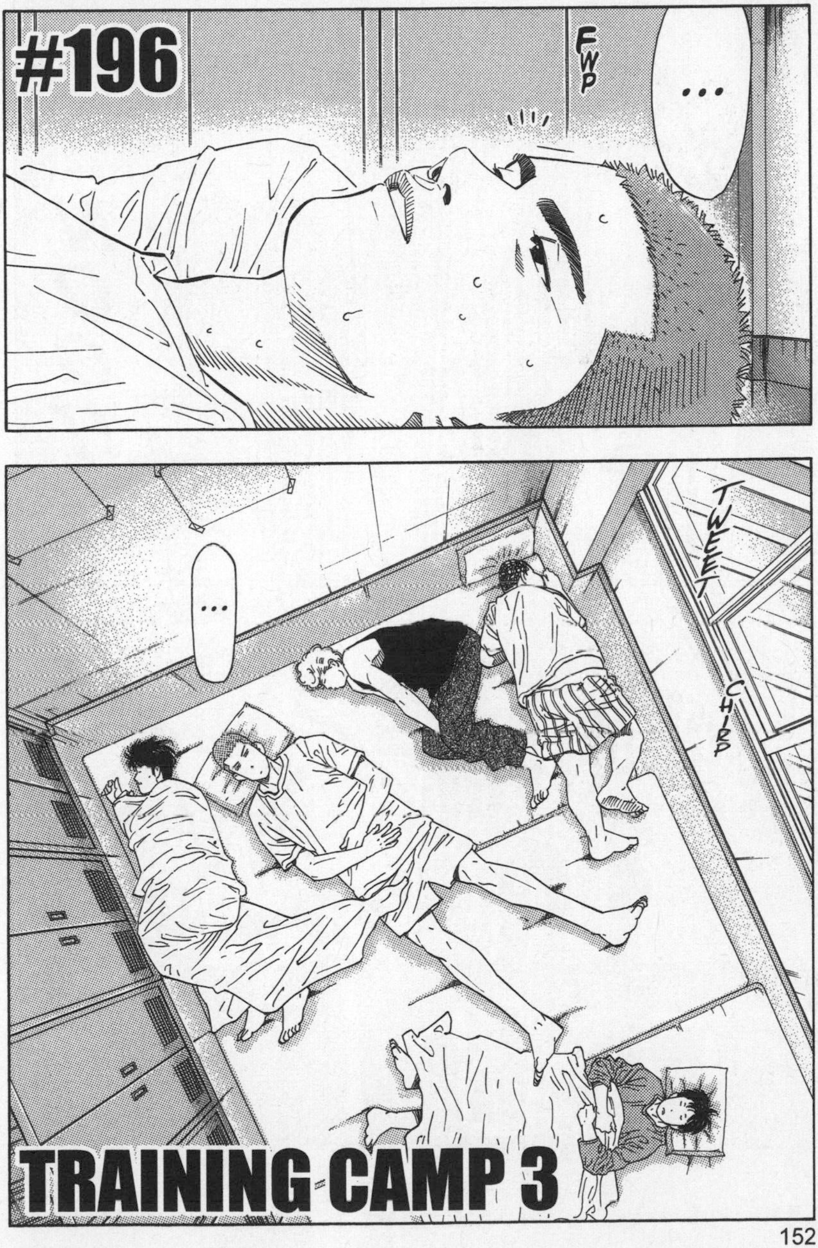
#196
...
FWP
TWEET
CHIRP
...
TRAINING CAMP 3

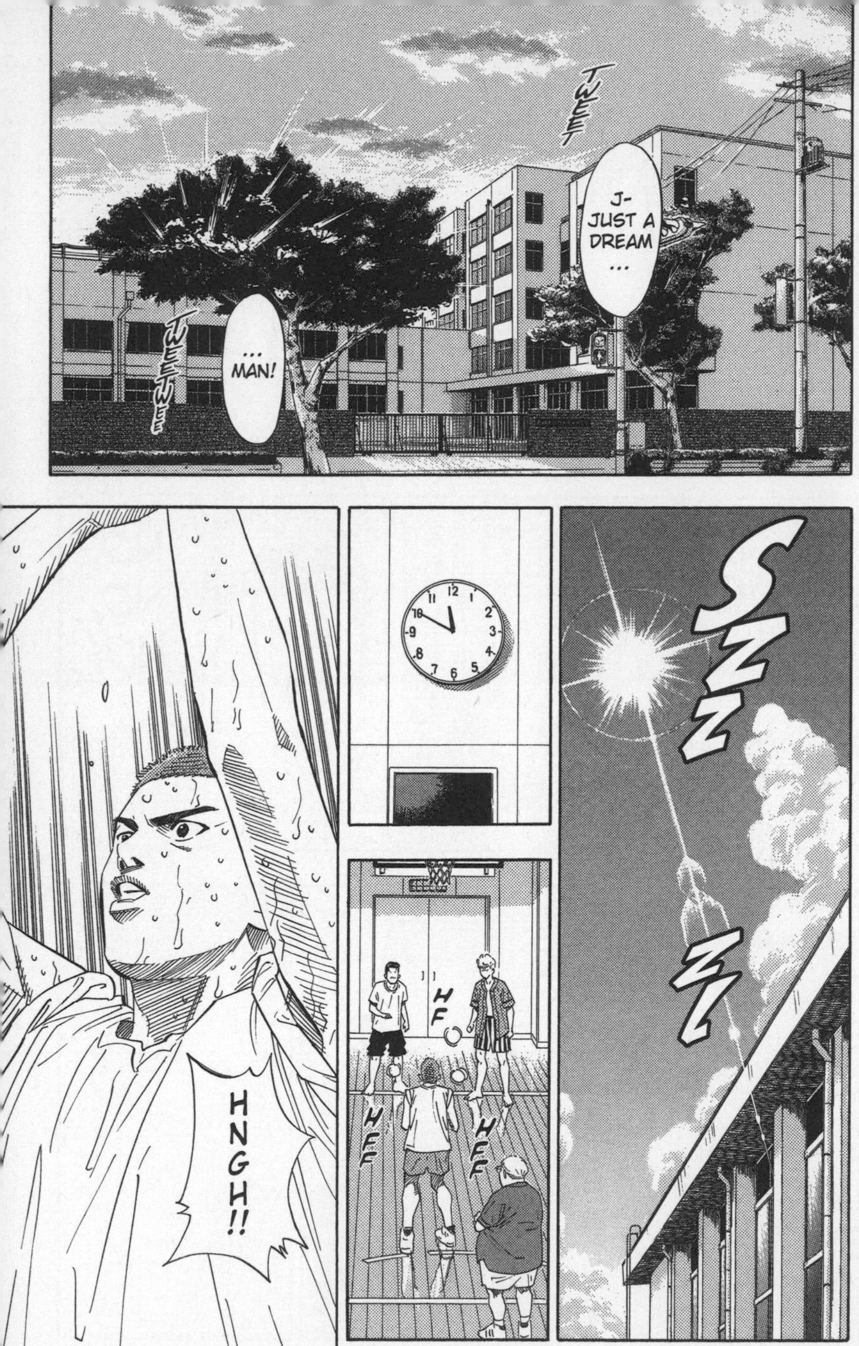
TWEET
J- JUST A DREAM ...
... MAN!
TWEETWEE
SZZZ
ZZ
HF
HFF
HFF
HNGH!!

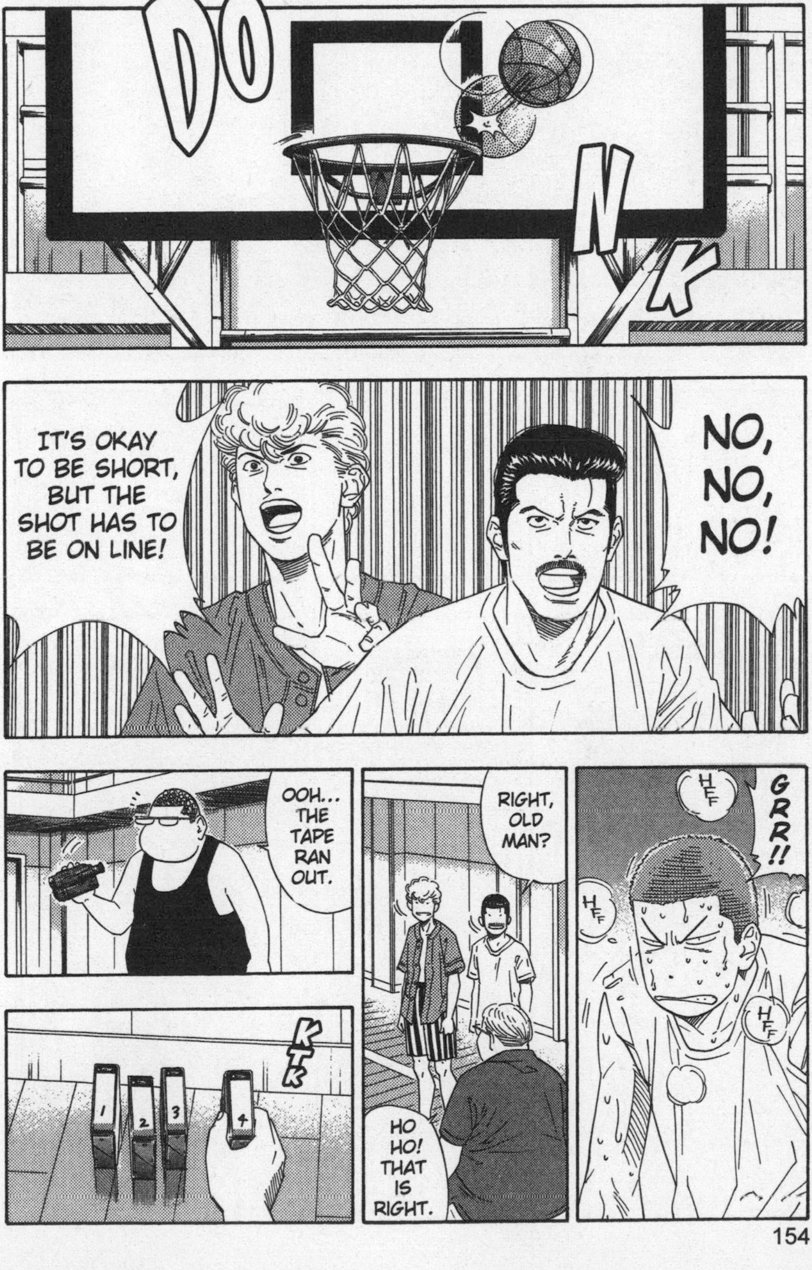
DONK
NO, NO, NO!
IT'S OKAY TO BE SHORT, BUT THE SHOT HAS TO BE ON LINE!
GRR!!
HFF
HFF
HFF
RIGHT, OLD MAN?
HO HO! THAT IS RIGHT.
OOH... THE TAPE RAN OUT.
KTK
1
2
3
4

READ THIS WAY

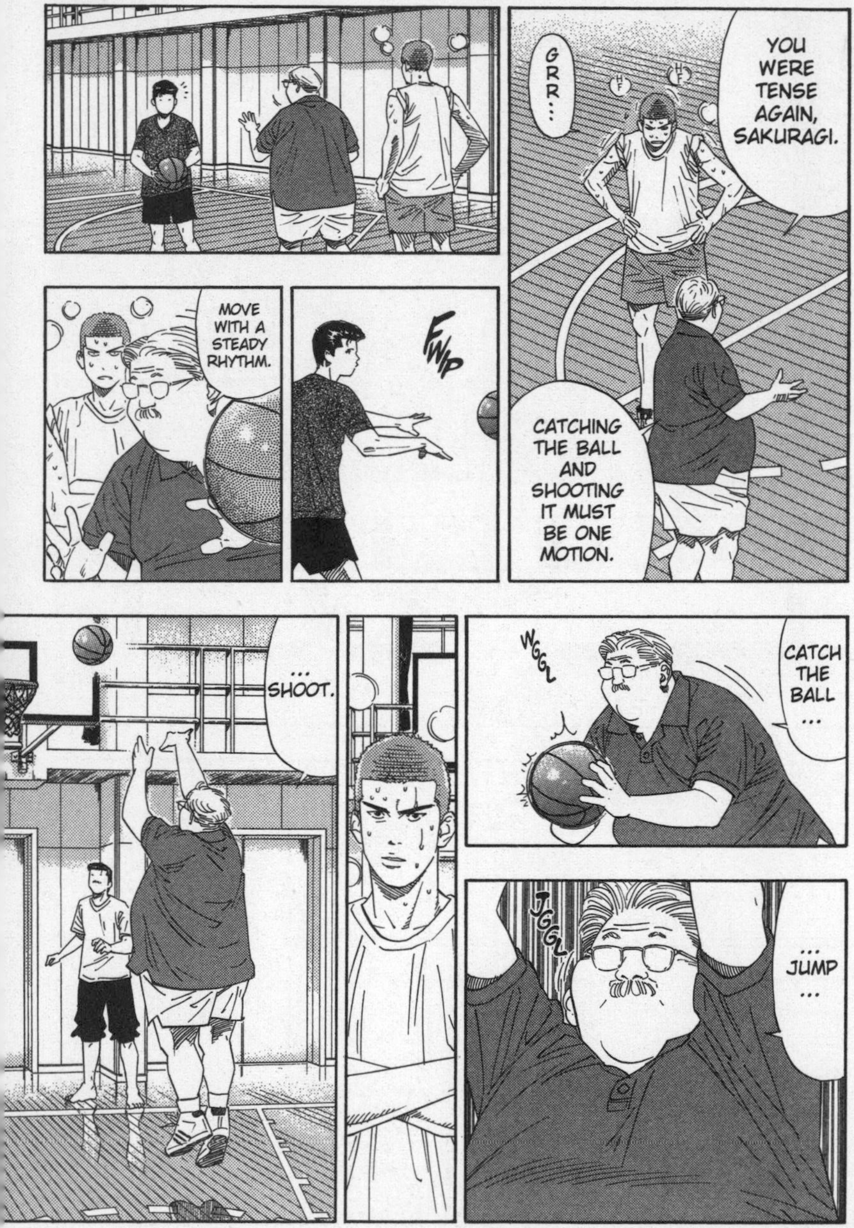
YOU WERE TENSE AGAIN, SAKURAGI.
GRR...
HF
HF
CATCHING THE BALL AND SHOOTING IT MUST BE ONE MOTION.
FWIP
MOVE WITH A STEADY RHYTHM.
CATCH THE BALL ...
WGGL
... JUMP ...
JGGL
... SHOOT.

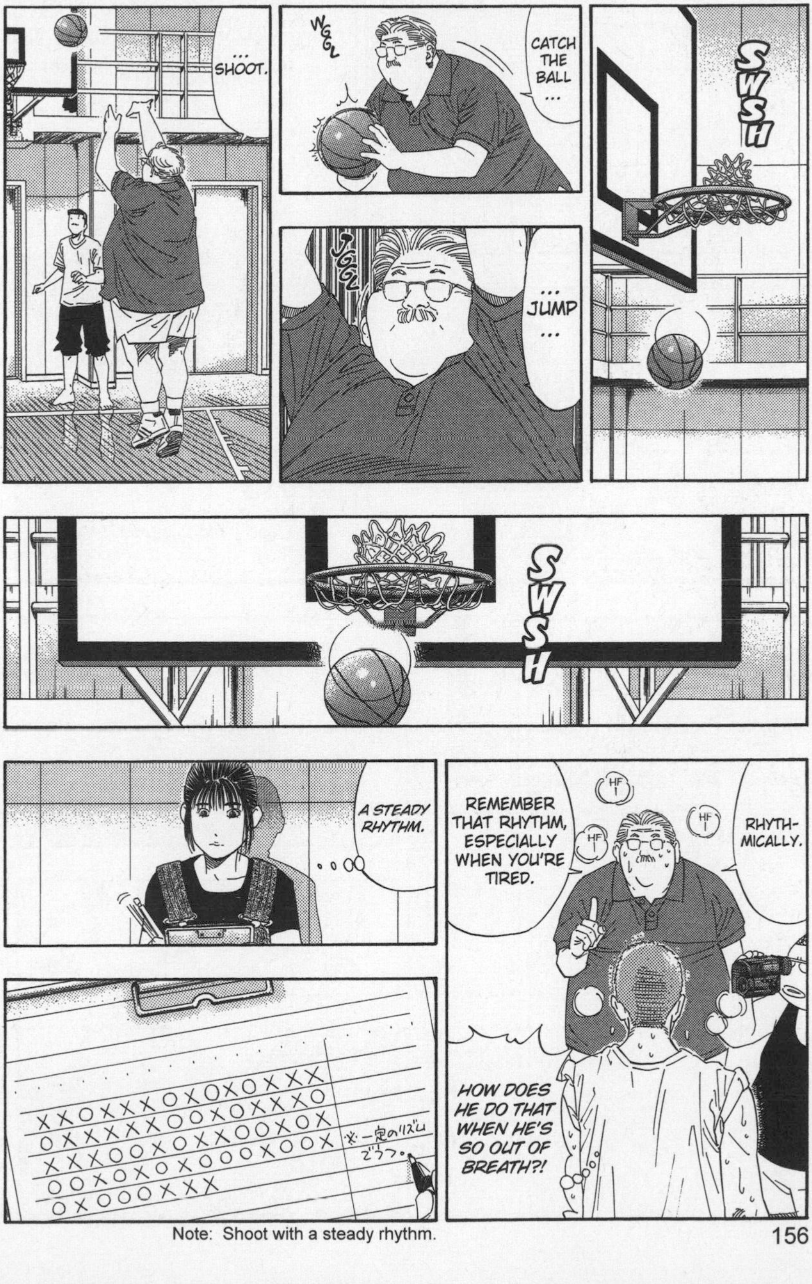
SWSH
WGGL
CATCH THE BALL ...
JGGL
... JUMP ...
... SHOOT.
SWSH
RHYTH-MICALLY.
HF
HF
REMEMBER THAT RHYTHM, ESPECIALLY WHEN YOU'RE TIRED.
HF
HOW DOES HE DO THAT WHEN HE'S SO OUT OF BREATH?!
A STEADY RHYTHM.
※一定のリズムで打つ。

Note: Shoot with a steady rhythm.

READ THIS WAY

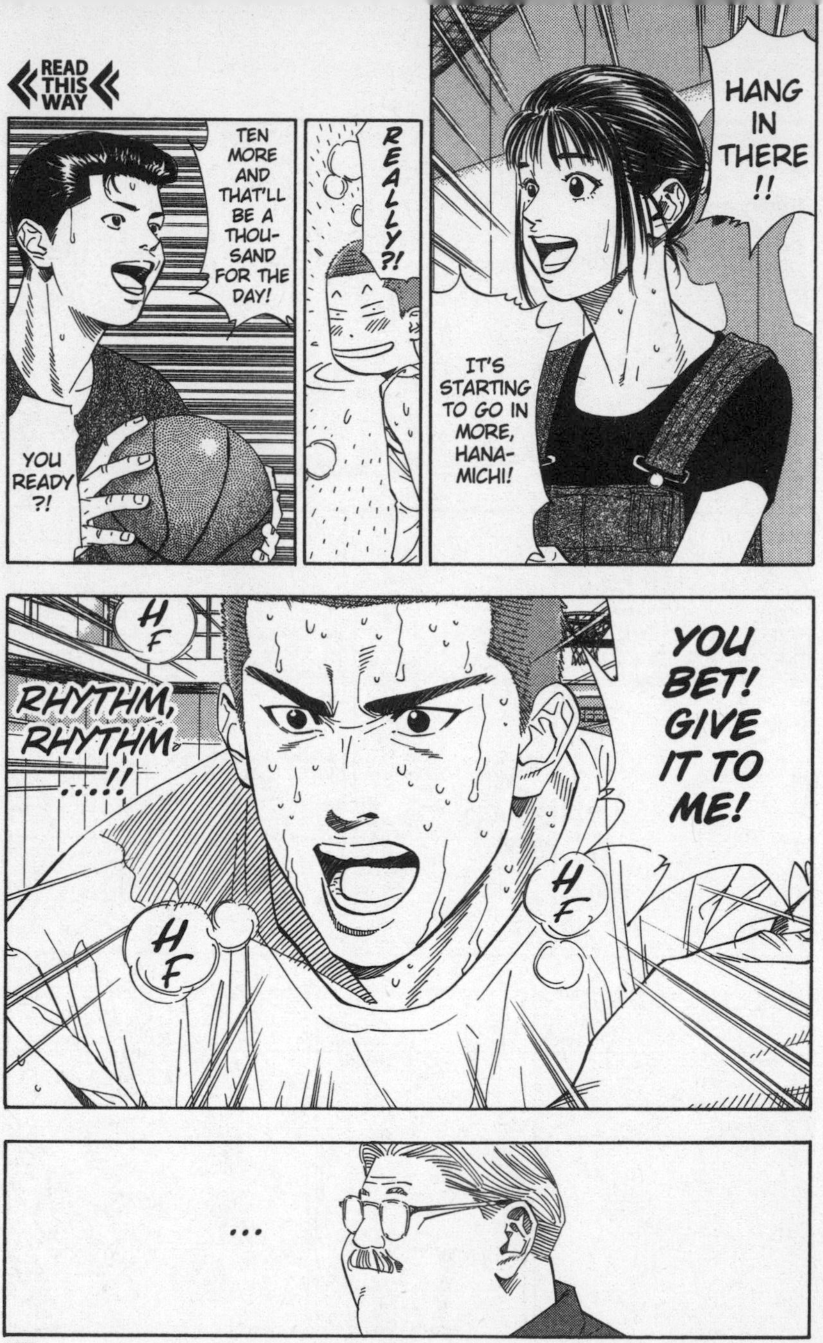
HANG IN THERE!!
IT'S STARTING TO GO IN MORE, HANAMICHI!
REALLY?!
TEN MORE AND THAT'LL BE A THOUSAND FOR THE DAY!
YOU READY?!
YOU BET! GIVE IT TO ME!
HF
HF
RHYTHM, RHYTHM...!!
HF
...

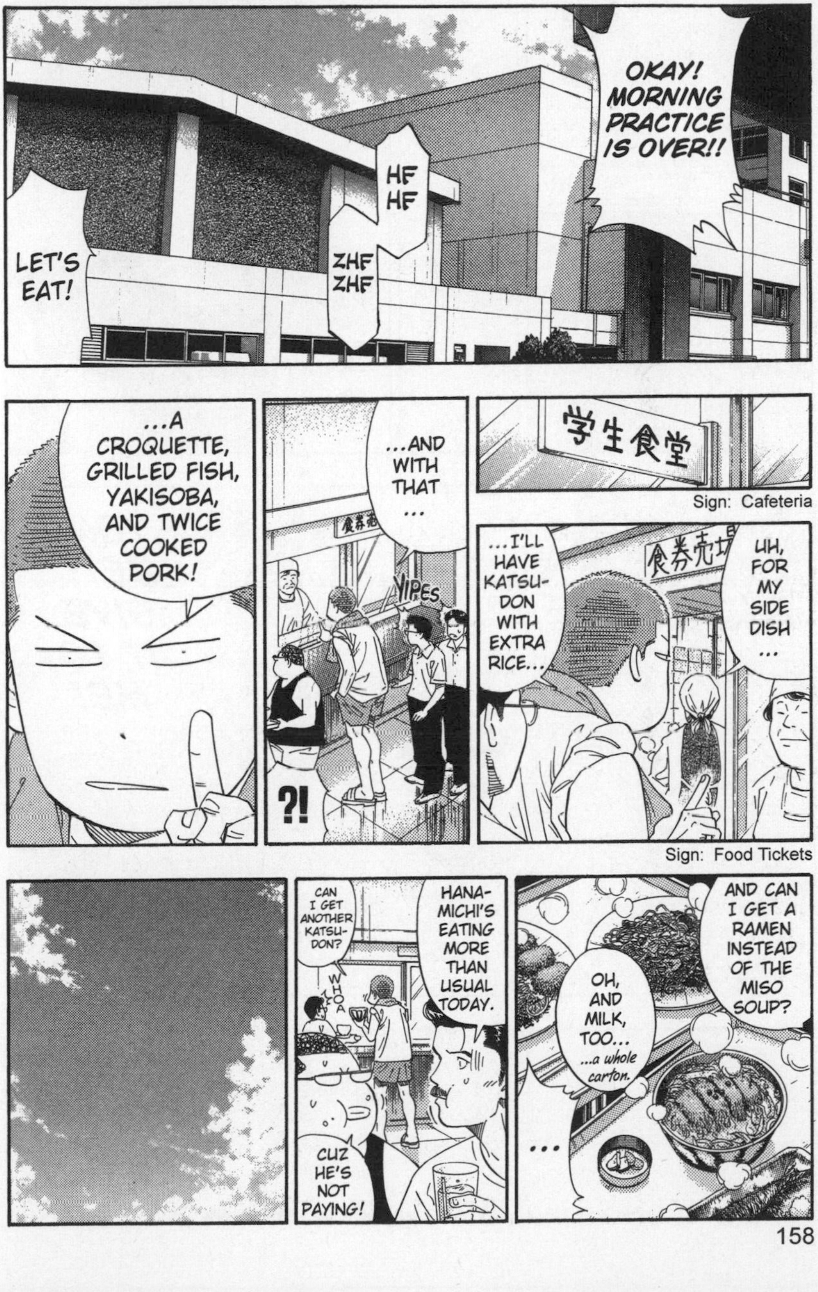
OKAY! MORNING PRACTICE IS OVER!!
HF HF
ZHF ZHF
LET'S EAT!
学生食堂
Sign: Cafeteria
UH, FOR MY SIDE DISH ...
...I'LL HAVE KATSU-DON WITH EXTRA RICE...
食券売場
Sign: Food Tickets
...AND WITH THAT ...
YIPES
?!
...A CROQUETTE, GRILLED FISH, YAKISOBA, AND TWICE COOKED PORK!
AND CAN I GET A RAMEN INSTEAD OF THE MISO SOUP?
OH, AND MILK, TOO... ...a whole carton.
...
HANA-MICHI'S EATING MORE THAN USUAL TODAY.
CAN I GET ANOTHER KATSU-DON?
WHOA
CUZ HE'S NOT PAYING!

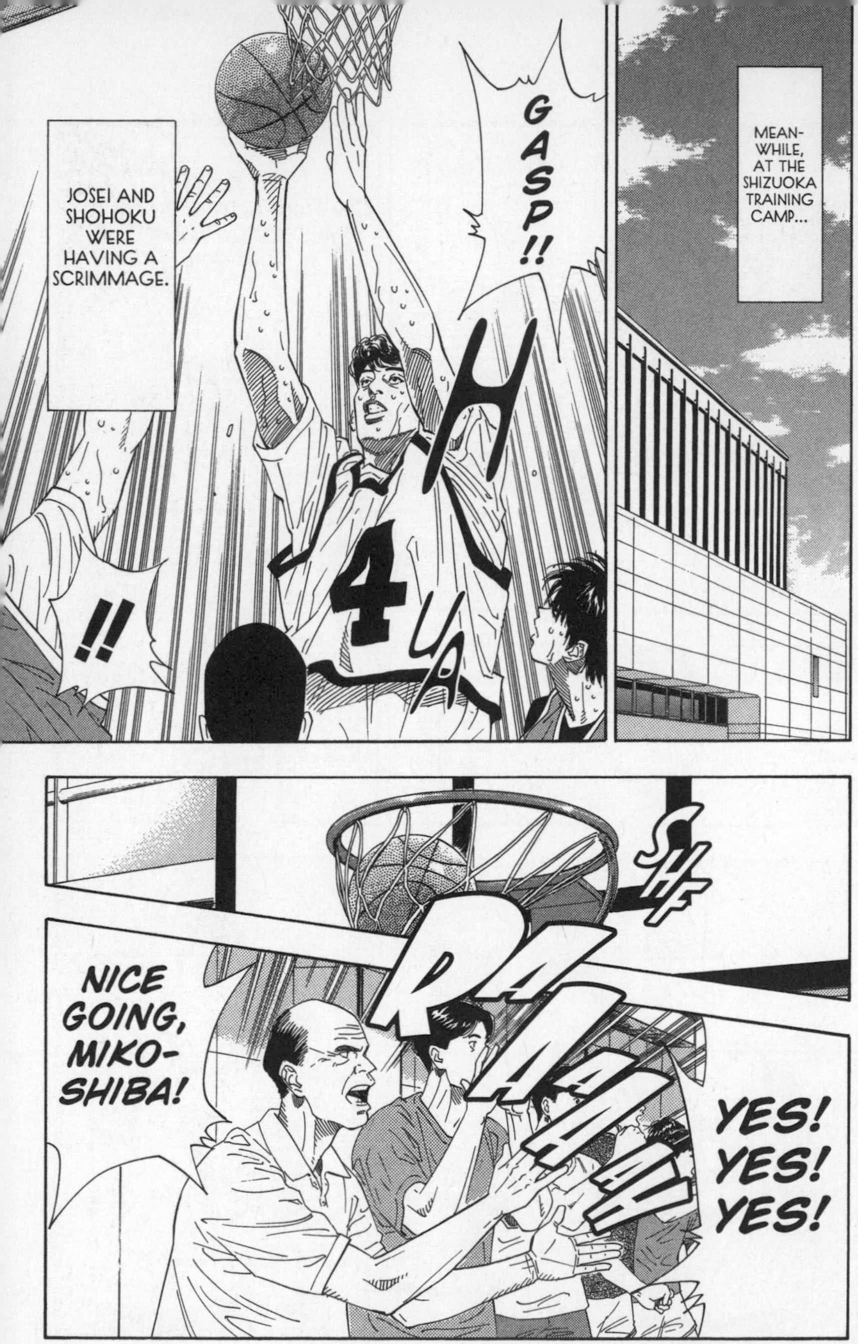
MEAN-WHILE, AT THE SHIZUOKA TRAINING CAMP...
GASP!!
HUA
JOSEI AND SHOHOKU WERE HAVING A SCRIMMAGE.
!!
SHF
DAAAAA
YES! YES! YES!
NICE GOING, MIKO-SHIBA!

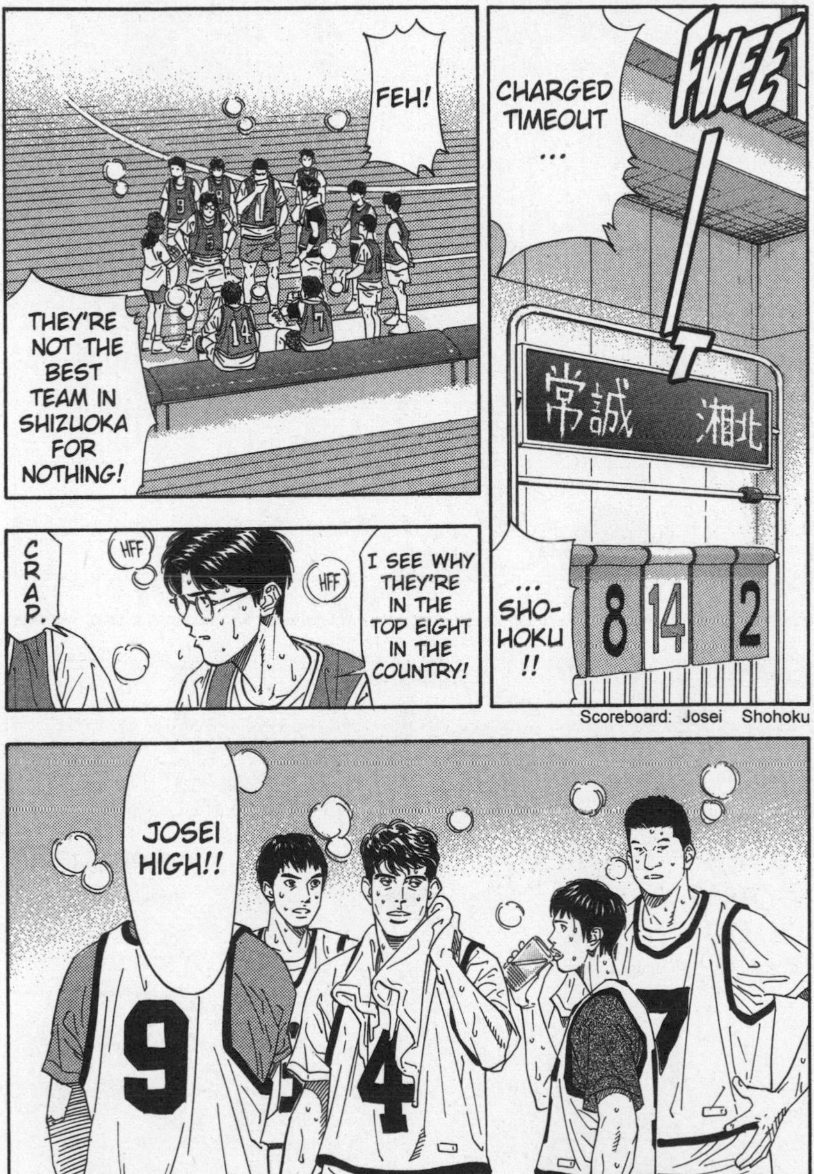
FWEET
CHARGED TIMEOUT ...
常誠 湘北
8 14 2
... SHOHOKU!!
FEH!
THEY'RE NOT THE BEST TEAM IN SHIZUOKA FOR NOTHING!
I SEE WHY THEY'RE IN THE TOP EIGHT IN THE COUNTRY!
HFF
HFF
CRAP.
JOSEI HIGH!!
Scoreboard: Josei Shohoku

READ THIS WAY

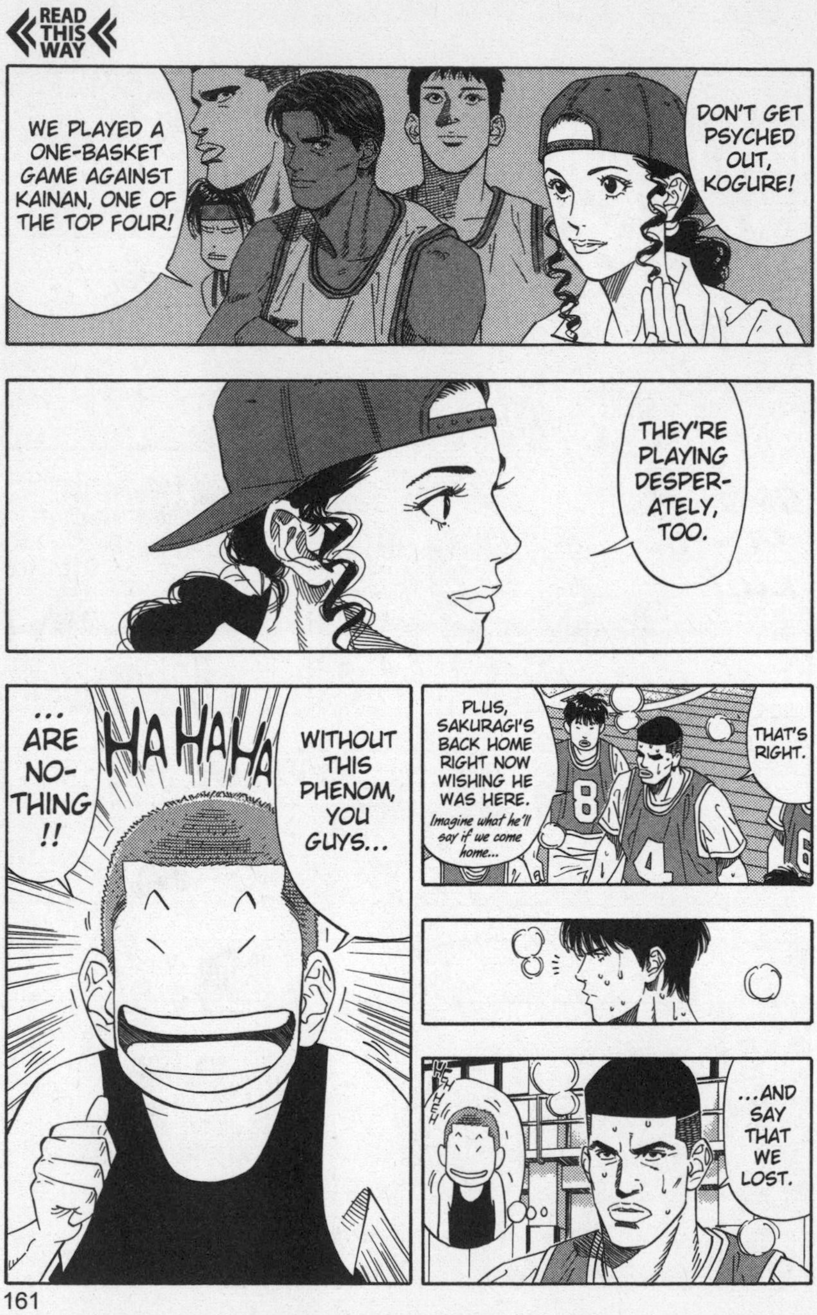
DON'T GET PSYCHED OUT, KOGURE!
WE PLAYED A ONE-BASKET GAME AGAINST KAINAN, ONE OF THE TOP FOUR!
THEY'RE PLAYING DESPER-ATELY, TOO.
THAT'S RIGHT.
PLUS, SAKURAGI'S BACK HOME RIGHT NOW WISHING HE WAS HERE.
Imagine what he'll say if we come home...
HEH HEH
...AND SAY THAT WE LOST.
WITHOUT THIS PHENOM, YOU GUYS...
HA HA HA
...ARE NO-THING!!

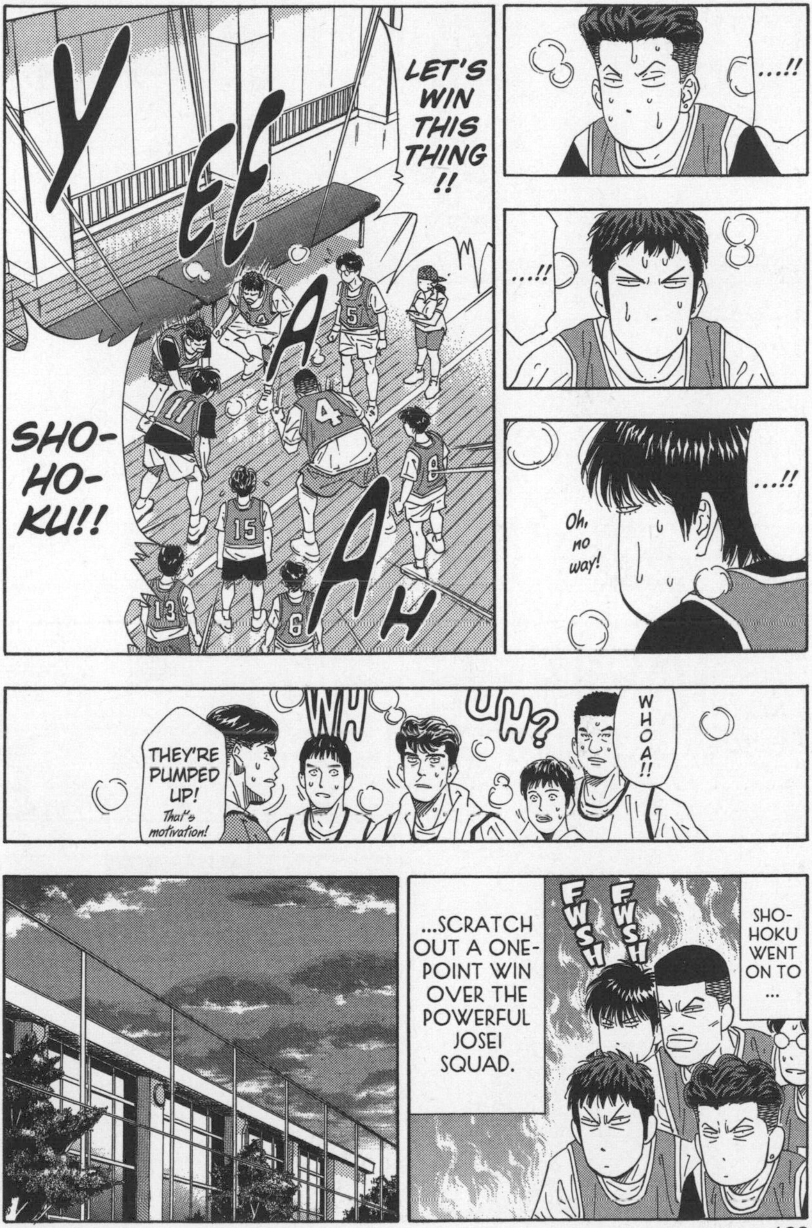
...!!
...!!
...!!
Oh, no way!
LET'S WIN THIS THING!!
YEEAAAH
SHO-HO-KU!!
WHOA!!
UH?
WH
THEY'RE PUMPED UP!
That's motivation!
SHO-HOKU WENT ON TO ...
FWSH
FWSH
...SCRATCH OUT A ONE-POINT WIN OVER THE POWERFUL JOSEI SQUAD.

READ THIS WAY

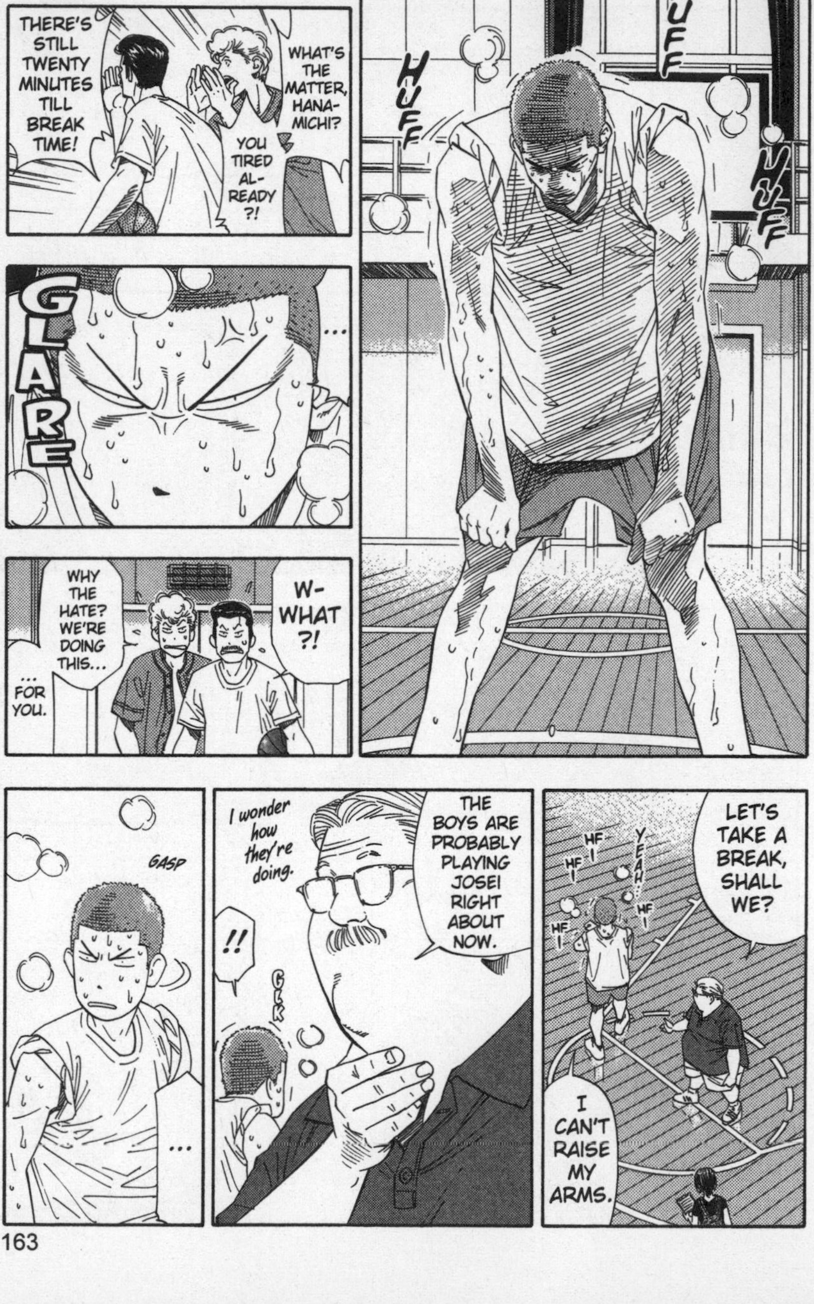

HUFF
HUFF
HUFF
HUFF
WHAT'S THE MATTER, HANA-MICHI?
YOU TIRED AL-READY?!
THERE'S STILL TWENTY MINUTES TILL BREAK TIME!
...
GLARE
W-WHAT?!
WHY THE HATE? WE'RE DOING THIS...
...FOR YOU.
LET'S TAKE A BREAK, SHALL WE?
HF
HF
YEAH...
HF
HF
I CAN'T RAISE MY ARMS.
THE BOYS ARE PROBABLY PLAYING JOSEI RIGHT ABOUT NOW.
I wonder how they're doing.
!!
GLK
GASP
...

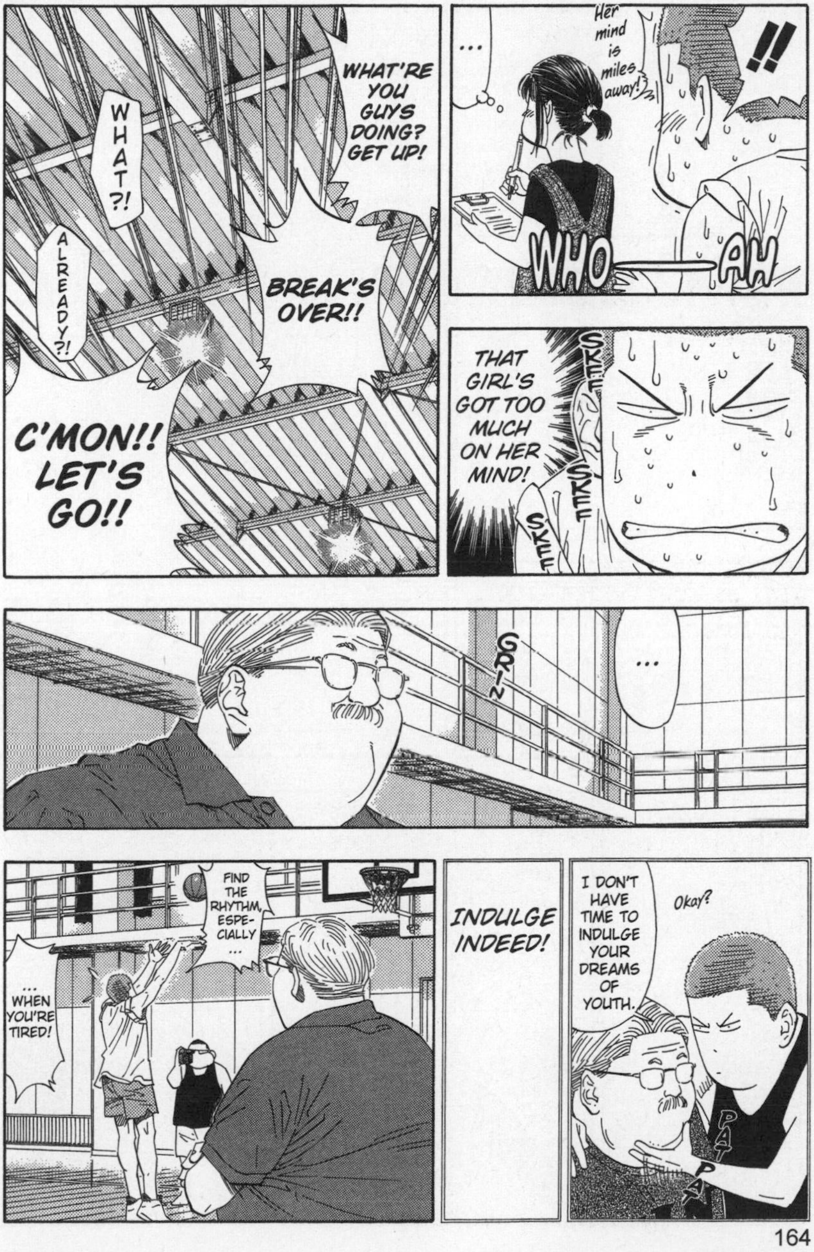
...
Her mind is miles away!
!!
WHO—AH
THAT GIRL'S GOT TOO MUCH ON HER MIND!
SKEF
SKEF
SKEF
WHAT'RE YOU GUYS DOING? GET UP!
BREAK'S OVER!!
WHAT?!
ALREADY?!
C'MON!! LET'S GO!!
...
GRIN
Okay?
I DON'T HAVE TIME TO INDULGE YOUR DREAMS OF YOUTH.
PAT
PAT
INDULGE INDEED!
FIND THE RHYTHM, ESPECIALLY ...
... WHEN YOU'RE TIRED!

READ THIS WAY

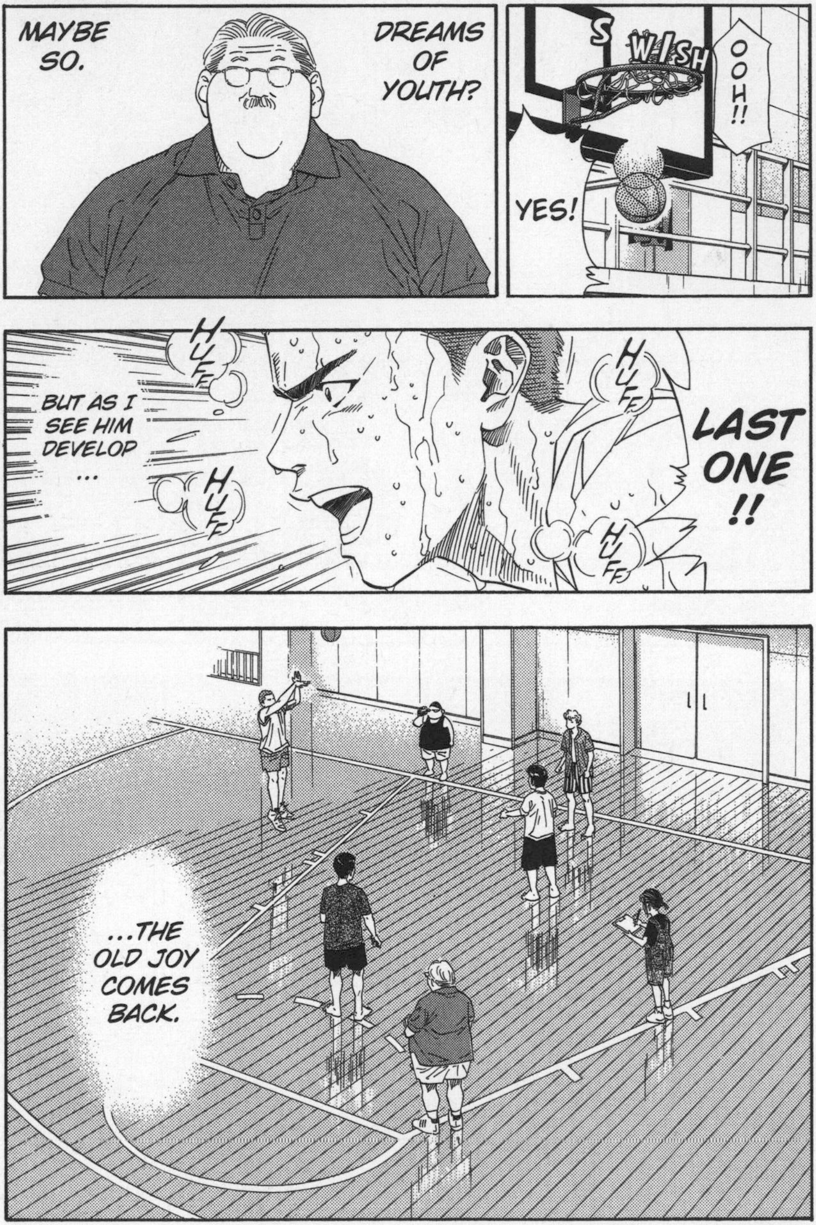
SWISH
OOH!!
YES!
DREAMS OF YOUTH?
MAYBE SO.
LAST ONE!!
HUFF
HUFF
HUFF
HUFF
BUT AS I SEE HIM DEVELOP...
...THE OLD JOY COMES BACK.

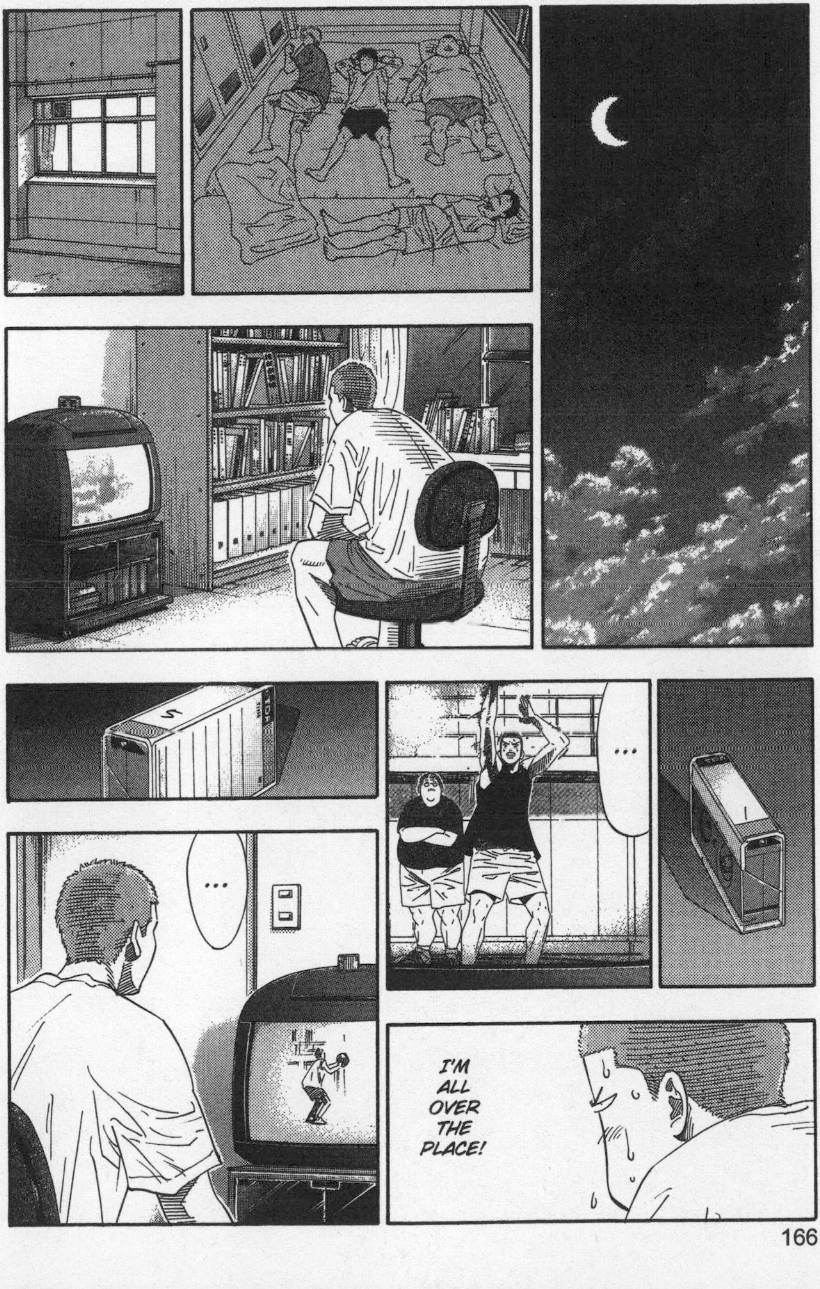
...
...
I'M ALL OVER THE PLACE!

READ THIS WAY

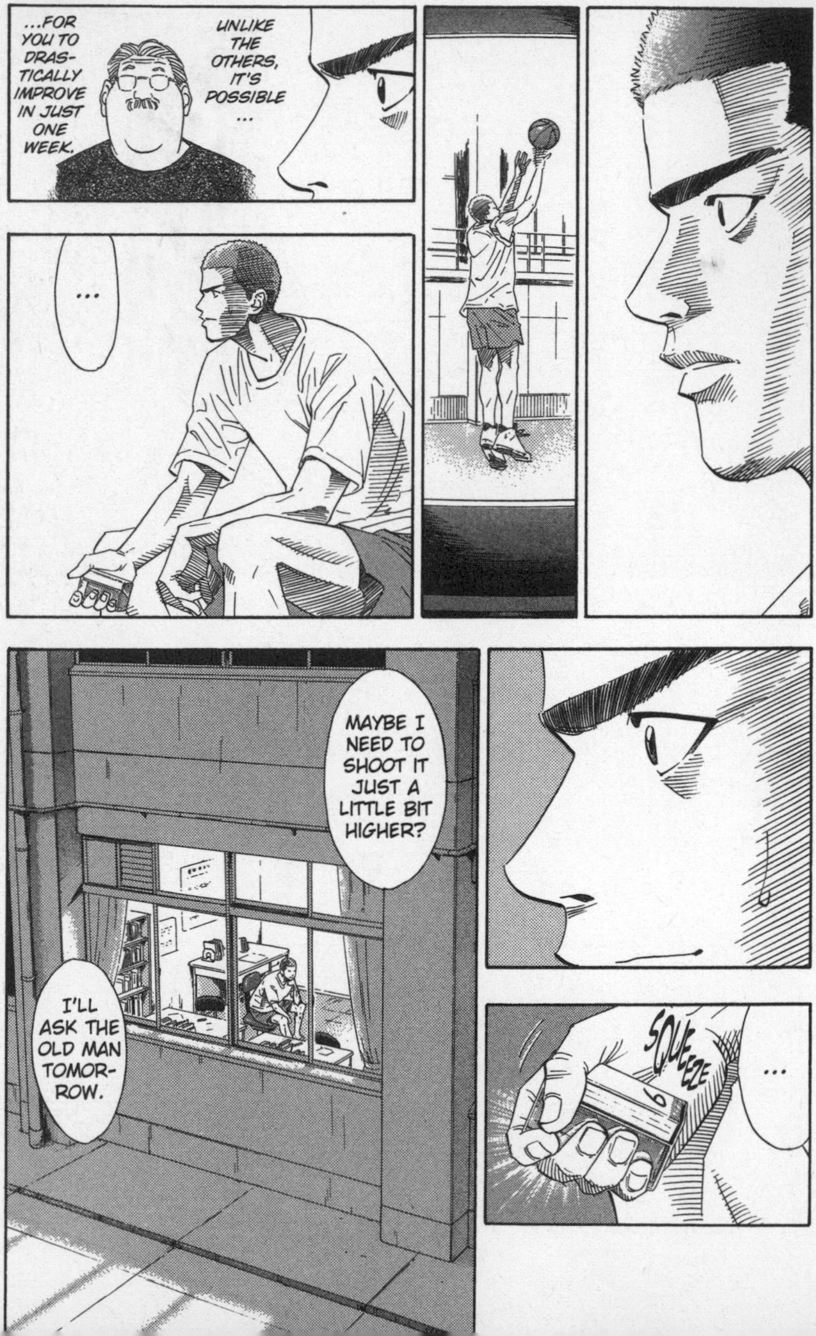
UNLIKE THE OTHERS, IT'S POSSIBLE ...
...FOR YOU TO DRAS-TICALLY IMPROVE IN JUST ONE WEEK.
...
SQUEEZE
...
MAYBE I NEED TO SHOOT IT JUST A LITTLE BIT HIGHER?
I'LL ASK THE OLD MAN TOMOR-ROW.

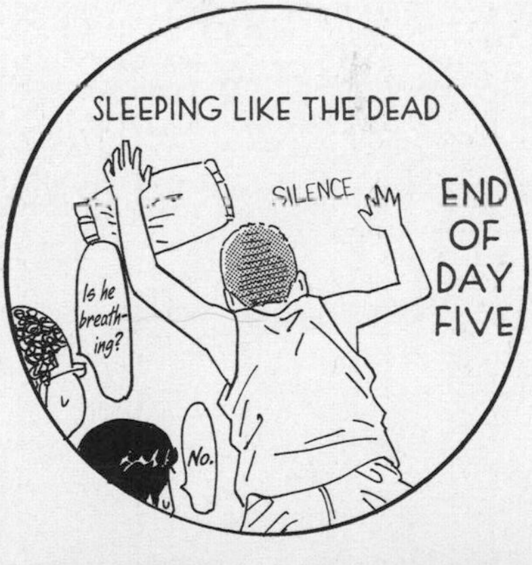
SLEEPING LIKE THE DEAD
END OF DAY FIVE
SILENCE
Is he breathing?
No.

SLAM DUNK

BRAND-NEW SHOES

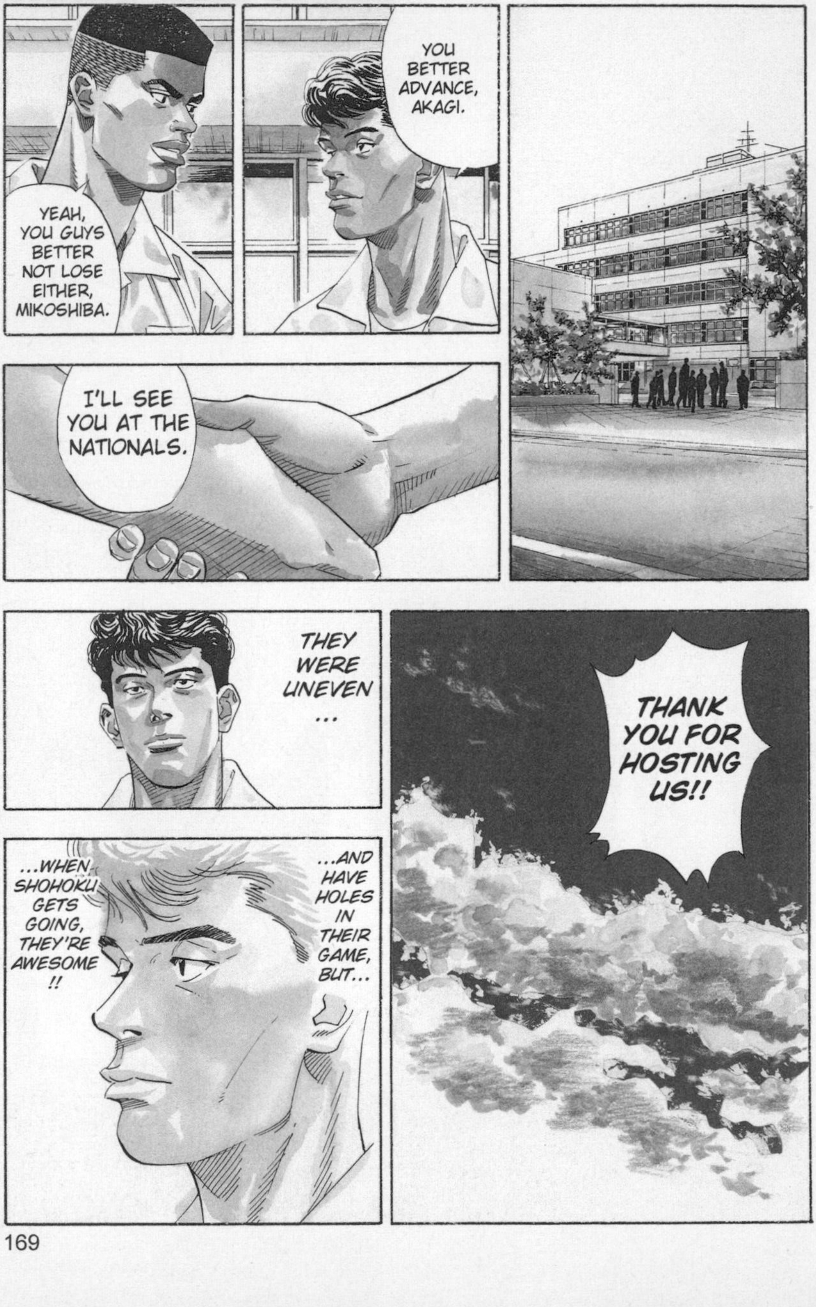
YOU BETTER ADVANCE, AKAGI.
YEAH, YOU GUYS BETTER NOT LOSE EITHER, MIKOSHIBA.
I'LL SEE YOU AT THE NATIONALS.
THANK YOU FOR HOSTING US!!
THEY WERE UNEVEN ...
...AND HAVE HOLES IN THEIR GAME, BUT...
...WHEN SHOHOKU GETS GOING, THEY'RE AWESOME !!

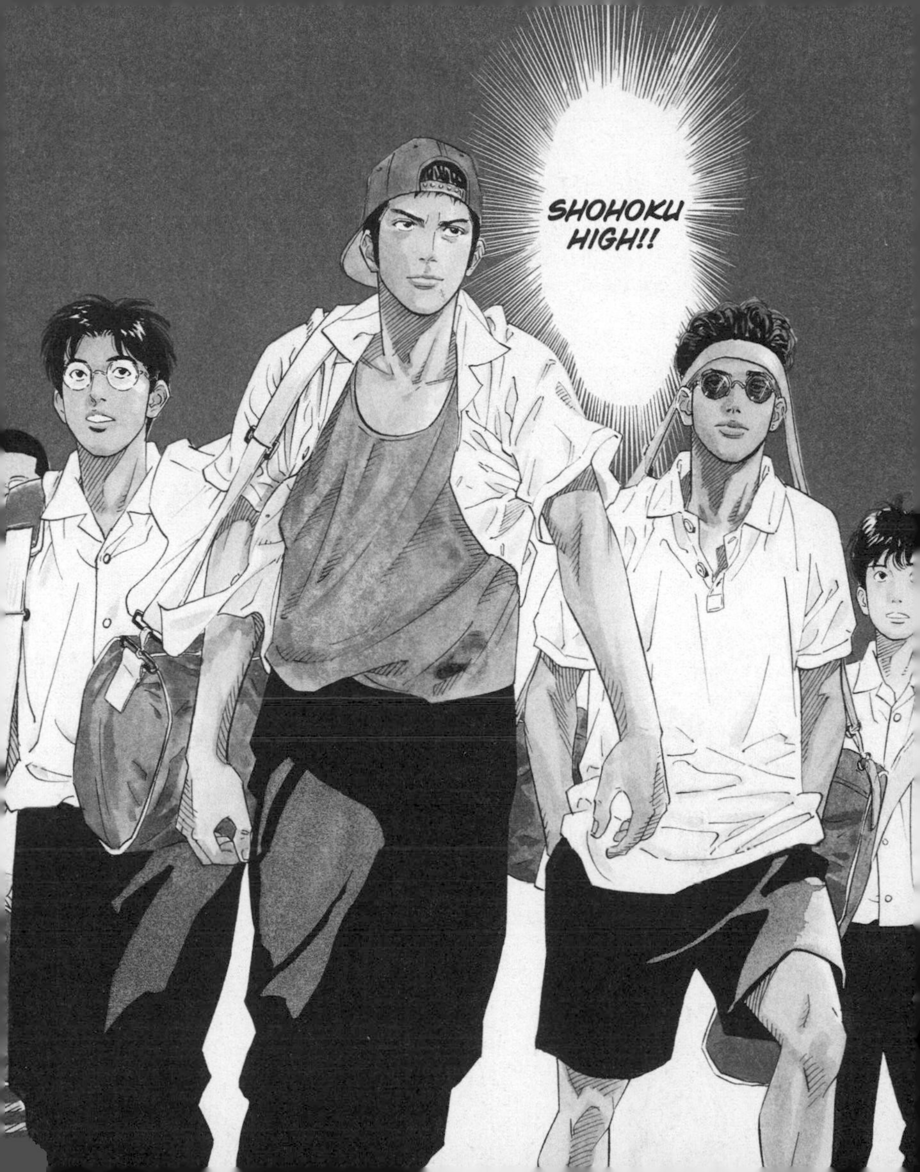
SHOHOKU
HIGH!!

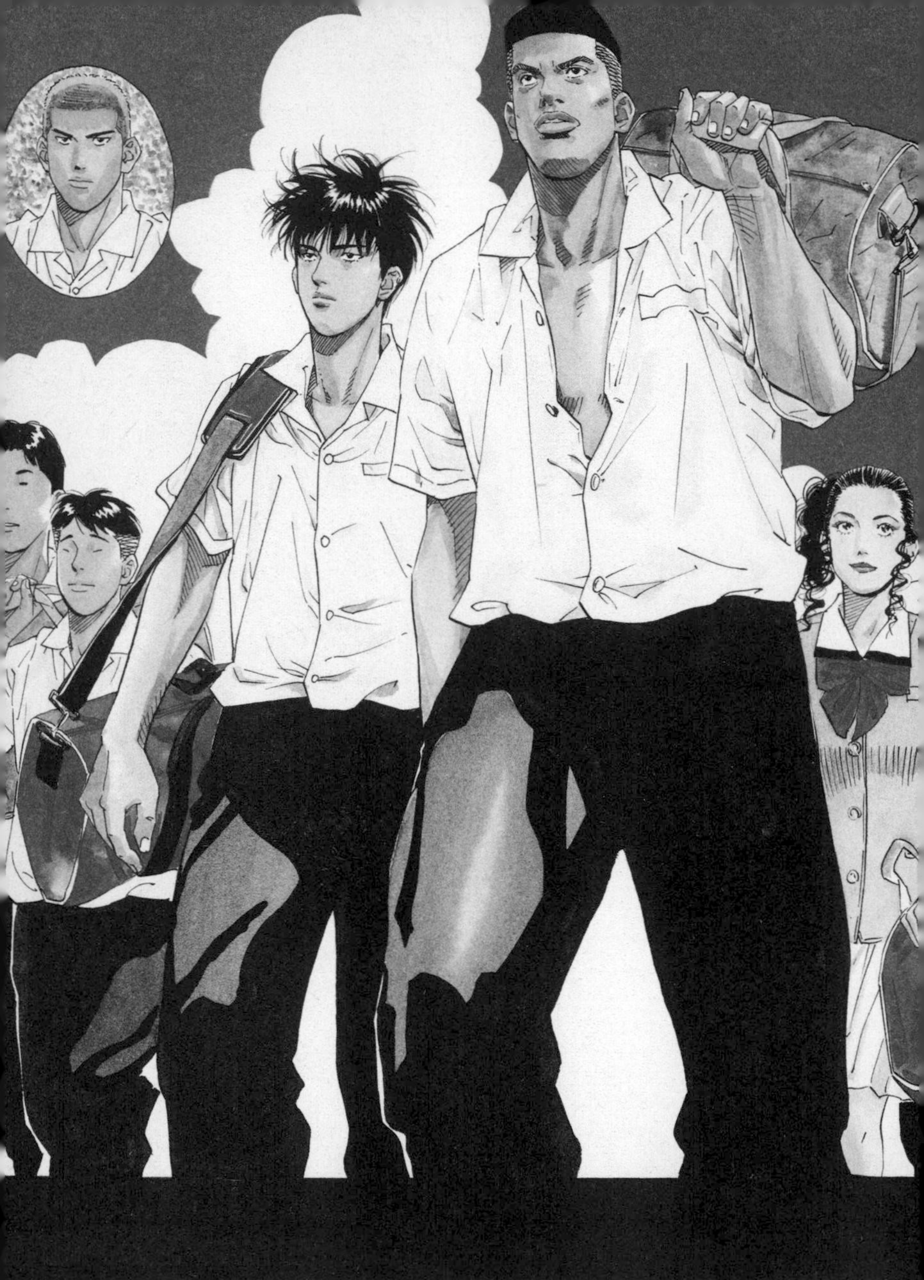

#197 BRAND-NEW SHOES

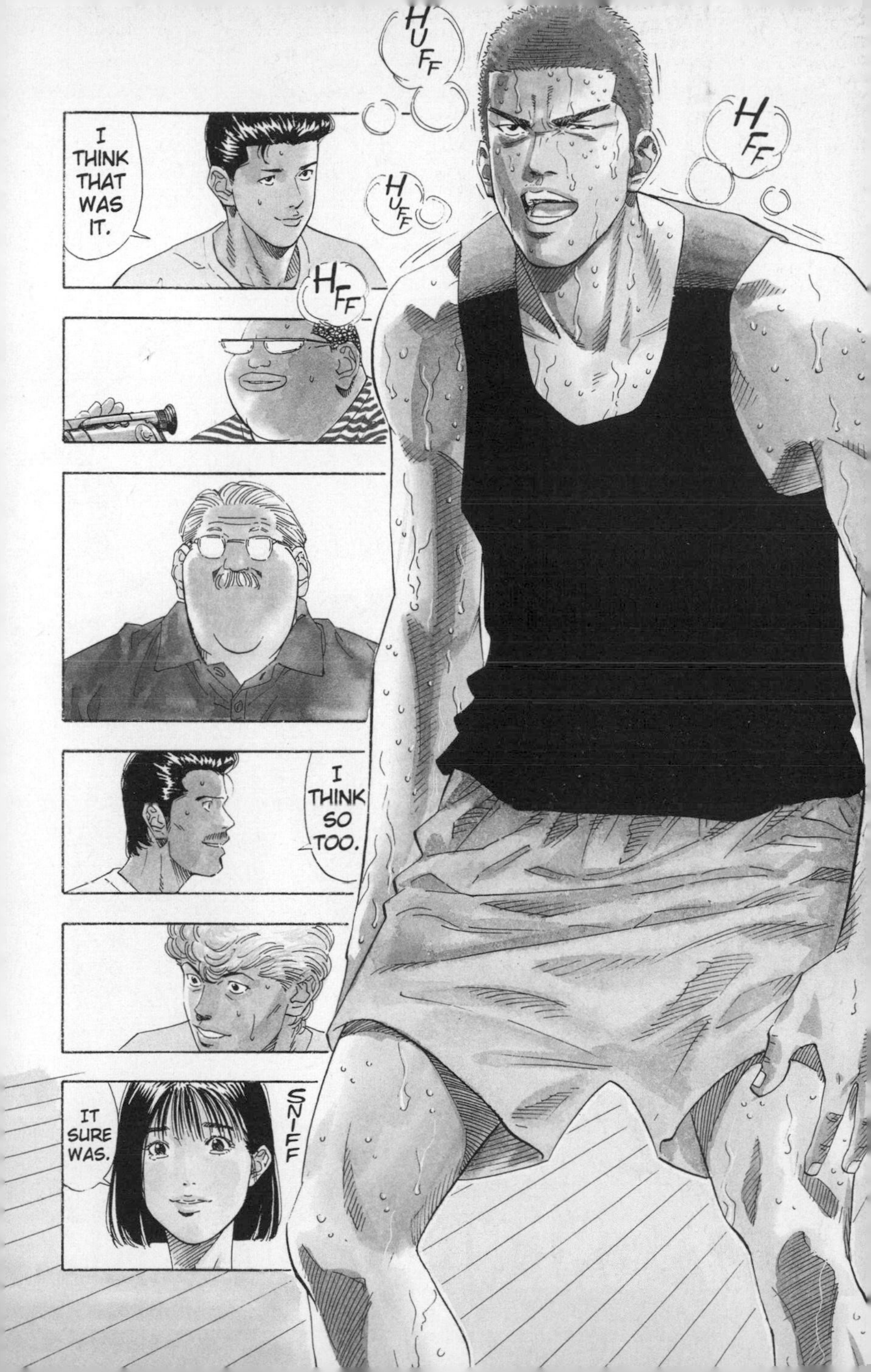
HUFF
HFF
HUFF
HFF
I THINK THAT WAS IT.
I THINK SO TOO.
SNIFF
IT SURE WAS.

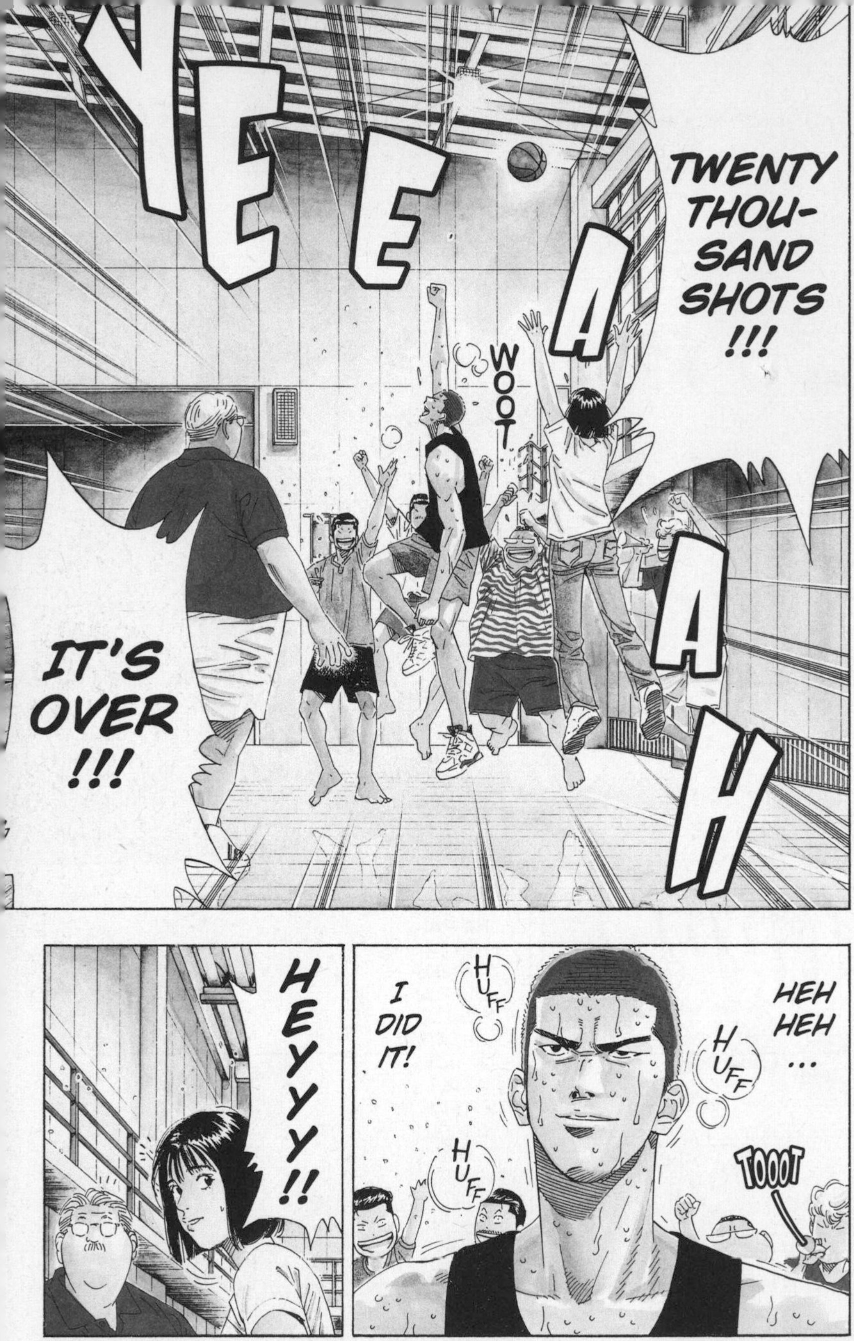
TWENTY THOUSAND SHOTS!!!
YEEAAAH
WOOT
IT'S OVER!!!
HEH HEH...
HUFF
HUFF
I DID IT!
HUFF
TOOOT
HEYYY!!

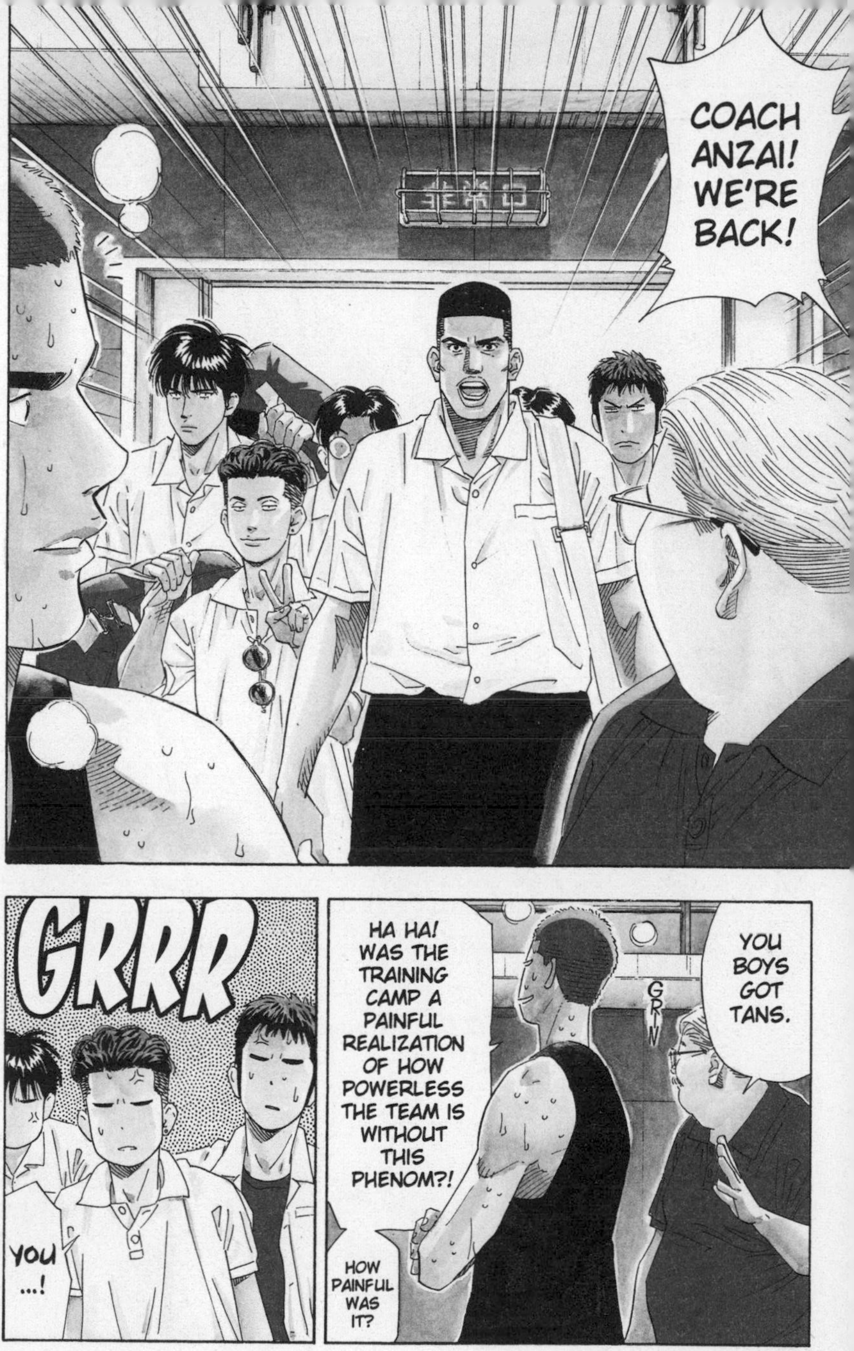
COACH ANZAI! WE'RE BACK!
YOU BOYS GOT TANS.
GRIN
HA HA! WAS THE TRAINING CAMP A PAINFUL REALIZATION OF HOW POWERLESS THE TEAM IS WITHOUT THIS PHENOM?!
HOW PAINFUL WAS IT?
GRRR
YOU ...!

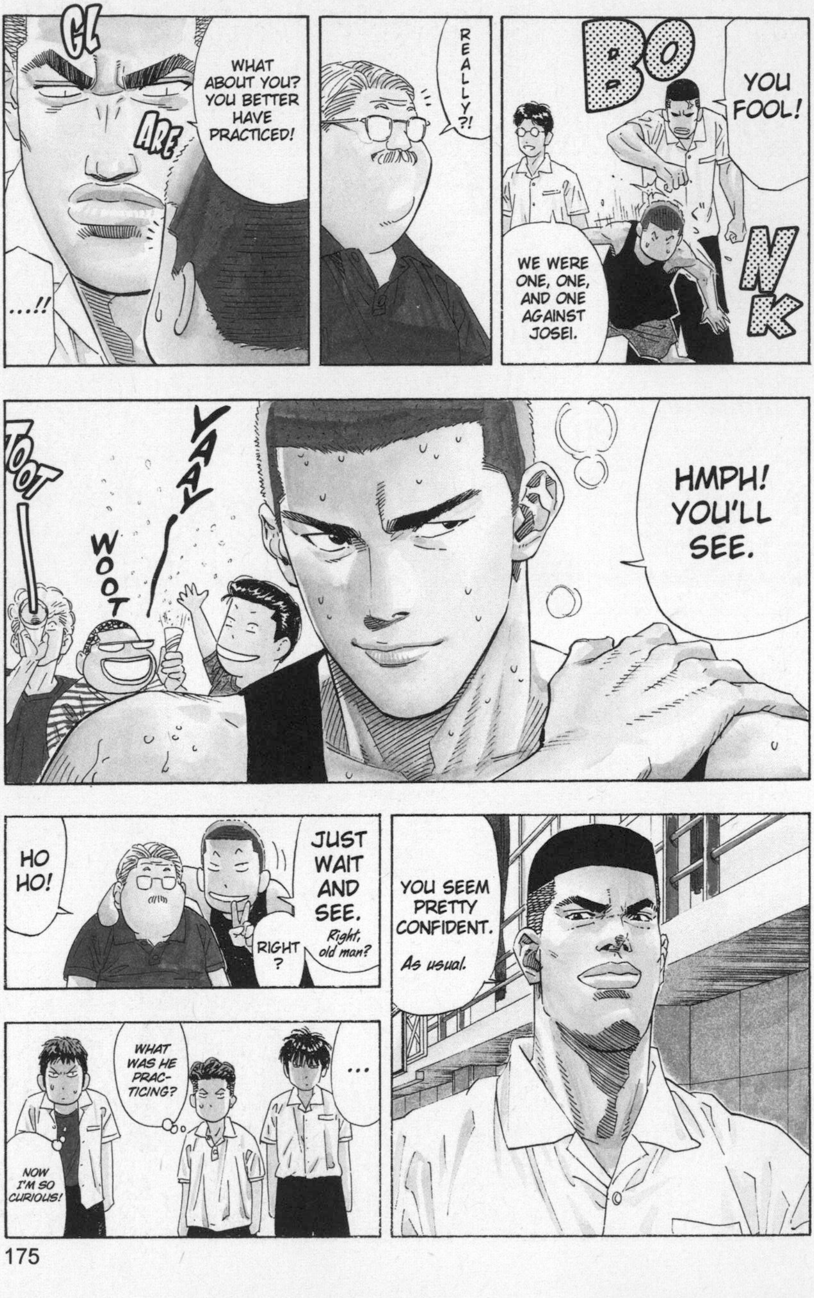
YOU FOOL!
BO
NK
WE WERE ONE, ONE, AND ONE AGAINST JOSEI.
REALLY?!
GL
WHAT ABOUT YOU? YOU BETTER HAVE PRACTICED!
ARE
...!!
HMPH! YOU'LL SEE.
YAAAY
WOOT
TOOT
YOU SEEM PRETTY CONFIDENT.
As usual.
JUST WAIT AND SEE.
Right, old man?
RIGHT?
HO HO!
...
WHAT WAS HE PRAC-TICING?
NOW I'M SO CURIOUS!

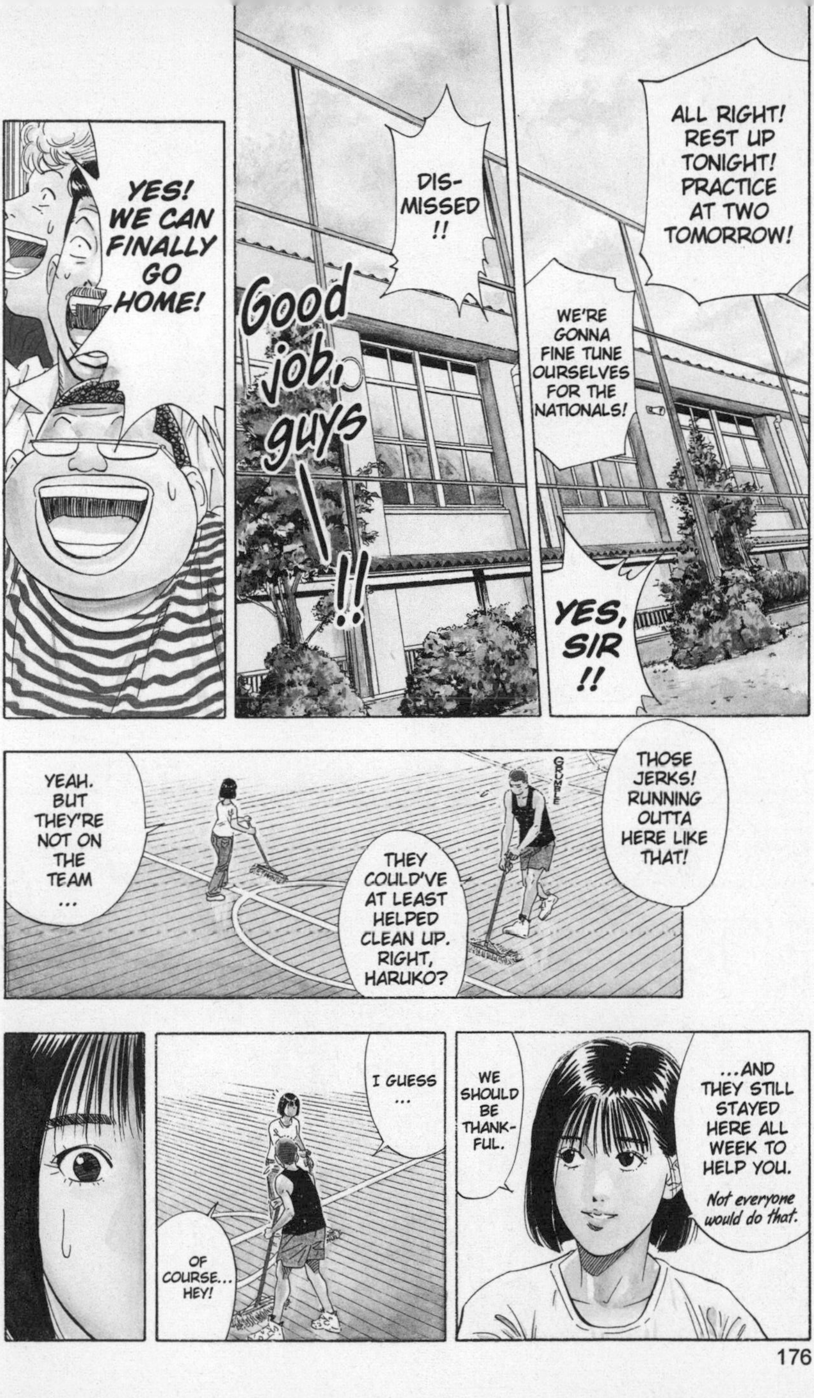
ALL RIGHT! REST UP TONIGHT! PRACTICE AT TWO TOMORROW!
WE'RE GONNA FINE TUNE OURSELVES FOR THE NATIONALS!
YES, SIR !!
DIS-MISSED !!
Good job, guys — !!
YES! WE CAN FINALLY GO HOME!
THOSE JERKS! RUNNING OUTTA HERE LIKE THAT!
GRUMBLE
THEY COULD'VE AT LEAST HELPED CLEAN UP. RIGHT, HARUKO?
YEAH. BUT THEY'RE NOT ON THE TEAM ...
...AND THEY STILL STAYED HERE ALL WEEK TO HELP YOU.
Not everyone would do that.
WE SHOULD BE THANK-FUL.
I GUESS ...
OF COURSE... HEY!

READ THIS WAY

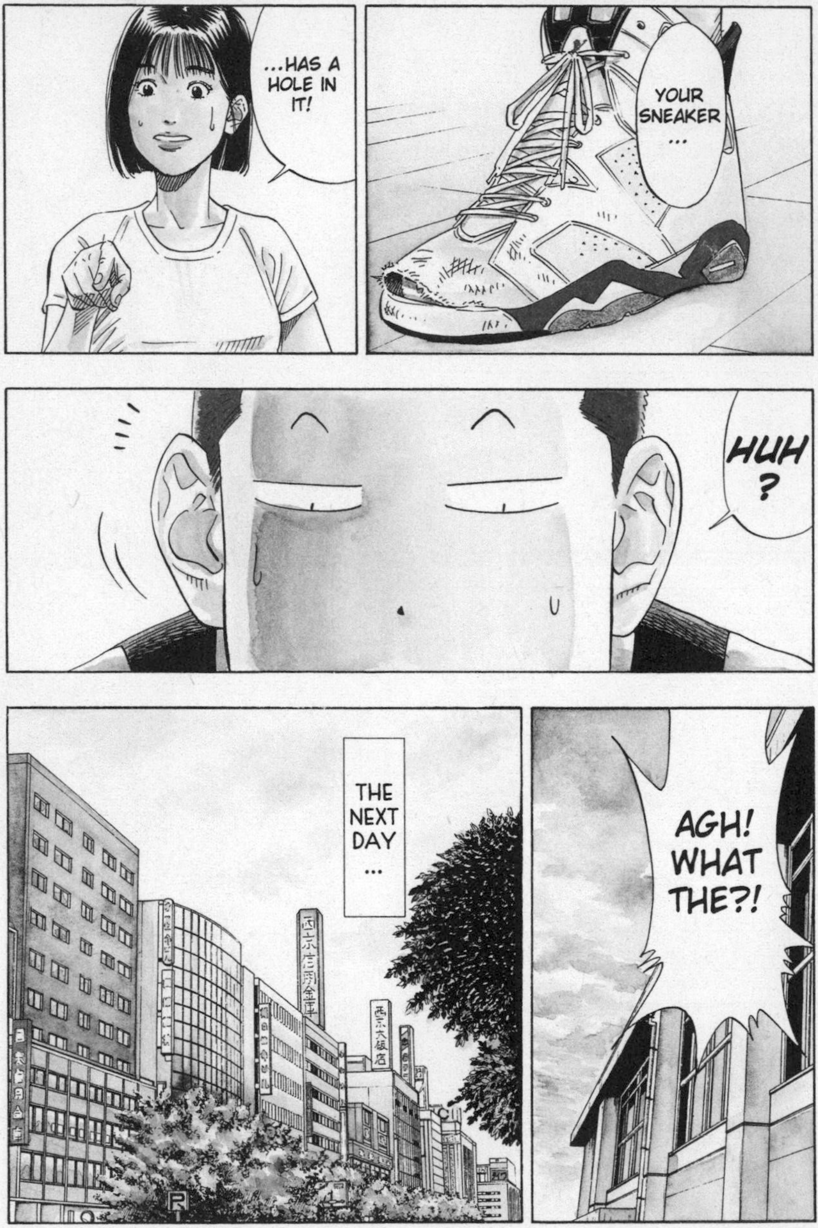
YOUR SNEAKER ...
...HAS A HOLE IN IT!
HUH ?
AGH! WHAT THE?!
THE NEXT DAY ...

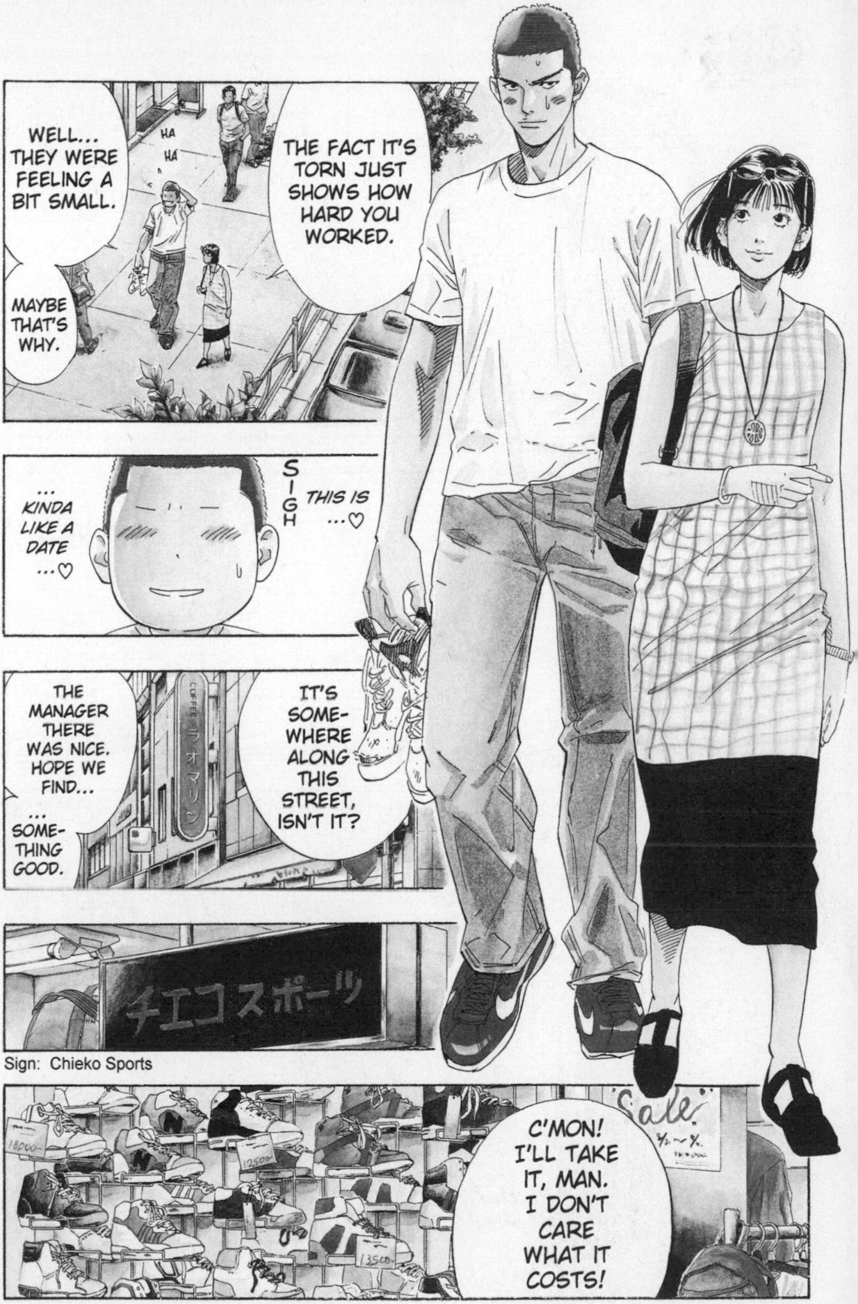
THE FACT IT'S TORN JUST SHOWS HOW HARD YOU WORKED.
WELL... THEY WERE FEELING A BIT SMALL.
HA HA
MAYBE THAT'S WHY.
SIGH
THIS IS ...♡
... KINDA LIKE A DATE ...♡
IT'S SOME-WHERE ALONG THIS STREET, ISN'T IT?
THE MANAGER THERE WAS NICE. HOPE WE FIND...
... SOME-THING GOOD.
COFFEE
チエコスポーツ
Sale
C'MON! I'LL TAKE IT, MAN. I DON'T CARE WHAT IT COSTS!

Sign: Chieko Sports

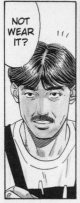

NOT WEAR IT?

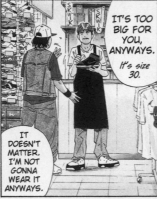

IT'S TOO BIG FOR YOU, ANYWAYS.

It's size 30.

IT DOESN'T MATTER. I'M NOT GONNA WEAR IT ANYWAYS.

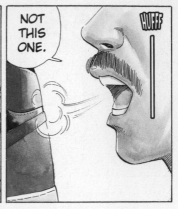

NOT THIS ONE.

HUFF

THAT COLOR'S THE LAST ONE I'M MISSING. SO PLEASE!

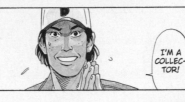

I'M A COLLEC- TOR!

I GOT EVERY JORDAN SERIES IN EVERY COLOR.

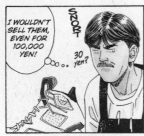

I WOULDN'T SELL THEM, EVEN FOR 100,000 YEN!

SNORT

30 yen?

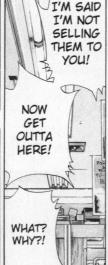

I'M SAID I'M NOT SELLING THEM TO YOU!

NOW GET OUTTA HERE!

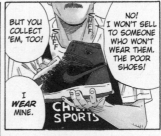

BUT YOU COLLECT 'EM, TOO!

I WEAR MINE.

NO! I WON'T SELL TO SOMEONE WHO WON'T WEAR THEM. THE POOR SHOES!

CHIEF SPORTS

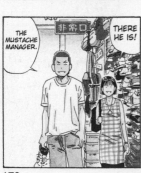

THE MUSTACHE MANAGER.

THERE HE IS!

WHAT? WHY?!

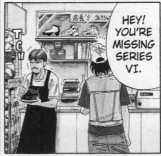

HEY! YOU'RE MISSING SERIES VI.

179

Case: Manager's Collection

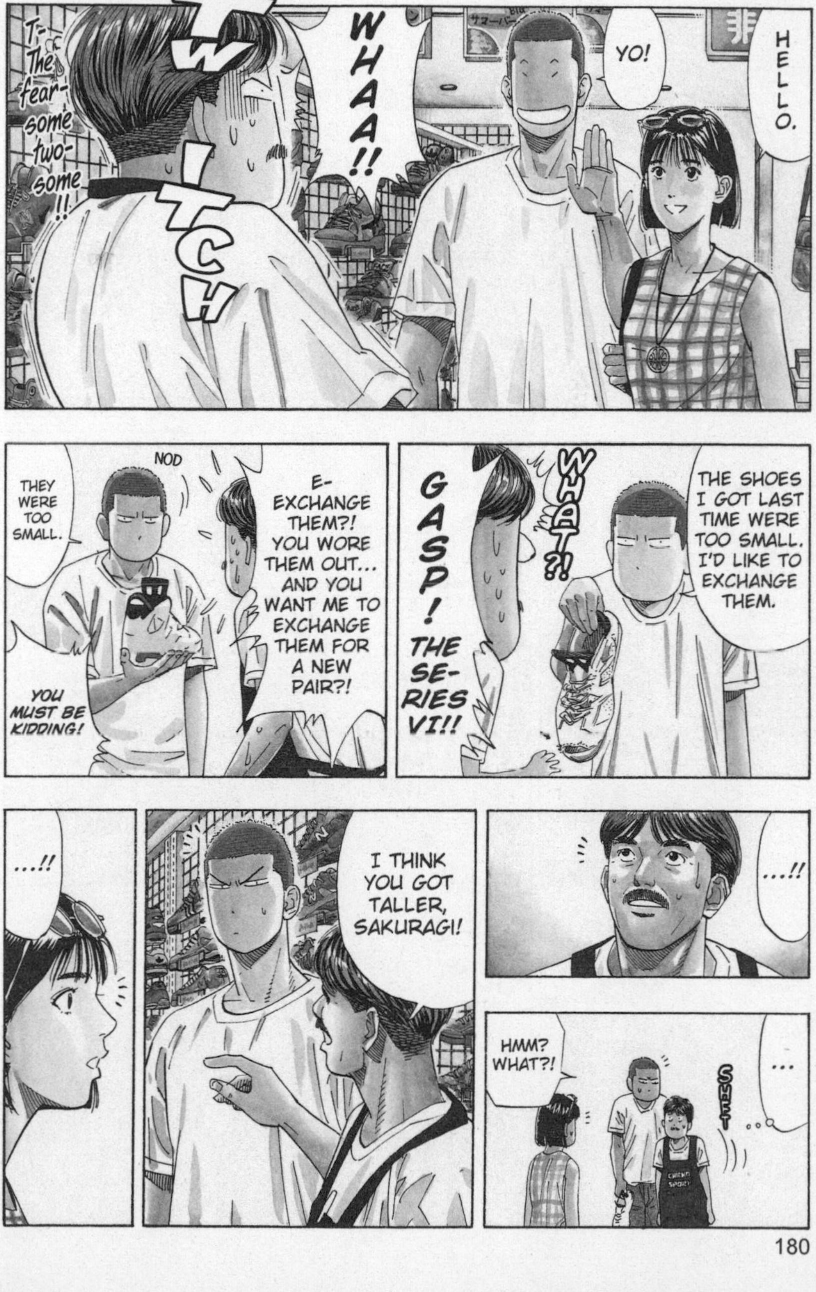
HELLO.
YO!
WHAAA!!
TWITCH
T-The fear-some two-some!!
THE SHOES I GOT LAST TIME WERE TOO SMALL. I'D LIKE TO EXCHANGE THEM.
WHAT?!
GASP!
THE SE-RIES VI!!
E-EXCHANGE THEM?! YOU WORE THEM OUT... AND YOU WANT ME TO EXCHANGE THEM FOR A NEW PAIR?!
NOD
THEY WERE TOO SMALL.
YOU MUST BE KIDDING!
...!!
...
HMM? WHAT?!
I THINK YOU GOT TALLER, SAKURAGI!
...!!

READ THIS WAY

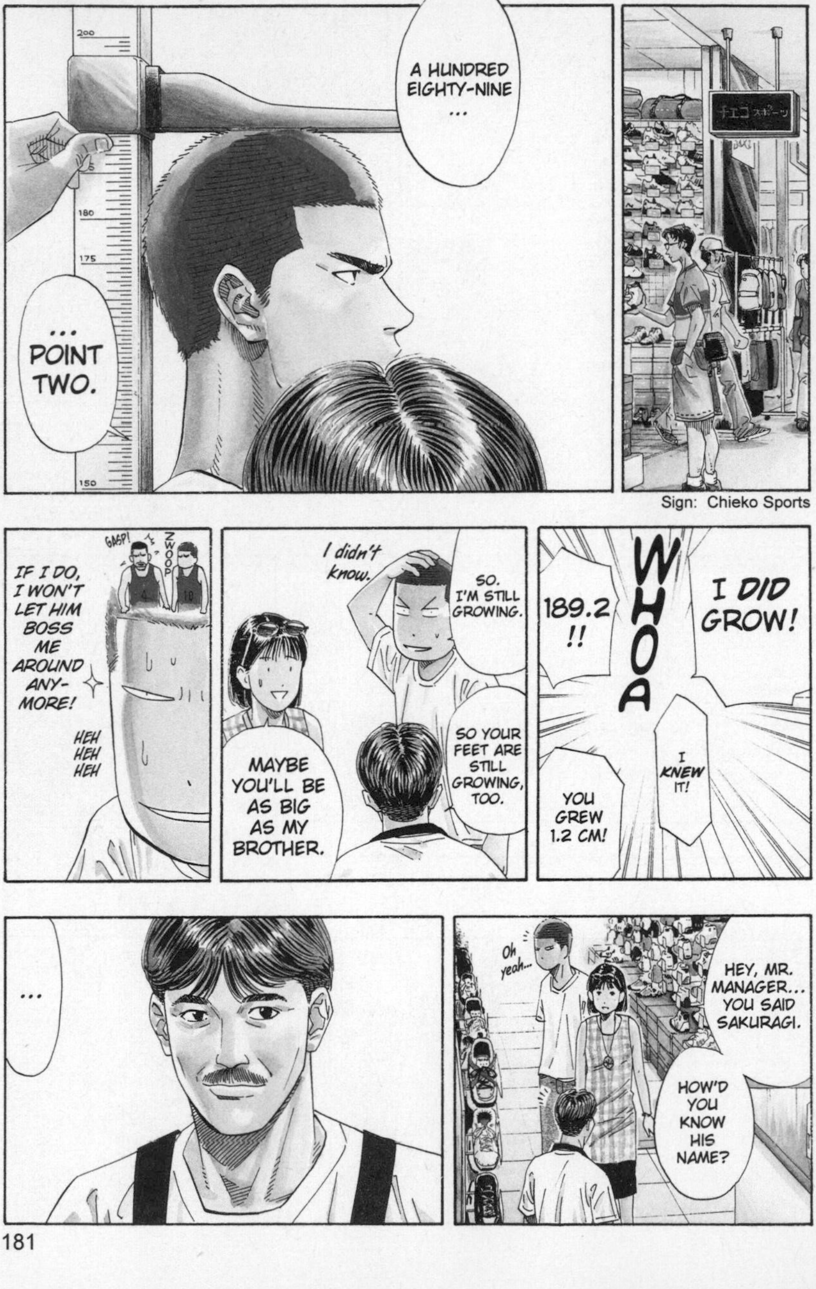

A HUNDRED EIGHTY-NINE ...
... POINT TWO.
I DID GROW!
WHOA
189.2 !!
I KNEW IT!
YOU GREW 1.2 CM!
SO. I'M STILL GROWING.
I didn't know.
SO YOUR FEET ARE STILL GROWING, TOO.
MAYBE YOU'LL BE AS BIG AS MY BROTHER.
GASP!
ZWOOP
IF I DO, I WON'T LET HIM BOSS ME AROUND ANY-MORE!
HEH HEH HEH
HEY, MR. MANAGER... YOU SAID SAKURAGI.
Oh yeah...
HOW'D YOU KNOW HIS NAME?
...

Sign: Chieko Sports

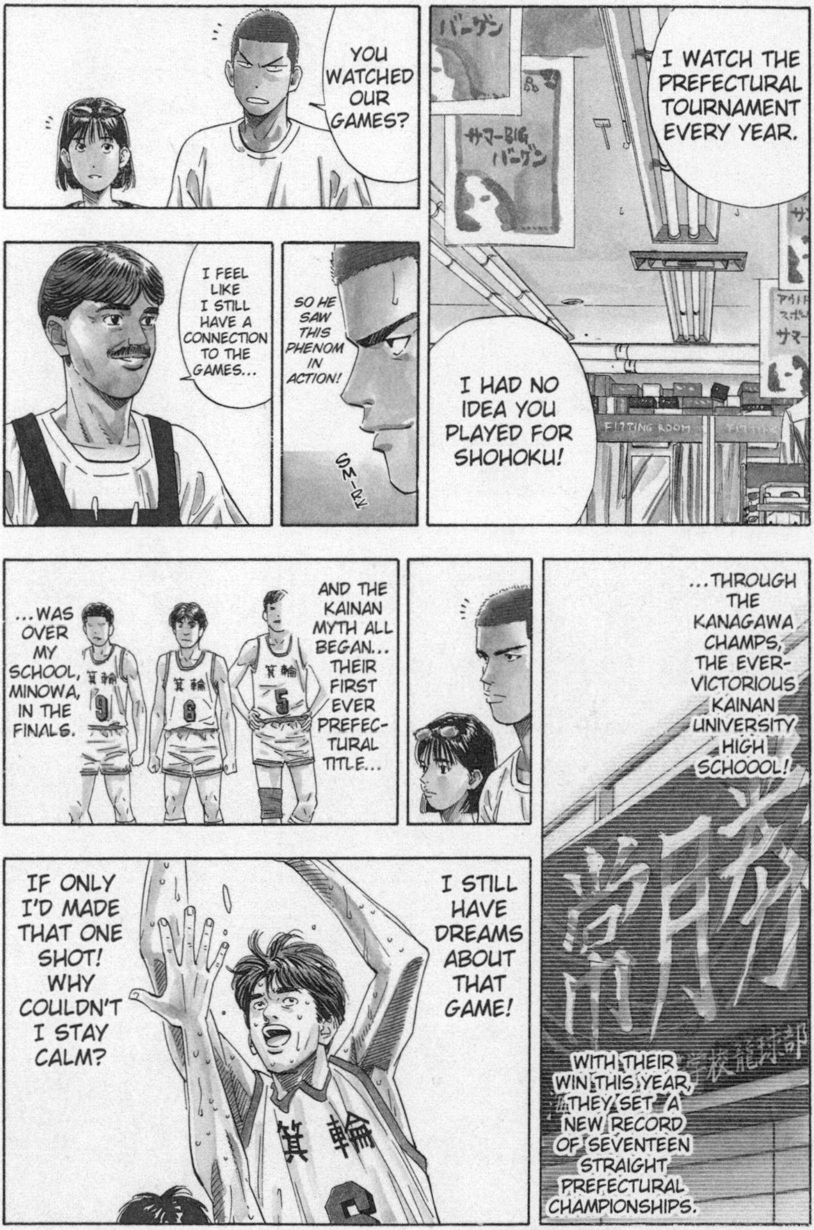
I WATCH THE PREFECTURAL TOURNAMENT EVERY YEAR.
I HAD NO IDEA YOU PLAYED FOR SHOHOKU!
YOU WATCHED OUR GAMES?
SO HE SAW THIS PHENOM IN ACTION!
SMIRK
I FEEL LIKE I STILL HAVE A CONNECTION TO THE GAMES...
...THROUGH THE KANAGAWA CHAMPS, THE EVER-VICTORIOUS KAINAN UNIVERSITY HIGH SCHOOOL!
WITH THEIR WIN THIS YEAR, THEY SET A NEW RECORD OF SEVENTEEN STRAIGHT PREFECTURAL CHAMPIONSHIPS.
AND THE KAINAN MYTH ALL BEGAN... THEIR FIRST EVER PREFECTURAL TITLE...
...WAS OVER MY SCHOOL, MINOWA, IN THE FINALS.
I STILL HAVE DREAMS ABOUT THAT GAME!
IF ONLY I'D MADE THAT ONE SHOT! WHY COULDN'T I STAY CALM?

Banner: *Josho* (ever victorious)
Kainan Dai Fuzoku High School Basketball Team

READ THIS WAY

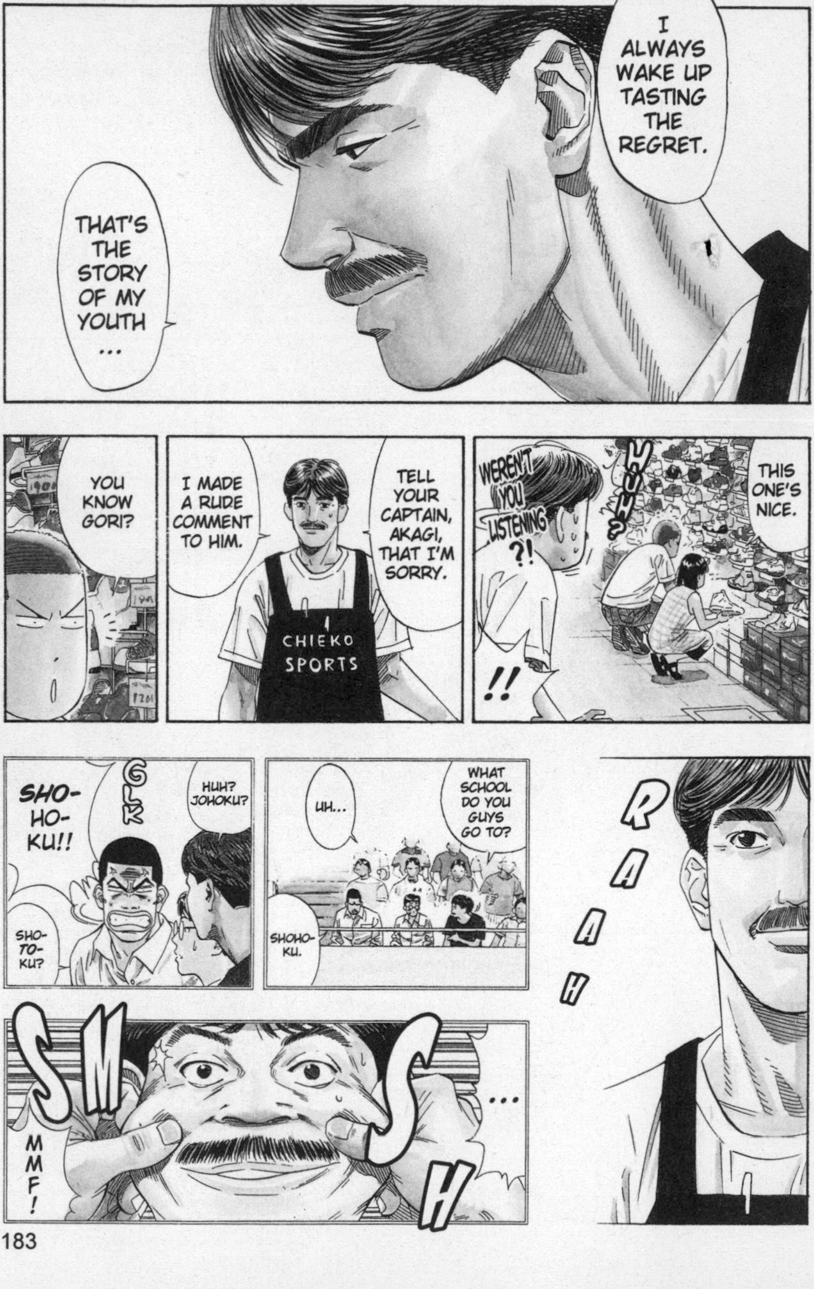

I ALWAYS WAKE UP TASTING THE REGRET.
THAT'S THE STORY OF MY YOUTH ...
THIS ONE'S NICE.
HUH?
WEREN'T YOU LISTENING ?!
!!
TELL YOUR CAPTAIN, AKAGI, THAT I'M SORRY.
I MADE A RUDE COMMENT TO HIM.
CHIEKO SPORTS
YOU KNOW GORI?
RAAAH
WHAT SCHOOL DO YOU GUYS GO TO?
UH...
SHOHOKU.
HUH? JOHOKU?
GLK
SHO-HO-KU!!
SHO-TO-KU?
...
SMSH
MMF!

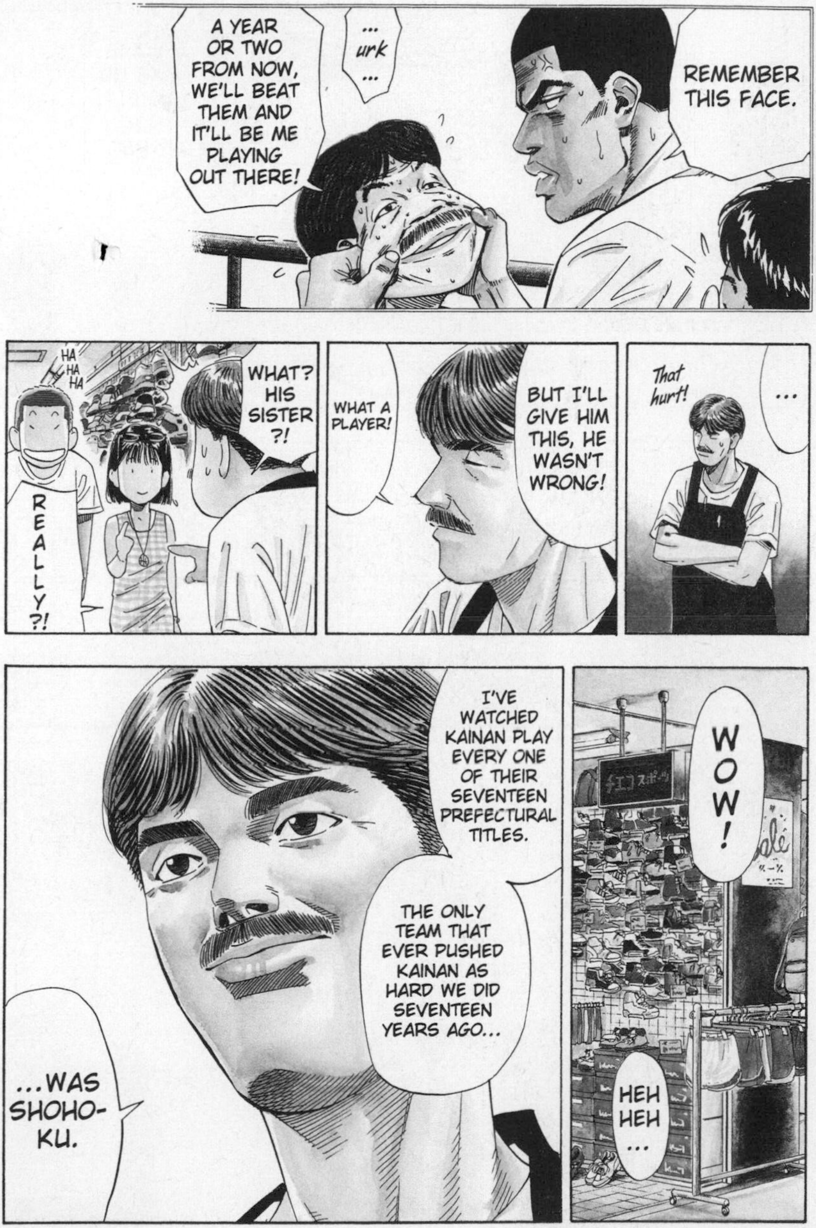
REMEMBER THIS FACE.
... urk ...
A YEAR OR TWO FROM NOW, WE'LL BEAT THEM AND IT'LL BE ME PLAYING OUT THERE!
...
That hurt!
BUT I'LL GIVE HIM THIS, HE WASN'T WRONG!
WHAT A PLAYER!
WHAT? HIS SISTER?!
HA HA HA
REALLY?!
WOW!
HEH HEH ...
I'VE WATCHED KAINAN PLAY EVERY ONE OF THEIR SEVENTEEN PREFECTURAL TITLES.
THE ONLY TEAM THAT EVER PUSHED KAINAN AS HARD WE DID SEVENTEEN YEARS AGO...
...WAS SHOHO-KU.

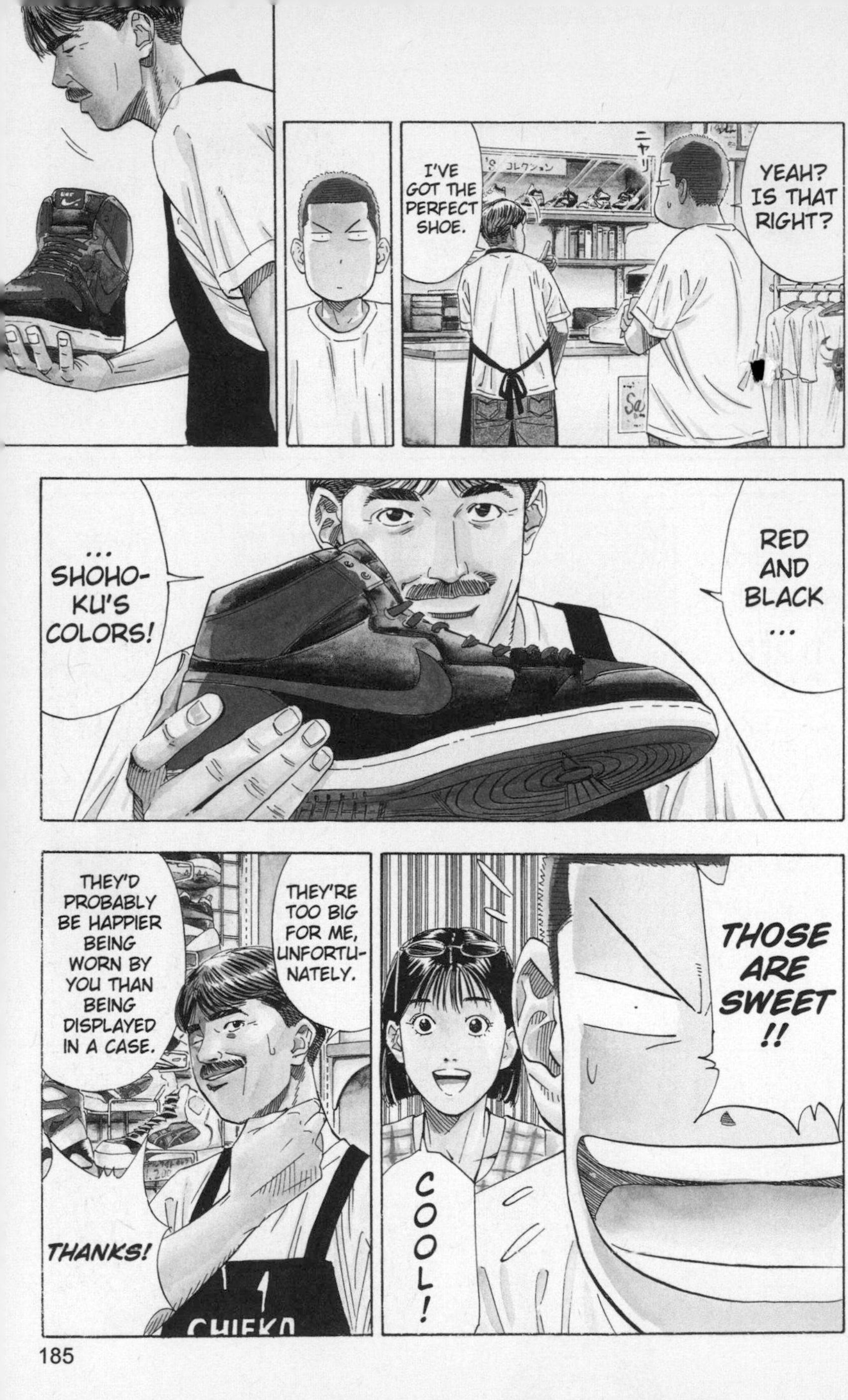
ニヤリ
YEAH? IS THAT RIGHT?
I'VE GOT THE PERFECT SHOE.
RED AND BLACK ...
... SHOHO-KU'S COLORS!
THOSE ARE SWEET !!
COOL!
THEY'RE TOO BIG FOR ME, UNFORTU-NATELY.
THEY'D PROBABLY BE HAPPIER BEING WORN BY YOU THAN BEING DISPLAYED IN A CASE.
THANKS!

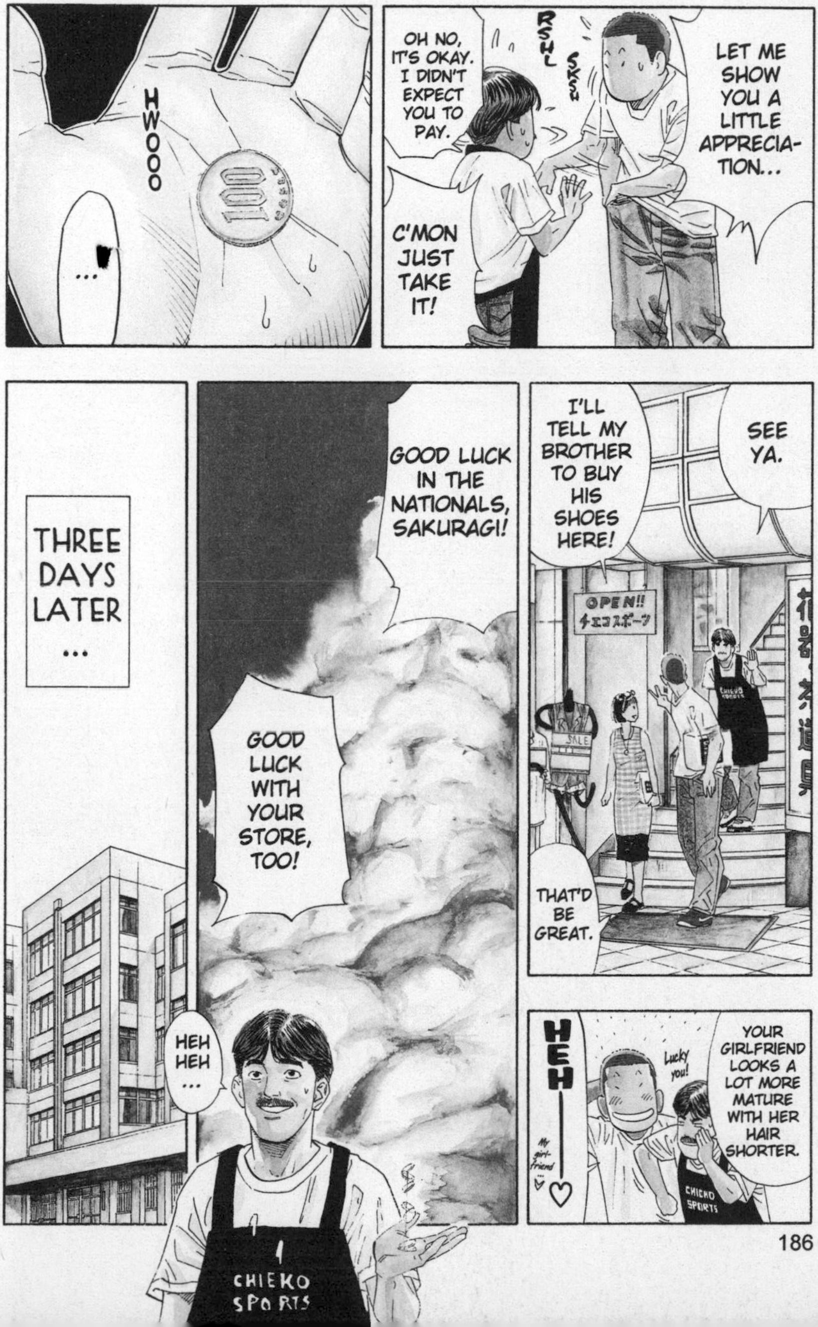
LET ME SHOW YOU A LITTLE APPRECIATION...
RSHL
SKSH
OH NO, IT'S OKAY. I DIDN'T EXPECT YOU TO PAY.
C'MON JUST TAKE IT!
HWOOO
...
SEE YA.
I'LL TELL MY BROTHER TO BUY HIS SHOES HERE!
OPEN!!
チエコスポーツ
THAT'D BE GREAT.
YOUR GIRLFRIEND LOOKS A LOT MORE MATURE WITH HER HAIR SHORTER.
Lucky you!
HEH—♡
My girlfriend...
GOOD LUCK IN THE NATIONALS, SAKURAGI!
GOOD LUCK WITH YOUR STORE, TOO!
HEH HEH...
CHIEKO SPORTS
THREE DAYS LATER...

READ THIS WAY

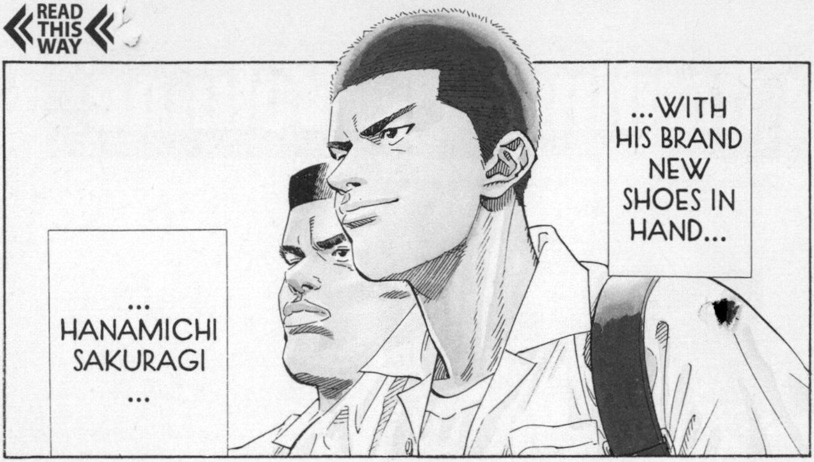
...WITH HIS BRAND NEW SHOES IN HAND...
... HANAMICHI SAKURAGI ...

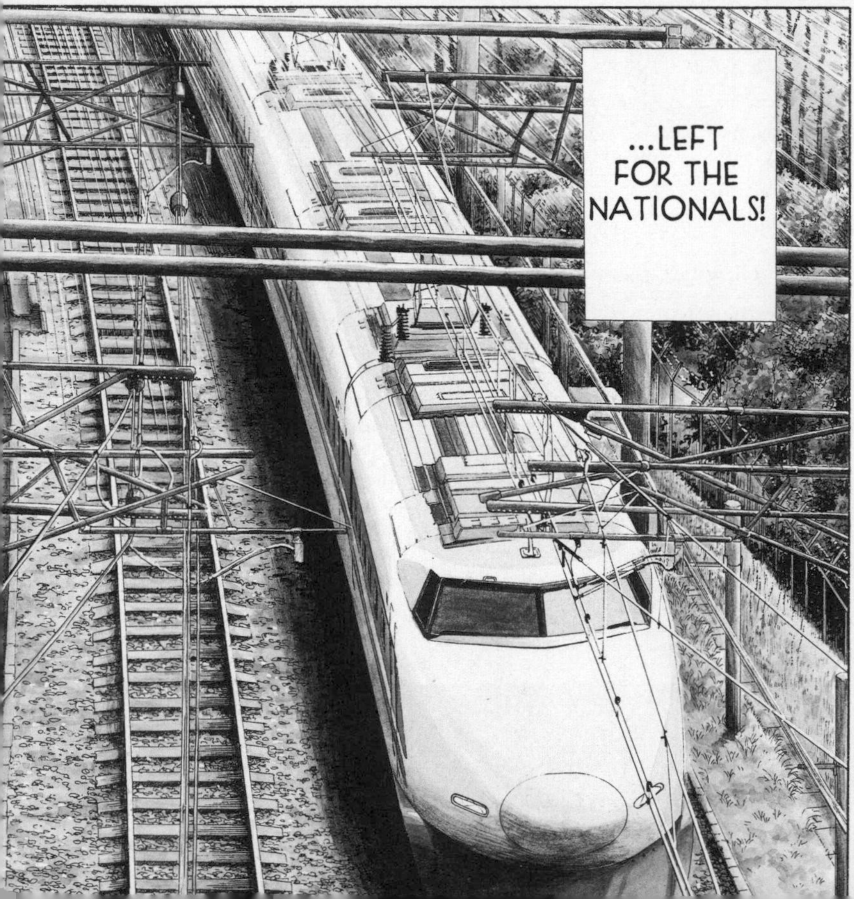
...LEFT FOR THE NATIONALS!

Coming Next Volume

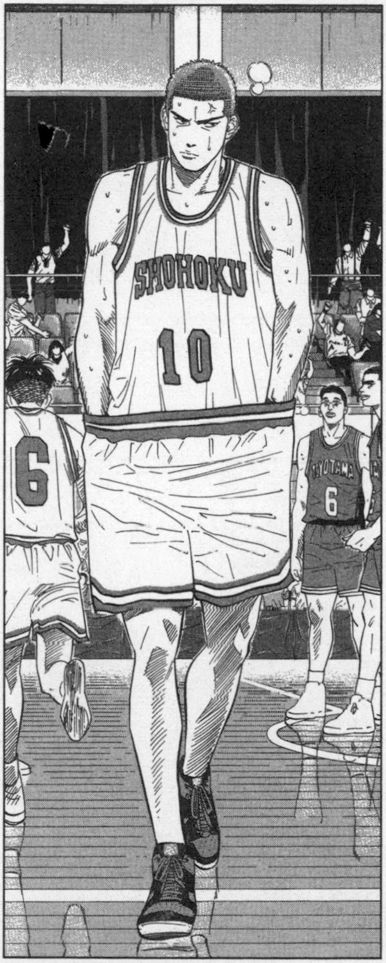
SHOHOKU
10
6
TOYOTAMA
6

Now that they've made it to the Nationals, Shohoku learns exactly where they rank in the overall standings compared to some of the other teams, and they don't like it! Shocked to learn that they're only a C-ranked team, they've got to get their game on to beat their A-ranked first round opponent, Toyotama. And even if they beat Toyotama, Shohoku's opponent in the second round is last year's champion, Sannoh Kogyo. For Sakuragi, Akagi, Rukawa and the boys of Shohoku High, the real game begins now!

ON SALE NOW

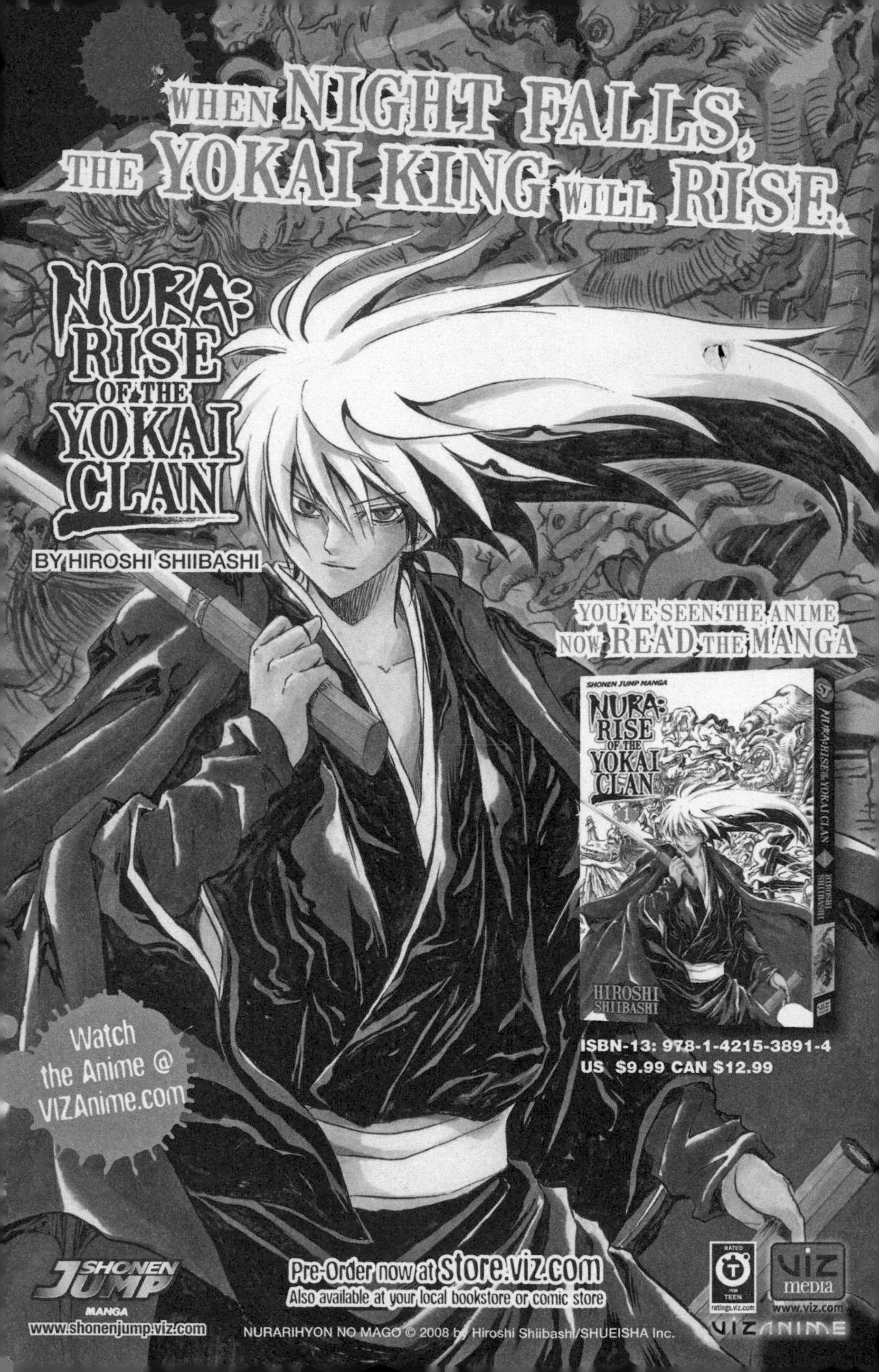

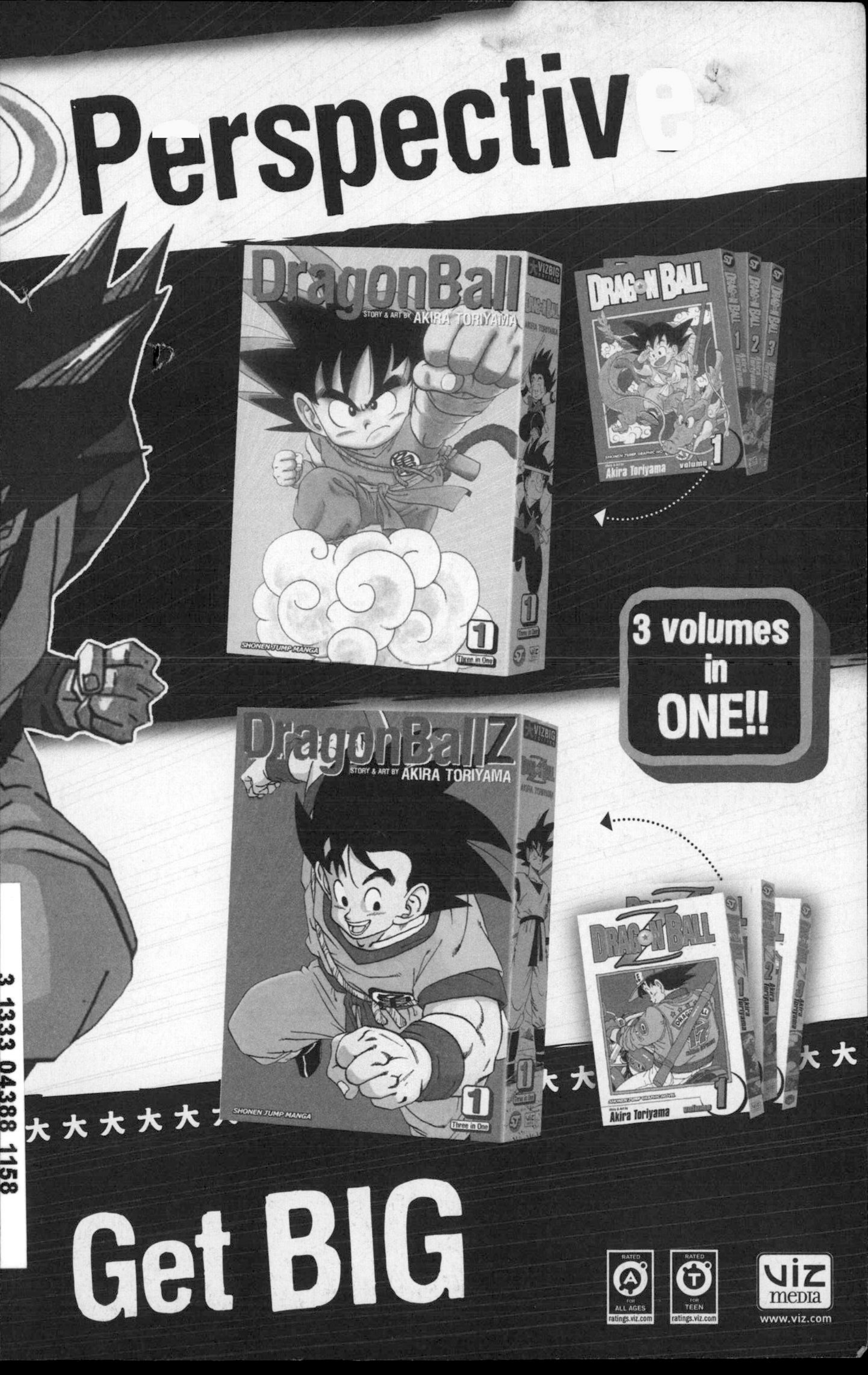
Perspective
DragonBall
STORY & ART BY AKIRA TORIYAMA
SHONEN JUMP MANGA
1
Three in One
VIZBIG
DRAGON BALL
Akira Toriyama
volume 1
3 volumes in ONE!!
DragonBallZ
STORY & ART BY AKIRA TORIYAMA
SHONEN JUMP MANGA
1
Three in One
DRAGON BALL Z
Akira Toriyama
Get BIG
RATED A FOR ALL AGES ratings.viz.com
RATED T FOR TEEN ratings.viz.com
viz media
www.viz.com

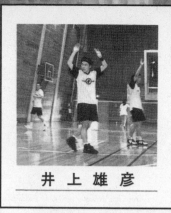

井上雄彦

Takehiko Inoue

THE 1994 JAPANESE BASEBALL SEASON WAS EXCITING. WAS IT BECAUSE I'M A TOKYO GIANTS FAN? MAYBE SO... BUT IT'S ALL OK NOW.

I REALLY DO BELIEVE IT WAS AN EXCITING YEAR. I WAS SO ANGRY WHEN THE GIANTS KEPT LOSING LATE IN THE SEASON, BUT THE JAPAN SERIES WOULDN'T HAVE BEEN AS EXCITING AS IT WAS WITHOUT THAT IN THE BACKGROUND. WITH THE POSSIBLE EXCEPTION OF GAME 1, EVERY GAME OF THE SERIES WAS INCREDIBLE. (OF COURSE, THE ONLY GAME I WENT TO WAS GAME 1.) THIS WAS THE FIRST TIME I EVER FELT SAD TO SEE THE SEASON END.

Takehiko Inoue's *Slam Dunk* is one of the most popular manga of all time, having sold over 100 million copies worldwide. He followed that series up with two titles lauded by critics and fans alike—*Vagabond*, a fictional account of the life of Miyamoto Musashi, and *Real*, a manga about wheelchair basketball.

SLAM DUNK
Vol. 22: The First Round

SHONEN JUMP Manga Edition

STORY AND ART BY TAKEHIKO INOUE

English Adaptation/Stan!
Translation/Joe Yamazaki
Touch-up Art & Lettering/James Gaubatz
Cover & Graphic Design/Matt Hinrichs
Editor/Mike Montesa

Some scenes have been modified from the original Japanese edition.

Printed in the U.S.A.

Published by VIZ Media, LLC
P.O. Box 77010
San Francisco, CA 94107

10 9 8 7 6 5 4 3 2
First printing, June 2012
Second printing, June 2014

viz media
www.viz.com

RATED T FOR TEEN

PARENTAL ADVISORY
SLAM DUNK is rated T for Teen and is recommended for ages 13 and up. This volume contains realistic violence and crude humor.
ratings.viz.com

THE WORLD'S MOST POPULAR MANGA
SHONEN JUMP
www.shonenjump.com